This book examines the efforts of France, Britain, and the United States to extend imperial dominion over the Ohio Valley, focusing on relations between Europeans, Euroamericans, and Indians to tell the story. It treats empires as cross-cultural constructions whose details were negotiated by their participants and argues that three models of empire competed for acceptance in the region: empires of commerce and of land, which both the French and the British sought to build, and an empire of liberty, which grew out of the American Revolution and eventually became the basis for Euroamerican occupation of the valley. Though European trade dramatically reshaped Native American communities in the Ohio Valley, France and Britain each failed to impose territorial dominion there. The American Revolution invented a new organizing principle of empire, one that empowered middling white landowners while it decisively undermined the sovereignty and independence of Native American communities in the west.

ELUSIVE EMPIRES

June 1997

For Luann,

In the hope you can
find something useful
here —

Eric Hinderaker

Elusive Empires

CONSTRUCTING COLONIALISM IN THE OHIO VALLEY, 1673–1800

Eric Hinderaker

University of Utah

CAMBRIDGE
UNIVERSITY PRESS

PUBLISHED BY THE PRESS SYNDICATE OF THE UNIVERSITY OF CAMBRIDGE
The Pitt Building, Trumpington Street, Cambridge CB2 1RP, United Kingdom

CAMBRIDGE UNIVERSITY PRESS
The Edinburgh Building, Cambridge CB2 2RU, United Kingdom
40 West 20th Street, New York, NY 10011–4211, USA
10 Stamford Road, Oakleigh, Melbourne 3166, Australia

First published 1997

Printed in the United States of America

Typeset in Sabon

Library of Congress Cataloguing-in-Publication Data
Hinderaker, Eric
    Elusive empires : constructing colonialism in the Ohio Valley, 1673–1800 /
Eric Hinderaker.
        p.   cm.
    Includes bibliographical references.
    ISBN 0 521 56333 X (hardcover)
    1. Ohio River Valley – History – To 1795. I. Title
F517.H55   1997   96-20230
977 – dc20   CIP

A catalogue record for this book is available from
the British Library

ISBN 0 521 56333 X hardback

For Carrie,
Michael, and Samuel

Contents

Maps and Figures

Preface

WHAT are the ends of empire? There is no simple answer. This book examines the efforts of France, Britain, and the United States to extend imperial dominion over the Ohio Valley, and contends that three distinct models of empire competed for acceptance in the region. The first two – empires of commerce and empires of land – accompanied French and British colonization. Empires of commerce sought to trade for economic resources with native populations; empires of land sought to export European populations across the Atlantic and thus exploit American resources more invasively. In practice the line between these competing views of empire was often blurred; they are entirely distinct only as analytical constructs. Separating them, however, allows us to develop a clearer appreciation for their discrete and often conflicting characteristics. In the American Revolution a third type of empire was born in the Ohio Valley: an empire of liberty, which departed fundamentally from earlier European conceptions of empire-building.

It is important to emphasize at the outset that I use the concept of empire somewhat differently than many other writers have. I treat empires more like processes than structures, and more as creations of the people immediately engaged in colonization than of policy directives originating in London, Paris, Philadelphia, or Washington. The empires of the Ohio Valley were negotiated systems; individuals could shape, challenge, or resist colonialism in many ways. They were also sites for intercultural relations. In the Ohio Valley, Native Americans actively participated in the European imperial systems that connected them with France and Britain. So, too, did thousands of individual colonists, whose ties to the sources of imperial authority in Europe were by no means simple or direct. If we regard empires as cross-cultural constructions that were shaped by the opportunities, constraints, and crises facing the people who participated in them, we can understand them as organic systems instead of abstracted, ideal forms. The definition of empire in the Ohio Valley was not an inevitable outgrowth of demographic forces, historical laws, or institutional developments; it was a mutable process, responsive to the choices of individuals and the contingencies of events.

Part One examines the trading empires that connected the Native American populations of the Ohio Valley with France and Britain. The first chapter explores them in broad outline; it describes the circumstances under which valley residents first established trading ties with European powers, and then explains the systemic patterns of their trade networks. Chapter two characterizes the social and cultural effects of this trading system on Ohio Valley communities. I argue that trade had the power to transform Indian towns, polities, and cultures, but that its effects were difficult for imperial adminstrators to control or channel. Trade served local interests much more effectively than metropolitan imperial ones.

Part Two explores the efforts of the European powers to extend firmer territorial control over the Ohio Valley. Chapter three considers French settlement in the Illinois country, at the western end of the valley, and compares it with the colonization of Pennsylvania. Pennsylvania's experience deeply influenced events in the Ohio Valley, both because many of the valley's residents, Indian and European, migrated from Pennsylvania and because events there prefigured and directly influenced later developments in the valley. Chapter four discusses the effects of the Seven Years' War in Pennsylvania and the Ohio Valley, and considers Britain's attempt to extend comprehensive territorial control over the valley after the war. In the end, that attempt failed; Britain's western empire collapsed in the years just before the outbreak of the American Revolution.

Part Three analyzes the origins, progress, and effects of the Revolution in the Ohio Valley, where the war with Britain intersected with the breakdown of imperial authority and intensified conflicts over control of the land. As the Revolution progressed, it justified and accelerated the process by which Euroamericans drove Indians off the land and claimed it for themselves. In the years after the war, the national government claimed the loyalties of the valley's inhabitants by supporting their aggressive pursuit of western expansion, while the definition of American citizenship hastened the process by which Indians could be dispossessed of their lands.

Whatever their differences, the British and French empires in America shared in common a fundamental constraint on their ability to exploit the Ohio Valley: the need to justify imperial development by the benefits it conferred on the European metropolis. Whether they were primarily interested in trade or in land development, the ministers who decided colonial policy tried to restrain and channel imperial growth so the benefits of empire would flow across the Atlantic, and so its costs would not outweigh them. The trading systems of the Ohio Valley threatened this conception of empire because of their anarchic tendencies: both European and Indian traders were notoriously difficult to control, and the boundaries separating the French and British trading spheres were easily blurred by their activities. Land development was equally hard to manage, because its success depended on harnessing the energies of thousands of ordinary settlers to an imperial framework. This required proprietors to manage expansion, clearly defined boundaries to establish its limits, unambiguous agreements with Indians to dampen the potential for conflict, arrangements for purchasing and surveying land, paying quitrents, and organizing communities. All of these things demanded a comprehensive administrative vision that consistently eluded the ministers of both empires. Nevertheless, despite the persistent failures of imperial administration, the logic of European empires – in which peripheral societies existed to serve the core – required that they control, direct, and limit the activites of their subjects.

The American Revolution overturned these constraints by inventing a new ideology, and a new organizing principle, of empire. Until 1775 government had been a restraining force in the Ohio Valley, but the collapse of royal authority liberated Euroamericans and encouraged settlers to take land where they could get it. For both strategic and ideological reasons, Revolutionary governments chose to support and legitimize their efforts. The consequences for Native Americans in the valley was devastating. While Revolutionary ideology freed American citizens from the constraints of the older European imperial systems, it correspondingly degraded the status of Indians. The growth of frontier violence in the second half of the eighteenth century heightened racial animosity among both Indians and Euroamericans. By the end of the Revolutionary era, Ohio Indians discovered that the terms of their relations with Euroamericans had shifted fundamentally as they were progressively denied recognition as independent, sovereign peoples.

For over a hundred years, the Ohio Valley was a crucible of imperial experimentation. Its diverse Indian population, rich natural resources, and geographical proximity to New France, British America, and the newly United States made it a natural focus for contests of imperial power. Its vast expanse and distance from the Atlantic seaboard meant that France and Britain could never gain more than a tenuous hold on its resources. The Revolution invented a powerful new engine of imperial expansion: the liberty of its people, freed to act outside older constraints of public authority. Widespread economic opportunity became the glue of post-Revolutionary American nationalism, but the promise of opportunity demanded that the national government support extraordinarily rapid expansion and exploitation of an open-ended national territory. The Revolution established a dynamic national empire in the Ohio Valley, and left an indelible legacy of violence and conquest that shaped the development of the region and the nation for generations to come.

*   *   *

This book has been many years in the making, and in the course of its writing I have incurred innumerable debts. During long years in graduate school, the generosity and good cheer of many friends sustained me. Betsy Glade, Liz Dennison, and Bill Myers made Temporary Building One seem a more than temporary home. Michael Prokopow, Vince Tompkins, Alison Carnduff, Steve Biel, Jean Kolling, Mark Peterson, Bruce Venarde, and Tom Siegel served as a vital network of friendship and support and offered a delightful combination of stimulation and diversion. Kim Acworth designed several graphs for the dissertation, two of which survive in the book.

Financial support for research and writing came from the History Department and the Charles Warren Center at Harvard University; the Artemas Ward Dissertation Fellowship at Harvard; the Robert Middlekauff Fellowship at the Huntington Library; and the National Endowment for the Humanities. I am also grateful for countless hours of helpful staff support at Widener Library, the Historical Society of Pennsylvania, the American Philosophical Society, the Historical Society of Wisconsin, the Clements Library at the University of Michigan, the John Carter Brown Library, the National Archives of Canada, the Filson Club in Louisville, Kentucky, the Kentucky Historical Society, the Huntington Library, the Ohio Historical Society, and Marriott Library – where I am especially indebted to Paul Mogren and Walter Jones – and the Law School Library at the University of Utah. The maps were prepared by Michael Foulger and Tom Zajkowski at the University of Utah's DIGIT Lab.

Many people have read parts of the manuscript and offered valuable suggestions and criticisms. Ernest May, Peggy Pascoe, and Richard White read my entire dissertation and offered thoughtful and extended suggestions for revision. I have been fortunate to join a remarkably collegial and supportive history department at the University of Utah; Rebecca Horn, Paul Johnson, Dorothee Kocks, Colleen McDannell, and

Jeff Garcilazo all commented on drafts of one or more chapters. Ed Countryman, Peter Mancall, Drew Cayton, and Ed Gray read chapter drafts and improved them considerably. Peggy Pascoe patiently read several drafts of an early introduction and outline of chapters, and shared her ideas and research on the legal definition of race, for which I am particularly grateful.

I am especially indebted to two people who advised and directed my development as a historian in broader ways. One of these is Bernard Bailyn, who directed my doctoral dissertation. The example of his scholarship and his powerful historical imagination served as an early inspiration for my own work. By encouraging me to follow my curiosity, broaden my focus, and ask harder questions until I came up with something genuinely interesting, he helped make this project satisfying to me and, I hope, compelling for its readers. My other adviser, to whom I owe more intellectual and personal debts than I can begin to recount, is Fred Anderson. At the very beginning of my graduate studies Fred extended encouragement, friendship, and a glimpse of what the life of a scholar implied. As my dissertation took shape he offered criticism and support; at times he understood the significance of my work much more clearly than I did. His penetrating critique of the manuscript's penultimate draft led to several crucial revisions and helped me to clarify and focus my argument throughout. I have benefited in countless ways from his unfailing friendship and aid.

My family has been especially supportive in this project. My parents helped me in every way during many years of productive but unremunerative labor. My brother John offered valuable advice about narrative voice, in addition to material aid of his own. James and Susan, and Paul and Carol, Hinderaker and their families, and my in-laws the Egglestons and McKisics, all offered hospitality that enlivened research trips. My greatest personal gratitude is reserved for Carrie, who has read chapter drafts when I've asked her to, but has more often, and more importantly, offered welcome relief from research and writing. I am also grateful to Michael and Samuel, who remind me every day that history begins with the lives and experiences of real people. For them I have reserved a page of their own.

ELUSIVE EMPIRES

PART ONE

Empires of Commerce

COMMERCE is among the most universal, and the most dangerous, of all human activities. Foreign exchange, in particular, has always been hedged round by taboos and special provisions designed to protect the hearth culture from alien hostilities and impurities.[1] Yet the allure of exchange seems nearly always to triumph over the fear of danger: this fact gave shape to much of the history of intercultural contact in North America.

In 17th-century Europe, fears relating to foreign trade were embodied in the principles of the mercantilists, theorists of state power who jealously guarded the national wealth. Mercantilists wanted their kingdoms to be self-contained and impregnable as they competed with one another for control of valuable resources.[2] These principles shaped the early period of state-sponsored colonization in England and France and drove both powers to seek wealth on the North American continent. Competitive, acquisitive, fearful of foreign power, Europeans entered into the search for exploitable resources in the Americas. They sought to fashion empires of commerce, understood as mercantilists would understand them. They regarded colonial commerce as a one-way flow of wealth, from the margins of empire to its center, and they believed

---

[1] For a particularly suggestive version of this idea, see Jean-Christophe Agnew, *Worlds Apart: The Market and the Theater in Anglo-American Thought, 1550–1750* (New York, 1986), ch. 1, "The Threshold of Exchange."

[2] For an insightful account of the triumph of mercantilist over free-trade doctrine in 17th-century England, see Joyce Appleby, *Economic Thought and Ideology in Seventeenth-Century England* (Princeton, 1978); the classic analysis of mercantilism, which emphasizes its relation to the competition for power among hostile nations, is Eli Heckscher, *Mercantilism*, trans. Mendel Shapiro, 2 vols. (London, 1935).

fiercely in the importance of maintaining the integrity – the purity – of their respective colonial spheres.

One source of colonial wealth was the trade for furs with Native American societies. In these exchanges the fears and desires of non-European cultures came into play as well. Indians, like Europeans, saw themselves as competitors with their neighbors; despite their misgivings, they usually chose to pursue trade with strangers as a means of gaining advantage over rivals. Thus for Indians and Europeans alike, trade inspired both fear and desire; initially it was necessary to establish rituals that could dampen the participants' fears and channel their desires. In the earliest meetings between Europeans and Indians, before such rituals were in place, powerfully conflicting sentiments about outsiders were paraded in high, sometimes comic, relief. When Verrazzano sailed down the coast of North America in 1524, he encountered natives who would not allow his party to come ashore to trade; instead, the Indians stood on rocks where the breakers were crashing and it was impossible to land a boat, and "sent us what they wanted to give on a rope." When the exchange was complete, the Indians, according to Verrazzano, "made all the signs of scorn and shame that any brute creature would make, such as showing their buttocks and laughing."[3] In a myriad of ways during the earliest years of intercultural contact, the participants in trade sought to capitalize on the benefits that might be conferred by strangers and protect themselves from the consequences of contact at the same time.

But however much Europeans and Native Americans may have wanted to preserve their autonomy as they drew one another into trading relationships, the history of intercultural relations offers a thorough refutation of that possibility. Nearly every feature of the empires of trade constructed in the Ohio Valley during the late 17th and 18th centuries worked against the preservation of insularity; like trading contacts everywhere, they tended instead to create powerful channels of intercultural influence and to blur the lines of power and interest.

Initially the competition between England and France in the Ohio Valley was defined almost entirely in commercial terms. Later, territorial considerations would become paramount; but it was as empires of commerce, in the first place, that both European powers began to reshape the contours of native life in the continental interior.

---

[3] Quoted in James Axtell, "At the Water's Edge: Trading in the Sixteenth Century," *After Columbus: Essays in the Ethnohistory of Colonial North America* (New York, 1988), p. 156.

CHAPTER ONE

Networks of Trade

I

For more than a millennium before the Columbian voyages, the Ohio River Valley served as one of the great conduits of human civilization in North America. Each of the main prehistoric culture complexes of the central continent was communicated through the Ohio Valley along the region's network of waterways: the Hopewell, Adena, and Mississippian cultures each left its mark in the valley and contributed to a rich and complicated prehistoric legacy. The Ohio Valley emerged then, and has persisted ever since, as a distinctive cultural and economic zone. Influences and contacts flow through the region like blood through the back of a hand; its tributary rivers, united by the great artery of the Ohio River, have always tended to make travel, communication, trade – and conflict – defining features of Ohio Valley communities.

To begin with, there is the landscape. The Ohio River falls from its origins in the Allegheny foothills to the south and west for nearly a thousand miles, fed along the way by nine major rivers and dozens of smaller streams. On its southern bank, the Ohio Valley embraces both the hardscrabble hills of northern West Virginia and the fertile plains of the Kentucky bluegrass, a region marked off by the Alleghenies on the east and the Tennessee River to the south. On the north side of the Ohio the valley is especially accessible through an intricately branching pattern of subsidiary rivers. The big river ties the entire region together at the same time that it divides it in two.

If the Ohio Valley has a kind of internal coherence and unity, the watercourses that surround and feed into the valley have always helped connect it to the rest of the continent. The Mississippi River is the valley's most important conduit to the outside world; it connects with the Southeast, the Gulf coast, and even the peoples of Mexico and the Yucatan. To the west, the Missouri River serves as a means of communication with much of the Great Plains as far as the Rocky Mountains; on the north, the Great Lakes act as a natural point of intersection between residents of the Ohio Valley and their northern neighbors. Less directly, the Allegheny and Tennessee Rivers provide routes of contact to the eastern woodlands as well. Along all of these routes, indigenous peoples traveled and interacted from at least 400 B.C. until Europeans arrived on the scene. They left a complicated archaeological legacy that scholars have labored for years to disentangle in order to make sense of the region's prehistoric past.

The Ohio Valley was never home to great, centralized empires. In contrast to other regions of the Americas – central Mexico, the Andean highlands, and parts of southeastern North America, for example – the Ohio Valley was too porous and easily penetrated to withstand external influences.[1] Instead the region was inhabited for at least a thousand years by relatively small, independent clusters of communities that periodically entered coordinated phases of economic, social, and cultural development.

During the Hopewell period (ca. 300 B.C.–A.D. 300), broadly shared culture patterns emerged throughout the Ohio Valley. They are revealed in distinctive mound burial sites, earthworks, and artifact styles, and taken together they suggest widespread contact and influence throughout the region. The mound site at Chillicothe, Ohio, has long been regarded as the prototype, and perhaps the point of origination, for Hopewell influence. But significant local variations remained; the Hopewell culture complex offers evidence, not of the formation of a unified empire of military or adminstrative domination, but instead of a period of cultural interaction and borrowing shared by a wide variety of communities, each developing according to its own dynamic. Similarly with the Adena complex, which emerged at roughly the same time in the central Ohio Valley. It is identified by a distinctive mortuary style, and Adena communities also probably shared a ceremonial complex in common, but they were not united under the kind of coercive imperial system that would have placed them under the rule of a single elite class or imposed regular tributes or common structures of community organiza-

---

[1] Considerable work has been done in recent years on the late prehistoric and early historic native populations of the southeast; for an introduction to this literature, see Peter Wood, Gregory Waselkov, and M. Thomas Hatley, eds., *Powhatan's Mantle: Indians in the Colonial Southeast* (Lincoln, NE, 1989).

tion upon them.[2] If we allow the term "empire" to apply only to a dominant, coercive administrative-military complex, these culture systems do not qualify. If, on the other hand, we define empire more flexibly to include broadly shared economic, social, and cultural patterns – an empire, in other words, defined not by the dominance of a ruling elite but by patterns of activity and meaning that were common to the region at large – then the culture systems of the Ohio Valley could also be described as empires. They were, in fact, very much like the systems I have termed empires of commerce, which will be considered at greater length below.

The last great cultural efflorescence of the pre-Columbian period conforms to this same pattern. The Mississippian culture complex (ca. 800–1500 A.D.) was widely dispersed, long-lived, and deeply influential in the period just before European contact. Its sites ranged throughout the Southeast, the Gulf Coast, and the Mississippi and Ohio Valleys; though their extraordinary scope and variety make them particularly difficult to describe comprehensively, some characteristics were common to them all. Mississippian communities were located in the "meander-belt zones" and alluvial floodplains of major rivers in eastern North America, which placed them in ecosystems that could support substantial populations. Mississippian peoples pioneered the corn-beans-squash agricultural complex that would become so important to Native Americans throughout the midcontinent and eastern woodlands, and the richly silted alluvial lands they settled were especially well-suited to that pattern. The oxbow lakes and marshy backwaters of the meander-belt zones also made fish and wildfowl easily available.[3] Alongside this settlement pattern, distinctive Mississippian cultural forms arose and spread across a wide area. They are identified by telltale artifacts, especially a certain type of earthen mound, usually rectangular and truncated, and distinctive shell-tempered pottery. As Mississippian communities grew more complex, differences in status and power became more pronounced: the spatial organization of Mississippian towns and the rich artifacts found in some burial sites both indicate that clearly ranked social hierarchies were common to Mississippian communities.[4]

---

[2] For an introduction to the Hopewell and Adena, see James E. Fitting, "Regional Cultural Development, 300 B.C. to A.D. 1000," in William C. Sturtevant, gen. ed., *Handbook of North American Indians,* vol. XV: *Northeast,* ed. Bruce G. Trigger (Washington, DC, 1978), pp. 44–57.

[3] Bruce D. Smith, "Variation in Mississippian Settlement Patterns," in Smith, ed., *Mississippian Settlement Patterns* (New York, 1978), pp. 479–503.

[4] On the origins of Mississippian culture generally see especially Bruce D. Smith, ed., *The Mississippian Emergence* (Washington, DC, 1990).

But although Mississippian culture supported the rise of local elites, they never functioned as agents of a centralized administrative empire. Instead the Mississippian system was a network of interlinked regions bound together by patterns of material and cultural exchange. Whether the connections among Mississippian communities were forged by conquest, by trade, or by some combination of the two, the archaeological record of Mississippian culture varies significantly from site to site.[5] Within each region, various kinds of societies and communities received and absorbed Mississippian influences in a variety of ways. The backbone of Mississippian culture was the Mississippi River, and its core was in the lower Mississippi Valley. As one of the great feeders of the Mississippi River, the Ohio was ideally situated to receive and disseminate the influences of the Mississippian cultural core. And as with the region's earlier culture complexes, Mississippian traits filtered into the region and spread throughout its settlements. One of the most important centers of Mississippian influence anywhere on the continent (and the greatest single prehistoric site north of Mexico) was at Cahokia, Illinois. There, within an area of nearly six square miles, a complex of more than a hundred man-made mounds – the largest covering almost sixteen acres – was constructed during the early period of Mississippian development.

From about A.D. 800–900 until at least 1250, Cahokia was one of the great centers of public and ceremonial life in the western hemisphere. By A.D. 1200, Cahokia served a community with a population of perhaps 30,000. In its immediate hinterland, a dozen or more satellite communi-

---

[5] For a thoughtful analysis of site variations and the evolution of archaeological interpretations of the Mississippian era see Jon Muller, *Archaeology of the Lower Ohio River Valley* (Orlando, FL, 1986), pp. 169–272. It has been argued that the Mississippians were a distinct people who came as conquerors and displaced preexisting populations. Certainly there is something to this view – the spread of Mississippian culture, and perhaps a distinctive Mississippian population, could not have proceeded without conflict where it was displacing older ways and, in some places at least, other peoples – but even if the spread of Mississippian culture is interpreted as a manifestation of conquest it is important to recognize the limits of that conquest. Unlike the more familiar empires of conquest – the Aztec empire in central Mexico, or the Roman empire of an earlier period – the Mississippians apparently did not create centralized systems of administration or tribute collection, nor did they establish a central ruling class. For discussions of the Mississippians that emphasize conquest, see Francis Jennings, *The Founders of America: How Indians Discovered the Land, Pioneered in It, and Created Great Classical Civilizations; How They Were Plunged into a Dark Age by Invasion and Conquest; and How They Are Reviving* (New York, 1993), and in an account that focuses on the coastal region of the Carolinas, James Merrell, *The Indians' New World: Catawbas and their Neighbors from European Contact Through The Era of Removal* (Chapel Hill, 1989), pp. 13–18.

ties grew up alongside it.[6] These were not insular, inward-looking settlements; on the contrary, given the enormous range and influence of Mississippian culture, it may be most useful to think of Cahokia as a "gateway center," a cultural focus from which rays of influence diverged across the countryside, touching many thousands of people living beyond the American Bottom. Artifacts from widely scattered sources throughout North America have turned up at Cahokia, suggesting that traders were traveling an astonishingly expansive circuit by the height of the Mississippian period. To Cahokia they carried superbly crafted artifacts and raw materials from Mexico, the Great Lakes, the Atlantic coast, and the central Great Plains.[7] In the final phase of the Mississippian period (ca. A.D. 1250–1500), Mississippian influences were everywhere in the Ohio Valley: at the Fort Ancient sites, clustered around the mouths of the Miami and Scioto Rivers; throughout the central Illinois River Valley; at the Kincaid sites, near the confluence of the Cumberland, Tennessee, and Ohio Rivers; and at the Angel and Caborn-Welborn sites near the mouth of the Wabash.[8]

At the moment of Columbus' first landfall in the Americas, the greater Ohio Valley thus seems to have been home to a sizable, interconnected indigenous population governed by well-developed systems of authority and meaning. There is evidence for ruling elites at most of its sites; for complex religious and ceremonial patterns; highly developed craft skills; and an extensive hinterland of interdependent communities linked by networks of exchange.[9]

What accounts for the collapse of Mississippian culture in central North America? To some extent, its rapid fall remains a mystery. Since the nineteenth century, archaeologists have entertained many possibilities: External invasion; a series of crop failures; a successful revolt against a ruling caste. Recent advances in our understanding of the epidemiology of European contact in the Americas suggest another possibility: the decline may have been caused, or at least hastened, by the ef-

---

[6] Melvin L. Fowler, "Cahokia and the American Bottom: Settlement Archaeology," in Smith, ed., *Mississippian Settlement Patterns*.

[7] John E. Kelly, "Cahokia and Its Role as a Gateway Center in Interregional Exchange," in Thomas Emerson and R. Barry Lewis, eds., *Cahokia and the Hinterlands: Middle Mississippian Cultures of the Midwest* (Urbana, IL, 1991), pp. 61–80; for a general discussion of long-range patterns of exchange, see William A. Turnbaugh, "Wide-Area Connections in Native North America," *American Indian Culture and Research Journal*, 1 (1976), 22–28.

[8] Smith, ed., *Mississippian Settlement Patterns*, throughout.

[9] The complicated interrelations between core settlements like Cahokia and hinterland communities cannot be characterized simply; for a general view, see the excellent collection of essays in Emerson and Lewis, eds., *Cahokia and the Hinterlands*.

fects of the first Spanish landfalls in Mesoamerica. If trading networks and travel routes connected the population of the Ohio Valley with Mexico and the Gulf coast, it is entirely possible that, from about 1500 on, devastating waves of epidemic disease could have swept through the continent along the great waterways that connected its population centers.[10] If smallpox, typhus, measles, and other European pathogens thus found their way to the Ohio Valley periodically, rapid depopulation would have been the result. We now have reliable information about the effects of European disease on Indian populations who were continuously exposed to them. During the first generation of exposure, they generally declined by something approaching 50%; after a century of sustained contact, population decline would have been on the order of 90%.[11] With intermittent rather than sustained exposure, the demographic catastrophe of the sixteenth century in the Ohio Valley would not have been so severe; nevertheless, even isolated waves of epidemic disease would have carried away a significant proportion of the region's population.

The advance of alien pathogens along the principal travel and communication routes of the central continent would have converted the blessings of geography in the Ohio River Valley into a curse of unparalleled proportions. The network of rivers which had heretofore facilitated contact and cultural diffusion would suddenly have become, inexplicably, a transmitter of disease and death. One natural reaction for survivors would have been to flee to other communities; they, too, would then become agents of disaster, visiting mysterious ailments upon their neighbors. Eventually, experience would provide communities with a rationale for withdrawal and isolation. It is easy to imagine how parties of messengers or traders arriving from the south might have been shunned by the increasingly fearful and suspicious clusters of surviving villagers: under the pressure of rapid and substantial population decline,

[10] This possibility has been suggestively explored by Alfred Crosby, in *Ecological Imperialism: The Biological Expansion of Europe, 900–1900* (New York, 1986), pp. 209–215; I am also indebted for the following discussion to Ralph J. Coffman, "Pre-Columbian Trade Networks in the Missouri, Ohio and Mississippi River Valleys and Their Importance for Post-Columbian Contact," paper presented at the Missouri Valley History Conference, Omaha, NE, March 1992. For an alternative interpretation of Mississippian decline in the Cahokia hinterlands, which places less emphasis on European diseases and argues for a period of "chronic, deadly warfare" in the 15th century, see Neal Salisbury, "The Indians' Old World: Native Americans and the Coming of Europeans," *The William and Mary Quarterly*, 3rd Ser., 53 (1996), 435–458.

[11] Two recent works carefully summarize and assess the work of a generation of historical demographers of Native America; see William Denevan, ed., *The Native Population of the Americas in 1492*, 2nd ed. (Madison, WI, 1992), and Russell Thornton, *American Indian Holocaust and Survival: A Population History Since 1492* (Norman, OK, 1987).

people are likely to have turned in on themselves and allowed the commercial, ceremonial, and tribute ties that had bound them into a larger culture system to lapse in the interest of survival. Like islands exposed by the receding tide of Mississippian influence, the surviving fragments of population may have passed the last half of the 16th century and the first part of the 17th regrouping along kin- and clan-based lines, beginning again to construct a social world for themselves out of the rudimentary building blocks of civilization.

In the 1650s, French missionaries and traders began to extend their contacts beyond the Great Lakes for the first time. When they asked about the people of the western Ohio Valley, native informants described them as a formidable and unified power. One report indicated that Frenchmen would encounter a great confederacy of Illinois Indians which embraced sixty villages and towns and was capable of putting twenty thousand warriors into the field.[12] As Frenchmen gained firsthand knowledge of these peoples, however, they discovered that the western Ohio Valley was occupied, not by a single, politically unified population, but instead by numerous confederacies, tribes, and bands of Indians, each of which sought to deal with the French independently, on its own terms.

As Richard White has recently argued, the French were encountering, without fully realizing it, a shattered social world in the Ohio Valley. On top of the dissolution of Mississippian culture and the devastation by disease that may have accompanied it, the region was also beginning to feel the effects of sustained and brutal Iroquois attacks by the 1650s and 1660s.[13] These attacks were pushing some groups from the Great Lakes region westward, devastating or destroying others, and scrambling earlier definitions of territory and identity throughout the Great Lakes and the Ohio Valley. The arrival of French traders and missionaries gave to the Indians occupying the western half of the Ohio Valley – the Illinois country, as the French called it – a means to reconstruct a social universe with a meaningful focus. Perhaps Onontio, the symbolic father figure of the French alliance, was powerful and appealing to the native occupants of the Illinois country in part because he helped to revive echoes of an earlier, more fully developed culture system which had given shape and meaning to past generations in the region, and which survived into the middle of the 17th century as a residual social memory. Perhaps. For whatever reason, French traders and missionaries were welcomed into

---

12 [Gabriel Dreuillettes], "Relation of 1657–1658," in Reuben G. Thwaites, ed., *The Jesuit Relations and Allied Documents*, 73 vols. (Cleveland, 1896–1901) [hereafter *JR*], vol. XLIV, p. 247.

13 Richard White, *The Middle Ground: Indians, Empires, and Republics in the Great Lakes Region, 1650–1815* (New York, 1991).

the Ohio Valley during the second half of the 17th century. With their arrival, the island communities of the interrelated but fragmented peoples who survived the fall of Mississippian culture could be bound together once again in a wider system of commerce, mediation, and cultural exchange.

II

When French traders and missionaries first ventured beyond the Great Lakes and into the Illinois country, they encountered a bewildering array of peoples. In part the problem was simply a profusion of names: dozens of tribal labels appear in the earliest documents, many of them only once or twice. In part, too, the confusion stemmed from the scrambled and apparently deteriorating lines of political authority in the region. Ostensibly these were tribal peoples, so that lines of authority should have run through channels of family, kin, and tribe, but individual villages often contained members of more than one tribe and the allegiances of their residents were sometimes far from clear. This was the fractured social world of post-Mississippian culture; now as in the 17th century, it defies easy description or comprehension.[14] Nevertheless, broader patterns of social organization still exerted some influence; the earliest French explorers encountered two weakly unified confederacies of tribes in the Illinois country – the Illinois confederacy and the Miami confederacy – and began to cultivate relations with each of them.

The Illinois and Miami Indians together dominated the territory bounded by the Mississippi River on the west, the Ohio River to the south, the Miami River to the east, and the lower tip of Lake Michigan to the north – essentially the western half of the Ohio Valley. Both participated in what anthropologists describe as the Central Algonquian culture complex. They were patrilineal and patriarchal societies. They relied for food primarily on agriculture, and particularly on corn, and they supplemented their crops with hunting, especially for deer and buffalo.[15]

Each of these two confederacies was comprised of a number of dis-

---

[14] By far the best comprehensive account of this region in the French period is in White, *Middle Ground*.

[15] The anthropological literature on the Illinois and Miamis is uneven, and sources are unsatisfactory, precisely because they were experiencing such upheaval during the era of early contact; see White, *Middle Ground*, pp. 16–17 and following. The most useful anthropological analysis is Charles Callender, *Social Organization of the Central Algonkian Indians*, Milwaukee Public Museum Publications in Anthropology no. 7 (Milwaukee, 1962).

tinct tribal units, though in each the number of member tribes was unclear at first and seemed to diminish gradually through the first several
decades of contact. The earliest French travelers identified at least 12
different groups as members of the Illinois "nation," but by the end of
the 17th century the number had dropped to four: the Kaskaskias, the
Peorias, the Cahokias, and the Tamaroas. Sometime around 1700 a fifth
tribe, the Michigameas, moved into Illinois territory from the south and
was incorporated into the confederation. Though they remained allies,
these tribal groups grew steadily more independent of one another in
the years after the arrival of the French.[16]

Similarly, early chroniclers named six different constituent groups as
members in the Miami confederation, but by 1700 there were only four;
the "disappeared" groups coalesced into the Miami tribe. The other
three tribes of the confederacy were the Piankashaws, the Ouiatanons
(known later in British sources as the Weas), and the Pepikokias, who
were absorbed into the Ouiatanon tribe around 1745. The members of
the Miami confederacy, like those of the Illinois, remained allies
throughout the colonial period, but the strength of this connection
could be tenuous. Each tribe maintained a distinct territory and autonomous political leadership.[17]

These confederacies were less units of political organization than
sources of social and cultural identity. When the first French explorers
visited the Illinois confederacy, it maintained a central community on
the upper Illinois River – known to the French as the "Great Village" of
the Illinois – where all the constituent tribes gathered during the summer. The Great Village served as their principal agricultural, political,
cultural, and ceremonial center; here the Illinois tribes affirmed their
shared identity in lacrosse matches, social, political, and religious rituals, planting and harvesting, hunting, and feasting. In fall, the confederacy dispersed into small hunting bands that wintered in a series of
camps scattered between the Illinois and Mississippi Rivers. The Miami
confederacy lacked such a central settlement; although the Miami tribes
recognized their common origin, there appears to have been little to
bind them together in the postcontact period.[18]

The timing of Frenchmen's first contacts with the Illinois and Miami
Indians was crucial in shaping the Indians' reaction to them. To begin

[16] For an introduction to the anthropological and historical literature on the Illinois, see
Charles Callender, "Illinois," in Trigger, ed., *Handbook*, p. 673.

[17] Callender, "Miami," in Trigger, ed., *Handbook*, pp. 681–689.

[18] Margaret Kimball-Brown, *Cultural Transformations Among the Illinois: An Application of a Systems Model*, Publications of the Museum, Michigan State University, vol. 1
no. 3 (East Lansing, 1979), pp. 227–229.

with, the confederacies were disintegrating as effective units of political organization by the middle of the 17th century, leaving the Illinois and Miami Indians increasingly vulnerable in their relations with outsiders. The two confederacies had been united in a single, larger confederation until very shortly before French contact.[19] Whether the dissolution of this larger Illinois–Miami confederacy was a late stage of Mississippian decline or the result of a localized dispute, it is symptomatic of a broader pattern: the region's Indian population was becoming steadily less unified. On its own terms such disunity should not be read as a failure of the political or social order; it may reflect a dynamic sense of independence among the constituent groups of the confederation. But in times of crisis there is strength in numbers. Whatever else it might indicate about the communities of the Illinois and Miami Indians, the dissolution of their joint confederacy could pose a severe threat to their ability to defend themselves against outside aggression.

The problem of defense became a matter of urgent concern beginning in the 1650s, when the Illinois country was first visited by war parties from the Five Nations of the Iroquois. The Iroquois had reached a crisis point in their relations with neighboring European and Indian powers by the early 1640s. They responded by embarking on a half-century of particularly destructive and wide-ranging warfare. The Iroquois sought to capture and monopolize the trade in beaver pelts throughout the Great Lakes and the Ohio Valley, to terrorize their enemies, and to carry captives back to Iroquoia to help offset their own rapid population decline. In these efforts they were astonishingly successful. They destroyed or displaced a succession of Indian tribes – the Wenros, the Hurons, the Petuns, the Neutrals, the Eries – claiming domination over conquered territories and either dispersing or absorbing their populations. By the 1650s Iroquois warriors were making their way into the Illinois country, and they brought with them a terrifyingly destructive pattern of warfare to which the Illinois and Miami Indians were ill-equipped to respond.[20]

The Iroquois raids raised the stakes of war to a new level. The most familiar form of war in the Illinois country was a mourning war, a local-

---

[19] Both oral tradition and anthropological research confirm the hypothesis of a single united confederacy in the immediate pre-contact period; for the former, see Thomas Forsyth, "An Account of the Manners and Customs of the Sauk and Fox Nations of Indians Tradition," in Emma H. Blair, ed., *The Indian Tribes of the Upper Mississippi Valley and Region of the Great Lakes*, 2 vols. (Cleveland, 1911), vol. II, pp. 199–201, and for the latter, Callender, *Social Organization*, p. 1; Kimball-Brown, *Cultural Transformations Among the Illinois*, pp. 228, 233–235; Emily J. Blasingham, "The Depopulation of the Illinois Indians," *Ethnohistory*, 3 (1956), 361–362.

[20] Daniel Richter, *The Ordeal of the Longhouse: The Peoples of the Iroquois League in the Era of European Colonization* (Chapel Hill, 1992), especially pp. 50–74.

ized, limited, and personal style of warfare that was intended to exact revenge for an earlier death. Mourning and revenge were often inseparable for the Illinois and Miami Indians, and the mourning war took on an almost ritualized form. With few exceptions, war was not intended to inflict mass destruction on an enemy people. Thus, even after the Illinois and Miami Indians began to receive French guns in trade sometime around the mid-1650s, they did not immediately conceive of them as efficient instruments of death. Instead, in keeping with their limited pattern of warfare, they used guns "to inspire, through their noise and smoke, terror in their Enemies." This was entirely fitting in the context of a mourning raid, but it would not serve them well in the face of a concerted Iroquois attack.[21]

The Illinois and Miami Indians soon discovered what such an attack could mean. During a raid on the Great Village of the Illinois in 1680, an Iroquois war party came upon the town at a time when most of its young men were away hunting. Following a prolonged series of skirmishes, the Iroquois raiders finally fell upon an unprotected group of seven hundred people, predominantly women and children, killing hundreds of them and taking many more as captives.[22] Even for a strong and united people, the Iroquois threat would have presented a formidable challenge; the fragile, disordered world of the western Ohio Valley was especially vulnerable to its terrors.

The first Frenchmen to visit the Illinois country thus encountered a beleaguered people. Pressured by the Iroquois from the east – and, at the same time, by the Sioux from the west – the Illinois and Miami confederacies were weakened and disunified. When French missionaries and traders ventured into Illinois and Miami villages for the first time, they were received practically (even literally) as gods by Indian leaders who recognized in their arrival the possibility of deliverance. When Father Jacques Marquette and Louis Joliet made their famous trip down the Mississippi in 1673, they visited an Illinois village where they were greeted enthusiastically by a party of elders. "Never has the earth been so beautiful," one of the Illinois men is supposed to have told them, "or the sun so Bright as today."[23] Nicholas Perrot, one of the first French traders to venture into the Illinois country, was reportedly told by a

---

[21] Kimball-Brown, *Cultural Transformations*, pp. 244–245; "Marquette's First Voyage," *JR*, vol. LIX, p. 127.

[22] "Cavelier de la Salle de 1679 a 1681," in Pierre Margry, ed., *Découvertes et Établissements des Français dans l'Ouest et dans le Sud de L'Amérique Septentrionale (1614–1754): Mémoires et Documents Originaux*, 6 vols. (Paris, 1876–1886), vol. I, pp. 503–513.

[23] "Marquette's First Voyage," *JR*, vol. LIX, p. 121.

Potawatomi chief, "You are one of the chief spirits because you use iron. It is for you to rule and protect all men. Praised be the sun, who has taught you and sent you to our country." A year later Perrot became the first Frenchman ever to visit a Miami village, and he promised its leaders,

You will become another nation when you know us. I am the dawn of that light, which is beginning to appear in your lands; which precedes the sun; which will shine brightly and will cause you to be born again, as if in another land, where you will more easily find all necessities in greater abundance.[24]

Though we might read these reports skeptically, the solar metaphors were more plausible under the circumstances in which they originated than they appear today. The French could, indeed, offer the Illinois and Miami Indians a center of gravity and a source of material aid and sustenance. Perrot's inflated prophecy was partially fulfilled in 1683, when Réné-Robert, Cavelier de La Salle, and his lieutenant, Henri Tonti, erected the first French fort and trading post in the Illinois country. With the permission of the Illinois confederacy, they selected a site on a high, rock-faced bluff overlooking the Illinois River near the confederacy's Great Village, erected several cabins and storehouses, surrounded them with palisades, and named the result Fort St. Louis (Fig. 1).

Again French timing was good, because in the early 1680s the frequency and intensity of Iroquois attacks accelerated. In the previous year the Illinois Indians suffered what must have been one of the most devastating assaults of their entire history. Iroquois warriors reportedly returned from their 1682 raid with about 700 Illinois prisoners; they claimed that they "killed and ate" another 600 on the spot. With the fort serving as a center of defense, the population of the Great Village ballooned from perhaps 12,000 to as many as 20,000. This enlarged population included the Miami tribes, who chose to overlook their differences with the Illinois Indians in exchange for French protection, and about 1000 Shawnees who had recently been driven out of their homeland between the Ohio and Tennessee Rivers by Iroquois attacks.[25]

[24] Charles Claude Le Roy, Bacqueville de la Potherie, "History of the Savage Peoples Who are Allies of New France," in Blair, ed., *Indian Tribes*, vol. I, pp. 309, 330. I have modernized the translations of these passages.

[25] "Cavelier de La Salle de 1679 a 1681," Margry, ed., *Découvertes et Établissements*, vol. I, p. 469; Richter, *Ordeal of the Longhouse*, pp. 144–145. For the pre-fort population, Louis Hennepin wrote that the village contained 460 cabins, with four to five fires per cabin and one or two families per fire; see *Description of Louisiana Newly Discovered to the Southwest of New France by Order of the King*, Marian E. Cross, trans. (Minneapolis, 1938) [orig. pub. Paris, 1683], p. 65. For the population after the construction of the fort see Franquelin's map, which gives estimates of warrior populations for the villages surrounding the fort. It is reproduced in Fig. 1.

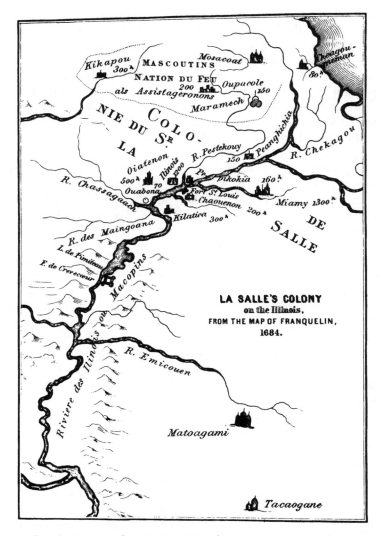

Figure 1. Fort St. Louis and environs, 1684, showing approximate location and estimated warrior propulation in nearby Indian villages. From an engraving published in Francis Parkman, *La Salle and the Discovery of the Great West* (London, 1869), based on a manuscript map by Jean Baptiste Louis Franquelin.

When Iroquois war parties arrived in the Illinois country in the spring of 1683, the local Indian population was well-fortified and well-armed and the Iroquois were driven out. In the following year Iroquois warriors returned; encountering a party of French traders, they inquired warily whether La Salle and Tonti were at the fort, and how many men they might have with them. They decided to proceed with the attack, but once again they were driven off. Beginning in 1685 New France and its Indian allies took the offensive against the Iroquois, and the focus of hostilities shifted to the east. With the immediate threat of war relieved, the population around Fort St. Louis began to disperse.[26]

As the fort's military importance declined, its commercial value grew. By bringing French traders, known as *coureurs de bois*, directly into contact with Illinois Indians for the first time, it gave a tremendous boost to the power and status of the Illinois. Even before Fort St. Louis was built, the Illinois Indians had developed limited trading ties with the Green Bay post through Ottawa middlemen, with whom designated Illinois emissaries exchanged animal pelts and slaves for French merchandise. The slave trade probably grew out of the traditional practice of taking captives as replacements for fallen warriors in battle – a common variation on the mourning-war theme – but the enticement of European trade goods soon encouraged the Illinois warriors to increase their take of live captives and use them as a commodity. Their victims in the slave trade came principally from among the Illinois' traditional enemies west of the Mississippi, especially the Pawnees and the Sioux. By 1670, Marquette could report that the Illinois "take a great many Slaves," for whom they received from the Ottawas "Muskets, Powder, Kettles, Hatchets and Knives."[27]

With the construction of Fort St. Louis, the Illinois Indians' involvement in trade grew and the confederacy's status in the eyes of its neighbors was transformed. From a people in decline, the Illinois once again became a considerable power in the region; after fearing for its territorial integrity and even its survival in the face of earlier Iroquois and Sioux attacks, the confederacy could again make war on and exact tribute from a host of nearby peoples. The scope of Illinois slave raids continued to expand, until they became a source of considerable concern and aggravation to French colonial officials.[28] At the same time, the Illinois

[26] "Tonti's Memoir [1693]," in Louise Kellogg, ed., *Early Narratives of the Northwest, 1634–1699* (New York, 1917), pp. 305–306, 308–311; M. de Beauvais et al., "Relation d'un Voyage dans le pays des Ilinois . . . ," 28 Mai 1684, Archives des Colonies, Série C¹¹A, vol. 6, pt. 1, National Archives of Canada, Ottawa.

[27] Marquette to Father Superior, 1669–1670, *JR*, vol. LIV, p. 191.

[28] See André Pénicaut, *Fleur De Lys and Calumet: Being the Pénicaut Narrative of French*

also began to serve the same middleman role for other Indian tribes that the Ottawas had once served for them. Members of the Osage and Missouri tribes, for example, established a trading alliance with the Illinois Indians and made annual visits to their villages to trade for French goods, especially hatchets, knives, and awls.[29] Such trading alliances were conducted according to a well-established protocol, in which representatives of the Illinois Indians consistently interposed themselves between traders from outlying tribes and the French *coureurs de bois*. This subsidiary trading pattern further profited the Illinois Indians, whether profits are calculated in prestige or in material rewards. Probably the former gain was more important; their middleman status solidified the dominant position of the Illinois Indians among their neighbors and confirmed them as a vital link to French markets.

The Miami Indians, too, benefited from their contact with New France. Leaving Fort St. Louis in several waves during the 1680s, the Miamis established new settlements, first on the lower shores of Lake Michigan and then on the Maumee and Wabash Rivers. There they controlled a particularly rich field for hunting and trapping fur-bearing animals, and became prodigious traders in the European market. The political economy of the Miami tribes was fundamentally altered by their ties with French traders, and their level of fur production soon tested the capacity of the French market to absorb it.[30] When Perrot first visited the Miamis in the 1660s they were embarrassed that they had no beaver pelts to offer him; until that time, they had hunted beavers only for their

Adventure in Louisiana, trans. and ed. Richebourg McWilliams (Baton Rouge, 1953), pp. 122–123; Blasingham, "Depopulation of the Illinois Indians," 376–377; Ramezay and Begon to the Minister, 7 Nov., 1715, in Reuben G. Thwaites, ed., *Collections of the State Historical Society of Wisconsin*, vol. XVI (Madison, 1902), p. 332. The only study of slavery in French Canada is Marcel Trudel, *L'Esclavage au Canada français: Histoire et Conditions de l'Esclavage* (Quebec, 1960); although he did not examine records from the Illinois country or Louisiana, Trudel gives some idea of the magnitude of slaveholding in Canada (he has definitely identified a pool of 2,472 Indian slaves); links the slaves, where possible, to their tribal backgrounds; and describes the Canadian market in Indian slaves. He estimates that nearly 70% of Canada's Indian slaves were Pawnees, although it is difficult to be confident of that number since, by the third decade of the 18th century, the term "*panis*" had become a synonym for "slave" in New France.

[29] Raymond E. Hauser, "Warfare and the Illinois Indian Tribe During the Seventeenth Century: An Exercise in Ethnohistory," *The Old Northwest*, 10 (Winter 1984–1985), 378.

[30] See, e.g., Jean Bochart de Champigny, "Mémoire pour le castor à Québec," 26 Oct. 1694, quoted in Harold A. Innis, *The Fur Trade in Canada: An Introduction to Canadian Economic History*, rev. ed. (Toronto, 1956), pp. 70–71.

meat.[31] They quickly learned the value Europeans placed on the animal's pelt, however, and just as quickly improvised a variety of commercial arrangements that allowed them to exploit European demand.

The economic benefits of the Miami alliance with New France comprised only one dimension in a larger pattern of aid and support; during the first several decades of the 18th century they enjoyed an unusually strong position in their relations with the French. In part, this was because they occupied territory strategically situated in the borderlands separating French and British claims to territory in the Ohio Valley. As a result, the Miamis were recognized as vitally important to French efforts to control the central continent. This strategic centrality permitted the Miami tribes to dictate the terms of their relations with New France in important ways. For example, when they resisted the efforts of imperial administrators to make them settle near the trading post at Detroit, the governor of Canada had no choice but to approve the creation of two new trading posts on the Wabash and Maumee Rivers, in close proximity to the main towns of the Miami and Ouiatanon tribes. The Miami confederation also benefited, as did many of their neighbors, from French military support in their conflicts with other Indian groups. The most notable case was in the war waged against the Fox Indians. In that war most of the peoples of the western Great Lakes and Ohio Valley, including the Miamis and Illinois, succeeded in drawing the French into a military alliance to drive the Fox, Mascoutens, and Kickapoos from the lands around Detroit. In this conflict the Indians, much more than the French, forced events and dictated their outcome.[32]

In a variety of ways, the Illinois and Miami Indians thus managed to use the new opportunities presented by French explorers and traders as sources of renewed power and autonomy. These strategies of accommodation had their costs, but initially they offered important forms of protection to previously endangered communities.

III

The Iroquois raids that inflicted so much damage on the Illinois Indians were even more devastating for another Ohio Valley population. Early French accounts suggest that many Shawnee villages – 15 in one source, 38 in another – were clustered south of the Ohio in the Cumberland

---

[31] La Potherie, "History of the Savage Peoples," in Blair, ed., *Indian Tribes*, vol. I, pp. 331–332.

[32] For the strategic importance of the Miami Indians, see Yves Zoltvany, "The Frontier Policy of Philippe de Rigaud de Vaudreuil, 1713–1725," *Canadian Historical Review*, 48 (1967), 227–250; for Miami resistance to resettlement at Detroit, see Father d'Ave-

River watershed; less reliable evidence also places some Shawnee communities north of the river in the upper valley. Some historians and archaeologists have argued that the Fort Ancient sites, which date from about 1400 to 1650 and share Mississippian traits, may in fact have been pre-contact Shawnee settlements. During the 1660s and 1670s, however, Iroquois warriors descended on Shawnee communities to inflict their characteristic terrors; by the early 1680s the Shawnees had begun to splinter, abandon their homeland, and search for new and safer territories. One group of perhaps 1000 Shawnees migrated north, where in 1683 they were received by La Salle's traders and the Illinois and Miami Indians gathered around Fort St. Louis. Others moved east to the Carolinas, where they already had trading ties, took up residence on the Savannah River, and became known locally as the Savannah Indians.[33]

Soon the Shawnees at Fort St. Louis were on the move again. One group left the fort in 1688 or 1689, and after a period of migration that apparently lasted several years, turned up in Maryland in 1692. The Maryland council was alarmed by the appearance of an unfamiliar group of Indians on the borders of its colony, particularly when they discovered that a Frenchman was traveling with them. Martin Chartier was a *coureur de bois* from the fort who had decided to throw in his lot with the Shawnee band; by the time they arrived in Maryland he was married to a Shawnee woman. The council quickly determined that Chartier was no spy, and soon he and the Shawnees had moved up the Susquehanna River into south central Pennsylvania where they settled the town of Pequea, apparently with the permission of the Unami Delawares who resided nearby. Two years later, in 1694, the rest of the Shawnees at Fort St. Louis were invited to settle among another group of Delawares, the Munsees, who lived along the Delaware River in

naut to Cadillac, 6 June 1702, *Michigan Pioneer and Historical Society Collections*, vol. XXXIII (Lansing, 1904), p. 123; for Miami relocation and new posts, see Vaudreuil to Council, 12 Dec. 1717, in Frances Krauskopf, ed., "Ouiatanon Documents," *Indiana Historical Society Proceedings*, vol. XVIII (Indianapolis, 1955), pp. 160–161; and for an account of the Fox wars generally, see White, *Middle Ground*, pp. 149–175.

33 The most reliable account of the Shawnee migrations is in James Howard, *Shawnee! The Ceremonialism of a Native Indian Tribe and Its Cultural Background* (Athens, Ohio, 1981), pp. 1–8 and following; a more comprehensive, but confusingly presented and occasionally inaccurate account can be found in Charles Hanna, *The Wilderness Trail*, 2 vols. (New York, 1911), vol. I, especially ch. 4. The population estimate is based on Franquelin's 1684 map of the fort, which gives a warrior count for each tribal group encamped in the vicinity. He estimates 200 Shawnee warriors, which would suggest a total Shawnee population at the fort of between 800 and 1,000. For the Savannahs, see Verner Crane, *The Southern Frontier, 1670–1732* (New York, 1981 [orig. pub. 1928]), pp. 19–21 and following.

northeastern Pennsylvania. The two Pennsylvania settlements became the core of a new Shawnee homeland; over the course of the next several decades most of the Shawnees on the Savannah River gradually migrated north to join their kinsmen. Initially the Shawnees were delighted with their new surroundings. One of their leaders told a Pennsylvania official that they were "happy to live in a Countrey at Peace, and not as in [those] Parts, where we formerly liv'd; for then upon our return from hunting, we found our Town surprized, and our women and children taken prisoners by our Enemies."[34]

The Pequea Shawnees found themselves in the middle of a rapidly growing trading system in the Susquehanna Valley. It originated several years before their arrival, in part through the initiative of Jacques Le Tort, his wife Anne, and their son James, Huguenot refugees who fled from France to England in 1685. In London, Le Tort met Sir Matthias Vincent, a partner in the New Mediterranean Sea Company. The company was founded by Dr. Daniel Coxe, a governor and great landholder of West Jersey, who hoped to exploit the Pennsylvania charter to bypass Iroquois control of the Great Lakes and engross the fur trade around Lake Erie – the "New Mediterranean." William Penn granted Coxe, Vincent, and their associates 100,000 acres within his colony in exchange for their promise to establish a new trading venture. Vincent then hired Le Tort to manage his estate within the company's grant, and the Le Torts left for Pennsylvania. In the meantime, however, the scheme was blocked by the Albany traders, who were well-represented in the court of King James (since James was New York's proprietor), and who depended on the Iroquois trade for their livelihood. Coxe's company collapsed; in place of his grand enterprise, he hired Le Tort simply to act as his private agent in the Pennsylvania Indian trade.[35]

Le Tort quickly found that the Schuylkill River trade with the Delaware Indians offered few opportunities to a newcomer; it was dominated by a host of well-established Swedes, Germans, and Englishmen. At about this time he crossed paths with Peter Bizaillon, an experienced *coureur de bois* who had served with Henri Tonti, lived in the Illinois country, and traveled the Mississippi. Bizaillon guided Le Tort on an ex-

---

[34] William Hand Browne et al., eds., *Archives of Maryland*, 63 vol. (Baltimore, 1883–1915), vol. VIII, pp. 341–345; Peter Schuyler to Iroquois, 6 Feb. 1694, and Arent Schuyler's journal, 10 Feb. 1694, in E. B. O'Callaghan and Berthold Fernow, eds., *Documents Relative to the Colonial History of the State of New York*, 15 vols. (Albany, 1856–1887) [hereafter *NYCD*], vol. IV, pp. 90, 98–99; *Minutes of the Provincial Council of Pennsylvania*, 16 vols. (Harrisburg, 1838–1853) [hereafter *Pa. Col. Recs.*], vol. II, p. 388.

[35] Evelyn A. Benson, "The Huguenot Le Torts: First Christian Family on the Conestoga," *Journal of the Lancaster County Historical Society*, 65 (1961), 92–105.

traordinary westward odyssey. They followed the Schuylkill and Susquehanna Rivers and their tributaries until they could portage to the Allegheny, which flows into the Ohio; they continued to the Mississippi, where they turned upstream and paddled a short distance up the Missouri before retracing their steps to the Schuylkill. Along the way they reportedly contacted more than forty Indian nations, "who all treated them very kindly and gave them many furrs." It was a long and arduous trip (some historians have dismissed accounts of it as too fantastic to believe), but Le Tort was not the first to take it – the Shawnees, Chartier, and Bizaillon had all followed essentially the same route – and he would be by no means the last.[36]

Shortly thereafter the Le Torts moved to the Susquehanna Valley, where they were soon trading with "strange Indians." Their mysterious contacts, many of them with French-allied tribes, aroused suspicion (and probably envy) among their competitors in Pennsylvania. A group of fellow traders petitioned the Governor's Council in 1694 to bar the Le Torts from trading "in remote and obscure places with the nativs." Instead, the council required Le Tort to take an oath of loyalty and to "acquaint the governm[en]t with all matters hee can hear of or observe concerning the Natives & the enemies of the countrie."[37]

Two years later Le Tort died at sea, but by that time he had drawn a nucleus of traders to the Susquehanna Valley that included his wife and son, Bizaillon, and John Dubrois, another Huguenot in Le Tort's employ. Thus the Pequea Shawnees discovered congenial trading contacts in their new home – contacts who were familiar with the west and who even spoke French. The Le Torts and their associates had established a tantalizing, but still tenuous and irregular, trade; the Shawnees helped put their business on a more reliable footing, one built on contacts between partners close at hand. The Shawnees were ideally suited to the developing Susquehanna Valley trade: they knew the hunting grounds of

[36] Coxe reportedly gave William Penn a journal and map of the trip in 1693. In 1719 he presented a memorial to the Board of Trade that described the expedition; though its credibility has been questioned, the accuracy of its descriptions and Le Tort's association with Bizaillon make Coxe's claims plausible. The memorial appears, along with a skeptical assessment, in Clarence Alvord and Lee Bidgood, *The First Explorations of the Trans-Allegheny Region by the Virginians, 1650–1674* (Cleveland, 1912), pp. 231–249; quote: p. 245. For more positive assessments of Coxe's claims, see Benson, "Huguenot Le Torts," pp. 99–100, and Francis Jennings, "The Indian Trade of the Susquehanna Valley," *Proceedings of the American Philosophical Society*, 110 (1966), 409–410. For extracts of the memorial and related documents, see also Albright Zimmerman, "Daniel Coxe and the New Mediterranean Sea Company," *Pennsylvania Magazine of History and Biography*, 76 (1952), 86–96.

[37] Council minutes, 6 Feb. 1694, *Pa. Col. Recs.*, vol. I, pp. 435–436.

the west; they had lived and traveled in the Ohio Valley. Moreover, in contrast to the Delawares and Iroquois whose experience with the fur trade centered on beavers, the Shawnees were seasoned deer hunters; those who had traded in the Carolinas had even hunted deer and prepared hides for the transatlantic market. While the founders of the New Mediterranean Sea Company envisioned the Susquehanna Valley as a conduit to the north, where Pennsylvania traders might challenge the Iroquois' control of the Great Lakes beaver trade, the westward-oriented trading system that developed in the lower Susquehanna specialized in deer hides rather than beaver pelts and opened the rich game populations of western Pennsylvania and the upper Ohio Valley to the English market for the first time.

James Logan quickly emerged as the Philadelphia merchant most closely identified with the Susquehanna trade. Logan was a precocious young Scotsman of twenty-five, just embarking on a career in trade, when he caught William Penn's eye and was recruited to accompany the proprietor to his colony in 1699. Penn made him his personal secretary and agent in colonial affairs. Logan soon became a dominant figure in Pennsylvania's public life, and usually appears in historical accounts as the prominent merchant and leading intellectual light that he eventually became. But focusing on the older Logan, a man of accomplishments, wealth, and ease, obscures the ambitious achievements of his first years in the colony, when he successfully wed his desire for personal wealth with the pressing need to grasp and shape affairs on Pennsylvania's western frontier.[38]

Though he began his private career in Pennsylvania as a planter, Logan soon became a factor, or wholesaler of agricultural products, on behalf of his neighbors. He specialized in buying, cutting, packing, and shipping tobacco; at the same time he entered into the dry goods trade, selling manufactured products from England back to the planters in return. But his returns were marginal, and by 1707 his creditors were worried about his prospects. Sometime in the second decade of the century he discovered the Indian trade, and through a patchwork of transactions he gradually shifted his attention to the west. By 1717 the trade

[38] Though various works have focused on certain aspects of Logan's career, he remains a neglected subject. Brief sketches can be found in Wilson Armistead, *Memoirs of James Logan* (London, 1851) and Irma Jane Cooper, *The Life and Public Services of James Logan* (New York, 1921); his early career is considered in Joseph Johnson, "A Statesman of Colonial Pennsylvania: A Study of the Private Life and Public Career of James Logan to the Year 1726" (Ph.D. diss., Harvard Univ., 1943); and his role in shaping provincial culture is treated in Frederick Tolles, *James Logan and the Culture of Provincial America* (Boston, 1957).

in skins and furs dominated his account book; in that year, his principal suppliers were Anne and James Le Tort, Peter Bizaillon, Joseph Smith, Martin Chartier, and John Cartlidge – names that would persist in all of Logan's surviving financial records. Logan's personal entry into the fur trade coincided with the rise of fur and skin exports in Pennsylvania's commerce with London. Customs records indicate that the volume of the trade fluctuated widely from 1699 to 1713: although there were three years in which more than £1000 worth were shipped, there were also three years in which the total value of the trade was less than £100. In 1714 these figures began to stabilize. Over the next ten years the annual value of fur and skin exports never fell below £1000, and it averaged more than £1750 per year (Fig. 2).[39]

Logan soon controlled the Susquehanna trade, and the trading cycle followed an increasingly predictable pattern. Logan delivered merchandise to the colonist-traders at the town of Conestoga, a short distance north of Pequea. The traders received the goods on credit, and then delivered them, again on credit, to their Indian customers. The Indians carried away their merchandise and went west to winter hunting camps, which were strung across western Pennsylvania as far west as the Allegheny and the headwaters of the Ohio. The Indians traded mostly for durable goods; cloth items like strouds, blankets, duffels, and "half thicks" predominated, along with decorative items like gartering and silk handkerchiefs. Iron mouth harps were also in high demand, as were rings, beads, steels and flints, vermillion, and pipes. Guns were not yet articles of trade in Pennsylvania, and rum changed hands in only token amounts – indeed, the small amounts that Logan shipped may have been kept by the traders for their own consumption. In the spring Indian hunters returned from their camps with the fruits of their winter hunt – primarily deerskins and bearskins, with a few pelts from smaller animals like beaver. The colonist-traders then carried the packs of furs to Logan's post at Conestoga, where they were loaded on a wagon, owned by Logan, and shipped to Philadelphia at the traders' expense. In the process, nearly every trader at Conestoga fell chronically into Logan's

[39] James Logan Receipt Book, 1702–1709, Logan Papers, Historical Society of Pennsylvania, Philadelphia; Logan to John Askew, Aug. 1706 and 2 Jan. 1707, James Logan Letter Book, Logan Papers, vol. II, HSP; James Logan Account Book, 1712–1720, Logan Papers, vol. IX, HSP; Stephen H. Cutcliffe, "Colonial Indian Policy As a Measure of Rising Imperialism: New York and Pennsylvania, 1700–1755," *The Western Pennsylvania Historical Magazine*, 64 (1981), 240–242, Table 1: "Fur and Skin Exports from New York and Pennsylvania to London by Constant Value in £." The figures are based on a constant value to correct for price fluctuations, so the table provides a roughly accurate gauge of the number of skins and furs shipped.

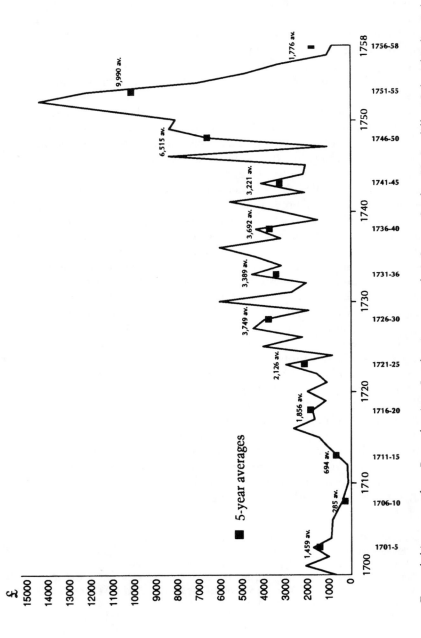

Figure 2. Fur and skin exports from Pennsylvania to London (constant value). Source: Stephen H. Cutcliffe, "Colonial Indian Policy As a Measure of Rising Imperialism: New York and Pennsylvania, 1700–1755," *The Western Pennsylvania Historical Magazine*, 64 (1981), 237–268, Table 1. No data was available for 1705 and 1712.

debt; by the mid-1720s many carried debts of between £300 and £650 apiece.[40]

While Logan the merchant profited handsomely from the trade, Logan the public official gained a valuable window into Indian affairs through his connections with the Susquehanna traders. He turned many of the traders into unofficial deputies of the governor's council, asking them to serve as interpreters, informants, and even, occasionally, as informal diplomats in intercultural relations. In return, Logan favored many of the most cooperative traders with generous grants of land from the colony, as well as with other forms of support.[41]

With the opening he gained from the traders, Logan became the chief architect of Pennsylvania's Indian policy in the west. His partner in this process was the Iroquois confederacy. The Iroquois interest in the lower Susquehanna Valley was rooted, perhaps unsurprisingly, in conquest. In the middle of the 17th century the region was controlled by the Susquehannocks, who were regarded by early English visitors as one of the most powerful nations on the continent. (In 1624 John Smith wrote that they were so "great" and "well proportioned" that "they seemed like Giants to the English.") But beginning in the 1660s the Susquehannocks were victimized by a series of Iroquois attacks; in 1674 they were forced south into Maryland, where a few years later they were caught in the backlash against Bacon's Rebellion in Virginia. Reeling with defeats, the surviving Susquehannocks found refuge in various Iroquois villages, and for nearly two decades the lower Susquehanna was largely unoccupied. In about 1690 a remnant band of Susquehannocks, accompanied by a

---

[40] For accounts with traders see James Logan Ledger, 1720–1728, Logan Papers, vol. X, HSP; for breakdown of merchandise see James Logan Day Book, 5 Sept. 1722–16 Jan. 1723, Logan Papers, HSP, and Logan's Account Book, 1712–1720, Logan Papers, vol. IX, HSP. For Logan's rise in the Indian trade see also Evelyn Benson, "The Earliest Use of the Term 'Conestoga Wagon,'" *Papers of the Lancaster County Historical Society*, 57 (1953), 109–119, and Jennings, "Indian Trade."

[41] Interpreters: see, e.g., *Pa. Col. Recs.*, vol. II, pp. 388–391; vol. III, pp. 45–49, 78–80, 92–98, 123–125; informants: e.g., *Pa. Col. Recs.*, vol. II, pp. 131, 145, 121–122; vol. III, pp. 295–298; diplomats: Logan to Bizaillon, 28 Oct. 1713, Logan Papers, vol. III, p. 239, American Philosophical Society, Philadelphia. Land grants: see surveys in the Taylor Papers, vol. XII, nos. 2399, 2426, and vol. XIII, no. 2731, HSP; William Egle, ed., *Pennsylvania Archives*, 2nd Ser., 19 vols. (Harrisburg, 1874–1893), vol. XIX, p. 496; James Steel's Letter Book, p. 83, Logan Papers, HSP; and Jennings, "Indian Trade," p. 418. This argument is developed in more detail, and the materials listed in this note are discussed more fully, in Eric Hinderaker, "The Creation of the American Frontier: Europeans and Indians in the Ohio River Valley, 1673–1800" (Ph.D. diss., Harvard Univ., 1991), pp. 186–191. See also the parallel discussion in Jennings' "Indian Trade," which stresses more than my account Logan's efforts to enrich himself personally through his relations with the traders.

group of Iroquois overseers from the Seneca tribe, returned to found a village at the mouth of Conestoga Creek; as a result of their location the combined Seneca/Susquehanna group was known by colonists as the Conestoga Indians. During the next several decades, as Iroquois war parties turned south, refugees streamed north out of the backcountry of Virginia and the Carolinas to take up residence in Iroquoia. Conoys, Tutelos, Nanticokes, and Tuscaroras, among others, followed the Susquehanna River toward Iroquois country; some settled for a time in or around Conestoga, creating what one historian has described as "a veritable united nations of Indians" there.[42]

The Conestoga Indians and the other southern refugees on the Susquehanna were Iroquois dependents; the Shawnees, on the other hand, had an uneasy, ill-defined relationship with the Iroquois. They considered themselves guests and allies of the Delawares, not the Iroquois. By 1700 a shared Shawnee–Delaware town named Paxtang had been settled on the Susquehanna, and the Shawnee groups on both the Susquehanna and the upper Delaware Rivers developed close political and kinship ties with the Delawares among whom they lived. The political relationship between the Iroquois and Delawares is itself problematic and controversial. It is clear that the Delawares recognized a debt of tribute to the Iroquois that dated to sometime in the 17th century, but it is equally clear that the Delawares were not refugees – they still retained control of their territory along the Delaware River – and thus they were not in the same position of complete subjection to the Iroquois council that the refugee groups on the Susquehanna were.[43] Nevertheless, in a

---

[42] John Smith, *Generall Historie of Virginia, New England, and the Summer Isles* (1624), in Edward Arber, ed., *Travels and Works*, 2 vols. (New York, 1966 [orig. pub. 1910]), vol. I, p. 350 and following. The best discussion of these displacements and migrations is in Barry C. Kent, *Susquehanna's Indians*, The Pennsylvania Historical and Museum Commission, Anthropological Series, no. 6 (Harrisburg, 1984). Quote: Francis Jennings, "Iroquois Alliances in American History," in Jennings et al., eds., *The History and Culture of Iroquois Diplomacy* (Syracuse, 1985), p. 41.

[43] Both the Delawares and, after their arrival in Pennsylvania, the Shawnees, formally acquiesced to the Iroquois in political affairs; for a description of a Delaware mission to offer tribute, see *Pa. Col. Recs.*, vol. II, p. 546–549; for a sketchy account of the Iroquois settlement with the Shawnees, ibid., vol. II, pp. 145, 155, 158–159. The precise terms of these relationships have been a subject of much controversy among historians; for various interpretations, see Anthony F. C. Wallace, "Woman, Land, and Society: Three Aspects of Aboriginal Delaware Life," *Pennsylvania Archaeologist*, 17 (1947), 1–35; Francis Jennings, "The Delaware Interregnum," *Pennsylvania Magazine of History and Biography*, 89 (1965), 174–198, and *The Ambiguous Iroquois Empire: The Covenant Chain Confederation of Indian Tribes from its Beginnings to the Lancaster Treaty of 1744* (New York, 1984), pp. 214–219, 301–303. My view is that both groups recognized a formal obligation of tribute, but did not understand that obliga-

process that will be described in more detail in chapter three, beginning in 1721 Logan and the Iroquois placed increasing pressure on the Indians of Pennsylvania to accept the Iroquois as their spokesmen and political superiors in all their dealings with the colony.

Beginning in the mid-1720s, parties of Shawnees and Delawares chose to leave the Susquehanna Valley to escape domination by Pennsylvania and Iroquois officials. They moved to a series of new villages, most of which grew up on the sites of old winter hunting camps, on the Allegheny and upper Ohio Rivers. In 1725 Pennsylvania's Shawnee and Delaware Indians each had one village site west of the Susquehanna Valley: Opessa's Town was a Shawnee settlement on the upper Potomac, while the Delaware town of Kittanning stood on the Allegheny River a short distance above the headwaters of the Ohio. During the next several years Shawnees and Delawares began to move west in larger numbers.[44] The migratory stream accelerated rapidly after 1728, and by 1731 more than half a dozen new towns had already been founded on the Allegheny and upper Ohio Rivers.

Pennsylvania's Governor Patrick Gordon, alarmed by the rapid outmigration of the colony's Indian population, questioned three traders late in 1731 who were familiar with the developing cluster of western settlements. Already, the traders estimated that between four and five hundred men, many with families, had moved west. The principal Delaware towns, according to Gordon's informants, were Kittanning, Kiskimenitas Town, Shannopin's Town, and Assunepachla, or Frankstown. The Shawnee settlements, in addition to Opessa's Town, included Black Legs Town, Conemaugh Town, James LeTort's town, and Ohesson, which lay on the Juniata River midway between the older Susquehanna settlements and the new ones on the Allegheny and Ohio.[45]

tion to entail abject political subjection. It was not until the 1720s that the Iroquois council tried to parlay their vague authority over the Delawares and Shawnees into absolute political superiority; see, e.g., the letter from several Shawnee chiefs to Governor Gordon claiming that the Iroquois first put "pettycoats" on them, an act that implies political subjection, in about 1726: Samuel Hazard, ed., *Pennsylvania Archives* [1st Ser.], 12 vols. (Philadelphia, 1852–1856), vol. I, pp. 329–330.

44 James Logan dated the first removal of members of these tribes to about 1724; see his letters to Gov. Clarke, 4 Aug. 1737, and Gov. Gooch, 11 May 1738, Logan Papers vol. IV, pp. 13–16, APS.

45 Examinations of Jonah Davenport, James Le Tort, and Edmund Cartlidge, 29 Oct. and 7 Dec. 1731, *Pa. Arch.* [1st Ser.], vol. I, pp. 299–302, 305–306. The best available map for locating these towns is Barry C. Kent, Janet Rice, and Kakuko Ota, "A Map of 18th Century Indian Towns in Pennsylvania," *Pennsylvania Archaeologist*, 51 (1981), 1–18 and endpaper. See also William Scull's excellent map of the colony published in 1770.

This migration stream would reach a flood stage by midcentury. The earliest Shawnees and Delawares were joined by successive waves of other Indian migrants: additional Shawnee and Delaware bands, many of whom had lost their Pennsylvania lands by treaty and sale to the colony; other members of the Iroquois protectorate, including Mahican refugees who had been pushed steadily westward from their original homelands in New England and New York, and bands of southern Indians, especially Nanticokes, who were driven off their lands by Cherokee and Catawba attacks; and a growing population of Iroquois hunters. Ostensibly the function of the Ohio Iroquois was to oversee the other Ohio Indians; Queen Aliquippa was the first Iroquois-appointed overseer for the region. But in reality, Aliquippa's Town was primarily a hunting and trading town like all the others. Queen Aliquippa was surrounded by young men who had come west for better access to game, much as the Shawnee and Delaware hunters had. In Aliquippa's Town originated the Ohio Valley band known as the Mingos, western Iroquois (mostly Senecas) who became notorious among colonial officials for their troublesome independence from the Iroquois council at Onondaga.[46]

For Pennsylvania officials and Iroquois leaders alike, the westward migration that began in the 1720s threatened the order they were trying to impose on Indian affairs. Above all, Pennsylvania officials feared that the western Indians might unite with the French in opposition to the colony's interests. But when they encouraged the Shawnees to return to the Susquehanna Valley and offered them a parcel of land as an enticement, Opakethwa, one of a new generation of Shawnee chiefs who reveled in their newfound autonomy, asked that the land be held for them in trust but insisted that, in the West, they could "live much better . . . than they possibly can any where on the Sasquehannah." He tried to ease the governor's fears by pointing out that, in moving west, "they did a Service to this Province, in getting Skins for it in a place so far remote."[47]

---

[46] For a more detailed discussion of this migration see Michael McConnell, *A Country Between: The Upper Ohio Valley and Its Peoples, 1724–1774* (Lincoln, NE, 1992), ch. 1. McConnell overemphasizes the communal and tribal cohesion of these migrations, in my view, and underestimates the extent to which Seneca villages in the Ohio Valley were populated by Indians from various backgrounds, but his is nevertheless an invaluable account.

[47] The Shawnees were invited to send a delegation to Philadelphia in the spring of 1732 by Governor Gordon, and in response he received vague assurances in a letter from five chiefs that some Shawnee representatives would visit Philadelphia sometime during the summer; see *Pa. Arch.* [1st Ser.], vol. I, pp. 329–330. Four delegates – Opakethwa,

When a direct appeal to the Shawnee leaders failed, the governor and his advisers still hoped that the Iroquois council might intervene to stem the tide of outward migration among the colony's Indians. The Iroquois reported that they had tried to persuade both Shawnee and Delaware leaders to "come back from the Ohio," but persuasion had so far proven insufficient. Believing that the Iroquois exercised "absolute Authority" over the Indians of Pennsylvania, the governor pressed them to enforce their order. When the Iroquois finally did try to pressure the Ohio Indians to return to Pennsylvania, a colonial official reported that the Iroquois' "Great Men received . . . ill usage instead of the expected success." Indeed, a Shawnee faction took offense at the arrogance of one of the visiting chiefs, and after the Iroquois delegation departed they traveled to Iroquoia, murdered the despised leader, and then fled down the Ohio River to found a new town at the mouth of the Scioto River – the town that would later become the center of Shawnee settlement in the Ohio Valley.[48]

The hierarchical structure of Indian diplomacy that leaders of Pennsylvania and the Iroquois were trying to impose on the colony's Indians paralleled the structure of the Covenant Chain, the diplomatic system that connected the Iroquois with New York. The metaphor sounds egalitarian, but within the logic of the Covenant Chain the first link was the strongest; the Iroquois exercised preeminent authority over every Indian group subject to their leadership. Instead of accepting the Covenant Chain, which would have placed them at the bottom of this hierarchy, Shawnee leaders sought to distance themselves from Pennsylvania and the Iroquois. To this end they established ties with New France – not in the interest of replacing one overlord with another, but to facilitate a play-off relationship that would balance their own interests between those of the European powers. In the early 1730s the Shawnees met with traders and colonial officials from New France, and soon Shawnee delegates visiting Philadelphia warned that they had now moved so far west that they were in danger of "going over to the French" unless Pennsylvania offered them arms and ammunition. Governor George Thomas despaired of the Shawnees' "Inconstancy." Although he acknowledged that Pennsylvania's "most valuable Trade for Skins is with them," he feared that the Shawnees had become ungovernable. Clearly, the Iroquois were not the answer; "the closer our Union has been with

Opakeita, and two younger men – finally arrived in the city at the end of September; for their visit, see *Pa. Col. Recs.*, vol III, pp. 491–496; quotes: pp. 494–495.

[48] *Pa. Col. Recs.*, vol. III, pp. 426–429, 464–483; Logan to Gooch, 11 May 1738, Logan Papers, vol. IV, pp. 13–16, APS; *Pa. Col. Recs.*, vol. III, pp. 607–609.

the Six Nations," he noted, "the greater distance they [the Shawnees] have kept from us."[49]

In contrast to the desire of colonial officials to dominate and control the Shawnees, the Shawnees sought a middle way that would allow them to develop roughly equivalent diplomatic and economic ties with each imperial power. Leaders in Philadelphia and Iroquoia imagined the western Indians as the final link in a chain that began with them; the Shawnees put forward an alternative metaphor, one that placed them at the center of an international trading nexus. Shawnee spokesmen admitted to the governor of Pennsylvania that they had established ties with New France from their new base in the Ohio Valley, but insisted that this did not imply an intention to "leave their brethren the English, or turn their backs upon them." On the contrary, Opakethwa claimed that the governor of New France himself had advised the Shawnees to maintain ties with the English, since they "were much better furnished with Cloathing, and other things necessary for the Indians, than his people were"; furthermore, according to Opakethwa, the French governor hoped "that in time the French and English Traders would meet at Allegheny, exchange goods, and trade together." This was a blatant misrepresention of Governor Beauharnois' wishes; he consistently and emphatically urged the Ohio Indians to sever their ties with the English.[50] But Opakethwa's misrepresentation perfectly described the relationship the Shawnees hoped to cultivate with the two European powers. By establishing economic ties with both France and Britain and avoiding diplomatic domination by either, they sought to maximize their independence and power.

The newfound political leverage of the Shawnees and their western neighbors was complemented by the growth of their trade. The move west lifted earlier constraints on the process of hunting for the market. While they lived on the Susquehanna, where game was scarce by the beginning of the 18th century, Indian hunters had to travel many miles through rough terrain to their winter camps and then carry the furs and skins they collected back to the Susquehanna trading posts. Since they did not employ pack animals, the practical limit on the number of skins

[49] For the Covenant Chain see especially Richter, *Ordeal of the Longhouse*, Jennings, *Ambiguous Iroquois Empire*, and Richard Aquila, *The Iroquois Restoration: Iroquois Diplomacy on the Colonial Frontier, 1701–1754* (Detroit, 1983); Council minutes, 10 Aug. 1737, *Pa. Col. Recs.*, vol. IV, pp. 233–235; Speech of Gov. Thomas to Assembly, 31 July 1744, ibid., vol. IV, pp. 737–740.

[50] *Pa. Col. Recs.*, vol. III, pp. 491–496; Beauharnois to the Minister, 15 Oct. 1732, and Indian Council speeches, 1732, in Sylvester Stevens and Donald Kent, eds., *Wilderness Chronicles of Northwestern Pennsylvania* (Harrisburg, 1941), pp. 5–11.

they traded was the number they and their families could transport. This pattern kept the volume of the trade quite modest, and guaranteed that hunting for the market would never be more than a sidelight to the economic activities of the Susquehanna Indians.

As Indians moved west, the structure of the trade was revolutionized and its volume jumped immediately and dramatically (Fig. 2). The burden of transporting skins, furs, and merchandise began to fall on the Pennsylvania traders, who were forced to travel to the western country to trade with the Indians.[51] This change demanded a more vigorous and capital-intensive form of business enterprise, fraught with risk. Traders used pack animals, employees, servants, and slaves to bear the added physical burdens, and took on partners to share the financial ones. These requirements made the Indian trade more challenging, but as its volume increased it also became potentially more lucrative. For the Indians, the change brought a new level of affluence and a new importance as producers and customers in the British commercial system. The western Shawnees and Delawares, along with the other groups being drawn into the trading network they pioneered, became Pennsylvania's most important source of deerskins and furs. Game was abundant, since the valley lands had been left largely uninhabited for two generations after the Iroquois wars; thus, when a Shawnee band settled near the mouth of the Scioto River they gave it a name that signified "Hairy River," because "when they first came to live here, deers were so plenty, that in the vernal season, when they came to drink, the stream would be thick of hairs."[52]

Although these developments were intimately tied to the Ohio Indians' growing reliance on transatlantic markets, they seemed to create a renaissance of traditional pursuits. The first several decades following the westward migration were halcyon days for previously embattled hunters and warriors. Both the Shawnees and the Delawares had struggled with displacement from traditional territories, shrinking success in hunting, and periodic failure and frustration in warfare. In the Ohio Valley they entered an expansive territory, free of the encroachments of settlers and their livestock, where they could spread out in search of ideal village sites.[53] Women planted extensive fields without worrying

[51] This change forced most of the Susquehanna traders out of the business. Of the twenty traders who were operating in the Allegheny and Ohio River towns and were identified by name in the Letter Respecting Traders, 1 May 1732, *Pa. Arch.* [1st Ser.], vol. I, p. 425, only four were doing business with Logan a decade earlier.

[52] David Jones, *A Journal of Two Visits Made to Some Nations of Indians on the West Side of the River Ohio, in the Years 1772–1773* (New York, 1865 [orig. pub. 1774]), p. 46.

[53] On colonial livestock in Indian fields see, e.g., *Pa. Col. Recs.*, vol. II, p. 554; vol. III, pp.

whether pigs and cattle would trample and forage in them, while men enjoyed unparalleled opportunity as hunters and traders.[54] For a time, the new communities on the Allegheny and Ohio thrived.

IV

French and British officials envisioned the Indian trade as a zero-sum competition for furs and skins, for trading partners, and by extension for neatly defined territorial claims. In practice, patterns of trade in the Ohio Valley did more to confuse than to clarify imperial pretensions to power. The region's commercial system developed according to a logic all its own – one that no administrator of empire could wholeheartedly endorse. As Indians and colonists pursued their own ends, the empires, contrary to all expectation, became the pawns in a complex of processes that neither could do much to control. While colonial officials tried to keep the British and French spheres in the Ohio Valley separate and distinct, the region's geographic unity and the dynamics of commercial expansion tended to blur the boundaries of national difference. Trading ties crossed artificially defined boundaries and increasingly knit the entire valley together into a single, unified commercial zone. The more trade refused to conform to national interests, the more aggressively French and British officials pushed to clarify imperial boundaries in the Ohio Valley, a process that culminated in the outbreak of the Seven Years' War. In the end, the struggle to create exclusive zones of commer-

---

49, 323–324. On the problem of encroachment more generally see especially the controversies over Conestoga and the Tulpehocken lands, in ibid., vol. III, pp. 216 and following and vol. III, p. 318 and following. For a fuller discussion of livestock, fences, and Indian lands, see William Cronon, *Changes in the Land: Indians, Colonists, and the Ecology of New England* (New York, 1983), pp. 127–156, and for livestock in particular as a source of intercultural conflict see Virginia DeJohn Anderson, "King Philip's Herds: Indians, Colonists, and the Problem of Livestock in Early New England," *WMQ*, 51 (1994), 601–624.

[54] On the tendency for settlement to sprawl and, particularly with the Delawares, for villages to be small and dispersed, see, e.g., Christopher Gist's first journal, 1750–1751, in Lois Mulkearn, ed., *George Mercer Papers Relating to the Ohio Company of Virginia* (Pittsburgh, 1954), pp. 99–114, in which he recorded visits to a dozen Indian communities. Of these, half were Delaware settlements, and of the four whose size he noted, the largest contained only twenty families. Another included half that many, and two were tiny villages of only four to six families, or perhaps thirty residents. The principal Shawnee towns, which tended to be much larger, were noteworthy for the size and productivity of their fields; the Governor General of New France called the Shawnees "an industrious tribe, cultivating much land." Beauharnois and d'Aigremont to Maurepas, 1 Oct. 1728, Stevens and Kent, eds., *Wilderness Chronicles*, pp. 3–4.

cial activity in the Ohio Valley only clarified the inherent limitations of a colonial system conceived along these lines.

Ironically, the Ohio Valley trade was not particularly profitable for either empire. It nevertheless drew each into a complex tangle of Indian alliances, and once they were involved they had no choice but to follow out the logic of these connections. Thus when the Illinois and Miami trade first opened to French markets, the result, measured purely in economic terms, was disastrous. On the one hand, the *fermiers* who held the royal monopoly in furs could not begin to absorb the sudden dramatic increase in the supply of beaver pelts, and during the first two decades of the 18th century enormous overstocks of furs slowly mouldered and rotted in Paris warehouses as hatmakers struggled to put them to profitable use. On the other hand, the beaver pelts acquired from the Ohio Valley were neither as thick nor as well-prepared as those traded further north. In order to compensate for the loss of quality associated with the Ohio Valley trade, the French government was forced to create a grading system that distinguished between higher- and lower-quality pelts and valued them accordingly.[55]

The colony of Pennsylvania, and the British empire it was supposed to serve, also benefitted in only limited ways from the western trade. Since trade was not conducted through monopolies, as it was in New France, neither colony nor empire collected fees from traders. In the decentralized system of enterprise favored by the British, benefits accrued to the crown less directly, through customs revenues and the growth of imperial markets. In the grand scheme of 18th-century empire, the Indian trade was a minor contributor to Britain's national wealth; and within Pennsylvania's robust commercial economy it was a small sidelight to the principal channels of trade.[56] The risks of the Indian trade, extraordinary even by colonial standards, meant that a few merchant firms emerged as specialists that dominated the field, while the most established Philadelphia partnerships generally chose to steer clear of such an uncertain enterprise.[57] Even on the eve of the Seven Years' War, when the volume of skins and furs exported from Pennsylvania reached unprecedented heights, the risks of the Ohio Valley trade were so high that very few participants could consistently make it pay. Nevertheless, offi-

[55] Innis, *Fur Trade in Canada*, pp. 63–73.

[56] Alice Hanson Jones, *Wealth of a Nation to Be: The American Colonies on the Eve of the Revolution* (New York, 1980), Table 2.8, "Major Commodity Exports by Region, 1770," p. 48.

[57] On risk generally see Thomas Doerflinger, *A Vigorous Spirit of Enterprise: Merchants and Economic Development in Revolutionary Philadelphia* (Chapel Hill, 1986), especially pp. 135–164; and on the Indian trade in particular, pp. 148–151.

cers of both empires invested untold time, energy, and resources in the effort to sustain and expand the Indian trade, because they equated trading alliances with imperial ascendancy. To compete with one another, the French and British empires supported trade networks whose dynamics ultimately threatened to ruin them both.

But if the economic benefits of the interior Indian trade were questionable when viewed from an imperial perspective, many promoters and traders were enthusiastic about its possibilities. The alluring myth of American abundance, even the intoxicating attractions of remote and exotic regions, were enough to draw certain kinds of adventurers into the field to test their fortunes and seek opportunity in an often uncomprehended enterprise. Entering the fur trade, like playing a lottery, was a gamble that not everyone could hope to win; nevertheless, with the right combination of skill and luck, some traders might do remarkably well. In the French empire the activities of the *coureurs de bois* have been relentlessly romanticized, until they have taken on legendary proportions in early American history. Britain's middle colonies, and especially Pennsylvania, gave rise to their own class of strenuous traders, who also expended enormous effort and took great risks in the pursuit of profits and adventure. Though their occupations were unusual, the peripatetic Indian traders were responding in their own way to a universal European fascination with the abundance of American resources. Drawn to the far margins of the known world, they were frequently entranced – and just as often deceived – by the apparent prospect of easy and unlimited wealth. The remote, temperate, and beautiful Ohio Valley was a particularly strong magnet for traders in search of such esoteric opportunity.

The *coureurs* of New France first entered the region from the Great Lakes, following (and in a few cases apparently even anticipating) the explorations and discoveries of Marquette and La Salle. While a restrictive licensing system permitted a small number of colonists to carry on a trade in furs by permission of the crown, other *coureurs* who entered the field in the last two decades of the 17th century did so essentially as outlaws. This status perhaps contributed to their tendency toward creative freelancing as commercial agents. From a surprisingly early date, *coureurs de bois* from the Illinois country began to experiment with trading routes to the English colonies on the Atlantic seaboard as alternatives to the much nearer French outposts; their experiments were further encouraged when Louis XIV temporarily outlawed the activites of *coureurs* altogether in 1696.[58]

---

[58] The 1696 edict is printed in part in *NYCD*, vol. IX, p. 636; for its context, see William Eccles, *The Canadian Frontier, 1534–1760* (New York, 1969), pp. 125–128.

Martin Chartier and Peter Bizaillon were both introduced to the Illinois country as associates of La Salle and Tonti, but soon helped pioneer trading routes that carried furs and skins from French-allied Indian tribes into English markets. They were not alone. In the first place they apparently had collaborators, especially among the Miami Indians, where Bizaillon's brother Michel resided as a trader and probably helped to facilitate trade contacts between the Miami Indians and the Le Tort group. In 1714 an official of New France lamented to his superior that Bizaillon and his associates were leading "a life not only scandalous but even Criminal in many ways" among the colony's Indian allies in the Ohio Valley.[59]

At roughly the same time some of the Miami villages were being approached by English traders from the Carolinas, again thanks in part to the early travels of a wandering *coureur*. Jean Couture also came to the Illinois country with La Salle and Tonti, and also deserted them to make a long trip through the continental interior. He followed the Tennessee River eastward, crossed the Alleghenies, and made his way toward the coast until, in the early 1690s, he arrived in Charles Town, South Carolina, where he caused a sensation by telling exaggerated tales of gold deposits and pearl fisheries. These stories, predictably, came to nothing, but in 1700 Couture led a party of South Carolina traders west along the Tennessee and Ohio Rivers to make contact with the French-allied Indians of the Mississippi and western Ohio Valleys. For perhaps a decade Carolina officials and traders sought to make the Tennessee an important trading route, and in 1701 18 *coureurs* requested permission to establish a regular trade in furs at Charles Town. In the end the Carolinians failed to make significant inroads in the region, but their efforts were not entirely ephemeral. As late as 1714, a group of Carolina traders had several storehouses on a tributary of the Wabash River, where they traded among the Miami tribes, especially the Ouiatanons and Piankashaws.[60]

The Miamis were not passive observers of these developments. They quickly learned that they could receive European manufactures on better terms from the English than they enjoyed with the French, and they soon acted on their own to take advantage of the fact. When they abandoned the Chicago mission in 1702 in favor of village sites on the Wabash and Miami Rivers, French officials suspected that they wanted

[59] Claude de Ramezay to the Minister, 18 Sept. 1714, *CSHS-Wisc.*, vol. XVI, pp. 300–303.
[60] Verner W. Crane, "The Tennessee River as the Road to Carolina: The Beginnings of Exploration and Trade," *Mississippi Valley Historical Review*, 3 (1916), 5–14;

to be closer to their English connections. The resident missionary at Chicago wrote that the Miamis "have never been seen more eager in hunting the beavers than since they received fine belts from the English." During the next several years, the presence of Miami Indians was noted in western Pennsylvania and also at Albany, where they first visited in 1708. They were so pleased by the terms of trade at Albany that they promised to return again the following year.[61]

Such trans-imperial trading contacts suggest that, from the very earliest years, commerce and empire were uncomfortably matched: an expanding sphere of contacts and trade could as easily undermine as promote stable imperial growth. Administrators in both colonial systems were beginning to learn this lesson in the first several decades of the 18th century, and no career drives home the point as clearly as that of the uncommon, enigmatic French adventurer Étienne de Véniard de Bourgmont.[62]

Bourgmont began his life as a well-born ne'er-do-well in Normandy, where as a young man he was caught poaching game on monastery lands. He fled to Canada and entered military service rather than pay his fine, and in 1706 he was assigned to the Detroit garrison. Within months he deserted from the service with two fellow soldiers and a woman named Madame Tichenet, who left a husband and several children behind at Detroit;[63] for more than a decade thereafter Bourgmont's movements cast only an occasional shadow across the documentary record. He and his companions briefly formed an outlaw colony on Lake Erie, but they scattered when one of the deserters was caught,

---

CSHS Wisc., vol. XVI, pp. 208–210; vol. XVII, 475n.

[61] Mermet to Cadillac, 19 Apr. 1702, *Michigan Pioneer and Historical Society Collections*, vol. XXXIII (Lansing, 1904), p. 118; references to the Miamis in western Pennsylvania appear periodically, but see, e.g., *Pa. Col. Recs.*, vol. II, pp. 121–122 (the Miamis are often called Twightwees in the English records of this period); Lord Cornbury to the Board of Trade, 20 Aug. 1708, *NYCD*, vol. V, p. 65.

[62] The best account of Bourgmont's life is Frank Norall, *Bourgmont: Explorer of the Missouri, 1698–1725* (Lincoln, NE, 1988); although I differ from Norall on certain points of emphasis, what follows is based primarily on his account. See also Louise Dechêne's essay in George W. Brown, gen. ed., *Dictionary of Canadian Biography* (Toronto, 1966–), vol. II, pp. 645–647, and Milo M. Quaife, "Detroit Biographies: The Sieur de Bourgmont," *Burton Historical Collection Leaflet*, 6 (1928), 49–63.

[63] This was only one episode in the long and storied life of Madame Tichenet. Within a few years she had resurfaced in Albany, where she became known as Madame Montour. She soon married an Oneida chief and began to serve the governor of New York as an interpreter. Eventually she and her husband moved to the vicinity of Shamokin, where their friend and associate Shickellamy was serving as an Iroquois overseer to the Pennsylvania Indians. For decades she and her son, Andrew, were prominent figures in the colony's intercultural relations.

tried, and sentenced to death. For the next several years Bourgmont was apparently active as a *coureur de bois*, headquartered perhaps among the Miami tribes but traveling widely along the Ohio, Mississippi, and Missouri Rivers. He soon became one of the first Frenchmen to establish trading connections with the Missouri tribes independently of Illinois middlemen; by 1714 he had married a daughter of a Missouri chief and they had a newborn son.

Between 1713 and 1718 Bourgmont was also making contacts in official circles in New Orleans and publicizing his wide-ranging travels and connections. By the end of the decade the governor of Louisiana, Jean-Baptiste Le Moyne de Bienville, decided to employ Bourgmont as an official ambassador to the Missouri tribes; in 1720 he was sent to Paris, knighted, and named commander of a new post to be erected on the Missouri River. From such a base, Bourgmont assured his superiors, he could make "peace among all the Indian tribes between Louisiana and New Mexico in order to open a safe trade route."[64] In exchange for his service, Bourgmont requested that the king admit him to the ranks of the French nobility. The Duc d'Orleans, acting as regent for Louis XV, accepted his terms and, after a two-year delay, sent him back to Louisiana. A decade and a half after Bourgmont ignominiously deserted his post at Detroit, he had thus parlayed his wide-ranging knowledge of the North American landscape and its inhabitants into a knighthood, the command of a new outpost, and the promise of a noble title.

The Duc d'Orleans and his advisers were pursuing two complementary goals in the Bourgmont mission. On the one hand, if he was successful the French trading sphere in North America would be dramatically expanded; on the other, an alliance with the Padouca tribe in the southwest would provide a valuable buffer between the French outposts on the Mississippi River and the Spanish presence in New Mexico. Armed with a royal commission, Bourgmont finally left New Orleans for the Missouri River early in the spring of 1723, accompanied by a small (and discontented) group of Frenchmen and his son, now nine years old. During the first winter they built Fort d'Orleans on the north bank of the Missouri, midway between the mouths of the Osage and Kansas Rivers. In the following year, after a long and difficult journey, Bourgmont and his party finally made peace with the Padoucas on behalf of Louisiana and its allies on the Missouri.

Bourgmont still had one task left. His final instruction was to persuade "some of the chiefs of the principal Indian tribes to travel with him to France, in order to give them an idea of the power of the

[64] Quoted in Norall, *Bourgmont*, p. 34.

French."[65] In November 1724, he set out from the Missouri post with a delegation of chiefs from the Missouri, Osage, and Oto tribes and the daughter of a Missouri chief. On their way through the Illinois country they were joined by a Jesuit superior, Father Nicolas-Ignace Beaubois, and five Illinois chiefs. To reduce expenses, 10 of the 15 Indians were sent home once they reached New Orleans. The other five set sail along with Bourgmont and Beaubois for Paris, where they were fêted by the nobility and caused a great sensation with the public. The climax of the visit came when they were invited to Fontainebleu for an audience with the fifteen-year-old Louis XV. Three days later he invited them to hunt with him in the royal woods, and before they left to return to America he gave each of them tokens by which to remember their visit.[66]

The Indian embassy orchestrated by Bourgmont may have been the social event of the season in Paris, but as a substantive diplomatic mission it accomplished nothing. The Indian tribes contacted by Bourgmont on his long trek into the interior made only a faint and fleeting impression on the minds of his superiors in France; the Padoucas were quickly forgotten altogether, and the Missouri post just as quickly became the exclusive province of *coureurs* who were criticized for their lawless ways. Nor were the descriptions of Paris offered by the Indian delegates given much weight among their people. In the Illinois country, where Frenchmen were commonly associated with smelly clothes, squalid huts and log forts, a traveller reported that "[e]verything which *Chikagou* [Agapit Chicagou, the Michigamea chief who made the trip] has related to his countrymen, with regard to France, has appeared to them incredible. 'They have bribed you,' said some to him, 'to make us believe all these beautiful fictions.'" Even his relatives and friends, who would not contradict him directly, concluded that the French must have given him some charm that made him imagine carriages that seemed to float above the ground, gardens and fountains of unimaginable ingenuity and beauty, and a capital city that stretched farther than the eye could see. Nothing in their own experience with the French even hinted that they might be capable of realizing the wonders he described.[67]

---

[65] Quoted in Norall, *Bourgmont*, p. 36.

[66] See Norall, *Bourgmont*, pp. 81–88; Jacob P. Dunn, ed., "The Mission to the Ouabache," *Indiana Historical Society Publications*, vol. III (Indianapolis, 1902), pp. 289–293.

[67] For a contemporary Parisian account of the visit, see the *Mercure de France*, Tome IX, Decembre 1725 (repr. Geneva, 1968), 2827–2859; for complaints about the Missouri post, see, e.g., [Anon.], "Memoire concernant les Ilinois," 1732, MG 1, série F³, vol. 24, partie 3, 603–612, NAC [orig. Collection Moreau de Saint-Méry, Archives Nationales des Colonies, Paris]; for traveler, Le Petit to d'Avaugour, 12 July 1730, *JR*, vol. LXVIII, pp. 213–217.

But if Bourgmont's efforts in the name of the crown ultimately meant nothing to the empire, they served Bourgmont himself remarkably well. He never returned to America; instead, he married a Frenchwoman and retired to his family estate in Normandy, where they lived comfortably. He was elevated to the nobility and took as his coat of arms "a naked savage reclining on a mountain of silver."[68] No image could better have captured the spirit of Bourgmont's term of public service, but its meaning is ambiguous: the colonial enterprise, in part through Bourgmont's efforts, was supposed to provide France with a lucrative Indian trade and mountains of silver from phantom mines along the Mississippi and its tributaries. But these were unrealized hopes. Instead, riches and exotic adventure were Bourgmont's personal reward; they were never translated into meaningful gains for the empire.

*   *   *

Just as New France's *coureurs* became free agents in the continental interior, pursuing their own interests with little regard for the imperatives of empire, Pennsylvania's Ohio Valley traders created a world unto themselves in the west. In so doing, they often flaunted the interests of creditors; ignored the strictures of colonial officials against a variety of offenses, including the liquor trade; and casually risked triggering international conflicts as their commercial activities undermined diplomatic alignments and threatened to remake the map of the Ohio Valley.[69] Though the characteristics of the traders in the two empires were quite similar, the problems they caused were very different. Throughout the first half of the 18th century, New France was plagued by *coureurs* and Indian allies who carried their trade to British markets, where they could almost always get better terms than they did at French posts. Britain's colonies suffered, in effect, from the opposite problem: as the Pennsylvania trading network stretched farther and farther into the Ohio Valley, the British empire was placed in the uncomfortable position of defending the consequences of their activities. By the early 1750s, Pennsylvania had established a tenuous string of Indian alliances connecting it with several groups about whom its officials knew, literally, almost nothing at all. In the end, the threat of British commercial expansion in the Ohio Valley was more than the officials of New France could bear; the opening act of the Seven Years' War was an attempt by the French to reclaim, through intimidation, what they had lost by virtue of a faltering overseas commercial empire.

[68] Norall, *Bourgmont*, pp. 87–88.
[69] For a perceptive study of the importance and effects of the liquor trade see Peter Mancall, *Deadly Medicine: Indians and Alcohol in Early America* (Ithaca, 1995).

Among the Britons drawn to the Ohio Valley, none exemplifies the
type so clearly as George Croghan, who quickly rose to dominate Pennsylvania's western trade. Croghan came to Pennsylvania from Ireland in
1741. He spoke with a thick brogue, and although he was a tireless
writer his orthography and spelling were so bad that he was accounted
nearly illiterate by at least one correspondent. He was a flamboyant,
hard-drinking man cut to the mold of his occupation, but he was not regarded, like fellow trader Michael Teaffe, as "more bold than prudent."
On the contrary, Croghan won allies among Indians and colonists alike
(and even, late in his career, in the leading circles of London society)
with an unusual combination of shrewd calculation and open-handed
affability. When he was among the Indians, a traveling companion
found him "most enterprising," but the commentator was also dis-
turbed by Croghan's dissembling manner; he noted that Croghan "can
appear highly pleased when most chagrined and show the greatest indif-
ference when most pleased."[70]

As a businessman Croghan was an energetic self-promoter with little
regard for order, careful recordkeeping, or, to hear some of his associates tell it, fair dealing. Croghan was supplied in the Indian trade by at
least four Philadelphia dry goods merchants, and he was periodically in
debt to each of them; his ventures were heavily capitalized by several
other Philadelphians, especially Richard Hockley and Richard Peters;
and he formed trading partnerships for specific undertakings with
William Trent, Robert Callender, and Michael Teaffe. In turn, he employed, at times, more than a score of men, kept numerous servants and
slaves, and on occasion used over a hundred packhorses to carry on his
trade. The tangle of obligations and debts created by these arrangements
would have been difficult for even the most assiduous bookkeeper to
follow; for Croghan, it was utterly impossible. Whether he intentionally
slighted the interests of his partners and backers in favor of his own, as
his creditors occasionally charged, or he was simply too much the tireless adventurer to spend time poring over his accounts, his business
practices failed to keep up with his trading enterprise. Throughout his
career as a trader, Indian agent, and land speculator, Croghan was periodically forced to remain in the backcountry for fear that he would be
imprisoned for debt if he appeared in Philadelphia.[71]

[70] Albert T. Volwiler, *George Croghan and the Westward Movement, 1741–1782* (Cleveland, 1926), pp. 17–51; George B. Wainwright, *George Croghan: Wilderness Diplomat*
(Chapel Hill, 1959), pp. 3–46, quote: p. 10; George Morgan to his wife, in Clarence
Alvord and Clarence Carter, eds., *The New Regime, 1765–1767*, Collections of the Illinois State Historical Library, vol. XI (Springfield, 1916), pp. 316–317.

[71] Volwiler, *Croghan*, pp. 39–41; Wainwright, *Croghan*, throughout.

But if Croghan was a suspect figure in the Pennsylvania capital, he was admired and respected in the West. In the early 1740s he established a trading base among the Shawnees, Delawares, and Mingos on the Allegheny and upper Ohio which was soon unrivaled by any of his competitors. When Logstown, a multiethnic trading village on the upper Ohio, was founded in the mid-1740s, Croghan's position of preeminence was confirmed by the fact that the town's central trading house belonged to him. From his base at Logstown, Croghan quickly began to extend his trading contacts farther downriver. In addition to the Shawnee, Delaware, and Mingo settlements that were beginning to spread out through the valley, Croghan was also drawing French allies into the net of British trade. A Wyandot band from Detroit, under the leadership of a chief named Orontony (known to the British as Nicolas), built a new village for themselves on Sandusky Bay, on the south shore of Lake Erie, to be closer to the Pennsylvania traders. Others remained at Detroit but crossed the lake to trade with Croghan. On occasion, Croghan's men ventured within sight of the French fort at Detroit to trade with the post's ostensible allies.[72]

During the 1740s, France's overseas commercial empire grew steadily weaker; as it did, the Pennsylvania traders gained influence throughout the Ohio Valley. Developments in the Atlantic theater during the War of the Austrian Succession, known in the British colonies as King George's War (1739–1748), seriously disrupted the Indian trade throughout French North America. Between 1742 and 1748 the shipping lines that tied Canadian merchants to their suppliers in Paris were challenged by British seapower, and with the capture of Louisbourg by New England forces in 1745 – "the Gibraltar of the New World," which guarded the Gulf of St. Lawrence – the trickle of merchandise dried up almost entirely for several trading seasons. Canadian merchants effectively lost the capacity, for a time, to carry on the Indian trade in the Ohio Valley at all. In 1745 the governor of Canada begged traders to go west as a personal favor to him, and the next year he allowed the monopoly leaseholders at Ouiatanon to remain at the post free of charge, "in order to maintain the savages of the post until times change."[73] By the late 1740s

---

[72] Conrad Weiser's Journal, 30 Aug. 1748, Weiser Collection, HSP; Croghan to Richard Peters, 26 May 1747, *Pa. Arch.* [1st Ser.], vol. I, p. 742; *Pa. Col. Recs.*, vol. V, p. 72; Jonquière to Clinton, 10 Aug. 1751, *NYCD*, vol. VI, pp. 731–734; Croghan to William Johnson, 14 Mar. 1757, ibid., vol. VII, p. 267.

[73] Eccles, *Canadian Frontier*, pp. 141–153; Fred Anderson, *A People's Army: Massachusetts Soldiers and Society in the Seven Years' War* (Chapel Hill, 1984), 8; Beauharnois and Hocquart to the Minister of the Marine, 22 Sept. 1746, *IndHSProc*, vol. XVIII, p. 195; see also Hocquart à Monsieur le controlleur général, 16 Oct. 1744, in H. A. Innis,

the French trading empire in the Ohio Valley had completely collapsed; in its place, Pennsylvania traders gained new commercial partners along the entire length of the Ohio Valley, including many members of the Illinois and Miami confederacies.

Especially for the three Miami tribes, who had a long acquaintance with British markets, the opportunity to trade with the Pennsylvanians was difficult to resist. By the mid-1740s, the circuit that Croghan and his fellow traders followed took them as far as the Shawnee town at the mouth of the Scioto River. A faction within the Miami tribe soon considered moving to a new site, easily accessible to the Pennsylvania traders from the Shawnee town on the Scioto. In the principal Miami town of Kekionga the preeminent chief of the French alliance, Le Pied Froid, stood firm in his loyalty. But when a rival leader known as La Demoiselle abandoned Kekionga in the spring of 1748 to found the town of Pickawillany on the Great Miami River, 50 or 60 miles to the south, nearly the entire town – about 400 families – followed; only Le Pied Froid's own family remained with him in Kekionga.[74]

The Pennsylvania traders immediately added Pickawillany to their trading circuit. George Croghan, John Frazier, Hugh Crawford, and their associates and employees began to reap astonishing rewards from their new contacts with the Miamis, as the records of Pennsylvania's fur and skin exports for these years illustrate (Fig. 2). In the spring of 1749 two of Frazier's employees had to make two trips to Pickawillany because they received "more Skins than they could carry with their horses at one time." Soon the Miamis at Pickawillany were joined by defectors from the Piankashaw and Ouiatanon tribes as well. By early 1752, the commanding officer at the Vincennes post, which had been the principal home of the Piankashaws, wrote with alarm that "we have no more Indians at this post" since their removal to Pickawillany.[75]

Out of these lucrative trading connections developed an awkward diplomatic alliance between the Miami tribes and the Pennsylvania government. When the colony organized a large treaty for all its Indian allies at Lancaster, Pennsylvania in 1748, a party of Miami chiefs ap-

---

ed., *Select Documents in Canadian Economic History, 1497–1783* (Toronto, 1929), p. 414.

[74] W. Vernon Kinietz, *The Indians of the Western Great Lakes, 1614–1760*, Occasional Contributions from the Museum of Anthropology of the University of Michigan, no. 10 (Ann Arbor, 1940), pp. 164, 181.

[75] See, e.g., *Pa. Col. Recs.*, vol. V, pp. 437–438, 461–462, 482–483, quote, p. 482; St. Ange to Vaudreuil, 28 Feb. 1752, in Theodore Pease and Ernestine Jenison, eds., *Illinois on the Eve of the Seven Years' War, 1747–1755*, Collections of the Illinois State Historical Library, vol. XXIX (Springfield, 1940), p. 485.

peared along with the expected Iroquois, Shawnee, and Delaware spokesmen. Apparently with no misgivings, the governor accepted the former French allies as a new, westernmost link in the colony's increasingly tenuous "chain of friendship," which now extended more than 1000 miles beyond Philadelphia into the continental interior. This addition not only strained any reasonable definition of alliance, but also made the supposed preeminence of the Iroquois even more questionable. Three years later, spokesmen for the Piankashaw and Ouiatanon Indians at Pickawillany approached Croghan to request that they, too, be admitted to the Pennsylvania alliance. Without authorization of any kind, Croghan hastily "drew up an instrument" that confirmed those two tribes, as well as distant links in the Pennsylvania chain; the governor and council approved the treaty after the fact.[76]

The Illinois Indians also developed new avenues of trade to the east by midcentury. As the Pennsylvania traders transformed the Ohio River into a conduit to British markets, Illinois residents responded. In the summer of 1751, a group of traders joined forces in the Ohio Valley in a venture that illustrates the range of their options. The group included two Frenchmen, Moreau and La Mirande; the latter's wife; Lalande, their partner, who was a *métis* (born to one French and one Indian parent) from the town of Kaskaskia in the Illinois country; at least one, and perhaps several, Illinois Indians; an unspecified number of slaves; and later two more French traders, named Deguir and Paget. Together they took full advantage of their available markets: after a season of hunting, one party transported the skins and furs they had accumulated – which included more than 600 deerskins – to a British trading post. Another party carried three boatloads of fat, oil, and salt meat to New Orleans, where chronic food shortages would inflate their value. Nor were Moreau and his associates alone in the undefined borderlands between the French and British empires; they encountered, for example, two British traders at the falls of the Ohio in the company of a *métis* from Kaskaskia, along with several British-allied Indians. Moreau's report worried the French commander in the Illinois country, who wrote to inform Governor Vaudreuil of the group's activities. "It is these gentlemen, trading with the English," he warned, "who little by little are bringing the English into our rivers."[77]

In response to the growing perception that British traders had penetrated "far within our territory," in the words of one alarmed observer, French officials took a series of increasingly aggressive actions to intimi-

[76] *Pa. Col. Recs.*, vol. V, pp. 307–319, 522–524.
[77] Macarty to Vaudreuil, 18 and 27 Mar. 1752, CISHL, vol. XXIX, pp. 515–517, 550–551.

date their Indian allies and drive away the offending traders. These actions began with the famous expedition of Céloron de Bienville down the Ohio River in 1749. He was sent to observe and report on the state of the region's Indian population, to frighten away the British traders, and to bury a series of lead plates proclaiming French sovereignty – a weak and ineffectual effort to lay claim to the entire valley on behalf of the crown. Céloron and his associates warned colonial officials that British inroads cut very deeply into the region; Pickawillany, in particular, posed a grave threat to the empire.[78] The next action addressed the problem of Pickawillany directly: a force of about 240 French-allied Chippewas, Ottawas, and Potawatomis from Michilimackinac attacked the village in June 1752. Most of the town's hunters were absent, but the attackers found many women, some British traders, and about 20 older men and boys at home. The raiders cut out the heart of one British trader and took five more prisoner; they also killed five Indians, including La Demoiselle, whom they boiled alive and ate as the Pickawillany residents looked on. The town was temporarily abandoned after the attack; when a party of British traders visited the site a month later, they found it entirely deserted.[79]

By September, though, the Pennsylvania traders and their formerly French-allied trading partners had rejoined forces on the Wabash River, and this time they were well-armed. The traders brought two cannons, many guns, and three hundred horses to the Wabash, where the pro-British factions of the Miami tribes, in concert with members of several other Ohio Valley Indian groups, had constructed two forts for their protection.[80] Early in the following spring, the Marquis Duquesne, newly appointed governor of New France, dispatched more than a thousand soldiers and *habitants* from Canada to build a string of forts that would run from Lake Erie to the forks of the Ohio, which were intended to establish unambiguously France's claim to the Ohio Valley. This is the traditional starting point for a narrative account of the Seven Years' War, a beginning that clearly highlights the fundamental interconnections between the trading world of the Ohio Valley and the imperial pretentions of the European powers. But the escalation of conflict in the region also

---

[78] For Céloron's journal, see C.B. Galbreath, ed., *Expedition of Celoron to the Ohio Country in 1749* (Columbus, Ohio, 1921); quote: Father Bonnecamps, "Account of the Voyage of Celoron," *JR*, vol. LXIX, p. 185.

[79] *Pa. Col. Recs.*, vol. V, pp. 599–601; William Trent's Journal, in Hanna, *Wilderness Trail*, vol. II, pp. 291–299. The commanding officer at Detroit believed the number killed in the attack to have been about twenty-six; see Longueil to Rouillé, 18 Aug. 1752, CISHL, vol. XXIX, pp. 652–653.

[80] Macarty to Vaudreuil, 2 Sept. 1752, CISHL, vol. XXIX, p. 668.

clarifies the extent to which the world of intercultural trade had a logic and a dynamic all its own, which functioned independently of the colonial imperative and consistently defeated the efforts of imperial administrators to control it or direct it into useful channels.

By the eve of the Seven Years' War, the trading culture of the Ohio Valley was, in fact, an interdependent and interpenetrated world. Although it would be easy to conclude that Britain had won control of the region, this was true only in abstract, systemic terms. In fact, as we have seen, it was the interpenetration of the French and British spheres of influence in the region, and the mixed loyalties of Indians, *coureurs de bois*, and Pennsylvania traders alike, that were its most striking features. Commercial cross-currents ran in every direction, and the Ohio River had become a highway of international trade that united Indians and traders across the ostensible lines of European sovereignty.

Contacts between colonist-traders from both empires and among Indians from a variety of ethnic backgrounds reached a high-water mark in the late imperial period that was, in some ways, reminiscent of the Mississippian era. A new language of commerce, mediated by a developing core of common interests and concerns and marked by a distinctive material culture, had emerged that blunted the sharp edges of distinct ethnic, national, or tribal differences. In part, the landscape itself produced this result: the interlaced river systems of the Ohio Valley once again helped to create networks of linked communities, with blurred lines of cultural difference, out of the island societies left in the wake of the Mississippian collapse and the demographic catastrophe that followed the European discovery of America.

CHAPTER TWO

Communities of Exchange

A s COLONIAL commerce began to reshape the economic contours of the Ohio Valley, it also initiated wide-ranging changes in community life. For the Indian population that was already resident in the valley, trading opportunities often led them to relocate towns, take in European residents, and undertake sometimes dramatic cultural experiments in the interest of strengthening their ties with the colonies. For those who were moving into the valley, intercultural commerce structured new patterns of social and economic interaction and helped to erode the significance of tribal identity in determining patterns of residence and loyalty. In place of tribally defined political units, villages of mixed ethnicity operated with a substantial degree of independence from one another, even as colonial and Indian diplomats struggled to make old, tribally-based definitions of power and authority hold in the region. By the end of the colonial period, the Ohio Valley was characterized by widespread intercultural influence and contact, by far-reaching disruptions in the organizing patterns of Native American life, and by unprecedented innovations and experiments in social and cultural forms.

I

The reorientations of Native American life introduced by European contacts and trade in the Ohio Valley were fundamental enough to warrant an inquiry into the most basic elements of community. Everything from the siting and functions of villages and towns, to the dynamics of household and gender relations, to the structures of spiritual and political power that bound communities together were reshaped more or less directly in response to the European presence. This is not to discount the

influence of continuities and traditions in the region – tradition, as always, remained the most powerful force shaping community life – but
the catastrophic experiences that shaped the Ohio Indians' reception of
Europeans also made them particularly receptive to innovation.

To begin with, the map of the Ohio Valley was quite literally remade
by the trading routes of the French and British empires. In a reciprocal
process that operated without conscious direction, the growth of trading networks made it possible and desirable to re-site towns, villages,
and trading posts along the principal waterways of the region, while
new town sites encouraged traders to extend their circuits still farther.
By the end of the colonial period this process had helped to repopulate
the Ohio Valley from one end to the other, and encouraged a broadly
decentralized pattern of population distribution.

The earliest phase of contact between Frenchmen and Indians was
characterized by large, central outposts in and near the Illinois country.
At places like Green Bay or the Great Village of the Illinois, which were
already important centers of settlement or crossroads for large numbers
of people before the arrival of the French, the construction of a fort and
trading post only increased their magnetic effect. Particularly during the
era of sustained Iroquois hostilities in the Illinois country, these central
places drew such large numbers of people that local resources were
strained to the limit; at many French posts in the third quarter of the
17th century the massed groups of Indians struggled to support themselves on the land. The concentration of people at key central sites also
tended to intensify disagreements and hostilities among their residents.[1]
Thus, although these central places served an important purpose for a
time, there were also powerful centripetal forces at work that encouraged their populations to disperse. In more widely scattered communities, both the dangers of poverty, famine, and disease, and the possibility
of conflict, would be diminished.

As the threat of Iroquois invasion waned in the late 1680s in the Illinois country, Fort St. Louis lost some of its attractiveness. In part this
was because the fort's defensive capability was less crucial to survival; in
part, too, several years' contact with French traders had helped to create
intercultural ties that could be extended to new, decentralized settlement
sites. Over the course of the next two decades the Indian groups that

---

[1] For a general discussion of the problems associated with population concentration at
central posts see Richard White, *The Middle Ground: Indians, Empires, and Republics
in the Great Lakes Region, 1650–1815* (New York, 1991), pp. 40–49; and for a specific
account of tensions between Illinois and Miami Indians at the Great Village in the
1680s, see "Tonti's Memoir [1693]," in Louise Kellogg, ed., *Early Narratives of the
Northwest, 1634–1699* (New York, 1917), pp. 305–311.

had gathered at the Great Village began to disperse, and as they did so they drew French *coureurs de bois* directly into their new communities.

The case of the Miami confederacy illustrates with particular clarity the extent to which the dynamics of the region's trading network could shape preferences and terms of settlement. The French, for all of their influence with the Miamis, could not dictate new settlement sites to them; the Miamis, though they were anxious to maintain independence from the demands of their European allies, made proximity to traders a paramount consideration in their relocation process. Upon leaving Fort St. Louis, the Miamis scattered. Some, mostly Piankashaws, moved east to the Mississippi temporarily; another group, predominantly Ouiatanons but also including some Piankashaws, relocated to the Jesuit Mission of the Guardian Angel at Chicago; and a third contingent, which included primarily those groups that were coalescing into the Miami tribe, traveled still farther east to the St. Joseph mission on the St. Joseph River. None of these relocations lasted, and many of the Miami bands entered upon a period of repeated migrations that lasted as long as three decades. The Piankashaw-dominated group on the Mississippi was forced by pressure from the Sioux to move again in 1792, and moved several more times before they eventually came to occupy the lower Wabash River, from the Vermillion to the Ohio. Those at Chicago abandoned that post rather quickly in favor of a new site on the upper Wabash River, where they established the village of Ouiatanon. And although the community at the St. Joseph mission lasted a little longer than that at Chicago, by 1720 the center of Miami settlement was shifting east, to the town of Kekinga on the upper Maumee River.[2]

For a time, French officials entertained different ideas about Miami resettlement. In 1701 France's minister of the marine approved a proposal for yet another large central post in the region. The new post was to be constructed at a place known as Detroit: located on the straits between Lakes Huron and Erie, Detroit stood on the threshold separating the settled parts of New France from the vast western territories claimed by the colony. The plan was conceived by Antoine Laumet de la Mothe, Sieur de Cadillac, a director and prime mover of the newly reorganized company that enjoyed Canada's fur trade monopoly. Cadillac was igno-

---

[2] J. Joseph Bauxar, "History of the Illinois Area," in William C. Sturtevant, gen. ed., *Handbook of the North American Indians,* vol. XV: *Northeast,* ed. Bruce G. Trigger (Washington, 1978), p. 597; see also W. Vernon Kinietz, *The Indians of the Western Great Lakes, 1614–1760,* Occasional Contributions from the Museum of Anthropology of the University of Michigan, no. 10 (Ann Arbor, 1940), p. 163; Mary Borgias Palm, *The Jesuit Missions of the Illinois Country, 1673–1763* (Cleveland, 1931), pp. 27–30; Bert Anson, *The Miami Indians* (Norman, OK, 1970), pp. 30–31.

rant of the ecological and political constraints that made large, multiethnic settlement sites problematic, but he hoped that good terms of trade could attract a very large Indian population. In addition to the Miami tribes, Cadillac wanted the area around Detroit to become home to the Ottawas, Hurons, Potawatomis, Mascoutens, and Kickapoos. All of them might live in contiguous villages, he thought, and conduct all of their trade at Detroit. He also hoped to attract a substantial French farming population to the post, so that the Indians might be exposed to the civilizing influences of European social forms. To help make the Detroit post a reality, the minister of the marine ordered the evacuation of Michilimackinac, where many of these Indians currently traded. If they wanted to maintain a trading connection with New France, they would have no choice but to frequent Detroit.[3]

Initially Detroit attracted a large Indian population. Many Hurons, Ottawas, Potawatomis, and Mascoutens moved to the lands around Detroit, as did a substantial number of Miami Indians in the course of their wanderings. Within a few years of its founding Detroit had drawn nearly 6000 Indians to the area and Cadillac, in his enthusiasm, referred to his new settlement as the "Paris of America." But the Miamis were reluctant transplants, and they did not stay long. Their memories of deprivation and conflict from the years at Fort St. Louis were apparently still strong; even before moving to Detroit the Miamis expressed the concern that "amidst so great a number of people, . . . they would be reduced in a short time to starvation." Once they had taken up residence, it was not long until the Miami band was embroiled in a series of conflicts with the Ottawas there. They finally abandoned the post altogether in 1712 and requested that individual trading posts be established at their village sites on the Maumee and Wabash Rivers.[4]

Canadian officials were reluctant to build additional, decentralized outposts for the Miami tribes – Detroit was conceived partly in an effort to consolidate French activity in the west – but they recognized the very real possibility that the Miamis might otherwise opt for even stronger ties with the English colonies. They chose to comply with the request, and around the end of the second decade of the 18th century two new

[3] For the origins and early history of Detroit, see E.M. Sheldon, *The Early History of Michigan from the First Settlement to 1815* (New York, 1956).
[4] Louise P. Kellogg, *The French Régime in Wisconsin and the Northwest* (Madison, WI, 1925), pp. 271–272; Father D'Avenaut to Cadillac, 6 June 1702, *Michigan Pioneer and Historical Society Collections*, vol. XXXIII (Lansing, 1904), p. 123; Kinietz, *Indians of the Western Great Lakes*, p. 163; Vaudreuil to Council, 12 Dec. 1717, in Frances Krauskopf, ed., "Ouiatanon Documents," *Indiana Historical Society Proceedings*, vol. XVIII (Indianapolis, 1955), pp. 160–161.

posts were built: Fort Miamis, near the Miami towns on the upper
Maumee River; and Fort Ouiatanon, near the town of Ouiatanon on the
upper Wabash. A little more than a decade later, in 1731, a third French
post, called Vincennes, was established farther down the Wabash alongside the Piankashaw town of Chippekoke. These posts did not make the
Miami tribes absolutely loyal to the French alliance – they continued to
maintain connections with British traders, often through Iroquois intermediaries, throughout the colonial period – but they did help to confirm
and solidify the new spatial arrangement of Miami territories, while
they strengthened the force of the alliance between the Miamis and New
France.[5]

The exodus from Fort St. Louis thus extended and decentralized the
French presence in the Illinois country, at the same time that it helped
the region's Indians to reconstruct a more stable social world. The
Shawnees began to leave the vicinity of the fort at about the same time
the Miamis did. In 1691 the Starved Rock site was itself abandoned in
favor of another a short distance down the Illinois River alongside Lake
Peoria, where water and firewood were more plentiful. At Pimiteoui, as
the new post was called, four large log buildings were surrounded by a
palisade while a village of French traders and Indians, mostly from the
Peoria and Kaskaskia tribes, developed outside its walls. Meanwhile the
Cahokias and Tamaroas had chosen a new village site near the confluence of the Illinois and Mississippi Rivers, perhaps 150 miles downriver.[6]

Finally, in 1700, the Kaskaskias decided to separate from the Peorias
and leave Pimiteoui. In response to rumors of favorable trading conditions in the newly formed colony of Louisiana, they considered moving
all the way to the mouth of the Mississippi before the Jesuit missionary
who lived at Pimiteoui prevailed on them to reconsider.[7] Instead they
moved southwest as far as the Des Peres River; three years later they
continued on to the confluence of the Kaskaskia and Mississippi Rivers,
where they founded the town of Kaskaskia.

[5] Charles Callender, "Miami," in Trigger, ed., *Handbook*, p. 686; for the initiative to establish Post Vincennes, see Beauharnois and Hocquart to the Minister of the Marine, 15
Oct. 1730, *IndHSProc*, vol. XVIII, p. 179; and for ongoing contact between the Miamis
and British and Iroquois trade, Vaudreuil to the Minister, 6 Oct. 1721, and Sieur Dar-
naud [Renaud] to Beauharnois, 25 Oct. 1732, *IndHSProc*, vol. XVIII, pp. 172, 181–
182.

[6] James H. Howard, *Shawnee! The Ceremonialism of a Native Indian Tribe and Its Cultural Background* (Athens, Ohio, 1981), pp. 7–8; Clarence Alvord, *The Illinois Country, 1673–1818* (Springfield, Ill., 1920), pp. 98–102; Bauxhar, "History of Illinois
Area," in Trigger, ed., *Handbook*, p. 595.

[7] "Gravier's Voyage, 1700," in Reuben G. Thwaites, ed., *The Jesuit Relations and Allied*

In all of these moves, individual groups of Indians chose to take advantage of the end of the Iroquois wars, and the possibility of an extended network of French alliances and trade, by spreading out along the region's principal travel routes. In much the same way, the British trading circuit grew throughout the Ohio Valley from the east as Indian towns proliferated along its principal waterways. By creating an integrated network of discrete but interrelated settlements, the Ohio Indians entering the valley from the east and northeast, like those dispersing throughout the Illinois country, gained strong commercial ties at the same time that they achieved a substantial degree of autonomy from the continent's European powers.

The occupation of the Ohio Valley by British-allied Indians began on the Allegheny and upper Ohio Rivers, and proceeded steadily downriver until every major watershed feeding the Ohio was dominated by communities bound into Britain's network of trade. The earliest settlements of westward-migrating Delawares, Shawnees, and Iroquois Mingos were concentrated along the Allegheny River; throughout the 1730s most of the activity of the Pennsylvania traders in the west took place between Kittanning on the north and Aliquippa's Town on the south. Although this region had nothing like the density of population clustered around Fort St. Louis, for a time it exercised comparable influence over regional trade, and attracted large numbers of inhabitants. Beginning around 1740 some Indians began to move farther west. In 1744 Logstown was established by a band of Shawnees migrating from eastern Pennsylvania, and within a few years it had become the most active trading center in the eastern Ohio Valley – a development that reflected the westward shift in both human and game populations.[8]

Soon the banks of many of the principal tributaries of the Ohio River were dotted with strings of new villages and towns. For a time in the 1730s and early 1740s the Cuyahoga River near the southern rim of Lake Erie attracted large numbers of westward-moving Iroquois and French-allied Indians from Detroit, especially Ottawas. By the mid-1740s most of the Iroquois population in the valley was concentrated farther south and west, particularly in the Beaver River watershed, where they settled the towns of Kuskuski, Buckaloons, and Conawango. Orontony and his band of Wyandots settled on the Sandusky River in the late 1730s. During this same period substantial numbers of Delawares were moving farther into the valley. Their villages tended to

---

Documents, 73 vols. (Cleveland, 1896–1901) [hereafter JR], vol. LXV, pp. 101 and following.
8 For a fuller account of these migrations see Michael McConnell, *A Country Between: The Upper Ohio Valley and its Peoples, 1724–1774* (Lincoln, NE, 1992).

be small and scattered, but many Delawares settled along the Beaver River, the Ohio itself, and in the lower Muskingum Valley. Shawnees were also to be found in small numbers on both the Beaver and Muskingum Rivers, but the center of Shawnee settlement was beginning to shift to the Scioto River, still farther to the south and west.

Gradually, most of these settlements became multiethnic in composition. While it is usually possible to identify the nominal tribal origin of any town in the Ohio Valley, in fact by 1750 nearly every community of any size in the valley contained a complex mixture of peoples who retained their tribal labels as a source of ethnic identity, but whose politics were more often driven by local concerns that cut across tribal identities. At Logstown in 1749, Céloron and his party encountered Mingos, Shawnees, and Delawares, along with smaller numbers of mission Iroquois, Nippisings, Abenakis, Ottawas, and others. "This assemblage forms a very bad village," Céloron wrote, "which, tempted by the cheap market which the English offered, were drawn into a very bad disposition for us." At the mouth of the Scioto they found Shawnees, Mingos, mission Iroquois ("whom licentiousness had made to retire there. Abundance of hunting and a cheap market – which the English gave them – are motives very seducing for them."), Delawares, Miamis, and others "from nearly all the nations of the upper country." Even in the case of small villages that remained ethnically homogeneous, their residents developed political connections that bound them into the region's larger centers, where multiethnic councils and alliances were being forged. European travelers who visited the region always commented on this phenomenon; however hard they might try to understand the Indian societies of the valley in terms of tribally defined political loyalties, the reality defied their efforts.[9]

What functions did these communities fulfill? Certainly they were not primarily defensive; one of the region's most remarkable features was the permeability of its territorial boundaries and the extent of interethnic contact. None of the Ohio Valley towns of the mid-18th century was fortified, or sited to take advantage of defensible terrain. Nor were they intended to bring together residents from a common background for cultural or social purposes, as the Great Village of the Illinois had once been. Some, like the Shawnee town at the mouth of the Scioto River, still retained a central longhouse for ceremonial and political purposes, but

[9] Journal of Captain Celoron, in Mary C. Darlington, ed., *Fort Pitt and Letters from the Frontier* (New York, 1971); quotes: pp. 35, 44–45. See also Bonnécamps' Relation, *JR*, vol. LXIX, pp. 150–199; Christopher Gist's First Journal, 1750–51, in Lois Mulkearn, ed., *George Mercer Papers Relating to the Ohio Company of Virginia* (Pittsburgh, 1954), pp. 7–31.

others contained no such structural evidence of their residents' shared cultural origins; often, in fact, their most prominent central buildings were trading posts.[10] Instead, these towns were designed primarily to facilitate commercial alliances, both among Indian groups and between Indians and European traders. In their siting, their populations, and their dominant activities they were trading communities, founded and frequented by hunters and traders who came together for the purpose of exchange.

This characteristic is reflected, particularly, in the way that European traders settled in considerable numbers in Ohio Valley Indian towns and, in effect, colonized them from within. In 1700, for example, a party of Frenchmen traveling up the Mississippi River came to the town of Cahokia and discovered thirty Canadian traders, who merrily greeted them by firing their guns. By 1715, there were reportedly about 150 traders in Cahokia, "living there at their ease." Their Indian slaves (who would have been captives, not Illinois Indians themselves) raised grain for them while they came and went according to the rhythm of the trading seasons. At Kaskaskia, too, a sizeable population of French traders settled with the Indians and made their homes among them, hunting, trading, and traveling throughout the region.[11]

Most French traders married into the communities they settled in, thereby stabilizing their local ties. This was a custom that conferred important benefits all around. For the bride's Indian father, usually a chief or at least a prominent man, the marriage brought honor and influence, since it guaranteed that his family would play an important role in acquiring and distributing European trade goods. The *coureur* established an enduring bond with his trading partners, at the same time that he gained both a companion and a laborer in his household. In addition to the traditional skills of European women – which would have included making clothes, preparing food, and maintaining the household – an Indian wife was also accustomed to working in the fields. Her husband was thereby freed for extended absences from his home to hunt or trade.

---

[10] Compare, for example, the description of the Shawnee town at the mouth of the Scioto, which was dominated by a large central council house, with that of Muskingum (or Conchake), where houses belonging to Orontony, the local chief, and George Croghan seemed to share a central place. Gist's First Journal, Mulkearn, ed., *Mercer Papers*, pp. 16, 11.

[11] André Pénicaut, *Fleur de Lys and Calumet: Being the Pénicaut Narrative of French Adventure in Louisiana*, trans. and ed. Richebourg McWilliams (Baton Rouge, 1953), p. 40; Ramezay and Begon to the Minister of the Marine, 7 Nov. 1715, in Reuben G. Thwaites, ed., *Collections of the State Historical Society of Wisconsin*, vol. XVI, p. 332; for cross-cultural marriage in Kaskaskia, see the discussion of community development there in chapter three.

For an Indian woman, marrying a trader brought easier access to European manufactures; it also conferred a unique form of social prestige,
since her husband and their children would comprise a new and growing link between Indian and European cultures. The *métis* children of
these marriages, originating at the intersection of European and Indian
societies, became central to the emerging system of intercultural commerce.[12]

Traders from the British colonies were slower and somewhat less
likely than their French counterparts to marry into the communities
they frequented and take up permanent residence there. Nevertheless,
by the late colonial period their influence in Ohio Valley communities
was everywhere. Travelers in the valley encountered British traders on
their routes as often as Indians, and every town seemed to have a substantial seasonal population of traders; Céloron's party was horrified by
their widespread presence and influence. "Each village, whether large or
small," wrote Father Bonnécamps, who accompanied Céloron, "has one
or more traders, who have in their employ engagés for the transportation of peltries."[13] Communities were linked by well-traveled pathways;
taken together, they constituted an integrated commercial circuit that
strung the communities of the Ohio Valley together like beads on a
string. In all of these ways, intercultural commerce was beginning to in-
troduce far-reaching changes into the region's settlements.

II

For the peoples of the Ohio Valley, spiritual and cultural power had always been mediated by rituals and talismans. Did this mean that new
sources of power would require new rituals and new talismans? The introduction of European artifacts that altered traditional equations of
power called upon the region's Indians to consider corresponding
changes in their formulas for invoking, preserving, and extending spiri-

---

[12] On the role of intermarriage and *métissage* in the fur trade in this region, see Olive Patricia Dickason, "From 'One Nation' in the Northeast to 'New Nation' in the Northwest: A Look at the Emergence of the Métis," in Jacqueline Peterson and Jennifer S.H.
Brown, eds., *The New Peoples: Being and Becoming Métis in North America* (Lincoln,
NE, 1985), and Jacqueline Peterson, "The People in Between: Indian-White Marriage
and the Genesis of a Métis Society and Culture in the Great Lakes Region 1680–1830,"
(Ph.D. diss., Univ. of Illinois Chicago Circle, 1981). For insightful discussions of this
subject that apply to different regions and contexts, see especially Sylvia Van Kirk,
"Many Tender Ties": Women in Fur Trade Society, 1670–1870 (Winnipeg, 1980), and
Jennifer S. H. Brown, *Strangers in Blood: Fur Trade Company Families in Indian
Country* (Vancouver, 1980).

[13] Bonnécamps' Relation, *JR*, vol. LXIX, p. 185.

tual power and cultural authority. In the French sphere the contest for cultural authority was intensified by the involvement of Catholic missionaries who sought to convert the native population to Christianity.

Their efforts met with a wide variety of responses. The activities of missionaries were quite important in some ways in shaping the dynamics of intercultural relations, particularly in the early period of French colonization, but it is possible both to overestimate their importance and to misread their significance. The tendency of both contemporary observers and modern apologists for mission work has been to regard conversion as evidence of a fundamental break with native traditions and with the past.[14] Critics, on the other hand, have argued that conversions were often forced on natives by "invading" priests, and tended in reality to be insincere or inconsequential.[15] But conversion implies neither a complete repudiation of the past, nor a unilateral imposition of European norms and attitudes. Like so many aspects of intercultural relations in the Ohio Valley, conversion was a negotiated process. It also served only as a single point of reference within a continuum of issues surrounding relations between Indians and Europeans. For groups that accepted Christianity, it could exercise considerable power over their social and cultural norms; but even devout converts did not become political tools for their missions, while those who rejected missionaries were by no means rejecting the full range of European influence.

French missionaries began operating in the Illinois country during the last quarter of the 17th century and persisted until the end of the French period in 1763. In the earliest years of their activity it is very clear that, although the missionaries themselves considered their enterprise to be in direct conflict with that of traders who were entering the region at about the same time, to the Indians the two dimensions of French activity were complementary.[16] Having been introduced to firearms and gun-

---

[14] The classic contemporary texts describing this process can be found in *The Jesuit Relations*; for modern apologists writing about the Illinois country, see, e.g., Palm, *Jesuit Missions of the Illinois Country*.

[15] See, e.g., Francis Jennings' account of Puritan missions in *The Invasion of America: Indians, Colonialism, and the Cant of Conquest* (New York, 1976), pp. 228–253. James Axtell has often employed martial metaphors to describe the missionaries' assault on native societies, and also emphasizes the coercive qualities of conversion: see *The Invasion Within: The Contest of Cultures in Colonial North America* (New York, 1985); "Were Indian Conversions *Bona Fide*?" in *After Columbus: Essays in the Ethnohistory of Colonial America* (New York, 1988), ch. 7; and "Agents of Change: Jesuits in the Post-Columbian World," in *Beyond 1492: Encounters in Colonial North America* (New York, 1992), ch. 6.

[16] Traders and missionaries frequently came into conflict on the frontiers of New France; for a particularly clear analysis of their divergent interests see Étienne de Carheil to Callieres, 30 Aug. 1702, *JR*, vol. LV, pp. 188–253.

powder, dyed cloth and brass kettles, many of the Illinois Indians were quite prepared to be initiated into the rites of power appropriate to the "god of iron." Thus they enthusiastically received the earliest Jesuit missionaries in the region, Jacques Marquette and Claude Allouez. When Marquette first traveled through the region with Louis Joliet in 1673, the Frenchmen were particularly impressed by the Illinois Indians; Marquette wrote that they possessed "an air of humanity which we have not observed in the other nations that we have seen upon our route." For their part, the Illinois peoples were disappointed that the Frenchmen were just passing through, and before Marquette left they made him promise to return and instruct them more fully in the mysteries of the Catholic faith.[17] Their expectations for a mission were certainly shaped by their knowledge of the French presence at Green Bay, where mission and trading post operated side by side; Christian instruction was thus inextricably linked in the natives' minds with access to the full complement of material artifacts associated with the fur trade, which were known but not widely available in the Illinois country in 1673.

Marquette returned to the Great Village of the Illinois in the early spring of 1675 and began to proselytize the local population. He was prepared for his visit with rudimentary instruction in the Illinois language by Claude Allouez, who had worked at the Green Bay mission and had some contact with Illinois traders and others who could help him work out an Illinois grammar. Allouez also armed Marquette with a 168-page bound manuscript of prayers, hymns, and services in the Illinois language, subdivided by French and Latin cues to guide the missionary through its pages. Drawing on the long experience of Jesuit missions in other parts of North America, Marquette began his course of instruction by talking with the local elders privately; in this way, he was careful not to violate the prevailing structure of authority within the Illinois community. To judge from the surviving accounts, they were a rapt audience.[18]

In Easter week, Marquette moved beyond his private consultations with Illinois leaders to address the whole community in a memorable pageant. On Maundy Thursday he invited the entire population of the Great Village to attend an outdoor service in a large meadow; his audience reportedly included 500 "chiefs and elders" seated on mats and robes in a circle around him, and behind them 1500 young men and a

[17] "Marquette's First Voyage," *JR*, vol. LIX, pp. 109–137, 161–163; quote: p. 125.
[18] The prayerbook, entitled "Cantiques en Langue Sauvage," is in MG18 C9, National Archives of Canada, Ottawa; on Allouez, see Palm, *Jesuit Missions*, p. 19; "Marquette's Journal" and "Marquette's Last Voyage," *JR*, vol. LIX, pp. 165–211.

large assemblage of women and children. Marquette worked in front of a backdrop of four pieces of Chinese taffeta stretched out upon lines, one facing in each direction, to which were affixed "four large Pictures of the blessed Virgin, which were visible on all sides." In a ceremony that gained substantial dramatic emphasis from this stage setting, Marquette made a ritual presentation of ten gifts to the Illinois people, each of which signified a principle of the Christian faith. By this method, according to his chronicler, Marquette "explained to them the principal mysteries of our Religion, and the purpose that had brought him to their country." Following this presentation he said a Mass. On Easter Sunday his visit culminated in another Mass; his commemoration of Holy Week complete, Marquette departed from the village.[19]

Marquette died on his return trip to Canada, but his place in the Illinois country was soon filled by Allouez, a veteran missionary in the Great Lakes region. Like his predecessor, Allouez concentrated on private instruction of the tribal elders; like Marquette, he also centered his teachings on physical artifacts that were presented as sacred mediums for spiritual power.[20] Crosses, medals, small pictures of the Virgin Mary, and portable or makeshift altars comprised of clusters of such artifacts became central to the faith as it was communicated to the Illinois Indians.

The early ministrations of Marquette and Allouez were apparently met with enthusiasm among the Illinois. How should we interpret this reception? To the missionaries, it seemed that the Indians were eager to become acolytes of the one true God, to throw over their superstitions and accept the teachings of Christ in their place. But this is too simple: in retrospect, it is clear that the Illinois Indians understood the missionaries on their own terms and to their own ends. Within a culture that identified gods with particular physical manifestations and regarded them as transcendent but finite beings, their interest in Christian instruction probably cannot be distinguished from their interest in the physical objects and powers that the Europeans carried with them. "You are one of the chief spirits because you use iron," the trader Perrot was supposed to have been told; the Illinois Indians wanted, above all, to gain entrance into the mysteries and rites surrounding European artifacts – particularly iron, that most useful and valuable substance.

But the idea of conversion, which implied a repudiation of the Indi-

[19] JR, vol. LIX, pp. 165–211.
[20] "Allouez in Illinois," JR, vol. LX, pp. 157–165. Allouez's account refers to a small altar he constructed from his portable chapel, which gave him a sacred space in which to work; it was there that he "exposed the crucifix" to his audience. Before leaving he planted a wooden cross, 35 feet high, in the center of the village.

ans' complex of spiritual beliefs and of their own universe of sacred artifacts, remained foreign and suspect. For the Illinois peoples, the process
of adding Christian objects and ideas to their own made sense in a way
that a more fundamental break with their past and their culture did not.
One particularly revealing episode suggests that the Illinois Indians
viewed their contacts with French missionaries in deeply traditional
terms. When Allouez was on his way to the Great Village in the spring
of 1675, he met a party of 80 warriors. Their leader drew Allouez aside
and pleaded with him for a blessing, explaining that he was afraid their
encounter would "prove fatal to me if I do not use it to my advantage."
For this man there was a clear connection between the god of the French
and the worldly power Frenchmen seemed to enjoy, and the Illinois warrior hoped to draw on this power: he wished to be accorded spiritual favor as a protection against his enemies. "If I lose this opportunity of lis-
tening to you, I shall be punished by the loss of my nephews [the assembled party of warriors], whom you see in so great number; without
doubt, they will be defeated by our enemies."[21] Just as clearly, though,
this war leader was no aspiring pious neophyte; he sought to add the
powerful new Christian god to his pantheon of protectors by accretion,
not to throw over his view of the world and his place in it to take up a
life of prayer in a Christian mission.

For the first two decades of contact between French missionaries and
Illinois Indians, Christianity was an accepted part of the European presence in the region but failed to win the exclusive allegiance of even a
small segment of the native population. Instead, missionaries and
traders coexisted in an uneasy partnership at Fort St. Louis. The Indians
at the post remained distant from the priesthood as they cultivated increasingly familiar relations with the *coureurs de bois*. Jesuit fathers reported with frustration that their prospective converts treated them with
politeness, attended services and prayers as casual observers, but failed
to embrace Christianity with their whole hearts.[22]

In fact, the local chiefs tried to strike a balance between Christian instruction and influence, on the one hand, and practices native to their
own cultures, especially associated with fertility and reproduction, on
the other. In one case a chief of the Peoria tribe instructed his followers
in the spring that "it was important for the public welfare" to stay away
from the Christian chapel "until the corn was ripe and the harvest over;
and that he would then exhort the people to go to be instructed." The

---

[21] *JR*, vol. LX, pp. 157–159.
[22] J. Joseph Bauxar, "History of the Illinois Area," in Trigger, ed., *Handbook*, pp.
594–595; Jacques Gravier's journal, 15 Feb. 1694, *JR*, vol. LXIV, pp. 161–163,
169–171, 201–203.

Peoria chief feared that attention to the Christian god, who seemed to be useful particularly in the masculine pursuits of hunting and war, might jeopardize the female-centered rituals associated with planting, tending, and harvesting crops.[23] In the same vein, Illinois leaders consistently resisted Jesuit attacks on polygamy and "sexual libertinage." Like most Algonquian cultures, the Illinois Indians encouraged sexual experimentation outside of marriage, especially among the young; in addition, perhaps in part because of their badly deteriorated sex ratio (estimated by one contemporary observer at one man for every four women in the late 17th century), it was not uncommon for Illinois men to have more than one wife.[24]

In response to their early lack of success among the elders of the Illinois tribes, the Jesuit fathers, following a strategy that had served them well in other mission fields, began to target young women in particular as prospective converts. In the eyes of the Jesuits young women were especially exploited and degraded by Algonquian sexual customs. To Europeans (particularly celibate priests), sexual purity was among the most highly prized traits of unmarried women. As a counterweight to Algonquian practice, Jesuit missionaries suggested religious devotions that highlighted the Virgin Mary and offered the possibility of a spiritual union with Christ as an alternative to marriage. In this way the Jesuit fathers made war on the gender system of the Illinois Indians. They held out alternative objects of adoration and worship, and an alternative symbol of ideal behavior, that could be especially potent and attractive to young women – and especially disruptive to Illinois culture. The ancestral practices of the Illinois Indians venerated fertility; the missionaries demanded instead that their followers protect their virginity. For young women, the Christian message implied a new route to social power and spiritual authority. Rather than using their sexuality to absorb and fructify male aggression and to domesticate dangerous and

---

[23] Gravier's journal, 15 Feb. 1694, *JR*, vol. LXIV, p. 163. Gravier probably misinterpreted these instructions when he wrote, "The period that he fixed was a long one, for he thought that I would offer him a present to shorten it." It is more plausible to conclude that the Peoria chief feared that Christian rituals might contaminate the rites of the growing season. Compare Ramón A. Gutiérrez, *When Jesus Came, the Corn Mothers Went Away: Marriage, Sexuality, and Power in New Mexico, 1500–1846* (Stanford, 1991), pp. 84–91.

[24] For polygamy see, e.g., Allouez in Illinois, [1676–77], *JR*, vol. LX, p. 161; for "libertinage," e.g., Binneteau to [?], [Jan.] 1699, *JR*, vol. LXV, p. 67, and Marest to Germon, 12 Nov. 1712, *JR*, vol. LXVI, p. 221; the sex ratio estimate comes from Louis Deliette, "Memoir Concerning the Illinois Country," Theodore Pease and Raymond Werner, eds., *The French Foundations, 1680–1693*, Collections of the Illinois State Historical Library, vol. XXIII (Springfield, 1934), p. 329.

alien forces in the natural world, the Jesuits insisted that they could triumph over nature only by stoically cultivating abstinence and an aloof disregard for the things of this world.[25]

The Jesuits' challenge was felt directly by male elders who had previously controlled patterns of meaning and authority in Illinois culture. Missionaries repeatedly attacked the shamans' practices and beliefs. Even the name they used to refer to shamans – they were almost always called "jugglers" by the Jesuit fathers – reflects the missionaries' belief that they were little more than tricksters and petty magicians. To Jesuit observers, the rituals, practices, and beliefs of native leaders were scarcely worthy of extended comment. They challenged the authority of shamans at every opportunity: In contests of wit and logic; in demonstrations of faithfulness and dogged perserverance; and occasionally in dramatic confrontations. In all of these actions they threatened to scramble the lines of political authority and to undermine the foundations of social stability among the Illinois Indians.[26]

Despite its disruptive aspects (or perhaps in part because of them), the attractions of Christianity for some young Illinois women could be very strong. Where wholehearted conversion occurred, it usually took root first among young women. The forms of female power ascribed by convention in Illinois society would, of course, be lost or at least jeopardized for a devout convert. Acceptance of Christian teaching might lead a young woman, for example, to reject an offer of marriage or refuse to participate in dances, feasts, and nocturnal celebrations. But in their place, as Jacqueline Peterson has argued, Christian devotion offered new and unconventional avenues to power. At the center of the faith was a mysterious and powerful female figure, paradoxically both virginal and fertile, who held out the promise of a kind of spiritual authority not normally available to Illinois women. For certain girls, the difficult strains associated with puberty and the transition to womanhood apparently made the ministrations of the Jesuit fathers, and the guidance of the symbolic virgin, especially appealing. Particularly in a society in which sexual relations were governed by male preferences and marriages were arranged by men, often without regard for women's

---

[25] For references to the centrality of young women to mission efforts see Deliette, "Memoir," CISHL, vol. XXIII, p. 361; Gravier's journal, 15 Feb. 1694, *JR*, vol. LXIV, p. 177; Binneteau to [?], [Jan.] 1699, *JR*, vol. LXV, p. 67. For women's capacity to domesticate dangerous and alien forces through their sexuality, see Gutiérrez, *Corn Mothers*, pp. 17–20.

[26] See, e.g., Binneteau to [?], [Jan.] 1699, *JR*, vol. LXV, pp. 65–67; Marest to Germon, 9 Nov. 1712, *JR*, vol. LXVI, pp. 233–235.

wishes, Christian conversion could offer young women an important refuge.[27]

The programmatic emphases of the missionaries strengthened the appeal of devotion and conversion for young women. The Jesuits, for example, encouraged converts to learn daily orders – catechisms and prayers – and bible stories by heart; in some cases they had accompanying pictures or engraved plates to serve as mnemonic devices. The most devout girls labored diligently to memorize the devotions word for word; they might even ask to borrow accompanying plates or pictures in order to learn them more quickly. Missionaries never failed to be impressed by alacrity in feats of memorization and recitation. Confession offered young women another unaccustomed opportunity to express themselves. Jesuit fathers discovered that some of them transformed the ritual of confession into an opportunity to fashion narratives of their lives. "There are many who confess frequently and very well," Father Jacques Gravier reported to his superiors; he described a system in which some "made use of little pieces of wood" and "as they mentioned everything of which they accused themselves, or which they considered a sin, they dropped one of these small pieces of wood, like the beads of a rosary." Illinois women were thus introduced to forms of public self-expression that would otherwise have been completely unavailable to them, and encouraged to use them to reflect on the meaning of their lives. In the process they took on new social roles that granted them an unusual degree of initiative and power.[28]

27 For the tendency of converted young women to shun dances and other "night assemblies," see Gravier's journal, 15 Feb. 1694, *JR*, vol. LXIV, p. 219; Jacqueline Peterson, "Women Dreaming: The Religiopsychology of Indian White Marriages and the Rise of a Metis Culture," in Lillian Schlissel, Vicki L. Ruiz, and Janice Monk, eds., *Western Women: Their Land, Their Lives* (Albuquerque, 1988), pp. 49–68. The most nuanced account of young women's centrality to the success of a mission is in Gravier's journal, 15 Feb. 1694, *JR*, vol. LXIV, pp. 159–237; its contents are analyzed further below. One observer of Illinois women wrote that, "according to their customs, they are the slaves of their brothers, who compel them to marry whomsoever they choose, even men already married to another wife. Nevertheless, there are those among them who constantly resist, and who prefer to expose themselves to ill treatment rather than do anything contrary to the precepts of Christianity regarding marriage." Binneteau to [?], [Jan.] 1699, *JR*, vol. LXV, p. 67.

28 Gravier's journal, 15 Feb. 1694, *JR*, vol. LXIV, pp. 225 [feats of memory]; pp. 227–229 [memory and plates]; pp. 177–179 [confessions and quote]. For the importance of pictures, see also Marest to [?], 29 Apr. 1699, *JR*, vol. LXV, p. 83. For the connection between conversion and new forms of public speech for women, see also Natalie Zemon Davis, "Iroquois Women, European Women," in Margo Hendricks and Patricia Parker, eds., *Women, "Race," and Writing in the Early Modern Period* (London, 1994), especially pp. 254–256.

The Jesuit fathers also offered their converts a new universe of material artifacts that gave substance to their newfound faiths. Children competed assiduously for such tokens of achievement as beads, needles, medals, crosses, knives, and rosaries. Devout converts treasured these tokens and invested the crosses, rosaries, and pictures of Mary or Christ with particular significance. They might construct altars or shrines in their homes to display them. In at least one case a particularly devout convert set aside an entire "apartment" to her Christian icons; in moments of crisis she retired to her "oratory" and knelt at the foot of a crucifix. She kept a picture of Christ crowned with thorns, the sight of which often made her weep; perhaps inspired by the image (and probably also by the example of the Jesuit fathers she knew), she made herself a girdle of thorns. "This she wore for two whole days, and she would have crippled herself with it," according to her priest, "had she not informed me of this mortification, when I compelled her to use it with more moderation."[29] In all of these processes – memorization and recitation; confessional self-construction; the creation of physical spaces rich with symbolic meaning; dramatic acts of self-abnegation – the Jesuits helped converts to build a powerful complex of associations that could serve as a foundation for their spiritual lives. Adoption of Christianity empowered young women, in particular, by giving them increased control over their sexual and spiritual selves and by offering them a rationale for challenging the dictates of their communities' male elders.

In one spectacular case, the success of missionaries among a devoted core of young women led, suddenly and unexpectedly, to the conversion of an entire Illinois tribe. Following two decades of limited achievements and frustrated ambitions during which conversions were relatively rare, the Jesuits in the Illinois country suddenly experienced a dramatic reversal of their fortunes when Marie Rouensa, daughter of the Kaskaskia chief, declared her allegiance to the Christian God. (She is the same young woman who fashioned for herself a Christian "oratory" and a girdle of thorns, and hers were also among the most prodigious feats of memory recorded in the Illinois country.) Her father arranged for Marie to marry Michel Accault, one of the traders who came to the Illinois country with LaSalle. Such matches were a familiar and traditional form of alliance. In this case, it was a marriage of great honor on both sides: the daughter of the chief of the most powerful tribe of the Illinois confederacy was being offered to one of the most prominent and

---

[29] Binneteau to [?], [Jan.] 1699, *JR*, vol. LXV, p. 77; Gravier's journal, 15 Feb. 1694, *JR*, vol. LXIV, pp. 231, 215–216, 223; quote: p. 215.

respected traders in the region. But, inexplicably in the eyes of her father, most of the rest of the Illinois Indians, and Accault himself, Marie Rouensa defied her father's wishes and refused the marriage. She attributed her decision to the influence of the resident Jesuit missionary, Father Jacques Gravier, and insisted that she was saving herself for God. In her ecstatic state, a wedding of convenience with a rather dissolute man appeared to her to be an unforgivable carnal evil.[30]

Marie Rouensa's refusal infuriated her father and threw the Kaskaskia village into turmoil. The chief railed against Gravier's influence and warned the entire community away from his services. For two days the standoff generated rancor and several episodes of near-violence, during which time the only members of the tribe to risk attending services were drawn from the core group of young women who were devoted to Gravier. Finally Marie became fearful that her show of piety might endanger Gravier's position in the village, and she decided to capitulate to the marriage. Even as she gave in, however, she proclaimed her hatred for her future husband "because he always speaks ill of my father, the black gown." To the missionary she confided her hope that the marriage might be a means for Gravier to gain more influence with her biological father, whom she reportedly regarded with "pity."[31] And indeed, the force of Marie's devotion and personality soon produced dramatic effects in both her parents and her new husband. All three turned over new leaves in the weeks and months following the wedding. Apparently humbled and inspired by Marie's example, they all converted and became devout Christians.

The conversion of the Kaskaskia chief and his family altered the most basic calculus of power within the tribe. Previously, the Christian message presented a face that was alien and hostile to the structure of social authority. Rouensa's conversion changed that, and in its wake the entire tribe's relation to the Jesuit fathers was transformed. During the winter following the Rouensas' baptism, attendance at Gravier's catechism classes jumped dramatically and the missionary was convinced that, for the first time, devotion replaced mere curiosity as the group's motive force. Within a year he had baptized 260 members of the tribe; a decade and a half later Gravier could report that nearly every member of the Kaskaskia tribe was baptized and "professed the catholic faith with the greatest piety and constancy."[32]

---

[30] This and the following paragraph are based on Gravier's journal, 15 Feb. 1694, *JR*, vol. LXIV, p. 193 and following.

[31] Quotes: ibid., p. 207.

[32] Gravier to Father General, 6 Mar. 1707, *JR*, vol. LXVI, p. 123.

No other community among the Illinois or Miami Indians responded with so much enthusiasm to the possibility of conversion. The Peorias, who were the most numerous Illinois tribe, stood at the other end of the spectrum from the Kaskaskias; they tolerated the Jesuit fathers out of a desire to maintain a trading connection with the French, but they successfully resisted their conversion efforts. During times when missionary efforts were especially pronounced, Peoria leaders occasionally lashed out at the fathers. Gravier's success with the Kaskaskias inspired one such occasion. "Let the *Kaskaskia* pray to God if they wish and let them obey him who has instructed them. Are we *Kaskaskia*? . . . [H]as this man who has come from afar better medicines than we have, to make us adopt his customs? His Fables are good only in his own country; we have ours, which do not make us die as his do." A decade later Gravier was attacked by a young man in the Peoria village and shot through the arm with an arrow; though he survived for a time, complications from the wound eventually killed him. French officials responded by forbidding traders from dealing with the Peorias. Under the pressure of this proscription, the Peorias soon apologized and asked that another missionary be sent among them.[33]

At the other end of the valley, more than half a century later, a comparable drama was played out among the Ohio Indians at the village of Goschgoschuenk on the Allegheny River following the arrival of two Moravian missionaries. Here the effect was even more pronounced because the community was more fragmented. It was a recently settled, multiethnic village, and its residents had all experienced prolonged contact with Europeans; many were refugees struggling to refocus their relationship with the world around them. One aspect of that struggle was the need to assess the relative validity of several competing sources of spiritual authority. In addition to the two missionaries and their core group of about a dozen followers, there were several other contending factions. At least three different Indian prophets preached their own gospels and urged the residents of the town to ignore the Christians. Even as they sought to discredit the Christian missionaries, they appro-

[33] Gravier's journal, 15 Feb. 1694, *JR*, vol. LXIV, p. 173; the story of the Peoria attack on Gravier is related in Mermet to the Jesuits in Canada, 2 Mar. 1706, *JR*, vol. LXVI, p. 51 and following. A comparable event occurred in the village of Cahokia, where the death of a missionary working under the auspices of the Seminary for Foreign Missions caused the local shamans to rejoice. "They gathered around the cross that he had erected, and there they invoked their *Manitou*, – each one dancing and attributing to himself the glory of having killed the Missionary, after which they broke the cross into a thousand pieces." In response, trade with Cahokia was curtailed, and as with the Peorias this caused the local headmen to apologize and seek reconciliation. See Marest to Germon, 9 Nov. 1712, *JR*, vol. LXVI, pp. 263–265.

priated their imagery. Two of the three claimed to have been to heaven themselves, and one said he had seen the Christian god. And there were other challenges as well: the Seneca chief with putative political authority over the village sent a message to warn the local Indians to "beware of the black coat," and a "baptized Jew" who originated in New England and now lived in Goschgoschuenk cautioned them "that whoever believes and is baptized becomes the servant of the whites."[34]

After three months in Goschgoschuenk, the Moravians concluded that their mission had made very little progress; the community remained distant and mistrustful. Nevertheless, the mere presence of the Moravians and the nature of their reception illustrate the challenges and transformations that European influence brought to Ohio Indian communities. In all of these cases, missionaries tested the strength of Indian communities by putting pressure on the fractal lines running through native societies. They tested individual leaders; they challenged the structures of social authority; they undermined the assumptions governing gender relations. Whether they were successful or not, the presence of Christian missionaries introduced the native residents of the Ohio Valley to an entirely unaccustomed phenomenon: a marketplace of ideas in the spiritual realm.

Contact with Europeans challenged Indian cosmologies simply by introducing other possibilities, and by radically democratizing access to spiritual power and authority in the process. The marketplace in spiritual ideas destroyed the unquestioning allegiance of Ohio Indians to traditional shamans and forced would-be spiritual leaders to prove their value against competing doctrines. Prolonged contact with Europeans and their ideas could lead Ohio Indians to demand new explanations and challenge older, insular religious traditions. Before the arrival of Europeans, the leadership of shamans in native cultures was presumably unquestioned; even where the pretensions of individual shamans to authority might be challenged, the framework in which they operated would have been relatively secure. By the middle of the 18th century, Ohio Indians enjoyed the bewildering luxury of being able to test the ideas and efficacy of shamans against other traditions.

Communities throughout the Ohio Valley witnessed an increasingly common spectacle in these years: holy men parading through their streets, calling upon the faithful – or the skeptical – to listen to their sto-

---

34 "Diary of David Zeisberger's and Gottlieb Sensemann's Jouney to Goschgoschink on the Ohio and their arrival there, 1768" [trans. typescript], Box 135, Folder 7, Records of the Moravian Mission Among the Indians of North America, Archives of the Moravian Church, Bethlehem, Penn. (microfilm), entries for 28 June, 4 July, 1 Aug., 24 June, and throughout.

ries. In town after town, European and Indian priests rubbed shoulders uncomfortably as they competed for souls. Father Gravier and his successors routinely marched through Illinois villages calling the residents to prayer; on occasion they were openly confronted by native chiefs or shamans who railed against them and warned the people away. Even in the communities at the eastern end of the valley, where missions were less systematically organized, at least occasional contact with Christian proselytizers was widespread. The effect was often to divide and fragment the villages; some residents were persuaded of the value of baptism and prayer and the efficacy of the missionaries' magic, while others looked upon their efforts with suspicion. In other places the presence of missionaries could strengthen the unity and resolve of a village. But in either case, the residents of the Ohio Valley were living in a changed world; no longer could the nature or context of spiritual authority be taken for granted. Those who claimed to possess spiritual authority had to respond creatively to the alternative traditions that were becoming available in the marketplace of ideas, even if it meant, in Goschgoschuenk, Indian prophets accepting the existence and power of the Christian god: by acknowledging him they could also claim the ability to comprehend him, and so maintain their own claims to authority.

III

Even where the formal efforts of Christian missionaries did not effect dramatic transformations, trading relationships with the French and British introduced a new calculus of power, a new universe of artifacts, and a new range of spiritual possibilities to Indian societies. The marketplace, in other words, brought its own rituals, talismans, and moral imperatives to the Indians who embraced it. Europeans never thought of the processes and artifacts of commerce in religious or spiritual terms (and neither, usually, do historians), but in fact trade introduced new avenues to power and distinction in Indian societies, dramatically revised the visible signs of status and authority, and created a framework for the transformation of Indian cosmologies. In all of these ways, throughout the Ohio Valley, trade with European empires introduced far-reaching changes into the connections native peoples perceived between the physical world and the spiritual one.[35]

[35] The debate surrounding the impact of the European commercial world-system on tribal societies is immense. Ethnohistorians have come to assume, correctly I think, that we cannot simply assume Indians' participation in the market is explained by universal models of economic behavior derived from Adam Smith. We must, instead, understand the meanings assigned to trade within their own cultural contexts. But historians have

In precontact Algonquian cultures, hunting apparently took place within a framework that emphasized the sacred qualities of animals and the importance of reciprocity and the propitiation of spirits. Hunting was intimately connected with the most pressing spiritual concerns of Indian peoples. It was central to the definition of male identity and status, and the interaction between men and other animals comprised one of the most important themes in visions and stories throughout native America. Eastern woodlands Indians believed that the behavior of animals was governed by their particular manitous, spiritual keepers or guardians to whom hunters must appeal for aid and express gratitude for successful hunts. Before beginning a hunt, men would pray to manitous and follow any guidance they might receive in dreams or visions. Interpreting those dreams and visions was the province of wise men in native cultures. Shamans understood the contours of the natural and supernatural worlds and made the universe coherent and explicable for their communities. After killing an animal, Indian hunters observed rituals that were intended to confirm their debt of obligation to the guardian spirit of the captured game. Central to this process was the belief that animals and men were closely related and connected, and the sacrifice of an animal for the sake of human survival was an extraordinary gift. It was crucial for men to honor such a gift properly if they were to maintain favor with the forces of the supernatural world.[36]

With the arrival of European fur traders in Indian country, old definitions of the meaning and purpose of hunting began to erode. It is difficult to describe this change precisely, and it certainly did not come overnight. But it is clear that hunting for the market did gradually undermine some of the ruling assumptions of earlier hunting practices. Within the traditional conception of the universe, for example, respect

been slow to ask how the rules and goods of the market themselves modified Indians' beliefs, behaviors, and cultures, except to say that in the long run it produced abject dependency.

[36] For a useful introduction to these ideas, see Ruth Underhill, *Red Man's Religion: Beliefs and Practices of the Indians North of Mexico* (Chicago, 1965); the best discussion of power and ritual in relation to the peoples under consideration here is in Gregory Dowd, *A Spirited Resistance: The North American Indian Struggle for Unity, 1745–1815* (Baltimore, 1992), pp. 1–22. The earliest ethnohistorical exploration of Indian-animal relationships is Calvin Martin's controversial *Keepers of the Game: Indian-Animal Relationships and the Fur Trade* (Berkeley, 1978); for critical responses see Shepard Krech III, ed., *Indians, Animals, and the Fur Trade: A Critique of Keepers of the Game* (Athens, GA, 1981). Martin's work relates to the Micmacs, who were hunter-gatherers; as he himself has noted, it would be inaccurate to analogize directly to horticultural peoples such as those considered in this work. Nevertheless, there is evidence that a comparable religious bond held between men and animals among the Ohio Valley Indians, even if it differed considerably in its details.

for animals and their manitous dictated that men hunt only for what
they needed to survive: the death of animals was a gift given to prevent
the death of men. One of the cardinal rules of the hunt was therefore to
take only what was needed for the sustenance of the group. The market
gradually reoriented this ruling presumption about hunting, and in one
region after another it caused Indians to overhunt game populations and
destroy ecosystems.

For the Shawnee and Delaware Indians moving west from Pennsylvania to the Ohio Valley, the shift to a more market-driven pattern of behavior in hunting appears, if we can judge by the volume of their trade,
to have roughly coincided with their removal. Before the move the volume of their trade was both small and inconsistent. But the Ohio Valley
was rich with game, and the surviving evidence indicates that the Ohio
Indians immediately began to overhunt its resources. In the 1730s the
Shawnees could name the Scioto "Hairy River" in honor of its apparently enormous deer population, but the commercial market for deerskins quickly depleted its numbers. Twice a year, from September or October until January and again in June and July, hunters in the Ohio Valley concentrated on gathering deerskins. A single accomplished hunter
might shoot between 50 and 150 deer in a single autumn hunt, usually
wasting most of the meat and collecting only the skins. Following the
autumn deer hunt, from February until April or May, men often spent
most of their time hunting beavers. By the early 1770s the populations
of both these animals had declined so sharply in the upper valley that
hunting parties sometimes had to travel hundreds of miles in search of
game. In 1773 a group of Delawares embarked on a hunting trip that
took them down the Ohio and the Mississippi all the way to New Orleans; from there they sailed back to Philadelphia, sold their skins, and
returned home overland. Those who remained closer to home felt the effects of the game shortage still more directly. During his visit to the
Delaware towns on the Muskingum River, David Jones commented that
"deer grow so scarce, that, [for a] great part of the year, many of them
rather starve than live."[37]

How could people deeply rooted in a tradition that attached sacred
meaning to the killing of animals undergo such a rapid and complete
transformation? The logic of the marketplace introduced an entirely unfamiliar set of pressures that favored overhunting, at the same time that

[37] For the increase in fur and skin production coinciding with removal, and the naming of
the Scioto River, see chapter one, p. 31 and following; Edmund de Schweinitz, *The Life
and Times of David Zeisberger* (Philadelphia, 1871), pp. 80–81; David Jones, *A Journal
of Two Visits Made to Some Nations of Indians on the West Side of the River Ohio, in
the years 1772 and 1773* (New York, 1865) [orig. pub. 1774], pp. 60, 89, 100.

it seemed to call upon, strengthen, and reward the most essential masculine traditions in native culture. Previously the connection between hunting and subsistence was direct and explicit; there was no reason to kill more game than could be consumed in the near future or carried home by the hunters. Within native subsistence economies, therefore, what was needed was a modest but steady supply of game. It is possible that this requirement made hunting a more personal, intimate, and therefore sacred activity than it would later become. Whether or not that is the case, it certainly made Indian populations quite sensitive to fluctuations in local animal populations. Moreover, when hunters needed to transport, not just skins or pelts, but whole animals, their effective range was considerably reduced. And it was necessary to be able to resort to hunting on a regular basis to supply food throughout the year. All of these considerations served to make hunting a limited activity, fraught with religious significance and constrained by ritual and taboo.

The market challenged the ethic of sacral restraint in hunting by rewarding prodigious short-term success. And the rewards it offered immeasurably enriched the material universe of Indian communities, a fact that seemed, for a time, to compensate more than adequately for the corresponding loss of sacred meaning – or rather, seemed to alter the calculus of sacred power. Cautious restraint was no longer rewarded as it had been; as European artifacts became coins of the realm in the Ohio Valley, hunting to excess brought the most dramatic success. The material transformation effected by the fur trade, in other words, generated a corresponding spiritual transformation, or at least created a crisis of spiritual values, in which older beliefs and patterns of behavior were challenged by the manifest efficacy of newer ones. Put simply, hunting for the market caused an unprecedented level of prosperity for the Ohio Indians. The artifacts of the fur trade came increasingly, by the middle of the 18th century, to dominate the material culture of the region. The changes were so sweeping and thorough, in fact, that they are difficult to catalog and assess adequately. One archaeologist has concluded that by 1760, Indians in the adjacent Great Lakes region had so fully embraced European goods that it is now impossible to distinguish sites by tribal group. In place of their distinctive material cultures, a single, pan-Indian culture had emerged that was defined primarily by European artifacts.[38]

Partly, of course, the effect of this material transformation was functional. Cloth replaced animal skins almost entirely as the basis for cloth-

[38] George I. Quimby, *Indian Culture and European Trade Goods: The Archaeology of the Historic Period in the Western Great Lakes* (Madison, WI, 1966).

ing; brass kettles supplanted pottery; guns, powder, and shot made bows and arrows increasingly obsolete. But to focus on the strictly functional importance of European artifacts is to miss their greatest significance, which was cultural and symbolic. The introduction of European trade goods in Ohio Indian societies created a whole new artifactual vocabulary of status: it revolutionized the nature and meaning of wealth. European artifacts introduced a new sense of personal style and ornamentation to Indian cultures. Cloth, glass, and silver largely replaced animal skins, feathers, and claws as marks of distinction among the Ohio Indians. Shirts and strouds made of English cloth were universally worn, and when men decorated their heads they used silk handkerchiefs or silver baubles. Glass beads, to judge from archaeological remains, were everywhere. Silver ornaments were especially popular; Shawnee women frequently wore silver earrings, and in one case a particularly affluent woman reportedly had "near five hundred silver broaches stuck in her shirt, stroud and leggins." A more modest example of this effect has been described by an archaeologist, who noted at a St. Joseph site "a fragmentary piece of trade cloth to which were attached about twenty-five or thirty small round brooches of silver so closely spaced or overlapping as to produce an appearance not unlike that of chain mail." Shawnee men also favored trade silver, and frequently wore silver armplates both above and below the elbows.[39]

It would be easy to dismiss such developments as insignificant ephemera, but in fact they run to the heart of far-reaching changes in Ohio Indian culture. Most importantly, they reflect the fact that the fur trade democratized access to marks of status. Previously, status and social authority flowed in channels that were structured by age and achievement and governed by tribal tradition. The shift to market-driven economies meant that older patterns of leadership and authority were eroded by the dominance of young men in the processes of hunting for the market. Among the Shawnees, for example, the move to the Ohio Valley coincided with the passing of an older generation of tribal leaders. In their place a generation of young hunter-warriors, distinguished for their prowess in taking game, rose in stature and authority. The Delawares, too, experienced a hiatus in seasoned political leadership when they moved west.[40] The practical efficacy of younger, more decentralized leadership was dramatically illustrated for Indian communities by the extended period of rising prosperity they experienced be-

---

[39] Jones, *Two Visits*, pp. 83–84; Quimby, *Indian Culture and European Trade Goods*, 145 and throughout.
[40] See pp. 75–76 below.

tween the 1730s and the 1760s. The widespread displays of silver, silk, colorful cloth, and other European items commented upon by visitors to the Ohio Valley were, in effect, displays of status. As with such displays in any culture, they were visible signs of power and influence; in this case, they demonstrated the valor and productivity of a community's young men. European clothing and extravagant ornamentation became marks of distinction, the new articles of conspicuous consumption, among the Ohio Indians.

Alcohol was perhaps the consummate luxury item in the Indian trade. It was useless rather than functional, consumable rather than durable, and notorious for its capacity to inflame the rash confidence of its partakers, particularly the same young men who were testing their hunting skills for the sake of the marketplace. When young Indian men chose to drink heavily, they were engaging in an especially visible form of conspicuous consumption. And the consumption of alcohol, not surprisingly, seems to have accelerated significantly among the Shawnees and Delawares following their removal to the Ohio Valley. Drinking came to be associated with skill in hunting; it was especially popular in the spring, immediately following the rigors of the winter hunt. During this era of rising prosperity, drunkenness became a common form of exuberant expression among the young males in the increasingly successful communities of hunter-warriors in the Ohio Valley.[41]

Thus the fur trade functioned for young men in much the same way that conversion did for young women. In both cases, the arrival of Europeans initiated a power shift in Indian communities, whose effect was to challenge the authority of elders and of tradition. Young men and women could now forge new alliances that opened new possibilities and challenged older conventions of age and gender that had previously structured power relations in their communities.

IV

The introduction of an imported material culture, like the challenge of European cosmologies, had significant implications for the structure of

---

[41] References to drinking are both commonplace and episodic, so it is difficult to prove that alcohol consumption increased in the west; when leaders among the western Indians communicated with colonial officials in Pennsylvania, however, they nearly always complained about the excess of alcohol in their communities. See, e.g., letter from the Allegheny Indians, 1 May 1734, in Samuel Hazard, ed., *Pennsylvania Archives* [1st Ser.], 12 vols. (Philadelphia, 1852–1856), vol. I, p. 425. In 1749 George Croghan wrote that the Ohio Indians "Complain very much that ye Governor Don't putt a Stop to his Traders bringing out Spirits to sell after ye Many Complaints Made on that ac-

political authority in the Ohio Valley. Older models of authority and
status were based on the wisdom of age and experience, on deference
and hierarchy. These principles were not entirely lost in the Ohio Valley
communities of the mid-18th century, but new sources of wealth – and
the power associated with it – undermined the stability of older hierarchies and created changes so fundamental that they caused what might
be described as a crisis of political leadership for the Ohio Valley Indians.

Throughout the colonial period, European goods passed into native
hands through two complementary but distinct processes. The first involved the ritual exchange of commodities in political or diplomatic
contexts. This kind of gift-giving was used to seal and sanctify agreements over such matters as land sales, peacemaking, and extending or
strengthening an alliance. Within the language of the Iroquois' covenant
chain, presents offered in diplomatic settings were used to "brighten the
chain," to confirm and strengthen the ties that bound together European and Indian allies. The protocol for these exchanges conformed to
Indian norms and practices; Europeans who entered into Indian country
had to learn new languages, new vocabularies, and new procedures for
intercultural relations if they were to avoid offending their hosts. The
participation of Europeans both validated and extended the usefulness
of native diplomatic structures, and at the same time exerted subtle (or
sometimes not so subtle) evolutionary pressures on the pattern of Indian
politics itself.[42]

The second means by which European and Indian societies exchanged goods was through the marketplace, a locus that was governed
by European norms and precedents. Here it was traders and merchants
who set the terms of exchange: they introduced Indians to such innova-

count," and noted that many Indians had been killed in "Drinking Spills." Croghan to
Richard Peters, 25 Nov. 1749, Box 5, Cadwallader Collection, Historical Society of
Pennsylvania [photostat; original held by the Indiana Historical Society]. Both these
documents, like most others of their kind, suggest that alcohol was a powerful source
of tensions between young hunter-warriors and their European trading partners, on the
one hand, and elders on the other, in the Ohio Valley communities. For an extended
analysis of the trade that considers alcohol's devastating effects on Indian communities,
see Peter Mancall, *Deadly Medicine: Indians and Alcohol in Early America* (Ithaca,
1995).

[42] For the creation of the covenant chain and the idea of "brightening" the chain, see
Daniel Richter, *The Ordeal of the Longhouse: The Peoples of the Iroquois League in
the Era of European Colonization* (Chapel Hill, 1992), pp. 134–142; for a comprehensive discussion of the ways that Indian practices could shape intercultural diplomacy,
see James Merrell, *The Indians' New World: Catawbas and Their Neighbors from European Contact Through the Era of Removal* (Chapel Hill, 1989), pp. 134–166.

tions as accounting precisely for credits and debts; using weights and measures to calibrate value; and relying upon international patterns of supply and demand to establish the worth of the articles of trade. The legitimacy of trade, like that of diplomacy, was confirmed in the ongoing willingness of members of both cultures to participate in exchange according to its rules.[43] And like intercultural diplomacy, trade exerted a transforming influence on the structures of political authority. In this case, it broadened access to wealth and thus tended to weaken the power of elders to control the behavior of their young hunters.

These new channels of wealth had a powerful impact on patterns of leadership precisely because the redistribution of material goods was so central to the role played by elders and leaders in Indian societies. As Marshall Sahlins has argued, structures of authority that reach beyond the household in non-state societies function in part as mechanisms for redistributing economic resources: "Kinship, chieftainship, even the ritual order, whatever else they may be, appear in the primitive societies as economic forces."[44] The ritual exchange that accompanied diplomacy complemented pre-existing patterns of authority, because it placed commodities into the hands of spokesmen who claimed political authority within their clans, tribes, or confederacies. Gifts were essential to successful diplomacy because they reinforced the authority of native spokesmen with their own people. Native leaders did not wield coercive power over their followers; they had to rely on persuasion and popular support for their authority. In this context, gifts were an essential source of influence, since Indian leaders could oversee their redistribution among the group. The value of an agreement was proven, in part, by the stock of goods leaders were empowered to distribute.

In practice, even the exchange that accompanied diplomacy could alter structures of authority by elevating individuals whose claim to status came not from within their own communities, but rather by virtue of their connections to Europeans. Diplomacy could confer leadership upon people who otherwise might not have enjoyed it. Thus, during the 18th century Indian societies throughout zones of intercultural contact in North America witnessed the rise of a new leadership class, some-

---

43 Indians often challenged aspects of market exchange which seemed arbitrary or tyrannical, especially fluctuations in value based on supply and demand (which could be exacerbated by the dishonesty of individual traders, since they were often operating without competitors in particular times and places); see, e.g., *Minutes of the Provincial Council of Pennsylvania*, 16 vols. (Harrisburg, 1838–1853) [hereafter *Pa. Col. Recs.*], vol. II, pp. 599–601. For a more general discussion, see Merrell, *Indians' New World*, pp. 49–91.

44 Marshall Sahlins, *Stone Age Economics* (New York, 1972), pp. 101–102.

times called "medal chiefs" in recognition of the fact that their status was conferred by marks of distinction which were distributed by Europeans. In most cases medal chiefs had an independent claim to influence within their own communities, but their contacts with colonial leaders boosted their status and made it more likely that their own interests, tied as they were to European sources, might not accord perfectly with those of the people for whom they spoke.[45]

For the colonial powers, the most desirable arrangement was to discover or create a small number of chiefs who could speak with unambiguous authority for a large and clearly defined tribal group. This was especially useful in arranging for land cessions, and because the British colonies were more expansive than the French it was on their borders, in particular, that the need for such chiefs was greatest. During the 18th century Anglo-American leaders established working relationships with chiefs whom they designated "kings" and "half-kings," labels that reflect the wishes of administrators rather than the reality of native politics. In some cases, colonial leaders were successful for a time in actually altering the structure of Indian politics through their diplomatic efforts. The Delawares, for example, were a loosely connected group with no tradition of leadership beyond the village level before they were drawn into diplomatic relations with Pennsylvania; but the leaders of the colony gradually helped to raise up a series of political spokesmen who were empowered to speak for the entire "tribe" – a term that had no effective political meaning for the Delawares before the colonization of Pennsylvania began. In a similar way, officials in New York and Pennsylvania cooperated with the Five Nations of the Iroquois to create a political confederacy for the purposes of intercultural diplomacy, which eventually exerted tremendous influence on Indian affairs throughout the entire northeast.[46]

In other cases, diplomatic gifts actually encouraged the proliferation and decentralization of political power. Often "medal chiefs" and recipients of occasional gifts were lesser figures in their communities, but circumstances brought them into a prominent role – often a short-lived one – in an intercultural alliance. This pattern was more common in the French sphere, where land cessions were less essential but where Indian allies were regularly encouraged to go to war in the interests of the empire. This meant that, in addition to the peace chiefs who treated with the French to strengthen the alliance, war leaders, and even common warriors with no claim to leadership status, were also singled out for fa-

---

[45] See, e.g., White, *Middle Ground*, pp. 177–179 and following.
[46] The case of the Delawares will be considered in more detail in chapter three, pp. 199–122 and following.

vors and gifts. Over the long run, in fact, the need to offer gifts to a proliferating circle of chiefs, war leaders, and faithful allies imposed crip-
pling administrative expenses on the French empire in the west. At the
same time, the wide distribution of gifts could all too easily cause fragmentation, rather than unity, within particular tribes and actually contribute to the breakdown of the alliance the French sought to create.[47]

But if the commodities that entered Indian societies through diplomacy could exert subtle pressures on structures of political authority, market exchange was an even more potent force for change. During the rise
of European trading networks in the Ohio Valley, two important developments affected Indians' access to resources. First, because people were
re-occupying a large, fertile region that was still well below its carrying
capacity, the possibility of famine declined and most communities were
able to provide for their subsistence with relative ease. And second, exchange for European commodities brought a dramatic increase in non-
subsistence, luxury goods that conferred prosperity and status on a very
broad segment of Indian communities. Under these circumstances the
power of chiefs and clan elders was diminished somewhat, and young
men, in particular, were empowered to act independently of their leaders. Especially when elders urged restraint in the face of expanding economic opportunities, they were likely to be ignored or opposed by
younger members of the community.

The Shawnee band that had settled on the Susquehanna River experienced just such a crisis in the years immediately before their large-scale
exodus to the Allegheny and Ohio Rivers began. In 1711 Opessa, who
had been until that time the preeminent leader of the band, abdicated
his position. A spokesman explained some years later that Opessa gave
up his role because "the People differed with him"; in particular, his
leadership was opposed by "the Young men who lived under no Government." Opessa was already experiencing the powerful solvent effects
of the marketplace on the social adhesives of ethnic solidarity and deference to authority. In response to his diminished status, he left the
Shawnee settlements on the Susquehanna and began a period of wandering; eventually he founded a new community known as Opessa's
Town on the upper Potomac, but he remained a secondary figure
thenceforward among his people. In 1714, after several years without
formal contact with the colony of Pennsylvania, a delegation of
Shawnees once again visited Philadelphia. This time it was a young

---

[47] See, e.g., Richard White, *The Roots of Dependency: Subsistence, Environment, and
Change among the Choctaws, Pawnees, and Navajos* (Lincoln, NE, 1983), pp. 52–54
and following. This pattern will be discussed in more detail in relation to the Miami Indians in chapter three, pp. 116–119.

group of leaders, unfamiliar to the colony's officials. They explained that Opessa had left them and others of their old men had died, and reported that the Shawnees' older leaders "are now succeeded by a younger Generation." The delegation presented a young man named Cakundawanna as the new chief spokesman of the Shawnees, and asked colony officials to recognize him as such. Cakundawanna did not remain a prominent figure among the Shawnees for long, a further indication that this was a period of instability in leadership. Six years later another Shawnee spokesman, named Sevana, was received as a chief of the Shawnees by Pennsylvania officials, but he lamented that "he had only the Name [of chief] without any authority, and could do nothing." When the Shawnees began to move west a few years later, they undertook the remove without any effective leader who could unify them or speak for them as a whole people.[48]

The opportunities presented by migration into the Ohio Valley affected both the Delawares and the Iroquois in a similar way. The carefully constructed hierarchies of the covenant chain and the designation of "kings" and "half-kings" were challenged by the possibility of westward migration, which tended to restore the political fragmentation those structures had been designed to combat. By the mid-1720s, two figures had risen to preeminence among Pennsylvania's Indians; both were leaders whose status was significantly enhanced by their contacts with Europeans. Olumapies was raised up as the first "king" of the Delawares, a status that was first clearly manifested in 1715; for nearly two decades thereafter he was the Delawares' chief spokesman in colonial affairs. His partner in intercultural relations was an Oneida chief named Shickellamy, who was appointed by the Iroquois council to act as overseer of the dependent Indian nations in the Susquehanna Valley.[49] The westward migrations of the Pennsylvania Indians carried them beyond the effective jurisdiction of these two leaders, and also of the Onondaga Council that set policy for the Iroquois confederation as a whole. From 1730 forward the independence of the western Indians became increasingly clear; by 1750 it had become a prime concern of British colonial officials.

In the French sphere as well, commercial opportunities helped to erode the strength of ethnic loyalties and tribal solidarities. New channels of trade made it possible for less established leaders to challenge more established ones for influence, especially once they were able to

---

[48] *Pa. Col. Recs.*, vol. II, p. 574; vol. III, p. 97.
[49] Olumapies and Shickellamy are considered in more detail in chapter three, pp. 119–128.

play off the British trading network against the French. It was in precisely such circumstances that La Demoiselle broke from the Miami town of Kekionga, under the leadership of Le Pied Froid, in the late 1740s to establish the town of Pickawillany.[50] The success of his power play relied, above all, on the attractiveness of the British trading connection. La Demoiselle had pretensions to chiefly leadership, but what is significant about the trading economy of the Ohio Valley is that it allowed hunters, as well as chiefs, to acquire the material sources of power. Throughout the region, communities of hunter-traders experimented with patterns of leadership that enhanced their access to the material resources offered by the European powers.

None of this is to say that political power became irrelevant to the Indians of the Ohio Valley; only that its communities saw the rise of a new kind of polity, whose strength came not from tribal solidarity but from intertribal linkages that facilitated the expansion of trade. If the various defections and revolts that brought Indian groups into the ambit of the British traders were to be successful, the Ohio Indians needed to cooperate among themselves, to lend strength and numbers to the region's new towns. Thus the intertribal communities of the valley, like Logstown and the Shawnee town on the Scioto, gained their importance precisely because they brought together spokesmen for so many different groups in the region; located along the Ohio itself or easily accessible from it, they became centers of a *de facto* alliance system among the trading populations of the valley.[51]

As political entities these communities, and the fragmented bands that occupied them, became increasingly unstable. Because political power in Indian societies stemmed primarily from the ability to control and redistribute property, trade both democratized and devalued political leadership. In a world of hunter-traders, chiefs could all too easily become troubling obstacles to prosperity, rather than facilitators of it. Thus, as Richard White put it, "The Ohio, a heaven to hunters, proved a purgatory to chiefs."[52] It remained possible for crises to re-energize more hierarchical structures of power as people were forced to choose sides and follow leaders; but in periods of peace, commerce tended to undermine the traditional bases of social authority.

---

[50] See chapter one, pp. 42 and following.

[51] Céloron and his party discovered that the residents of small, scattered villages congregated in the central trading towns for diplomatic purposes, and that the politics of these communities were shaped by interethnic coalitions of leaders. See Céloron's Journal, pp. 27–39, 41–50.

[52] White, *Middle Ground*, p. 189.

PART TWO

Empires of Land

EMPIRES are constructions of convenience, and the particular forms they take reflect the needs and desires of the people who constitute them. A "pure" mercantile empire would have had only very modest territorial requirements: garrisoned ports, perhaps established in conjunction with plantation colonies that might be relatively small and circumscribed; inland trading posts to serve as points of exchange. But a vital element of the European attraction to North America was the land itself, and more capacious development schemes emerged very rapidly. Alongside proto-modern visions of commercial exploitation and development, retro-feudal fantasies of vast landed estates became commonplace in seventeenth-century Europe. For a time America appeared to the nobles of England to be a place where the past glories of the great privileged families might be revived, where the steady erosion of noble status and influence might be reversed. In France, which had more successfully preserved noble prerogative, New World holdings still seemed suitable for extending aristocratic privileges overseas. As it turned out, nothing could have been more misconceived. The American colonies were too vast for their populations and resources to be carefully managed and controlled, the tie to Europe too tenuous to be closely bound. Rather than serving as bastions of social conservatism, they became hothouses of experimentation and change.

New France provides one kind of example of this pattern. There a neo-feudal world was created along the banks of the St. Lawrence River, where land was granted in *seigneuries*; Cardinal Richelieu, and later Louis XIV, viewed Canadian settlement as an extension of French feudal

responsibility and privilege. Yet nearly a half-century after the first concessions were made only 6,000 people had settled in Canada, and one
historian has estimated that no more than 4–5% of all the seigneurial
lands had been cleared for farming. The feudal system in Canada was a
failure: *seigneurs* were largely unsuccessful in recruiting *censitaires* for
their estates, they often exercised little practical control over the land,
and with only a few exceptions their profits were modest or nonexis-
tent. Chronic underpopulation in the French colony kept land values
low – indeed, most of the land in Canada was essentially worthless in
the French period – and also limited its potential for expansion. Despite
substantial population growth during the eighteenth century, Canada
never experienced real demographic pressure on the colony's landed resources.[1] As a territorial empire, New France placed small demands on
the landscape and its native inhabitants; in practice, the colony's landed
resources simply provided a subsistence base for its trading activities – a
pattern that emerged very clearly in its settlements in the Illinois country.

Feudal pretensions failed for different reasons in the English colonies.
In the years following the restoration of the crown in 1660, the feudal
ideal was embodied in the chartering of the four great proprietary
colonies – Carolina, New York, the Jerseys, and Pennsylvania. They
were conceived essentially as feudal estates, vast beyond the wildest
imaginings of the English nobility, which were granted to leading
courtiers surrounding the crown. Their early development presents a series of fascinating studies in the breakdown of received ideas in the face
of unforeseen and entirely unfamiliar circumstances. In Pennsylvania, it
was the unanticipated success of settler recruitment, rather than its unexpected failure (as in Canada), that overwhelmed the feudal ideal governing the original grant. By 1720 European immigrants were entering
the colony in numbers far greater than William Penn or his fellow promoters had ever anticipated, and the colony's institutions were strained
to the breaking point by the effort to absorb them all.

The story of Pennsylvania is an integral part of the story of the Ohio
Valley. As we have seen, many of the Indians and traders who entered
the valley from the east were coming from Pennsylvania; later, many of
the Euroamerican settlers who wanted to take up lands there originated

[1] Richard Colebrook Harris, *The Seigneurial System in Early Canada: A Geographical
Study* (Madison, WI, 1968); Peter Moogk, "Reluctant Exiles: Emigrants from France in
Canada before 1760," *William and Mary Quarterly*, 3rd Ser., 46 (1989), 463–505;
Leslie Choquette, "Recruitment of French Emigrants to Canada, 1600–1760," in Ida
Altman and James Horn, eds., *"To Make America": European Emigration in the Early
Modern Period* (Berkeley, 1991), pp. 131–171.

in Pennsylvania as well. For Indians, traders, and settlers alike, the past prefigured the future: earlier experiences in the colony shaped their relations to one another, established their attitudes toward the land and toward property rights, and gave each powerful memories that would mold their responses to one another in the years to come.

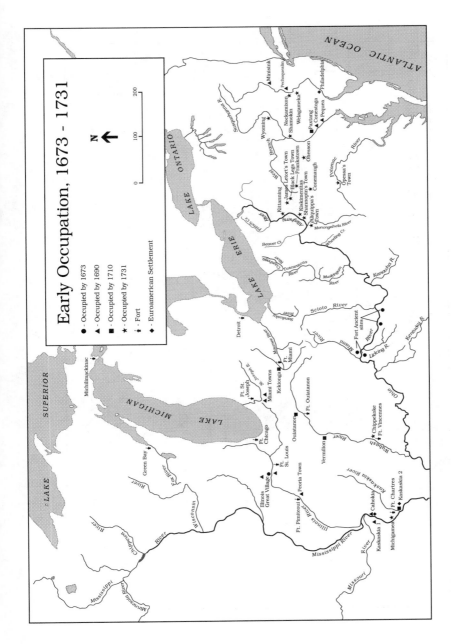

Early Occupation, 1673 - 1731

● - Occupied by 1673
▲ - Occupied by 1690
■ - Occupied by 1710
★ - Occupied by 1731
† - Fort
◆ - Euroamerican Settlement

N

0   100   200

LAKE SUPERIOR

LAKE MICHIGAN

LAKE ONTARIO

LAKE ERIE

ATLANTIC OCEAN

Michilimackinac

Green Bay

Fox River

Wisconsin River

Chippewa River

Minnesota River

Mississippi River

Missouri River

Illinois River

Ft. St. Joseph

St. Joseph R.

Miami Towns

Kekionga

Ft. Miami

Maumee R.

Detroit

Sandusky River

Ft. Chicago

St. Louis

Ouiatanon

Ft. Ouiatanon

Vermilion

Wabash River

Chippekoke
Ft. Vincennes

Kaskaskia River

Illinois
Great Village

Ft. Pimiteoui

Peoria Town

Cahokia

Michigamea

Ft. Chartres

Kaskaskia 1

Kaskaskia 2

Scioto River

Fort Ancient sites

Miami River

Licking R.

Kentucky R.

Kenawha R.

Ohio

Muskingum River

Tuscarawas River

Cuyahoga River

Wheeling Cr.

Beaver Cr.

Sandusky

Cuyahoga River

French Cr.

Allegheny River

Kittanning

James Lecort's Town

Black Legs Town

Frankstown

Kiskimentas

Shannopin's Town

Conemaugh

Alliquippa's Town

Monongahela River

Youghiogheny

West Branch

Wyoming

Nockamixon

Shamokin

Wehagameka

Paxtang

Obesson

Conemaugh

Opessa's Town

Potomac River

Susquehanna R.

Pechoquealin

Minisink

Philadelphia

Conestoga

Pequea

Map 1

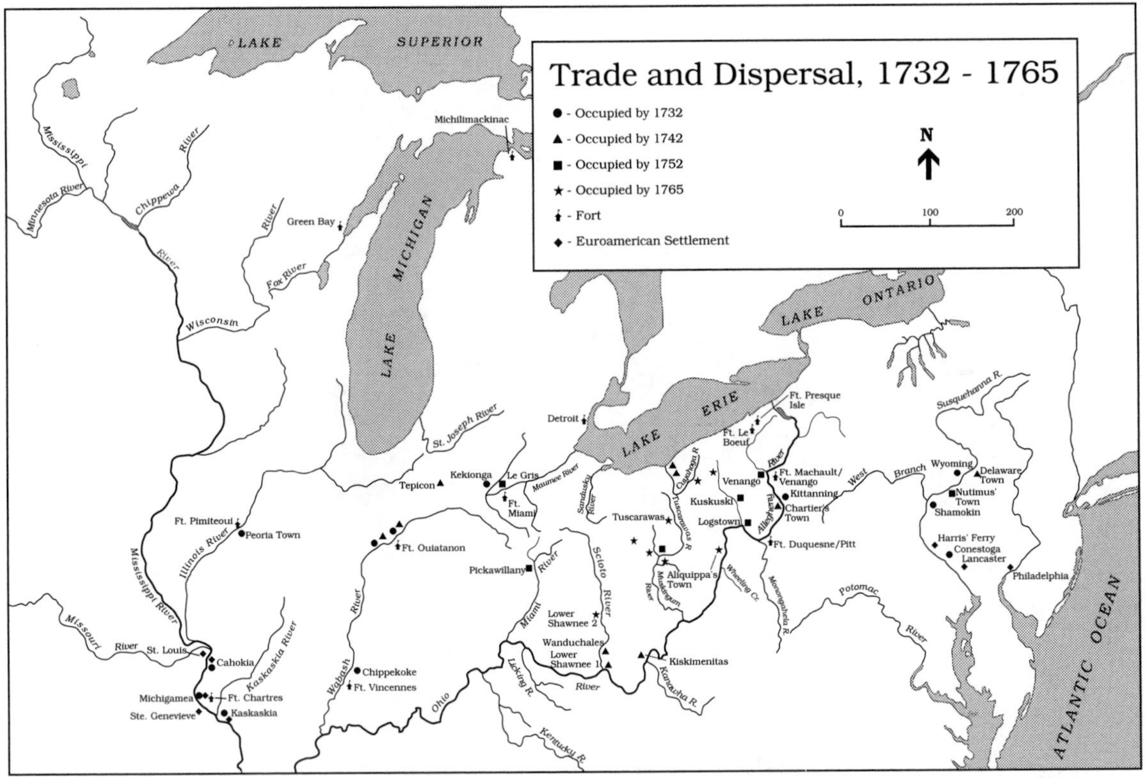

Trade and Dispersal, 1732 - 1765

- • - Occupied by 1732
- ▲ - Occupied by 1742
- ■ - Occupied by 1752
- ★ - Occupied by 1765
- ♦ - Fort
- ◆ - Euroamerican Settlement

N

0   100   200

LAKE SUPERIOR

LAKE MICHIGAN

LAKE ERIE

LAKE ONTARIO

ATLANTIC OCEAN

Michillimackinac

Green Bay

Fox River

Wisconsin River

Chippewa River

Mississippi River

Minnesota River

Missouri River

Illinois River

Ste. Genevieve

St. Louis

Michiganea

Ft. Chartres

Cahokia

Kaskaskia

Kaskaskia River

Wabash River

Ft. Vincennes

Chippekoke

Ft. Ouiatanon

Pickawellany

Tepicon

Kekionga

Ft. Miami

Peoria Town

Ft. Pimiteoui

Ft. St. Joseph River

Maumee River

Le Gris

Detroit

Sandusky R.

Kentucky R.

Licking R.

Lower Shawnee

Wanduchales Lower Shawnee

Lower Shawnee 2

Scioto River

Miami River

Ohio River

Kiskiminitas

Kanawha R.

Kiskiminitas R.

Muskegum

Aliquippa's Town

Wheeling Cr.

Tuscarawas

Tuscarawas R.

Kuskuski

Logstown

Kuskuski

Venango

Ft. Le Boeuf

Ft. Presque Isle

Ft. Machault/ Venango

Kittanning

Chartiers Town

Raystown

Ft. Duquesne/Pitt

Monongahela R.

West Branch

Susquehanna R.

Wyoming

Nutimus' Town

Shamokin

Delaware Town

Harris Ferry

Conestoga

Lancaster

Philadelphia

Potomac River

Map 2

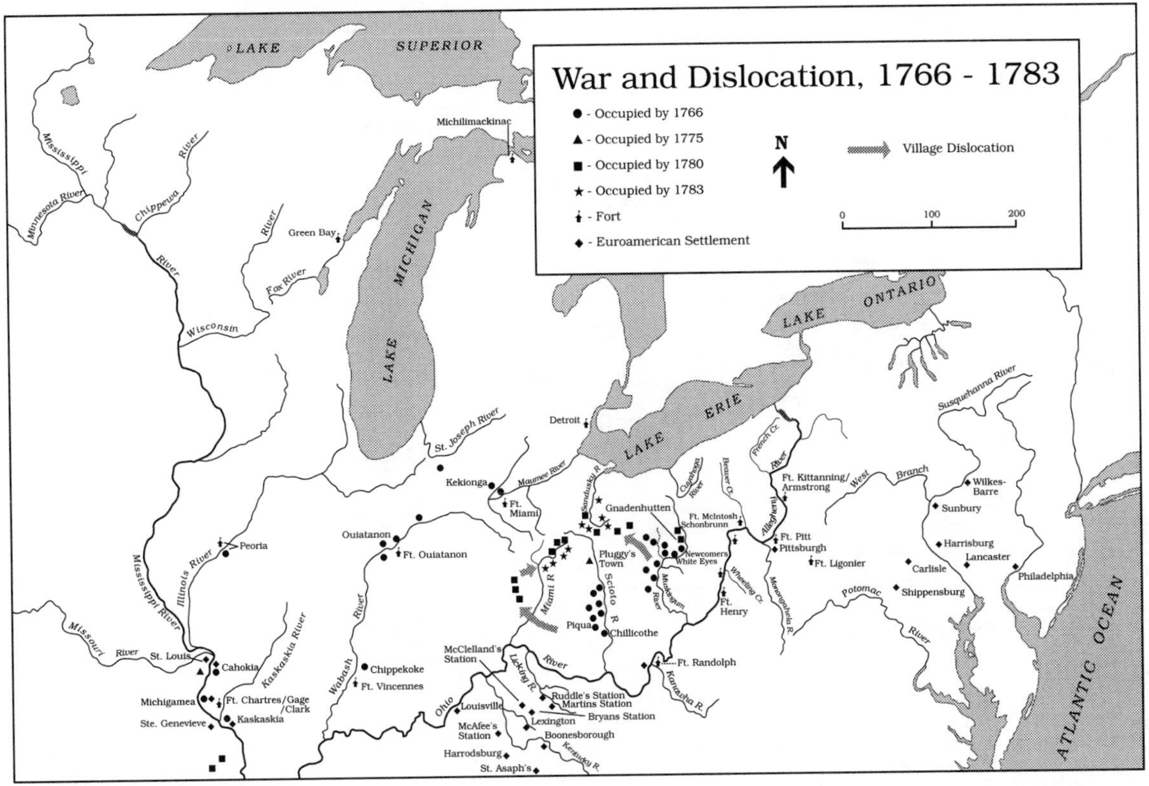

War and Dislocation, 1766 - 1783

● - Occupied by 1766
▲ - Occupied by 1775
■ - Occupied by 1780
★ - Occupied by 1783
⸸ - Fort
◆ - Euroamerican Settlement

N

⟶ Village Dislocation

0   100   200

Map 3

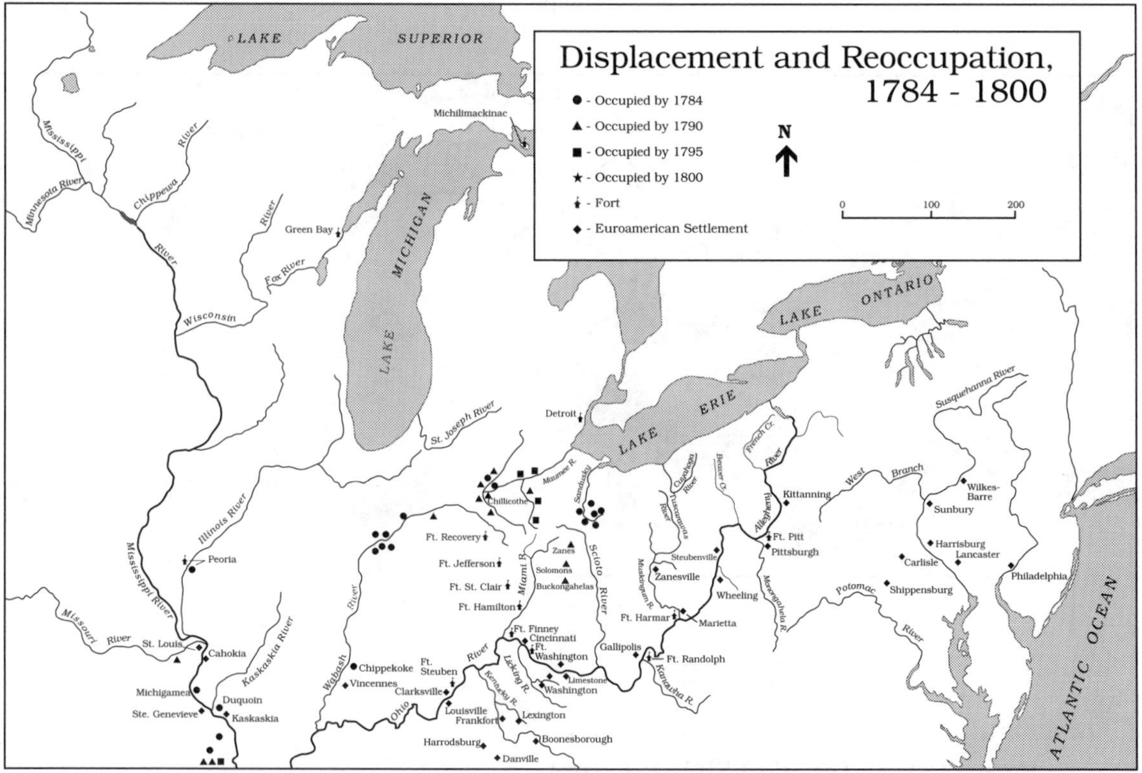
Displacement and Reoccupation, 1784 - 1800
● - Occupied by 1784
▲ - Occupied by 1790
■ - Occupied by 1795
★ - Occupied by 1800
Fort
◆ - Euroamerican Settlement
N
0
100
200
LAKE SUPERIOR
LAKE MICHIGAN
LAKE ERIE
LAKE ONTARIO
ATLANTIC OCEAN
Michilimackinac
Green Bay
Detroit
Mississippi River
Minnesota River
Chippewa River
River
Fox River
Wisconsin
Illinois River
Missouri River
St. Joseph River
Maumee R.
Sandusky
Cuyahoga River
Tuscarawas River
Beaver Cr.
French Cr.
Allegheny River
Muskingum R.
Scioto River
Miami R.
Wabash River
Ohio River
Kaskaskia River
Licking R.
Kentucky R.
Kanawha R.
Monongahela R.
West Branch
Susquehanna River
Potomac River
Peoria
St. Louis
Cahokia
Michigamea
Ste. Genevieve
Duquoin
Kaskaskia
Chillicothe
Ft. Recovery
Ft. Jefferson
Ft. St. Clair
Ft. Hamilton
Zanes
Solomons
Buckongahelas
Ft. Finney
Cincinnati
Ft. Washington
Chippekoke
Vincennes
Ft. Steuben
Clarksville
Louisville
Frankfort
Lexington
Harrodsburg
Boonesborough
Danville
Limestone
Washington
Gallipolis
Ft. Randolph
Ft. Harmar
Marietta
Zanesville
Steubenville
Wheeling
Ft. Pitt
Pittsburgh
Kittanning
Sunbury
Wilkes-Barre
Harrisburg
Lancaster
Carlisle
Shippensburg
Philadelphia

Map 4

CHAPTER THREE

Definitions of Value

IN THE waning days of 1718 Pierre Duqué, Sieur de Boisbriant, arrived in the trading village of Kaskaskia as the first French commandant of the Illinois country. He was appointed to the post after the Company of the Indies received a charter for the floundering colony of Louisiana in 1717; in the colony's reorganization, the bounds of Louisiana were redefined to include the Illinois towns.[1] Now, after a two-month voyage up the Mississippi from Mobile with a retinue of about a hundred men, Boisbriant disembarked at Kaskaskia and began to shape it to the wishes of the company and the crown. One such wish for the Illinois country was to settle *habitants* on the rich alluvial bottomland along the Mississippi River, where the towns of Kaskaskia and Cahokia already lay, so that it might serve as a breadbasket region for the lower settlements. To that end, Boisbriant's first priority upon his arrival was to lay a secure foundation for property ownership in the Illinois country; the creation of new *seigneuries*, it was hoped, would encourage the small French population already present to take up land under French auspices, and also help to attract other *habitants* from the agricultural settlements of Canada. Boisbriant began this process by expelling the Indians: The site of the existing town of Kaskaskia was to become a farming village on the French model, and a new Indian village was built about four miles away. By acceding to Boisbriant's wish that they relocate, the Kaskaskia and Michigamea Indians implicitly ceded land rights to the company

---

[1] The most reliable and comprehensive guide to the reorganization of Louisiana in this period is Marcel Giraud, *Histoire de la Louisiane française*, 5 vols. (Paris, 1953–1987); vols. 1, 2, and 5 have now appeared in English translation.

and to France – though apparently no formal agreement was ever made for the transfer of this property.[2]

Next Boisbriant devised an orderly land tenure system for the community. For each villager who would claim residence in his new town, he confirmed a title to land. In addition to these private holdings, Boisbriant also laid out a town commons and common fields. The local Jesuits were now expected to serve as parish priests as well as missionaries, and the commons became the property of the parish while the common fields were allotted to the individual residents of the town. The result, on paper at least, was a European-style *seigneurie*. The common fields were arranged in a traditional strip pattern, while the church's control of the commons emphasized its central position in the life and economy of the community. Finally, to secure imperial control over the vicinity Boisbriant dispatched a party of laborers to a site about sixteen miles north of Kaskaskia, where in the spring of 1720 they finished work on a wooden fortification that was named Fort Chartres.[3]

In Boisbriant's actions we can read the desire of French officials to create an orderly landed empire in the North American interior. In his effort to separate Frenchmen from Indian families and communities, in the seigneurial grants, in the ordering and fortification of the landscape, the wish for territorial dominion is unmistakable. But the Illinois country never fulfilled the original vision of the officers of empire. *Habitants* came to the Illinois country only in an intermittent trickle, and its villages remained small and underdeveloped; the local population did not separate neatly into French and Indian communities, but continued to trade, to marry, and to interact in ways that defy clear categories and easy description; and the region was never more than a remote backwater in the grand scheme of transatlantic colonization.

Contrast this experience with that of Pennsylvania, where from the beginning the colony's founder, William Penn, professed his desire for European immigrants to "sit downe Lovingly" among the Indians. With a series of negative examples before his eyes – especially the disastrous 17th-century Indian wars in Virginia and Massachusetts – Penn envisioned a much different, and more harmonious, pattern of Indian rela-

---

[2] Joseph Wallace, *The History of Illinois and Louisiana Under the French Rule* (Cincinnati, 1893), p. 270; Bienville to the Council [of the Marine], 20 Oct. 1719, Dunbar Rowland and Albert Sanders, eds., *Mississippi Provincial Archives, 1704–1743: French Dominion*, 3 vols. (Jackson, MS, 1927–1932) [hereafter *MPAFD*], vol. III, p. 275; Natalia Maree Belting, *Kaskaskia Under the French Regime*, Illinois Studies in the Social Sciences, vol. XXIX (Urbana, 1948), pp. 16–17.

[3] Belting, *Kaskaskia*, 18–21; Mary Borgias Palm, *The Jesuit Missions of the Illinois Country, 1673–1763* (Cleveland, 1931), pp. 49–50; Wallace, *Illinois and Louisiana*, p. 270.

tions for his own colony. Immediately after he received the charter for Pennsylvania, Penn composed a list of "Conditions or Concessions to the First Purchasers," in which five paragraphs were devoted to interactions between colonists and natives. Penn was especially concerned to protect the colony's Indians from sharp or dishonest trading practices, to guarantee them "Liberty to doe all things Relateing to the Improvem[en]t of their ground & provideing Sustenance for their Familyes, that any of the planters shall enjoy," and to ensure that disputes between colonists and Indians were adjudicated fairly. Perhaps most remarkable is his proposal that all such disputes would be resolved by a jury consisting of "Six Planters and Six Natives, that so wee may Live friendly Together."[4]

Penn also took care to cultivate peaceful relations directly with the local Indians. In the fall of 1681, as he began to organize the colonization enterprise, Penn wrote a letter to the "Kings" of the Delawares to inform them of his new grant and give them an idea of what to expect. He announced that his God and his king had given him the gift of a "great Province" in their lands, but stressed his "desire to enjoy it with your Love and Consent, that we may always live together as Neighbours and freinds." He knew all too well that Indians had often met with "unkindness and Injustice" at the hands of Europeans; but, he assured the Delawares, "I am not such a Man. . . . I desire to Winn and gain your Love & freindship by a kind, just and peaceable life; and the People I send are of the same mind, & shall in all things behave themselves accordingly." Finally, Penn proposed the same plan for resolving differences between colonists and Indians that he laid out in the First Concessions: "[I]f in any thing any shall offend you or your People, you shall have a full and Speedy Satisfaction for the same by an equall number of honest men on both sides." Nine months later he wrote a similar letter to the leaders of the Iroquois confederacy. Upon his arrival in the colony, Penn began to arrange for orderly land sales, and among the local Indians he quickly developed a reputation for honesty and generosity.[5] In all his preparations for settlement, Penn's solicitude toward the

[4] Penn's instructions to his commissioners, [30 Sept. 1681], and Conditions or concessions to the first purchasers, 11 July 1681, in Richard Dunn and Mary Maples Dunn, eds., *The Papers of William Penn*, 5 vols. (Philadelphia, 1981–1986), vol. II, pp. 118–123, 98–102; quote: p. 120.

[5] Penn to the "Kings of the Indians," 18 Oct. 1681, and to "the Emperor of Canada," 21 June 1682, *PWP*, vol. II, pp. 128–129, 261; for land sales, see the deeds in this volume, including the earliest recorded agreement between Penn and the Delawares dated 15 July 1782 (vol. II, pp. 261–269), as well as the many letters and instructions relating to land sales. The subject of Penn's land purchases, and of his reputation as a fair dealer

native population of his new colony contrasts sharply with Boisbriant's brusque dismissal of the Kaskaskias and Michigameas.

Yet by the 1720s the Delawares were largely displaced from southeastern Pennsylvania, and conflicts between settlers and Indians were becoming endemic in some areas; as we have seen, a steady westward exodus of Indians had begun; and with the infamous Walking Purchase of 1737, an enduring legacy of fraudulent dealings was introduced into the colony's Indian relations, whose implications would continue to echo through Pennsylvania's intercultural relations for the rest of the colonial period. By the time of the Seven Years' War, relations between Indians and European settlers in Penn's colony were irremediably poisoned by misunderstanding, conflict, and hatred. These developments were critically important in shaping relations in the Ohio Valley, both because so much of the valley's Indian population came from Pennsylvania and because the colony's experiences forecast, with remarkable accuracy, later developments in the Ohio Valley itself.

The great irony of these two stories is that, by the middle decades of the 18th century, Penn's vision of intercultural relations had been much more closely realized in the Illinois country, despite Boisbriant's strident efforts to impose a very different kind of order on the region; while in Pennsylvania a pattern of settlement and of Indian relations emerged that Boisbriant himself could have happily embraced. What had happened in the intervening years to reverse the intentions of Penn and Boisbriant, each in his own context a key proponent of the effort to secure a landed empire in North America? What follows is an attempt to answer that question.

I

Boisbriant's reform efforts were part of a larger push by French administrators to create a stronger territorial empire in North America. By 1713, New France had been at war with New York, New England, and their Indian allies for decades; most recently, the War of the Spanish Succession had endangered the colony's survival at several points during the first decade of the century. Under the pressure of these prolonged hostilities, the colony's rate of population growth slowed almost to a standstill and the extent of its cultivated land actually declined for a time.[6] With the Peace of Utrecht in 1713, several officers of the French

and friend to the Indians (a reputation which is as influential with modern historians as it was with his contemporaries) will be treated in more detail below, pp. 101–110.

[6] Yves F. Zoltvany, *Philippe de Rigaud de Vaudreuil: Governor of New France 1703–1725* (Toronto, 1974), p. 17.

crown advocated a new direction in imperial strategy in North America.

One of the foremost architects of this new strategy was Philippe de Rigaud de Vaudreuil, Governor of New France from 1703 until 1725 and, by 1716, a perceptive and experienced observer of events in the colony. In that year he argued that two measures would have to be taken for New France to survive. First, immigration to the colony must be encouraged. As it stood, New France could mobilize about 5,000 fighting men; by contrast, he estimated that the English colonies could place up to 60,000 men in the field. Second, according to Vaudreuil, the colony's Indian alliances should be strengthened. The empire needed to rein in *coureurs* who were acting as free agents in the continental interior, establish regular trading relations at a chain of newly created military outposts in the west, and increase the fund of diplomatic gifts available there for rewarding loyal allies. If New France could meet these requirements, Vaudreuil thought the colony could establish itself as a legitimate territorial power in North America.[7]

In France, the Council of the Marine took Vaudreuil's views seriously; at the same time, it turned its attention to Louisiana in a more sustained and focused manner than ever before. For French interests in North America to flourish, informed observers increasingly believed that it was essential to exploit the resources of this promising and still poorly understood region. The Council's new interest resulted in the chartering of the Company of the Indies in 1717, an action that placed the weight of crown authority behind the revival of Louisiana. Although the company encountered legendary financial difficulties, thousands of new migrants came to Louisiana under its auspices and collectively reinvigorated France's prospects along the southern Mississippi.[8]

The Illinois country was vital to the interests of both New France and Louisiana, and more generally to the interests of France. Positioned halfway between the two centers of the French empire in North America, administrators of New France and Louisiana fought to control it. Officials of the Company of the Indies argued that the Illinois settlements should be included in their grant because of rumored gold and silver deposits in the region, which would guarantee the company's financial success, and also because these villages could help feed the planta-

---

[7] Zoltvany, *Vaudreuil*, pp. 146–147 and following.

[8] Marcel Giraud, *A History of French Louisiana, Volume Two: Years of Transition, 1715–1717*, trans. Brian Pearce (Baton Rouge, 1993 [Fr. ed. orig. publ. 1958]), especially pp. 1–49, 115–131; Daniel H. Usner, Jr., *Indians, Settlers, and Slaves in a Frontier Exchange Economy: The Lower Mississippi Valley before 1783* (Chapel Hill, 1992), pp. 31–43; Usner, "From African Captivity to American Slavery: The Introduction of Black Laborers to Colonial Louisiana," *Louisiana History*, 20 (1979), 25–48.

tions further south, freeing them to devote more resources to growing tropical staples. To the dismay of Canadian officials, the Council of the Marine was persuaded by these arguments; in September 1718 the Illinois country (including the settlements tied to the Illinois Indians, but not those connected with the Miami confederacy) was placed under Louisiana's jurisdiction.

The jurisdictional conflicts between New France and Louisiana notwithstanding, anyone who viewed the French empire as a whole recognized the significance of the Illinois country to the imperial enterprise. If France controlled the Illinois country, it gained a strong, unified American empire; if not, it was left with two small colonies (one oppressively hot, the other unbearably cold) separated by a thousand miles of potentially hostile terrain. In addition to its strategic importance, the Illinois country was also singularly attractive as a center of settlement. Its climate was temperate in a way that neither the St. Lawrence Valley nor the lower reaches of the Mississippi were; here French immigrants could recreate, with relative ease, an agricultural society comparable to the one they left behind. The Illinois country, in short, could be viewed as the linchpin of French territorial expansion in North America.[9]

Yet within this new frame of official reference, the trading culture of the Illinois posts appeared inconsistent with imperial aims. French colonists had indeed already settled in the Illinois country, but the communities they helped to create were disorderly, and the alliances they forged were unreliable and unpredictable. Their very presence on the land was illegitimate: any claims French traders might make to land ownership had no foundation in French law. Instead the traders remained in the Illinois towns at the sufferance of their Indian hosts, and in most cases had accommodated themselves to native cultures to an alarming degree. For imperial administrators, the trading culture appeared to be shaped by a conspiracy between the natural inconstancy of the Indians and the inveterate scheming of the *coureurs de bois*.[10] If the Illinois country was to serve French interests, it required a more orderly pattern of social development and a more reliable and regulated system of Indian alliances.

---

[9] The most recent treatment of peasant society in the Illinois country, which emphasizes the favorable conditions for settlement, is in the work of Winstanley Briggs; see "The Forgotten Colony: *Le Pays des Illinois*" (Ph.D. diss., Univ. of Chicago, 1985); and "Le Pays des Illinois," *The William and Mary Quarterly*, 3rd ser. [hereafter *WMQ*], 47 (1990), 30–56.

[10] See, e.g., Louvigny to the Council, 15 Oct. 1720, in Reuben G. Thwaites, ed., *Collections of the State Historical Society of Wisconsin*, vol. XVI (Madison, 1902), pp. 389–390.

This was the context for Boisbriant's arrival in Kaskaskia in December 1718. His first task was to create new settlements, modeled on French precedents, from the straggling villages he discovered. The geography of the Illinois towns ideally suited the creation of farming communities: Kaskaskia and Cahokia both lay in the alluvial bottomland of the Mississippi River, so their soils were rich with silt and the *habitants* did not have to break the extremely tough sod of the Illinois prairie. Along this fertile strip, between five and ten miles wide on average, the residents of the early trading villages were already practicing subsistence agriculture. Cahokia stood at the northern extreme of the new French zone of settlement; Kaskaskia, about sixty miles downriver, at the southern. Along this axis the Company sought to transform the Illinois country from a remote outpost in an empire of commerce to a valuable center of settlement in an empire of lands.

Following Kaskaskia's reorganization, the surrounding countryside also began to take on the impress of a French landed empire. With Fort Chartres completed, the village of Chartres was founded outside its walls; there the Company of the Indies established its warehouse and installed a clerk and two assistants, the Jesuits created a new parish called St. Anne's, and a small core of settlers took up lands under Company auspices. In 1722 Boisbriant granted a *seigneurie* of four square leagues to the Cahokia mission, located just above the Indian town; part of the grant was farmed by the mission, the rest offered to prospective settlers. The Company sent a mining engineer, Philippe Renault, to the Illinois country to search for deposits of silver and gold. In 1723 he received a *seigneurie* one league square just north of Fort Chartres, where he founded the village of St. Philippe. Boisbriant also granted himself several thousand acres three miles east of Fort Chartres, which passed to his nephew, Jean St. Therese Langlois, in 1733. Langlois established the town of Prairie du Rocher on the site, which became, like St. Philippe, a personally held *seigneurie*. Around 1740 the community of Ste. Genevieve was founded on the west bank of the Mississippi as a satellite of Kaskaskia (Fig. 3).[11]

The region's character was gradually modified by the French settlers who began to arrive in the 1720s. Most prospective *habitants*, like the *coureurs* who were already there, came from Canada; a smaller but still

[11] Minutes of the Superior Council of Louisiana, 21 Apr. 1722, *MPAFD*, vol. II, p. 270; Wallace, *Illinois and Louisiana*, pp. 270–276; John McDermott, ed., *Old Cahokia: A Narrative and Documents Illustrating the First Century of its History* (St. Louis, 1949), p. 63; *MPAFD*, vol. II, p. 183; Carl J. Ekberg, *Colonial Ste. Genevieve: An Adventure on the Mississippi Frontier* (Gerald, MO, 1985).

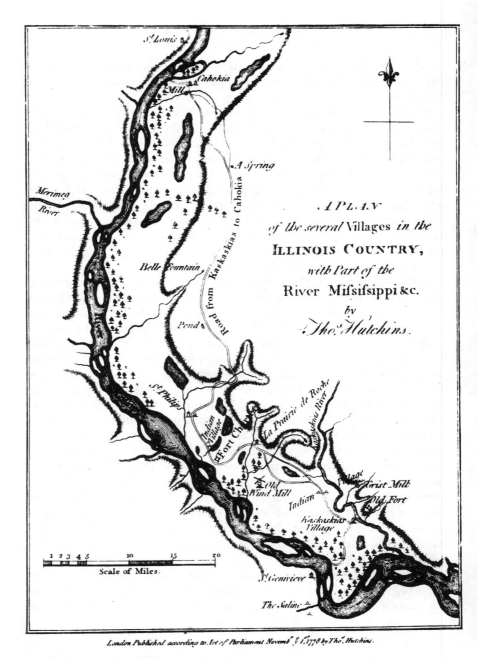

Figure 3. The French Illinois, 1765. From Thomas Hutchins, *A Topographical Description of Virginia, Pennsylvania, Maryland, and North Carolina . . .* (London, 1778). Courtesy of the John Carter Brown Library, Providence, Rhode Island.

considerable percentage came directly from France. Despite the administrative link between Illinois and Louisiana, only a scattered few settlers in Illinois originated in the lower Mississippi valley.[12] Nevertheless, Louisiana's growth affected the Illinois communities indirectly. Between 1718 and 1732, more than 7,000 colonists and another 7,000 black slaves arrived in the lower Mississippi Valley, of whom about 2,000 Europeans and 3,800 Africans remained in 1732. In addition to the settler population, a series of small military outposts was constructed between New Orleans and Fort Chartres during the first three decades of the 18th century; by 1731, more than a thousand soldiers manned these forts. All these people needed food. From the beginning, the settlers struggled to feed themselves; familiar European grain crops were especially scarce in the semi-tropical environment of the lower Mississippi. Though they gradually adapted to local food supplies, the demand for provisions, and especially flour, remained very high throughout the French period, and that demand was supplied primarily by the farming towns of the Illinois country.[13]

The agricultural output of the Illinois towns expanded steadily in response to the growing demand. In 1731, more than 220,000 pounds of flour were shipped down the Mississippi River from the Illinois country. Five years later, after a bad harvest, the Illinois farmers still managed to ship over 160,000 pounds of flour, which was reportedly less than a quarter of the region's normal output. Soon the Illinois towns could export nearly a million pounds of flour in a good year. Even in 1747, when the commandant of troops at Fort Chartres was forced to assemble the population of all the villages within the palisades at Kaskaskia at the height of King George's War, the governor of Louisiana described the Illinois harvests as "abundant," and the following June another "plentiful" supply of flour arrived in New Orleans.[14]

---

[12] Briggs estimates that in 1752 the French population of the Illinois country could be broken down by place of origin as follows: Canada, 58%; France, 38%; Switzerland, Italy, and Louisiana, 4%. "Le Pays des Illinois," 38.

[13] Usner, "From African Captivity to American Slavery," and "The Frontier Exchange Economy of the Lower Mississippi Valley in the Eighteenth Century," *WMQ*, 44 (1987), 171; Nancy M. Miller Surrey, *The Commerce of Louisiana During the French Régime, 1699–1763*, Columbia Studies in History, Economics and Public Law, vol. LXXI (New York, 1916), pp. 231–232; for the evolution of Louisiana foodways see Usner, *Indians, Settlers, and Slaves*, ch. 6.

[14] Belting, *Kaskaskia*, pp. 54–56; Vaudreuil to Maurepas, 20 Mar. 1748, in Theodore Pease and Ernestine Jenison, eds., *Illinois on the Eve of the Seven Years' War, 1747–1755*, Collections of the Illinois State Historical Library, vol. XXIX (Springfield, 1940), pp. 55, 73. The most careful examination of Illinois agriculture has been done by Briggs; see "Le Pays des Illinois," 51–52, and "The Forgotten Colony," ch. 9.

Who was responsible for this transformation of the Illinois economy? The region's social evolution can be traced in a general way through irregular censuses from the French period. Though sketchy and uneven, they help to clarify the changes that came after 1718. The first visitor to enumerate the local population was Diron D'Artaguiette, inspector of troops for Louisiana, who visited the Illinois towns in the spring of 1723. He found that Kaskaskia was the largest of the towns, with 64 *habitants* and 41 laborers, along with thirty-seven married women and 54 children. Cahokia, by contrast, remained more strictly the community of traders it had always been; only seven *habitants*, a single laborer, one married woman, and three children had settled on *seigneurie* lands, though many more Frenchmen presumably could be found in the nearby Indian town. The village of Chartres more closely resembled Kaskaskia; it included 39 *habitants*, 42 laborers, 28 wives, and seventeen children. Two companies of infantry were also stationed at the fort.[15]

Since D'Artaguiette was primarily interested in prospective militia members, he left both Indians and *coureurs* out of his census. He also passed over the slave population of the communities he visited, though the enslavement of captive Indians dated to the earliest years of the local trading towns and, with the growing influence of the Company of the Indies, African slaves were beginning to appear in the Illinois country as well.

Indeed, the institution of slavery was gaining strength in the Illinois towns in this period, as later censuses make clear. By 1732 the permanent, free population of the Illinois towns had changed very little; the number of *habitants* at Kaskaskia, in fact, had fallen: 159 Frenchmen were counted in Kaskaskia, Chartres, and Cahokia, along with 66 women and 190 children. But if the free farming population was only barely holding steady, its economic resources – in slaves, livestock, land, and capital improvements – were increasingly impressive. The combined value of landholdings for the three villages was calculated at 3,391 *livres*, and improvements included more than 100 houses, 55 barns, five stables, and 18 mills. The Illinois residents also owned 1,463 pigs, 431 cows, 407 oxen, and 202 horses. Slaveholding was by no means universal in the Illinois towns, but it was widely distributed. Of 111 households, 31 held black slaves and 50, or almost half, held Indian slaves; in all, there were 165 black slaves and 119 Indian in the three communi-

---

[15] Mémoire des Illinois, Juillet 1724, MG 1, série F³, vol. 24, partie 2, pp. 468–469, National Archives of Canada, Ottawa [orig. série F³ C¹³A8 fo. 226, Archives Nationale des Colonies, Paris].

ties.[16] The figures from the 1732 census allow us to refine our understanding of the region's agricultural output. The steady growth in wheat exports appears not to have been the result of a growing *habitant* population. Instead, between 1723 and 1732 a fixed or even slightly shrinking number of permanent landholders controlled a steadily expanding pool of labor, land, and capital.

The last complete census of the French period in the Illinois country, taken in 1752, confirms the impression that a relatively small group of substantial landholders controlled the region's agricultural resources.[17] Remarkably, the number of *habitants* in the Illinois country in 1752 had barely grown beyond that of twenty years earlier. In all six towns – Kaskaskia, Chartres, Prairie du Rocher, Ste. Genevieve, St. Philippe, and Cahokia – only 134 male heads of household and a hundred thirty-two women were counted, along with 352 children and 150 *volontaires*, or contract laborers. But the economic assets of the communities had continued to grow. The total land value in the Illinois country had approximately doubled since 1732, to 6,658 *livres*. The number of slaves grew by a comparable margin; in 1752, Illinois propertyholders owned 445 black bondsmen and 147 Indians. Livestock of every kind had multiplied as well: The Illinois farmers could claim 1,582 pigs, 1,063 cattle, 1,165 oxen, and nearly 700 horses.

A disproportionate amount of the region's wealth was concentrated in the hands of its most prominent residents. In Kaskaskia, for example, one man, Antoine Bienvenue, held over 22% of the community's land value. The census lists 33 landholders and 67 households for Kaskaskia; of these, the top 10% of the landholders controlled over 38% of the town's land value. If we consider the top 10% of the *households*, the impression of an extreme concentration of wealth is even greater: the six greatest landholders controlled over 53% of the land. A comparable pattern held in each of the Illinois towns, with the exception of Cahokia, where only the Seminarian missionaries had followed the trend toward agricultural development and established a relatively intensive farming operation. Half of Cahokia's households held no lands at all, and it was livestock-poor and had relatively few slaves.

For many of the great landholders of the Illinois towns, slaves were the key to their considerable economic success. Slave ownership was, of course, disproportionately a characteristic of the wealthiest elite. In

16 "Recensement des Illinois, 1732," MGi, série G¹, vol. 464, partie 2, 282–293, NAC [orig. A.N.C., Paris].
17 "Recensement General du Pays des Ilinoise de 1752," Loudon Papers, no. 426, Huntington Library, San Marino, CA.

Kaskaskia, Bienvenue owned 59 slaves (only four of whom were Indians), which amounted to more than 18% of the town's total. But a heavy reliance on slave labor was a matter of choice for Illinois landholders. The second-wealthiest Kaskaskia resident owned only five slaves, one black man and four Indian women. His household included four sons of military age and two daughters old enough to marry, as well as three *volontaires*. His family and the laborers who lived with them undoubtedly did most of the work throughout the year; in the spring and fall, he probably hired additional short-term laborers for planting and harvest. In Kaskaskia, Chartres, and Cahokia, the missionaries were among the largest slaveholders. The Kaskaskia Jesuits owned 37 slaves, three of whom were Indians; the missionary at Chartres held nine slaves, including four Indians; and the Cahokia mission owned ten African slaves and four Indians. Slave ownership was more widely distributed than was that of land, which suggests that slaves were not always employed in agriculture. In fact, though the evidence is very limited, it appears likely that a basic division of labor existed between Indian and African slaves. The former were probably employed as household labor, and perhaps also in operations related to the fur trade: preparing, bundling, and packing pelts, for example. The latter seem to have been used most often as field hands, though some Africans also became artisans. When the Kaskaskia mission was disbanded in 1763 the number of black slaves had risen to 68, of whom the men were reportedly "for the most part workmen, blacksmiths, carpenters, joiners, brewers, masons, etc."[18]

In general, despite the diversity of the slave population and the variety of its occupations, the institution was evolving unmistakably toward higher concentrations of Africans serving as field hands on the Illinois farms. Slaves constituted more than 43% of the enumerated population in 1752 – a percentage roughly comparable to that of the tobacco colonies of the Chesapeake in the same period. Even more strikingly, African slaves outnumbered male heads of households by more than three to one. By the 1740s Louisiana and Illinois planters competed fiercely for slave labor, and the governor of New France had concluded that the Illinois farmers were completely dependent on their slaves. "[T]here was no other means to induce the inhabitants of that country to cultivate their lands [except to provide them with slaves]," he wrote.

---

[18] Winstanley Briggs, "Slavery in French Colonial Illinois," *Chicago History*, 18 (1989–1990), 66–81; "Some Points on the Jesuit Mission in the Illinois," encl., Gen Thomas Gage to H.S. Conway, June 24, 1766, in Clarence Alvord and Clarence Carter, eds., *The New Regime, 1765–1767*, Collections of the Illinois State Historical Library, vol. XI (Springfield, 1916), pp. 326–328.

"As it was, they left the land entirely to the labor of their negroes and remained in an indolence from which nothing else could draw them." When the government outlawed the transportation of slaves to the Illinois settlements to protect the Louisiana planters, he observed that the "prohibition was a great prejudice to the welfare of the inhabitants of the Illinois who could no longer enlarge their farms." The agricultural productivity of the Illinois country, in short, was achieved on the backs of a steadily expanding population of bound labor.[19]

How did this pattern affect administrators' desire to create a landed empire along the inland arc of French occupation? That vision was not threatened by the creation of a slave-based economy *per se* – such an economy is perfectly compatible with a viable empire of lands – but it was endangered by the related fact that the Illinois country, like the rest of France's American holdings, persistently failed to attract colonists in any numbers. By 1755, 200 years after the first attempts to settle New France, the colony's population still did not exceed 62,000. The fundamental problem that Vaudreuil clearly recognized in 1716 – the need for bodies in New France – was never solved.

Why this should be the case remains a puzzle. Some commentators have stressed that New France was always subject to excessive state supervision of emigration, which prevented dissidents from settling in Canada, in contrast to the English colonies where settlement was less regulated. But this argument is misleading. For much of the 17th century settler recruitment was in the hands of a series of proprietary groups and individual *seigneurs*, who experimented with a wide variety of recruiting strategies. Only after their repeated failures did Louis XIV take control of recruitment; following his intervention matters improved somewhat, largely because Louis was more willing and able to absorb losses in the process. And to place too much emphasis on official prohibitions of Protestant or Jewish emigration gives too much credit to the formal power of such proscriptions. When such groups wanted to emigrate, Louis was willing to bend his own rules.[20]

---

[19] For the slave population of the Chesapeake, see Allan Kulikoff, *Tobacco and Slaves: The Development of Southern Cultures in the Chesapeake, 1680–1800* (Chapel Hill, 1986), p. 340; La Jonquière to Rouillè, 16 Sept. 1751, CISHL, vol. XXIX, pp. 369–380; quotes: p. 378.

[20] For the varieties of French recruitment, see Leslie Choquette, "Recruitment of French Emigrants to Canada," in Ida Altman and James Horn, eds., *"To Make America:" European Emigration in the Early Modern Period* (Berkeley, 1991), pp. 131–171, and for a more detailed survey of emigration, Choquette, "French Emigration in the Seventeenth and Eighteenth Centuries" (Ph.D. diss., Harvard Univ., 1988); for crown-ap-

Another possible explanation is cultural. Unlike the English colonies, it has been argued, which developed reputations as peasant havens, Canada remained a bad joke to the French. Despite considerable hardships at home in the 17th and 18th centuries – unemployment, distress, famine – French men and women remained surprisingly reluctant to emigrate. Nor were those who came much impressed by what they found; the most recent study of return migration concludes that at least 27,000 French people went to Canada in the colonial period, but that more than 68% of them returned.[21] This argument comes closer to a persuasive explanation, but it also begs two central questions. First, how did impoverished French laborers avoid Canada as a destination of last resort? After all, the English colonies of the 17th-century Chesapeake held no great attractions on the other side of the Atlantic; they were widely recognized in England as brutal, deadly places. Tens of thousands of English workers were nevertheless driven by the vagaries of the labor market into the transatlantic servant trade. The answer may lie in the structure of the French economy, which was perhaps large and various enough to absorb more displaced workers than the English economy could. Migration to other European countries – especially Spain – was another alternative open to poor French workers that would have been closed to their English counterparts.[22]

The second question that the cultural explanation begs, and the one that goes to the heart of the paradox of Canadian underpopulation, is why America's reputation remained so bad in France for such a long time. In the British colonies, recruitment accelerated in the 18th century once the hard work of establishing the colonies on a secure footing was completed. It was in this period that Europeans began to think of

---

proved Protestant emigrants, Peter Moogk, "Reluctant Exiles: Emigrants from France in Canada before 1760," *WMQ*, 46 (1989), 467–468.

[21] For the cultural argument, see Moogk, "Reluctant Exiles," 463–505; the return migration estimate is from Mario Boleda, "Les Migrations au Canada sous le règime français" (Ph.D. diss., Université de Montréal, 1983), cited in Moogk, 463.

[22] Olwen Hufton argues that temporary migrations of poor laborers were a central characteristic of the French economy during the 18th century, involving hundreds of thousands of workers annually by the end of the century. They included large-scale seasonal migrations into the grape-growing regions of southern France; an even larger flow of workers into Paris; and particularly by the end of the century significant migrations into the provincial cities. Temporary migrations to Spain, according to Hufton, had been one recourse of migrating French laborers since the late fifteenth century. See *The Poor of Eighteenth-Century France, 1750–1789* (Oxford, 1974), especially pp. 69–106. The French crown also experimented much more actively than the English with state-sponsored efforts to employ the urban poor; see Robert Schwartz, *Policing the Poor in Eighteenth-Century France* (Chapel Hill, 1988).

colonies like Pennsylvania as the "best poor man's country." Why was there never a comparable turnaround in French attitudes toward Canada? One answer is that Canada was too cold: given the short growing season, and the fact that the St. Lawrence River generally froze for a month or more during the winter, it did not enjoy the natural advantages that the English colonies did. But then – to return our discussion to its starting point – what kept the Illinois country from becoming a burgeoning center of French settlement in the mid-18th century? It was temperate, and the Mississippi linked it to other French colonies in the Americas and to the Atlantic world. Perhaps the weak reputation of Canada had by this time taken its toll, and could not be easily reversed; perhaps alternatives to emigration closer to home remained more attractive than the uncertainty of a trans-Atlantic move. Whatever the explanation, the Illinois farm settlements always maintained a somewhat tenuous existence. They were vitally important to the economy of Louisiana, but they never became anything other than isolated outposts on the far margins of Europe's America.

II

In Pennsylvania, by contrast, a very different dynamic drove the creation of a landed colonial establishment. As in the Illinois country, the earliest settlers in Pennsylvania (beginning perhaps half a century before Penn received his charter) focused on the Indian trade. The first effect of colonization was not to displace Indians, but to draw them toward European settlements and strengthen the groups that enjoyed close ties to European goods – again, paralleling the experience in the Illinois country.[23] But the landed development of Pennsylvania dramatically altered this early pattern and carried the colony in an entirely different direction from that of the Illinois country. The growth of European settlement transformed the colony's population, landscape, and Indian relations. This was less an intentional effect of colonization than an unanticipated and uncontrollable consequence of the fact that Pennsylvania succeeded where the Illinois country failed: in attracting large numbers of Europeans to the shores of North America.

In the colony's early years that outcome remained in doubt. William

---

23 For an introduction to the early Indian trade and its effects, see Albright Zimmerman, "European Trade Relations in the 17th and 18th Centuries," in Herbert Kraft, ed., *A Delaware Indian Symposium*, The Pennsylvania Historical and Museum Commission Anthropological Series, no. 4 (Harrisburg, 1974), and Francis Jennings, "The Indian Trade of the Susquehanna Valley," *Proceedings of the American Philosophical Society*, 110 (1966), 406–407 and following.

Penn is most familiar to historians for his "Holy Experiment," a principled attempt to settle diverse populations of persecuted peoples in a single colony whose founding principle would be mutual toleration.[24]
Though Penn was mostly concerned to create a haven for Quakers and
other radical Protestants, he hoped the spirit of toleration would extend
to the colony's Indians as well – he expected the colonists to "sit downe
Lovingly" among the Indians. Historians have generally taken Penn's
concern for the Indians at face value, without questioning its compati-
bility with a great colonization enterprise. Yet to understand Penn in all
his complexity, he must be seen not only as a benevolent Quaker, but
also as a visionary promoter of development. Penn was, after all, a great
landholder with floundering Irish estates and large family debts. After
he received the charter to his vast new proprietary estate, his first priority was to populate its lands so he could extract revenues from them.
From the beginning, this practical need abraded uncomfortably with his
benign intentions toward the Indians.[25]

Penn's imperial vision initially focused on two regions: the lower
Delaware Valley, in the southeastern corner of the colony, where European settlement had already begun and where the town of Philadelphia
would soon be founded; and the Susquehanna Valley, which connected

---

[24] See, for example, Sally Schwartz, *A Mixed Multitude: The Struggle for Toleration in
Colonial Pennsylvania* (New York, 1987).

[25] The myth of a benevolent Penn has been astonishingly durable. It originated among his
fellow Quaker leaders in Pennsylvania during the colonial era, received classic iconic
treatment in the paintings of Edward Hicks, and has been passed almost intact to contemporary historians, who tend to view him as a benign and exemplary manager of Indian affairs, while the practices of his successors, and especially his sons, are regarded
as reproachable perversions of Penn's ideals. Very little attention has been drawn to the
inherent potential for conflict between the place of Indians in his "Holy Experiment"
and the fundamental assumptions of his colonization enterprise. See, e.g., Frederick
Tolles, "Nonviolent Contact: Quakers and the Indians," *Proceedings of the American
Philosophical Society*, 107 (1963), 93–101; J. William Frost, "William Penn's Experiment in the Wilderness: Promise and Legend," *Pennsylvania Magazine of History and
Biography* [hereafter *PMHB*], 107 (1983), 577–605; and, for a creative approach to
the story that raises the myth of a benevolent Penn to its apotheosis, Daniel Hoffman,
Brotherly Love (New York, 1981). Even the normally irascible Francis Jennings has
consistently chosen to treat Penn favorably; see *The Ambiguous Iroquois Empire: The
Covenant Chain Confederation of Indian Tribes from its Beginnings to the Lancaster
Treaty of 1744* (New York, 1984), especially pp. 223–248, and "Brother Miquon:
Good Lord!" in Richard S. Dunn and Mary Maples Dunn, eds., *The World of William
Penn* (Philadelphia, 1986), pp. 195–214. For a more critical assessment of Penn, see
Thomas Sugrue, "The Peopling and Depeopling of Early Pennsylvania: Indians and
Colonists, 1680–1720," *PMHB*, 116 (1992), 3–31. For Penn's Irish estates and finan-
cial affairs, see Richard S. Dunn, "Penny Wise and Pound Foolish: Penn as a Business-
man," in Dunn and Dunn, eds., *World of William Penn*, pp. 37–54.

the Iroquois hunting grounds and the rich interior lands of his colony with the navigable waters of the Chesapeake Bay. In both areas he immediately began to pursue land purchases from the local Indians in order to secure unambiguous ownership of large, contiguous tracts for European occupation. On the lower Delaware Penn was reasonably successful.[26] But on the Susquehanna the Indian population was unsettled, and such purchases were much more difficult.

As recently as two decades before Penn's charter was granted, the Susquehannocks controlled the lower Susquehanna, and Penn might have been able to buy an unambiguous title to part of the region from them. But the Susquehannocks were driven out in the 1670s and the valley was not resettled until the early 1690s. As refugee populations moved back into the valley – the combined Seneca/Susquehannock group known as the Conestogas; the Shawnees; groups of Delawares moving out of the Delaware Valley; other Iroquois-sponsored refugee groups migrating north from Virginia and the Carolinas – their precise relationship to the land, and in some cases to one another, remained uncertain.[27]

During these same years Penn was trying to acquire a secure title to Susquehanna lands. Confusion and ambiguity clouded the question of ownership, but in a complex and cunningly expedient three-step process, Penn gained the upper hand in all subsequent land deals in the region. First, he purchased a title to the land from Thomas Dongan, former governor of New York, to whom the Iroquois had granted their claim to the valley in 1683. The Iroquois' "title" arose from their supposed conquest of the Susquehannocks; they transferred it to Dongan while they were negotiating for English protection in their war with the French. The highly irregular character of such a transfer of ownership to a crown official, instead of to the crown itself, was compounded by the fact that no document survived that Dongan could sign over to Penn; instead a new deed to the land was drawn up by Dongan in 1697. Once Penn obtained the title, he took the second step: to gain its confirmation from the residents of the valley. He found two old men among the Conestogas, Widaagh and Andaggyjunkquah – presumably Susquehannocks with long-standing ties to the valley – who were willing to accept his claim, but it is unclear upon what authority they acted. The surviving record of the meeting blurs this question. It first grants all the Susque-

---

[26] See, e.g., the deed from the Delawares dated July 15, 1682, *PWP*, vol. II, pp. 261–269. Much of this region had already been settled under the auspices of New Sweden and New Netherlands, which required Penn only to extinguish the right of New York to these lands by conquest of the Dutch; see *PWP*, vol. II, pp. 305–308.

[27] For these relocations, see chapter one, pp. 18–20, 25–26.

hanna lands "which are or formerly were the Right of the . . . Susquehanna Indians" on the men's personal authority, and then proceeds to
"ratifie and confirm . . . ye bargain and Sale of the said Lands" by Dongan to Penn.[28]

Though this document seems to perpetuate, rather than clarify, the
questionable nature of the Dongan deed, it did give Penn the legal form
of a title to the Susquehanna lands. With that in hand he was prepared
to take the third step in laying a foundation for his claims. In April,
1701, Penn invited representatives of the Conestoga and Shawnee Indians to Philadelphia to sign a treaty that can only be described as mutually beneficial, since it shored up dubious claims to the Susquehanna lands
on every side. The treaty stipulated that the current inhabitants of the
Susquehanna Valley would be granted "full & free priviledges & Immu-
nities of all ye Said Lands, as or any other Inhabit[an]t they duely owin-
ng & Acknowledg[in]g ye Authority of the Crown of England and Government of this Province."[29] Penn's claim to own the valley was confirmed, even as it was compromised, by this remarkable passage that
granted the Shawnees and Conestogas Englishmen's rights to the lands
they occupied. At the same time, the Shawnees and Conestogas were assured that they could stay on land – a valuable assurance, considering
how recently they had settled their new communities.

For the Conestogas, in particular, this agreement completed a
strangely circular process. The Susquehannocks lost control of the val-

---

[28] Penn's quest for a title to the Susquehanna actually began in 1683, when he purchased
two tracts in the lower valley from local Delaware headmen whose claims were vague
and somewhat dubious. As it turned out, nearly all of this land lay within Maryland's
boundaries; see Penn's declaration, 18 Oct. 1683, and map, *PWP*, vol. II, pp. 491–492.
In the same year Penn began to seek an agreement with the Iroquois, who could claim
the valley by right of conquest; see Penn to James Graham and William Haige, 2 Aug.
1683, and editorial comments, *PWP*, vol. II, pp. 422–424, and Haige to Penn, 29 Aug.
1683, *PWP*, vol. II, pp. 466–471. He was thwarted by the maneuvering of Dongan,
who won title to the valley for himself and then sold it to Penn for £100 in 1696; the
convoluted history of these transactions is recounted in detail in Gary Nash, "The
Quest for the Susquehanna Valley: New York, Pennsylvania, and the Seventeenth-Century Fur Trade," *New York History*, 48 (1967), 3–27. The confirmation deed between
Penn and Widaagh and Andaggyjunkquah is printed in Samuel Hazard, ed., *Pennsylvania Archives* [1st Ser.], 12 vol. (Philadelphia, 1828–1835), vol. I, pp. 133–134. Years
later, James Logan acknowledged the weakness of the Dongan title in a letter to the
proprietors, and the subsequent history of land purchases in the valley bear out his
skepticism. Logan to Penn's sons, 16 Nov. 1729, Logan Papers, vol. III, Historical Society of Pennsylvania; Paul A. W. Wallace, *Indians in Pennsylvania*, rev. ed., Pennsylvania Historical and Museum Commission Anthropological Series, no. 5 (Harrisburg,
1989), p. 131.

[29] Texts of the treaty appear in *Pa. Arch.* [1st Ser.], vol. I, pp. 144–147, and in *Minutes of*

ley to the Iroquois, who claimed it by right of conquest even though they never attempted to occupy it; the Iroquois sold the entire region to the then-governor of New York in an expedient but highly irregular way; he, in turn, sold it to Penn in another questionable bargain; finally, Penn, meeting with the refugee descendants of the Susquehannocks who now lived on Conestoga Creek, re-granted them the lands they lived on by the authority of the British crown. Though it met Penn's immediate needs, the agreement only deepened confusion over legitimate claims to Susquehanna lands.

In all, Penn's quest for a workable title to the Susquehanna Valley took nearly two decades to complete. In the meantime he pressed ahead with sales and development. He first advertised the opportunity to purchase shares in the region in 1690, and in 1696 he started assembling a group of subscribers to develop it. Five years later the project was finalized. The subscribers were granted control of a tract of about 100,000 acres along the east bank of the Susquehanna running north from Conestoga Creek, where they were expected to lay out a "chief town," erect a county, and subdivide the land into townships as the need arose.[30]

Development along the Susquehanna proceeded "not so briskly" following the initial subscriptions. Its sluggish progress urgently concerned Penn and James Logan, his agent in the colony, but until about 1710 very few Europeans who were not Indian traders ventured that far west. After 1710, groups of European settlers finally began to arrive and take up lands along the Pequea, Conestoga, and Swatara Creeks, in areas near Indian communities but not yet directly competing with them for land. For a time, Logan was able to arrange for surveys that ran far ahead of settlement, so that by 1714 more than 58,000 acres had been laid off, although only a small number of settlers had actually moved into the area. When settlement began to encroach on the Conestoga village and its fields, Penn instructed Logan to survey an Indian preserve (which was known as Conestoga Manor) and to fence the Indians' crops to minimize the potential for conflict.[31]

the *Provincial Council of Pennsylvania*, 16 vols. (Harrisburg, 1838–1853) [hereafter Pa. Col. Recs.], vol. II, pp. 15–18.

30 William Penn, *Some Proposals for a Second Settlement in the Province in Pennsylvania* [orig. pub. London, 1690], in Samuel Hazard, ed., *The Register of Pennsylvania*, 16 vol. (Philadelphia, 1828–1835), vol. I, p. 400; the 1701 concession is printed in F.R. Diffenderffer, "Early Local History as Revealed by an Old Document," *Papers of the Lancaster County Historical Society*, 2 (1897), 5–10.

31 The urgent need for further land sales is apparent throughout the correspondence between Penn and Logan during these years; see, e.g., Logan to Penn, 7 May 1702, Logan Papers, vol. I, HSP; quote: Logan to Penn, 2 Jan. 1702, Logan Papers, vol. I, HSP; H.M.J. Klein, ed., *Lancaster County Pennsylvania: A History*, 4 vols. (New York, 1924), vol. I, p. 16.

By 1719 the lands on Conestoga and Pequea Creeks were said to be fully surveyed. Logan had nowhere else to go without further instructions from Penn himself, who had sole authority to make land purchases from the Indians, or from Penn's Commissioners of Property, who were required to authorize further surveys and sales. That permission was not forthcoming, however. William Penn died in 1718, an event that vastly complicated land arrangements in the Susquehanna Valley. Penn's heirs wrangled among themselves for control of his estate for more than a decade following his death, creating a hiatus in proprietary authority that lasted until 1732.[32] In the meantime Logan was powerless to purchase land from the Indians, or to arrange for futher surveys and sales.

At precisely the moment when proprietary authority lapsed, the tide of incoming migrants suddenly rose to flood stage as large numbers of German refugees and displaced Scottish tenants began to arrive. The first Germans came to Pennsylvania by an indirect route, but word of their favorable circumstances soon redirected the immigration patterns of many of their countrymen who would follow. They were driven out of the Palatinate by a devastating combination of warfare, disease, famine, and despotic rule, and began to flee by the tens of thousands early in the 18th century. Most stayed on the continent, but some traveled to England. There they were received sympathetically by Queen Anne, but the huge influx of destitute immigrants into London (an estimated 13,500 arrived in 1709, 11,000 within a three-month period) demanded a bold resettlement plan. Anne and her councillors decided upon three destinations for the German refugees: Ireland, North Carolina, and New York. Nearly 3,000 were shipped to New York City – where the local population of fewer than 6,000 must have shuddered to see them arrive – and then taken north to the Hudson River estate of Robert Livingston, where they were to be employed making naval stores.[33]

The experiment in naval stores quickly failed – no one on the estate

---

[32] Klein, ed., *Lancaster County Pennsylvania*, vol. I, p. 16; the dispute among Penn's heirs over his estate and the proprietary hiatus in Pennsylvania is treated concisely in William R. Shepherd, *History of Proprietary Government in Pennsylvania* (New York, 1896), pp. 198–204.

[33] W.A. Knittle, *Early Eighteenth Century Palatine Immigration* (Philadelphia, 1937), pp. 1–12, 65–66, 82–110, 147–148, 155–156. Knittle is the classic and still indispensable account of the early Palatine migration; for a more general account of German migration in the colonial period see Marianne Wokeck, "Harnessing the Lure of the 'Best Poor Man's Country': The Dynamics of German-Speaking Immigration to British North America, 1683–1783," in Altman and Horn, eds., *"To Make America"*, pp. 204–243.

knew anything about making pitch – and the Palatines left *en masse* in 1712 for the Schoharie River, where they settled a string of farming villages with the permission of the Mohawks. When New York refused to recognize the legitimacy of their Schoharie claims, some of these farmers moved south, to the western fringes of settlement in Pennsylvania. Others followed, and they were soon joined by newcomers from Europe who began to migrate directly to Philadelphia in response to the positive reports they were hearing in the seaports of Europe.[34]

The other immigrant group arriving in Pennsylvania in large numbers was the Scots-Irish, mostly Ulstermen driven from their homes in Ireland by bad harvests and exorbitant rent increases. The majority of the migrants were originally Scottish Presbyterians who leased lands in Ireland from English landlords. They generally moved to Ireland following periods of English conquest and expansion on the island, especially in the 1650s and again in the 1690s, and usually signed 20-year leases on rented farms. As the leases came due in the second and third decades of the 18th century, high demand for Irish land drove up their rents and triggered waves of dislocation among the tenants; bad harvests between 1725 and 1727 added to the distress. From 1717 until 1728 the displacement of Scots-Irish was especially acute, and levels of migration to the American colonies, in particular Pennsylvania, were very high.[35]

Thus population growth in the lower Susquehanna Valley took off just as proprietary affairs ground to a halt. The earliest surviving tax lists from the Conestoga region illustrate this process, though they probably underestimate the magnitude of settlement (Fig. 4). In 1718, when the entire Susquehanna Valley was treated as a single township and most of its European residents were clustered on the upper Pequea and Conestoga Creeks, its population was perhaps 725 residents. The numbers increase steadily for each of the years recorded until 1726, the last year for which early records are extant. In 1720, the growing numbers on Conestoga Creek led the assessors to separate its records from those for Pequea, whose population remained much smaller. Conestoga became the center of German settlement in the region, and included nearly 1,000 recorded residents in 1720, when only about 132 people were assessed on Pequea. Two years later the assessors created yet another regional subdivision when they identified Donegal as an independent set-

---

[34] Knittle, *Palatine Immigration*, pp. 193–210.

[35] The classic, and still useful, general account of this relocation is James G. Leyburn, *The Scotch-Irish: A Social History* (Chapel Hill, 1962); see also especially Maldwyn A. Jones, "The Scotch-Irish in British America," in Bernard Bailyn and Philip Morgan, eds., *Strangers Within the Realm: Cultural Margins of the First British Empire* (Chapel Hill, 1991), pp. 284–313.

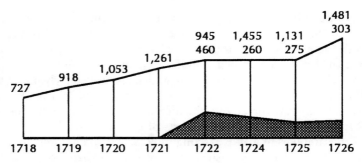

Figure 4. Population growth in the Susquehanna Valley, 1718–1728. Source: H. Frank Eschleman, "Assessment Lists and Other Manuscript Documents of Lancaster County Prior to 1729," *Papers of the Lancaster County Historical Society*, 20 (1916), 162–194. No data was available for 1723.

tlement. Located on a level plain along the Susquehanna about halfway between the Indian towns of Conestoga and Paxtang, Donegal became the primary destination for the rapidly increasing Scots-Irish migration to western Pennsylvania. In 1722 it had already attracted nearly 500 residents, about half as many as were settled on the Conestoga. The Conestoga population continued to grow to nearly 1,300 residents in 1726, while Donegal's taxpayers actually declined in number after their first year in the records.[36]

The decline in Donegal's taxpayers after 1722 probably reflects resistance to tax collection rather than a falling population, and this may only be the most visible instance of a more general pattern. The first Germans on the Conestoga arrived when they could still purchase lands from the proprietor, and others were able to buy land on Conestoga Creek from speculators who had engrossed large tracts there. But legal

---

[36] The tax lists are transcribed in H. Frank Eshelman, "Assessment Lists and Other Manuscript Documents of Lancaster County Prior to 1729," *Papers of the Lancaster County Historical Society*, 20 (1916), 162–194. To estimate population, I have calculated five residents for every taxpayer whose property is assessed, while counting freemen and those assessed at a head rate as single residents. Non-resident taxpayers are more difficult to convert into population estimates, since some may have rented to a number of families while others may have held most or all of their land as a speculative investment, in which case it would have remained in an unimproved state. Based on the fact that the 1720 assessment shows non-residents paying an average of 64 shillings while residents paid 30, I have concluded that non-residents, on average, held twice as much improved land as residents, and therefore supported twice as many settlers – or ten residents for each non-resident owner.

possession of the Donegal lands was difficult or impossible to obtain, so the late-arriving Scots-Irish were forced to occupy them illegally and hope that a fair acknowledgment of their *de facto* possession would one day win them title to the lands they had improved. In the meantime, as squatters they evaded tax assessments on property they could not claim to own.

As Penn's personal agent and land commissioner, James Logan was initially at the forefront of efforts to organize the settlement of this region. When the Scots-Irish began to arrive, he greeted them enthusiastically and shepherded them to the westernmost periphery of the colony. There, he reasoned, their experiences "bravely defend[ing] Londonderry and Inniskillen" would fit them for settlement in a spot where they could act "as a frontier, in case of any disturbance" along the Susquehanna. Thinking partly of the safety of the colony and partly of his own speculative interest in the lands along the Susquehanna, he directed a party of them to Donegal in 1718.[37] But with Penn's death that same year, Logan's plans for the development of Donegal Township were suddenly stalled, and both he and its new settlers were forced to await the outcome of events across the Atlantic.

Logan's enthusiasm for the newly arriving immigrants waned as their numbers rose, while he remained unable to perform his office of Commissioner of Property. By 1727, he was heartily tired of the large numbers of Germans, "many of them . . . a surly people, divers Papists amongst them and ye men generally well-arm'd," pressing in upon the colony.[38] He began lobbying for a bill in Parliament that would close off German immigration to the colonies, and at the same time urged the colonial assembly to prohibit their entry into Pennsylvania. Nor was Logan's distaste reserved for the incoming Germans; he saw the Scots-Irish immigrants, too (despite his own Scottish heritage), with an increasingly jaundiced eye. In a letter to a Scottish correspondent, he suggested that the experience of the Scots in Ulster must have perverted their character. Perhaps it was the "diffidence" with which they were forced to regard the native Irish that had "gradually introduced the same spirit universally & destroyed [their] opinion of each others honesty & honour," so

---

[37] Logan to James Steel, 18 Nov. 1729, quoted in Charles Hanna, *The Wilderness Trail*, 2 vols. (New York, 1911), vol. I, p. 162; James T. Lemon, *The Best Poor Man's Country: A Geographical Study of Early Southeastern Pennsylvania* (New York, 1976), p. 59.

[38] Quoted in Evelyn A. Benson, "James Logan as the First Political Boss of Lancaster County When it Was the Wild Frontier," *Papers of the Lancaster County Historical Society*, 59 (1955), 63; this essay provides an excellent account of Logan's efforts to deal with the problem of immigration during the proprietary hiatus, and my account owes much to its author's interpretation.

that they had become "tricking and contentious."[39] His carefully considered theory of Scots-Irish degradation masked a weary frustration with the endless succession of new arrivals who came to Pennsylvania to take up lands. "My life is at present intolerable," he confided to a correspondent in 1727. "I am obliged to sitt all day . . . to receive the continual senseless & fruitless applications of People for Lands." He could only reply "that they may proceed to such measures as they please."[40] With this small encouragement, boatloads of Germans and Scots-Irish traveled to the Pennsylvania frontier and settled, often without title, among their countrymen.

In 1729, James Logan sought to impress upon Penn's heirs the importance of making arrangements for the "Settlem[en]t of those vast numbers of poor but presumptuous People, who w[i]thout any License have entred on your Lands, & neither have, nor are like to have anything to purchase w[i]th." "[T]he Palatines," he warned, "crowd in upon us and the Irish yet faster, of which no less than Six Ships are arrived at Newcastle & this place [Philadelphia] within these ten days and many more are daily expected." In a separate letter to John Penn, Logan's preferred candidate to assume the role of proprietor, he emphasized that "[a]s the numbers of these people encrease upon us So will the difficulties of Settling them." Logan pleaded with Penn to come to his colony personally to settle the land disputes.[41]

Another three years passed before John Penn finally traveled to the colony to restore proprietary authority and undertake additional land purchases. By this time, certain fundamental patterns in Pennsylvania history – patterns that would shape experiences in the Ohio Valley as well – had been set: the tendency for the colonist population to grow in unforeseeably, almost incomprehensibly large surges; the corresponding difficulty government agents faced in trying to arrange for their settlement, and especially in making timely purchases of land; and the resulting tendency for discontents to develop among both Indians and colonists, with the potential for violence when provocations arose.

III

The very different trajectories of development in the Illinois country and Pennsylvania produced different calculations of value in colonization;

---

[39] Logan to James Kirkpatrick, 2 Aug. 1729, Logan Papers, vol. IV, p. 223, American Philosophical Society, Philadelphia.

[40] Quoted in Benson, "James Logan," 65.

[41] Logan to Penns, 16 Nov. 1729, Logan Letter Book, Logan Papers, vol. III, HSP; Logan to Penn, 11 Sept. 1728, Logan Papers, vol. I, HSP. Because Germans coming to Penn-

those differences, in turn, were reflected in the dynamics of intercultural relations by midcentury. In the Illinois country, value never inhered in the land because population pressures never made it a desired commodity. For those who could command the necessary capital resources and master the production routines of its fertile soils, it was possible to live very well in a kind of self-contained peasant utopia; but they were big fish in a small pond, producing food for local consumption and a limited regional market. The most valuable transatlantic commodities in the Illinois country still came from the Indian trade, and the majority of the region's always small colonist population remained fundamentally connected to the local Indians for its economic well-being. For political reasons as well as economic ones, these tenuous little communities, isolated as they were, remained dependent on the Indians. Their survival required that they maintain strong ties with their allies, shower the pro-French leaders among them with gifts, and support their warriors in battle against enemy Indian populations.

In contrast to the experience of English colonies in America, the arrival of farmer-colonists in the Illinois country failed to displace the region's trading culture. In some ways, in fact, the growth of farming strengthened the position of traders. Many successful planters in the Illinois settlements began to capitalize trading ventures, which gave the *coureurs de bois* who dealt with them reliable trading connections close at hand. Farming also gave *coureurs* temporary employment opportunities they would not otherwise have had: as agricultural laborers, as boatmen ferrying supplies to and from New Orleans, as hunters or guides, or as artisans. In economic terms, the presence of traders opened opportunities for successful farmers looking for ways to diversify their investments, while the high demand for farm labor offered traders well-paid short-term employment.

The social and cultural changes accompanying the growth of settled farm communities are harder to gauge. Certainly the opportunity to take up farming held little appeal to most *coureurs*; they remained as peripatetic as ever, and extended the range of their trading activities as farmers began to act as middlemen in the trade. Census-takers were consistently unable to account accurately for this essential dimension of local life, creating a sense of frustration that is often palpable in the records. The 1732 census includes the marginal note that there were "always a number of *voyageurs* coming and going who number about

sylvania had to be naturalized, their arrivals are noted in the Council Minutes. See, e.g., the lists, totaling about 400, of those who came in the summer of 1728: *Pa. Col. Recs.*, vol. III, pp. 327–332.

fifty men." Other evidence suggests that this was a very modest estimate of the region's floating population. Another description of the Illinois country, written in the same year, estimated that Kaskaskia alone had twice that number of seasonal residents; when the *coureurs* returned from their "winter trips in the high country," its author estimated that the number of men capable of bearing arms would jump from about 100 to about 200. Even prospective landholders in the Illinois country could be hard to pin down, as the Seminarians at Cahokia discovered. When they sent a description of their newly designed *seigneurie* to their superiors in 1735, they had to apologize for the document's appearance. "You will find, gentlemen," they wrote in explanation, "several erasures in this common letter which we wrote more than a month ago. These erasures come in part from changes in *habitants* who take land today and leave it tomorrow."[42]

As time passed, the problem of accounting for the full population of the Illinois country only became more acute. In 1752, the official census numbered the French *habitants* and their families at 768, but a memoir on the French settlements in Louisiana written in the same year estimated that the total population of the Illinois towns was 6,000. When British soldiers occupied the region following the Seven Years' War, Thomas Stirling was assigned the task of counting the local population. He echoed the exasperation of his predecessors when he wrote that he "had not been able to get an Exact Account of the Number of the Inhabitants, as there is always many of them at N Orleans, trading with the Indians, or Hunting, which they go to as regularly as the Savages."[43] Though French farmers had arrived in the Illinois country, they never displaced the local Indians, the *coureurs de bois* who depended upon them for their livelihoods, or the trading culture they had created together.

Which is not to say that no one tried. From the arrival of Boisbriant and his fellow officers and company employees, local officials sought to institute policies that would more clearly discriminate between Frenchmen and Indians. The distinction was illusory from the start, since a *métis* population was already growing in the Illinois country; and although French women began to arrive in the region in small numbers after 1718, Indian women continued to marry and bear the children of

---

42 "Recensement des Illinois, 1732," 293; [Anon.], "Memoire concernant les Ilinois," 1732, MG 1, série f³, vol. 24, partie 3, NAC [orig. Collection Moreau de Saint-Méry, ANC]; "Explanation of the Plan and Settlement of the Seignory of the Mission to the Tamaroa, 12 April 1735," in McDermott, *Old Cahokia*, p. 22.

43 Belting, *Kaskaskia*, p. 39; Stirling to Gage, 15 Dec. 1765, CISHL, vol. XI, pp. 124–127.

French men – of *habitants*, especially of the first generation, as well as *coureurs*. Nevertheless, colonial officials assumed, first, that there were two distinct populations, and second, that it was possible and desirable to maintain that distinction intact. One context for their efforts was in property law. With the creation of a formal system of landholding and property ownership, legitimized and regulated by French law, inheritance became an important issue for the first time during the 1720s. Given the relative scarcity of women in the Illinois country, local customs quickly developed that granted widows an unusual degree of control over local resources. The Superior Council of Louisiana alertly recognized that this could present a grave threat: if they did not act, Indian widows, their *métis* children, and even relatives with no legal ties to the community might soon hold a considerable share of the nominally French property in the Illinois country. Accordingly, in 1728 the Council decreed that widowed Indian women could not control the inheritance of their own estates (unlike their French counterparts), and that the property of Indian women who died without issue could not be passed to their families, but would instead revert to the Mississippi Company.[44]

Property was only the most manageable dimension of a much more general and baffling problem, however. At stake was not only the territorial coherence of the French empire in the Illinois country, but the coherence of its cultural identity as well. The disorder of the trading culture resided not just in its careless disregard for property rights, but also in its wholesale capitulation to native cultural forms. Nothing symbolized and accelerated this capitulation so clearly as marriage between French men and Indian women. Such unions blurred the lines that distinguished a civilized people from a savage one, creating instead a hybrid society that, some feared, had the virtues of neither of the original populations. In 1732 an anonymous commenator complained that the Illinois *coureurs* were extending their "libertinage" to the Illinois and Missouri Indians and threatening to ruin French policy in the west. Many French traders, he noted unhappily, had the "feebleness and laxity to marry Illinois women" – the cause, he thought, of many social evils in the Illinois towns. He called for the local missionaries to forbid such marriages in the future, in order to "thin out the mixed blood of half-

---

44 On women's autonomy and power in Illinois property law, see Winstanley Briggs, "The Enhanced Economic Position of Women in French Colonial Illinois," in Clarence Glasrud, ed., *L'Héritage Tranquille: The Quiet Heritage* (Moorhead, MN, 1987), pp. 62–69 (this essay is a distilled version of Briggs, "Forgotten Colony," ch. 5); Belting, *Kaskaskia*, 74–75; *Canadian Archives, Supplement*, 1899 (Ottawa, 1901), p. 135.

breeds, whose hearts are corrupted and who are in a way more dangerous than the pure Illinois."[45]

Despite such objections, many Jesuit missionaries in the Illinois country were convinced that marriages between French men and Indian
women were a useful way to draw nonbelievers to Christ, and also to
extend the regulation of the church over local affairs.[46] Nevertheless in
1735, by order of the king, such marriages were prohibited outright.
This decree placed the local clergy in an uncomfortable position, and a
Jesuit at Kaskaskia, Father Tartarin, articulated an impassioned objec-
tion to the new policy. The power to legitimate marriages between
Frenchmen and Indians, he argued, was essential to the preservation of
his community. If a child of mixed parentage was a legitimate heir, he or
she might be drawn successfully into the French community; then, according to Tartarin, the child would become more French than Indian.
But if the children of mixed marriages were considered illegitimate, and
could receive neither an education from the priests nor an inheritance
from their fathers, then they could only be a scourge to the community –
and, by extension, to the entire colonial enterprise.[47]

As he formulated his argument, Tartarin may have had in mind the
example of Michel, son of the devout convert Marie Rouensa and her
trader-husband, Michel Accault. Born into the trading community of
Kaskaskia, he remained in the French agricultural village along with his
mother after Boisbriant's reforms forced the removal of the Indian population in 1719. Sometime around 1725, however, the younger Michel
decided to leave the French community and move to the nearby Indian
town. His decision so infuriated Marie that she threatened to disinherit
him unless he returned to French Kaskaskia. Faced with the potential

---

[45] [Anon.], "Memoire concernant les Ilinois," 1732, MG 1, série F³, vol. 24, partie 3, pp.
603–612, NAC [orig. Collection Moreau de Saint-Méry, ANC, Paris].

[46] A fragmentary baptismal register from the earliest years of the Kaskaskia mission illustrates the extent to which early missionaries supported such unions. It records 83 baptisms between 1692 and 1735; of those, 51 were children born to an Illinois mother
and a French father. Considering only the baptisms through 1719 the pattern is even
clearer: 43 of 56 baptisms – about 75%—were of children born to Illinois women and
French men. See C.J. Eschmann, comp. and trans., "Kaskaskia Church Records," *Illinois Historical Society Transactions*, 1904 (Springfield, 1904), pp. 394–413. All of the
birth, marriage, and death records that survive from the Illinois parishes in the 18th
century have been rearranged alphabetically, compiled, and published in Marthe Faribault-Beauregard, *La population des forts français d'Amérique (XVIIIe siécle)*, 2 vols.
(Montreal, 1982–1984).

[47] Order of the king, 8 Oct. 1735, *Canadian Archives*, 1904 (Ottawa, 1905), App. K, p.
209; Belting, *Kaskaskia*, p. 75.

loss of his substantial family assets, her son chose to return.[48] In Michel's case, the combination of a legitimate marriage and his mother's power to control his inheritance was enough to draw him back to the French settlement; in effect, his propertied stake in the community "made" him a Frenchman rather than an Illinois Indian.

If the local clergy lost the power to sanctify marriages, Tartarin argued, young Frenchmen would continue to live illegitimately with Indian women – who were also, in some cases, their slaves – "to the scandal of the community," but these relationships would exist beyond the reach of the church and the French community. While marriage was an option, the missionaries had leverage in such cases; robbed of their authority to sanctify mixed marriages, the unions themselves would not cease, but the priests would lose their ability to regulate them.

Underlying the entire discussion was the problematic question of cultural identity. Did it make more sense to regard the younger Michel Rouensa as a Frenchman or an Indian? What about his father, the trader Michel Accault, a profane anti-cleric before his marriage who was content to live among the Indians beyond the reach of French authority? And what of his mother, Marie Rouensa, born the daughter of a Kaskaskia chief but also a devout convert both to Catholicism and, apparently, to her new status as a French wife? Her first husband died after fathering two children, probably in 1701 or 1702, and she remarried another Frenchman, named Michel Philippe. Philippe came to the Illinois country as a *coureur de bois*, but (influenced perhaps by his wife's tenacious identification with settled French Catholic life) soon took up land in Kaskaskia; he went on to become captain of the militia and one of the town's leading inhabitants. He and Marie had six children, who themselves married into the community and thus established kinship ties with several other prominent families. By the time of her death in 1725, Marie was among the leading matrons of Kaskaskia; in recognition of her great service to the parish, she was buried beneath her pew in the local church. Her children were divided: those fathered by Philippe stayed in Kaskaskia and helped to comprise the solid citizenry of the second generation, but the two fathered by Michel Accault (their mother's efforts notwithstanding) soon disappeared from the local record.[49] Whether the younger Michel Accault returned to the nearby Indian

---

[48] Briggs, "Economic Position of Women," 67.

[49] Belting, *Kaskaskia*, pp. 14–15; the oldest son of Michel Accault, Pierre, inherited his parents' house and lands but sold them in September, 1725, for 2,500 *livres*: Belting, *Kaskaskia*, p. 33.

town is uncertain, but in any case he seems to have inherited more of his father's character than his mother's – an inheritance that, ironically, drew him away from the settled life of a French peasant and toward an identification with the local Indian community.

The common incidence of Indian wives among the first-generation settlers of Kaskaskia gave way, after mixed marriages were outlawed, to a predominance of women with French surnames thereafter – though many of these, of course, were the *métis* children of first-generation mixed marriages. Even as the frequency of intermarriage apparently declined, however, the Illinois towns necessarily retained an intimate connection to the Indian communities around them. The towns, in fact, were buffeted by Indian affairs throughout the colonial period. Far from being impregnable outposts of empire, the Illinois communities were small, permeable islands, awash in circumstances beyond their control. Perhaps no series of events in the colonial period illustrates this as clearly as the prolonged war with the Chickasaw Indians.

The Chickasaws were an English-allied tribe closely connected with the French-allied Choctaws. War between them began in 1718; French officials soon recognized that hostilities between the Choctaws and Chickasaws served French interests better than peace would, and they encouraged the fighting to continue. The scope of the war expanded late in 1729, after a large party of Natchez Indians attacked the French settlement at Fort Rosalie. When some Natchez warriors took refuge among the Chickasaws, the governors of Louisiana and Canada and French post commanders encouraged their Indian allies throughout the Mississippi and Ohio Valleys to go to war against the Chickasaws.[50] For more than a decade thereafter the warriors of the Illinois and Miami confederacies, the soldiers at Fort Chartres, the Illinois militias, and on occasion the civilian townspeople themselves, were all involved periodically in the fighting.

By the mid-1720s, French administrators worried that the Chickasaws might bring English traders into the Ohio Valley. In response to this fear, the French commander at Ouiatanon, François Morgane de Vincennes, tried to persuade the Indians at his post to move farther down the Wabash River to a more strategic site, where he promised to build a new fort that could protect the confluence of the Wabash and Ohio Rivers. After two years of pleading, he finally convinced a large body of Piankashaws to accompany him south, and in 1731 he began to

---

[50] For brief accounts of the Chickasaw Wars, see Richard White, *The Roots of Dependency: Subsistence, Environment, and Social Change among the Choctaws, Pawnees, and Navajos* (Lincoln, NE, 1983), pp. 52–61, and Usner, *Indians, Settlers, and Slaves*, pp. 81–87.

build a new fort – later named Vincennes to honor its first commander – on the lower Wabash. Then colonial officials started a campaign among the Illinois and Miami Indians to stir up sentiment against the Chickasaws. In 1732, Governor Beauharnois (successor to Vaudreuil in Canada) wrote a circular letter urging the Illinois and Miamis to raise an expedition against the Chickasaws, "whom they should look upon as the common enemy of all the tribes." Beginning that fall, raids and counterraids between the Illinois and Miami tribes and the Chickasaws became commonplace occurrences.[51]

During the next several years hostilities steadily escalated, until in 1736 Bienville, governor of Louisiana, planned a coordinated, three-pronged attack on the Chickasaw towns. One body of troops would come from the Illinois country, where Diron D'Artaguiette raised a force of 33 regular soldiers stationed at Fort Chartres, 110 militiamen from the Illinois towns, and more than 300 Indian warriors, most from the Illinois and Miami tribes. This party was to join another raised in Cahokia and the Michagamea village near Fort Chartres, and then proceed to Chickasaw country, where its attack would be coordinated with an army from the south led by Governor Bienville himself. The campaign was a disaster: D'Artaguiette's company was the only one of the three to arrive on time; underestimating the strength of the Chickasaw village, he decided to attack alone. His forces were routed. Six of the seven officers in the company were killed (including both D'Artaguiette and Vincennes) along with thirteen soldiers, seventeen militia, and an unreported number of Indians. The French organized a grand campaign to avenge this defeat in 1739, which would have once again included detachments from the Illinois country, but it collapsed at the last minute because of supply problems.[52] Thereafter the Chickasaw Wars were characterized, as in the years before 1736, by sporadic and small-scale raiding.

Though the Chickasaw Wars began as a French initiative, they reflect

---

[51] Jacob P. Dunn, ed., "Mission to the Ouabache," *Indiana Historical Society Publications*, vol. III, pp. 257, 279–280; Beauharnois and Hocquart to the Minister of the Marine, 15 Oct. 1730, in Frances Krauskopf, trans. and ed., "Ouiatanon Documents," *Proceedings of the Indiana Historical Society*, vol. XVIII (Indianapolis, 1955), p. 179; Beauharnois and Hocquart, "Report of Trade for 1732," 1 Oct. 1732, and Beauharnois to the Minister, 31 July 1733, *Collections of the Michigan Pioneer and Historical Society*, vol. XXXIV, pp. 100, 110.

[52] "Account of the Battle Fought by D'Artaguiette with the Chickasaws, March 25, 1736," *IndHSPub*, vol. VIII (Indianapolis, 1930), pp. 107–123; preparations for the 1739 campaign are described and debated in detail in a long series of documents printed in Dunbar Rowland and Albert Sanders, eds., *Mississippi Provincial Archives, 1729–1740: French Dominion*, vol. I, pp. 314–469. For a brief account, see Usner, *Indians, Settlers, and Slaves*, pp. 83–85.

the extent to which the French empire was dependent on maintaining strong Indian alliances for its survival. In its origins, the war was encouraged to reduce the likelihood that the Choctaws and other French-allied Indians would be drawn into English trading alliances through the Chickasaws. But as the war progressed, Illinois and Miami warriors turned it to their advantage. Encouraged by post commanders to raid the Chickasaws, the warriors used their raids as leverage to exact a steady supply of gifts and rewards in recognition for their services – leverage that was especially important as the fur trade stagnated in the 1730s and 1740s. Thus Vincennes, commanding at the fort that would soon bear his name, noted that the Illinois and Miami warriors regularly expected gifts in exchange for their services. He worried about the cost of this policy, but it could not be helped: "I anticipate that I will be put to still greater expense when the tribes return," he wrote after the departure of a war party in 1733, "because all the prisoners which they bring will be given to us, and it is necessary to pay for this sort of thing."[53]

As the fighting progressed, the number of war chiefs steadily proliferated, since anyone who led a war party south could demand a gift for his services. Just as trade expanded access to European merchandise in the British sphere, war served the same function in the French empire. The cost of this policy to the French crown was enormous. In Canada the king granted a generous 20,000 *livres* a year to be used for alliance gifts, but soon discovered that this sum was far from adequate: In 1740 the gifts that were actually distributed cost more than three times that much. The colony of Louisiana had a similar experience: In 1707 the king granted 6,515 *livres* for gifts; by 1732 that grant had mushroomed to 20,000 *livres*. Much of this growth can be attributed to the proliferation of war chiefs. At Ouiatanon, in less than nine months – from September 1746 until May 1747 – at least fifteen chiefs received gifts. Only five of these gifts were given to tribal leaders as formal confirmations of the French alliance; the rest went to war leaders as rewards for service. In all, gifts were given on thirty-three different occasions and totaled over 6,500 *livres* in value. (And it should be noted that the fragmentary journal recording these costs does not cover the summer months, traditionally the warriors' most active season.) By comparison, the leasehold on the post's trading monopoly netted the crown only 3,000 *livres* a year.[54] French officials clearly recognized that the practice of showering

[53] White, *Roots of Dependency*, pp. 50–51; Vincennes to Governor Bienville, 7 and 21 Mar. 1733, *IndHSPub*, vol. III, pp. 302–307.

[54] White, *Middle Ground*, pp. 180–181; King Louis XIV to De Muy, 30 June 1707,

their Indian allies with gifts had ruinous implications for colonial fi-
nances, but they were powerless to disappoint the expectations they had
helped to create.

In the French empire, war made allies of colonists and some Indians,
even as it strengthened hostilities with others; In the Illinois country it
confirmed and extended connections originally forged between trading
partners. For much of the 18th century, colonial officials struggled to
create a landed empire in North America strong enough to stand on its
own: an empire that could rise above the confusing array of alliances
and hostilities that structured the politics of the Indians' worlds, that
could declare its independence from the natives and exert some control
over them. Such a vision was never realized. Instead, in the interest of
survival and out of the contest for advantage, Indians and Frenchmen
constructed a shared world, shaped by the practical necessity of accommodation, that persisted until the end of the colonial period.

IV

The Pennsylvania experience offers a sharp contrast to that in the Illinois country. There, land values increased dramatically as the population grew and its farms were integrated into intercolonial and transatlantic markets. Those drawn west by opportunities in the Indian trade
were overwhelmed during the 1720s by those who were coming for
land.[55] Colonists settling new farmlands in the Susquehanna Valley were
unfamiliar with the local Indians, and generally wanted as little to do
with them as possible. The natives remained an exotic and potentially
threatening presence, especially when disagreements arose over land
ownership. Alliances were always precarious, and even where relations

---

MPAFD, vol. III, p. 52; King Louis XV to Bienville and Salmon, 2 Feb. 1732, MPAFD,
vol. III, p. 576; Michel Gamelin, "List of Supplies . . . ," IndHSProc, vol. XVIII, pp.
195–205; the leaseholding fee for 1742 is recorded in IndHSProc, vol. XVIII, pp.
150–151. For the argument that reports of gift expenditures were exaggerated by ministers and were actually a reasonable imperial investment see Catherine Desbarats,
"The Cost of Early Canada's Native Alliances: Reality and Scarcity's Rhetoric,"
WMQ, 52 (1995), 609–630. Desbarats deals only with Canada, an omission that
makes her discussion of the cost of Chickasaw raids, for example, incomplete; and by
arguing that Indian alliances were cheap compared to the cost of maintaining a French
army, she concedes my essential point: that France's Indian allies became paid merce-
naries, and thus guaranteed a steady flow of merchandise to their communities.
[55] This transition is described especially well in Peter Mancall, Valley of Opportunity:
Economic Culture along the Upper Susquehanna, 1700–1800 (Ithaca, 1991), though it
comes somewhat later in the upper valley than it does in the area I am describing.

appeared cooperative they could quickly become adversarial and hostile.

Indian relations in Pennsylvania were driven by two complementary needs: to facilitate orderly and timely land sales, and to dampen conflicts between settlers and Indians. During the first third of the 18th century, colonial officials and Indian leaders created a framework for handling these problems; although they largely succeeded in imposing order on intercultural relations, their arrangements significantly compromised the autonomy that some of the colony's Indian groups, and especially the Shawnees and Delawares, had previously enjoyed.

The need to buy land placed constant pressure on Pennsylvania's Indian relations. The southeastern quadrant of the colony was controlled by the Delawares, but, as Penn and his agents soon discovered, the Delawares were inefficient sellers of real estate. The problem lay in Delaware political organization: There was no central Delaware council, or single recognized leader, that could speak for the Delawares as a whole. In fact, the term "Delaware" refers not to a single sociopolitical group, but to perhaps as many as four ethnically and linguistically related, politically independent groups: furthest south, around the mouth of the Delaware River, the Unalachtigo ("people near the ocean"); just to the north, around the site of Philadelphia, the Unami ("people down the river"); a little further north, near the confluence of the Lehigh and Delaware Rivers, the Unalimi ("people up the river"); and still further north, beyond the Delaware Water Gap, the Minsi or Munsees ("people of the stony country"). Pennsylvanians never understood these distinctions clearly, and they remain confused and inconsistent in the documentary record of colonization. Sometimes the term "Delaware" referred to all four groups, but not always. Even within each of these four subgroups, political authority was decentralized. Power resided primarily on the level of village leaders and family lineages. Generally there was no preeminent chief who could speak for all the villages or lineages of, say, the Unamis.[56]

This radically decentralized form of political organization caused considerable confusion in Pennsylvania's Indian relations; in particular, it made definitive land purchases very difficult. Initially Penn and his agents bought small parcels piecemeal from individual "chiefs" – village leaders, or men who claimed to speak for particular family lineages –

---

[56] Considerable confusion remains about the precise organization of early Delaware society. Here I follow C. A. Weslager, *The Delaware Indians: A History* (New Brunswick, NJ, 1972), pp. 31–49; see also Ives Goddard, "Delaware," in Trigger, ed., *Handbook*, pp. 213–239.

whose status and authority was often uncertain. After a purchase, other families or bands might appear, sometimes many years later, to claim partial ownership. Colonial officials needed a Delaware "king": someone whose signature on a deed could expunge the claims of all other Delawares to the land. A man named Olumapies came to fill that role for the Unami Delawares. He was first introduced to Governor Gookin and his council in 1712 as the first Delaware leader in more than a decade to be recognized by the other chiefs as a man of preeminent stature. Colonial officials seized on his prominence and made Olumapies the first "king" of the Delawares. In 1715 he claimed to speak for "all our Indians on this [the east] side of the Sasquehannah," and three years later he was the leading signatory of a treaty that confirmed all previous Delaware land sales in the colony. In the wake of this 1718 treaty, the Unami Delawares controlled only a single remaining tract of land in Pennsylvania: the Tulpehocken lands, a broad swath of fertile ground along the Tulpehocken and Swatara Creeks, which became the last center of Unami settlement east of the Susquehanna.[57]

Though a brief account of Olumapies' career can make him sound like a passive tool of English imperialism, the pressures of colonization made it increasingly important for the Delawares, too, to have a preeminent spokesman. As settlement and land sales advanced, Delaware leaders needed to speak with a single voice if they were to retain any power or influence with the colony. It was among the Delawares, after all, that Olumapies' preeminent status was created; only then could Pennsylvania officials use his power for their own purposes. Nevertheless, once he was established as a Delaware "king," his position was increasingly untenable. As a mediator, Olumapies' foremost responsibility was to preserve peace between the colony and his people; he consistently sought accommodation on the assumption that peace with the colony would best serve Delaware interests. He even went so far as to hope that all differences between the colonists and his people might be effaced – "that the Indians should be half English & the [English] make themselves as half Indians" – so that conflict could be avoided.[58]

The nadir of Olumapies' career came in 1731 and 1732. In 1731 Olumapies, who had become a heavy drinker, killed his cousin Shackatawlin in a drunken fight. His death was an especially crushing blow

---

[57] *Pa. Col. Recs.*, vol. II, pp. 546–549, 599–601; Wallace, *Indians in Pennsylvania*, pp. 131–134. For an insightful discussion of Delaware land use patterns, see Anthony F. C. Wallace, "Woman, Land, and Society: Three Aspects of Aboriginal Delaware Life," *Pennsylvania Archaeologist* 17 (1947), 1–35.

[58] *Pa. Col. Recs.*, vol. II, pp. 599–601.

since Shackatawlin was very highly regarded among his people – he was widely viewed, in fact, as Olumapies' likely successor as Delaware spokesman. A short time later Olumapies appeared remorsefully before the governor's council to request new and stricter alcohol regulations at the trading town of Shamokin. A year later, after a series of conflicts and piecemeal sales, Olumapies finally signed away all Delaware claims to the Tulpehocken lands, the last Unami Delaware territory east of the Susquehanna.[59] Thereafter he quickly became irrelevant. The murder of Shackatawlin largely destroyed his credibility among the Delawares, and without any more land to sign over he was of very little use to colonial officials.

As land changed hands and the number of colonist farmers in the Susquehanna Valley grew, so too did the potential for conflict with Indians. This possibility created the second great challenge in the colony's Indian relations. Newly arrived farmers, many just off boats from Europe, and Indians long familiar with the lands the farmers were settling, often made each other nervous; this was especially true when traveling bands of warriors crossed settled farmlands on their way to war. Just such an encounter occurred in 1720, when a party of Iroquois warriors arrived in Conestoga on their way south to raid Catawba settlements. They frightened and intimidated the nearby settlers, shooting "divers of our People's Creatures for their Diversion only[,] without touching them for food," and robbing one trader's stock of goods. Equally worrisome, several Cayuga warriors "had the Boldness to assert, that all the Lands upon Sasquehannah River belonged to them, and that the English had no Right to settle there."[60]

For Pennsylvania officials, these events dramatized the need to impose order on Indian relations in the Susquehanna Valley. The Iroquois council dispatched a delegation to Conestoga in the summer of 1721 to seek reconciliation for the warriors' affronts; there the Iroquois emissaries met with Governor Keith, James Logan, and three other members of the governor's council. In a three-day conference, Pennsylvania and Iroquois officials established a vague but far-reaching understanding that laid a foundation for their mutual cooperation for decades to come.[61]

The ruling principle of the conference, which embodied a fundamental social metaphor that was accepted by both sides, was the need for

[59] *Pa. Col. Recs.*, vol. III, pp. 404–406; Wallace, *Indians in Pennsylvania*, pp. 134–135.
[60] Gov. Keith to Gov. of NY, 19 July 1720, *Pa. Col. Recs.*, vol. III, pp. 99–102.
[61] The record of the conference, and all of the quotations in the subsequent paragraphs, can be found in *Pa. Col. Recs.*, vol. III, pp. 120–130.

councillors – wise, old men – to restrain the impulses of warriors and traders – foolish, young men. Governor Keith introduced this image when he told the Iroquois delegates that he would "forget the mistakes which some of their young men were guilty of," but he also stressed the responsibility of the Iroquois council to restrain its warriors. "I hope They will grow wiser with age," Keith said of the warriors, "an[d] hearken to the grave counsels of their old men whose Valour we esteem because they are wise; But the Rashness of [these] young men is altogether Folly."

The Iroquois spokesman for the conference, a Seneca councillor named Ghesaont, elaborated on Keith's metaphor. He expressed embarrassment over the warriors' behavior but refused to accept full responsibility for it. Traders, after all, were also prone to treat his warriors unkindly, and the liquor they offered to his young men affected the behavior of colonists and Indians alike. Nevertheless, he maintained the distinction between warriors, whose "hasty . . . Accident[s]" might cause misunderstandings, and councillors, who would be able to "treat amicably upon" any such problems as they arose. Drawing on the image of youthful irresponsibility, Ghesaont emphasized the reciprocal obligations that bound the colony and the Iroquois confederacy: I hope, he said, "[t]hat We may now be together as one people, treating one anothers Children kindly and affectionately on all occasions." Finally Ghesaont and Governor Keith renewed the "chain of friendship" – tentatively extended by William Penn to the Iroquois many years earlier – and promised to keep it "so well clean'd as to remain brighter and stronger than ever it was before."

The landmark 1721 conference marked a fundamental turning point in Pennsylvania's Indian relations. It established a commitment by both the colony and the Iroquois confederacy to keep the peace between Indians and colonists in the Susquehanna region. Pennsylvania officials took this role very seriously. When John and Edmund Cartlidge, two established and well-respected Susquehanna traders, were accused of murdering an Iroquois warrior in 1722, they were imprisoned for trial despite strong evidence that they had acted in self-defense. Governor Keith met with an Iroquois delegation in Albany that summer and reported on the progress of the Cartlidges' case; the Iroquois delegates, horrified at this development, pleaded that the traders be released. At their request, the Cartlidges were set free and legal proceedings against them were suspended. Six years later Keith's replacement, Governor Patrick Gordon, told a delegation from the Susquehanna that two colonists convicted of murdering several Indians had been put to death. "[W]e & you are as one People," he told his audience; "we treat you exactly as we do our own People."[62] By extending the colony's powers of justice to include protection of the Indian population, Pennsylvania officials acted on a vision of Indian relations that placed a premium on order, cooperation, and peaceful interaction.

The Iroquois embraced the new order in the Susquehanna Valley somewhat more hesitantly than the Pennsylvanians did. Convinced that the rapid expansion of the colony posed a direct threat to their interests, at least some Iroquois leaders apparently tried to organize an all-out war on Pennsylvania. The Susquehanna Indians resisted the idea – whether out of fear of the English, mistrust of the Iroquois, a preference for peaceful trade, or the lack of an immediate provocation is not clear – and the Iroquois promptly dropped the idea. From that time, the Six Nations took on the responsibility for overseeing affairs on the Susquehanna to ensure that no further conflicts between Indians and settlers would develop. They appointed an Oneida chief – Shickellamy, "the enlightener" – to act as a special overseer on the Susquehanna, where he could monitor and regulate the actions of his supposed dependents.[63]

His services were needed soon enough. In the late 1720s, contacts between colonists and Indians were becoming more frequent, and in places where unauthorized settlement impinged on Indian lands they could be fraught with mutual suspicion, mistrust, and incomprehension. Tulpehocken Creek was one such place: an important Indian pathway, which connected the Unami Delaware and Shawnee settlements on the Susquehanna with the Unalimi and Munsee lands on the upper Delaware, followed the course of the Tulpehocken. But as early as 1723, when Governor Keith suggested that a band of German emigrants take up lands on the Tulpehocken, the area was also becoming a center of farm settlement.[64] Such settlement parties generally reached an agreement or made a purchase from the local Indians, and presumably that happened here; nevertheless, especially as settlement encroached on an important travel route, Indians generally expected hospitable treatment from the newcomers. For the settlers, the sight of Indians along the Tulpehocken must

---

[62] *Pa. Col. Recs.*, vol. III, pp. 196–199, 336.

[63] The clearest direct evidence for this aborted conspiracy comes from a letter of five Shawnee chiefs to Governor Gordon, 7 June 1732, *Pa. Arch.* [1st Ser.], vol. I, pp. 329–330; see also the report of James Le Tort that the Iroquois tried to enlist the Miamis in the plot as well: *Pa. Col. Recs.*, vol. III, pp. 295–298; for its broader context, see Jennings, "Iroquois Alliances," pp. 42–43. For a brief sketch of Shickellamy, see Wallace, *Indians in Pennsylvania*, pp. 181–182; and for a fuller account of his role in Pennsylvania's Indian affairs, Paul A.W. Wallace, *Conrad Weiser: Friend of Colonist and Mohawk* (Philadelphia, 1945).

[64] Knittle, *Palatine Emigration*, pp. 205–207.

have been common. But newly arrived immigrants could also be disoriented and frightened by the sudden appearance of a party of Indians emerging from the woods, which could serve as an unwelcome reminder of their precarious hold on the landscape and of their inability either to control, or even fully to comprehend, their surroundings.

In early May, 1728, a party of 11 Shawnee warriors, painted and armed for war, appeared among the settlers on Manatawny Creek (a tributary of the Schuylkill near Tulpehocken Creek) as they made their way from the upper Delaware to the Susquehanna. They were investigating reports, as their leader later explained, that some Catawba warriors had come north into Pennsylvania. The Manatawny settlers knew nothing about the warriors' larger purpose, but they quickly discovered that the Shawnee party needed provisions to continue on their way. Apparently short on food, the warriors entered several settlers' houses and demanded hospitality. Armed, painted, and behaving belligerently, the Shawnees terrified the local farmers. The settlers even claimed later that the warriors' leader was speaking Spanish – a highly unlikely claim, though it might have been French – which raised suspicions about the Indians' loyalty to the colony. The settlers soon organized an armed party of their own, about twenty men in all, to catch up with the Shawnees and inquire about their intentions. Their meeting ended in gunfire that scattered both sides. No one was killed, but the leader of the Shawnees and two of the settlers were slightly injured. The Indian party immediately fled.[65]

Within days, reports of the encounter had traveled to other nearby farm settlements, the details twisted and exaggerated in the process. On Cocosing Creek, a tributary of the Tulpehocken about ten miles from Manatawny, Walter and John Winter heard that two white men were killed and three injured in an attack by hostile Indians. Then they learned that another party of Indians had just appeared unannounced at a neighbor's cabin, and they panicked. Accompanied by two other settlers, they hurried to the scene, where they found an Indian family, probably local Unami Delawares, speaking with their neighbor in his yard. The four men rushed to their friend's aid with their guns drawn. The startled Indian man, who carried no gun, raised his bow in alarm and reached for an arrow. The Winters and their friends shot him dead and turned on his family, two women and two young girls. They beat the women to death, then seized the girls as they tried to flee and beat one of them severely as well. They held the girls prisoner at the home of

---

[65] This account is pieced together from several partial descriptions; see *Pa. Arch.* [1st Ser.], vol. I, pp. 223–224; *Pa. Col. Recs.*, vol. III, pp. 303–305, 309.

one of the attackers, in the expectation – astonishing under the circumstances – that they might bring some reward.[66]

These encounters apparently dramatized, for many Pennsylvania Indians, the incompatibility of the growing colonial settlements with their
presence on the land. Individual parties of Shawnees and Delawares had
been migrating west to the Ohio Valley for several years, but beginning
in 1728 the Shawnees and many Delawares broke *en masse* with the
conciliatory policies of Shickellamy, Olumapies, and the Conestoga Indians. Between April and August of 1728, groups of Shawnees had violent run-ins with both Conestoga Indians and Pennsylvania traders on
the Susquehanna. The governor's council quickly contacted Olumapies
and the recently-arrived Shickellamy to mediate the crisis. The two Indian leaders agreed to come to Philadelphia, but they failed to persuade
any Shawnee chief to accompany them. Olumapies anxiously tried to
cover for the absence by claiming that the Shawnees were all away hunting. He asked that "the Gov[erno]r...not think strange of it, because at
this time of the year they [the Shawnees] cannot conveniently come; that
nevertheless, he now speaks in the Name & Behalf of them all." The ex-
cuse was accepted, since it remained useful to regard the Susquehanna
mediators as spokesmen for all the western Indians (at this meeting, his
first with colonial officials, Shickellamy received a special gift that included a gun, in recognition that his "Services had been & may yet further be of great advantage to this Government"), but the cracks in the
colony's system of Indian management were already being exposed.[67]

That system was strained to the breaking point less than a decade later, in the controversy that surrounded the so-called "Walking Purchase." The territory affected by the purchase lay near the confluence of
the Lehigh and Delaware Rivers, an area known as the Forks of the
Delaware. It had long been inhabited by Unalimi Delawares; as relatives
from New Jersey and southeastern Pennsylvania were pushed off their
lands, the number of Delawares living at the Forks grew. Just to the
north of the Delaware settlements was the Shawnee village of Pechoquealin, which had been settled with Delaware permission in the
1690s. Still further north, beyond the Delaware Water Gap, resided the
northernmost branch of the Delawares, the Munsees.

On the upper Delaware, as on the lower Susquehanna, a growing

---

[66] *Pa. Arch.* [1st Ser.], vol. I, pp. 215–221; Wallace, *Weiser*, p. 43.

[67] Accounts of the further disturbances can be found in Wright to Logan, 2 May 1728;
Sadowsky to Petty, 27 Aug. 1728; Smith and Petty to Gov., 3 Sept. 1728; in *Pa. Arch.*
[1st Ser.], vol. I, pp. 213, 227, 232. For the Council's summons, see *Pa. Col. Recs.*, vol.
III, pp. 329–331, and *Pa. Arch.* [1st Ser.], vol. I, pp. 228–229; the record of the conference is in *Pa. Col. Recs.*, vol. III, pp. 334–337.

concentration of Indian peoples began to face increasing pressure on their lands late in the 1720s. They responded in different ways. The Shawnee warriors who exchanged gunfire with settlers on Manatawny Creek in 1728 immediately moved to a more remote location; they built a new town, called Wyoming, on the north branch of the Susquehanna River. This settlement, perhaps 50 miles northwest of the Delaware Water Gap, seemed for a time to be entirely immune to encroachment. The Forks Delawares, on the other hand, were much more reluctant to forfeit their lands. But when Thomas Penn arrived in Pennsylvania in 1732 and finally restored proprietary authority for the first time in 14 years, he was eager, if not desperate, to compensate for the many years in which the Penns had gained nothing from the colony's development. The Forks lands were especially desirable, and they became a focus of colonial expansion in the 1730s as Penn and Logan tried to convince the Delawares there to sell out and leave.[68]

When the Forks Indians resisted these overtures and complained to Pennsylvania officials about the growth of illegal settlement on their lands, James Logan produced a copy of a 1686 deed by which, according to his reading, all the Forks lands had already been sold to the colony. The Forks Indians, led by a chief named Nutimus who had himself recently moved to the Forks from New Jersey, disputed Logan's interpretation of the deed's boundaries. They correctly insisted that the original signatories to the deed – Unami Delawares – would have had no authority to sell any land around the Forks. The sketch map on the deed was inconclusive; the resolution of the disagreement hinged on a very vague description of the tract in the text of the deed. It referred to land lying between the Delaware River and Neshaminy Creek, extending northwest from a clearly designated line "as far as a man can go in one day and a half." To resolve the question of how far this might be, a northwest course was laid out and cleared of all obstacles; at dawn on September 19, 1737, a team of three young men, accompanied by packhorses and two Indian observers, set off. They measured their walking time with a watch – 12 hours the first day, six the second – and pressed ahead at a pace that astonished and infuriated the Indian observers. Two of the walkers, in fact, were too exhausted to complete the course, but the third pushed on until, by noon of the second day, he had covered 55 miles. By the end of the first day the walkers were already beyond Nutimus' land; in the end, the Walking Purchase netted about 1,200 square miles. It established a foundation, however questionable, for the

[68] Hanna, *Wilderness Trail*, vol. I, pp. 154, 187; Anthony F. C. Wallace, *King of the Delawares: Teedyuscung, 1700–1763* (Philadelphia, 1949), pp. 18–21.

dispossession of not only the Unalimi Delawares at the Forks, but even of the Munsee Delawares, of their lands. It also came to represent, for later critics, a fundamental turning point in the colony's Indian relations: It marked the first time that the Delawares were brazenly defrauded in a dispute with the government.[69]

The Forks and Munsee Delawares initially resisted abandoning their lands and protested their treatment, but in the late 1730s and early 1740s many departed from the Delaware Valley. Most followed the Wyoming Shawnees to the north branch of the Susquehanna; then, beginning in the 1740s, many Shawnees and Delawares around Wyoming moved again, this time to the Ohio Valley. In 1744 most of the Shawnee band at Wyoming settled in the new village of Logstown, which quickly became the region's principal trading center. During the same decade parties of Forks Delawares also abandoned Pennsylvania altogether to test their fortunes in the Ohio Valley.[70]

V

Despite the rhetoric of intercultural unity that informed relations in Pennsylvania for many years – "that the Indians should be half English & the [English] make themselves as half Indians," "[t]hat We may now be together as one people," that "we & you are as one People" – the reality was that Indian and European interests were diverging sharply, and Indians were increasingly forced to adapt radically or pick up and move. Those who moved to the Ohio Valley experienced an apparent renewal of autonomy and a renaissance of traditional pursuits. The alternative was a strategy of radical accommodation. For a minority of Pennsylvania Indians, especially Delawares from around the Forks, it made more sense to adapt to European standards of religious identity and political economy and stay where they were. Their experiments in acculturation offered faint echoes of Penn's earliest, fondest hopes for the future of intercultural relations in his colony.

Some Delawares were especially resourceful in resisting efforts to remove them from the Forks. After their protests of the Walking Purchase failed, in November 1742 a group of self-proclaimed Christian Delawares petitioned the governor's council for a land grant from the colony. One of the petitioners was Moses Tatemy, a former interpreter for the colony who already owned a 300-acre tract granted to him by

---

[69] Wallace, *King of the Delawares*, pp. 21–30.
[70] Hanna, *Wilderness Trail*, vol. I, pp. 355–356; Goddard, "Delaware," in Trigger, ed., *Handbook*, pp. 220–223.

the proprietor. He was reportedly "farming in a small way" on this land, and sought a confirmation of his title; the other petitioners hoped to make purchases. For the council, religious identity was the crux of the matter: if the petitioners really were Christians, their request would be treated sympathetically. When they were questioned, however, most of the petitioners failed this test – "it appeared they had very little if any [knowledge of Christianity] at all" – and their request was denied. There were two exceptions; whether they demonstrated a better knowledge of Christianity or were singled out for their earlier services to the colony is not certain. Tatemy and a local headman named Captain John were granted land, provided they first received permission from the Iroquois and no one but their immediate families remained on the property.[71]

Captain John soon sold his land and moved on, but Tatemy stayed and adapted to Christian and European ways. In 1742 he was described as "a man of remarkably quiet and modest deportment, who spoke English well, and had regulated his housekeeping much in the European style." Two years later, he began to serve as an interpreter for the Presbyterian missionary David Brainerd, who baptized both Tatemy and his wife. In the new towns on the north branch of the Susquehanna, too, some Delawares experimented with partial acculturation. Nutimus, one of the most vocal opponents of the Walking Purchase, afterward moved to Nescopeck, where he and his family kept a plantation with the help of five black slaves. Other communities were noted by travelers for the apparent influence of Christianity among their leaders. At the mouth of the Lackawanna River stood a village whose chief was named Papoonhan, later baptized as John. He was described in one colonist's account as "a Very Religeous civilised man in his own way," and he and his followers were noted for their interest in the preaching of Christian missionaries.[72]

The Delawares who stayed behind often saw their social worlds disintegrate almost completely. The vulnerability created by that experience made some of them prime candidates for Christian conversion. Through more than half a century of contact with Quakers, the Pennsyl-

---

[71] *Pa. Col. Recs.*, vol. IV, pp. 624–625; the first quote is from Count Nicholas Ludwig von Zinzendorf, "Zinzendorf Among the Delawares," in William C. Reichel, ed., *Memorials of the Moravian Church*, 2 vol. (Philadelphia, 1870), vol. I, p. 26.

[72] Zinzendorf, quoted in William A. Hunter, ed., "John Hays' Diary and Journal of 1760," *Pennsylvania Archaeologist*, 24 (1954), 63n; for Brainerd's efforts among the Forks Delawares, see Brainerd to Ebenezer Pemberton, 5 Nov. 1744, in Reichel, ed., *Memorials*, vol. I, pp. 27–28n; Wallace, *Indians in Pennsylvania*, p. 179; "Hays' Diary and Journal," pp. 67–74.

vania Indians had never been exposed to missionary work, but in the 1740s other sects began to preach to them in earnest. The most success-ful was a band of radical Protestants from Moravia led by Count Nicholas Ludwig von Zinzendorf, a charismatic nobleman who was also the group's patron. The count and his followers were a mystically inclined, communal sect that took up Indian conversion as one of their principal activities in America. Zinzendorf, whose aristocratic back-ground, excellent education, and plain style appealed to Pennsylvania's Quaker elite, found an ideal setting for his grand designs in the Pennsyl-vania countryside. He bought 5,000 acres near the Lehigh River, which he hoped to expand into a broad swath of territory two miles wide and eight miles long. At one end of the tract he planned a town to be called Bethlehem, and at the other a second called Nazareth. In between, he proposed "to build small villages for ye Brethren to live in, the same in number, and to have the same names as are found on the maps of the Holy Land."[73] Though this plan was never fully realized, Moravian missions established in concert with the new villages of Bethlehem and Nazareth won Indian converts to the group's distinctive blend of ascetic communalism.

Not all Indians were equally receptive to the Moravian message, but Zinzendorf and his followers offered an appealing alternative to the un-certainties faced by many of the Delawares who remained in eastern Pennsylvania. When a new mission village named Gnadenhutten, or Huts of Grace, was built 25 miles north of Bethlehem, it grew quickly; by 1749 it housed 500 converts. On the simplest level, life at Gnaden-hutten eased the difficult transition in political economy that accultura-tion required. The Brethren laid out a farm for the mission and super-vised its grain cultivation and livestock management according to Euro-pean custom, thus introducing the converts to the routines of farm life; the Indians typically served as agricultural laborers and woodcutters for the village. As the Brethren added gristmills and sawmills, the mission village became largely self-sufficient in the production of food and building supplies. The Indians also had access to the services of black-smiths and other craftsmen whose skills were highly valued by the con-

---

[73] James Logan to Gov. Clarke [NY], 30 Mar. 1742, and Richard Peters to Thomas Penn, 9 July 1742, both quoted in Reichel, ed., *Memorials*, vol. I, pp. 14–16n; for general ac-counts, see August Gottlieb Spangenberg, *The Life of Nicholas Lewis Count Zinzen-dorf*, trans. Samuel Jackson (London, 1838); Arthur James Lewis, *Zinzendorf, the Ecu-menical Pioneer: A Study in the Moravian Contribution to Christian Mission and Uni-ty* (Philadelphia, 1962); Gillian Lindt Gollin, *Moravians in Two Worlds: A Study of Changing Communities* (New York, 1967).

verts.[74] In all these ways, Gnadenhutten schooled eastern Delawares in the esoteric arts of a European-style farming community.

The Moravians also deeply affected the spiritual lives of at least some of their converts. They preached a version of the Christian gospel uniquely suited to the circumstances of the eastern Delawares. They emphasized, above all, the misery of the human condition, the inevitability of suffering and pain, and the power of Christ alone to redeem humanity from its sins. Moravian preaching was vivid and dramatic; it reflected a fascination with blood imagery – the blood of the lamb, the blood of Christ – which heightened the emotionalism of the message and the intensity of a listener's response. Approached by a prospective convert, the "Br[ethre]n painted the Lamb before him most sweetly in his bloody Hue." Like the evangelical preachers of the Great Awakening, Moravian preachers sometimes induced conversion experiences, moments of great emotional release for the Indians who had them. Thus a Delaware with the Christian name of Gottlieb "was powerfully touch'd in his Heart" by a sermon, "& shed many Tears, under a Sence of his miserable Condition." At the same time, the Moravians' characteristic Christian emphasis on sin and repentance encouraged Indian converts to accept responsibility for the confusion and suffering they experienced.[75]

Though many mission Indians became deeply attached to their new lives, conversion placed them in a vulnerable position. Caught between two very different cultures, they could never win full acceptance with either. The Moravians, though dedicated to their Indian converts, regarded them as morally and socially inferior beings whose sufferings were a divine judgment against their traditional ways. When the Brethren reflected on "the poor condition of the Indians inwardly & outwardly," they concluded that their only hope lay in conversion and a complete repudiation of their native cultures. But despite their emphasis on spiritual and cultural regeneration, the Moravians never drew Indian converts into their own communities as equals. They maintained separate Indian settlements ("Our brown D[ea]r flock," in one missionary's phrase), in-

74 John Heckewelder, *A Narrative of the Mission of the United Brethren Among the Delaware and Mohegan Indians, from Its Commencement, in the Year 1740, to the Close of the Year 1808* (New York, 1971 [orig. pub. 1820]), pp. 34–36; "Appraisement of the United Breth[re]ns Loss . . . ," 4 Feb. 1756, Box 119, Folder 4, Records of the Moravian Mission Among the Indians of North America, Archives of the Moravian Church, Bethlehem, Pa. (microfilm); John F. Oberlin and August H. Francke, "The Case . . . ," 15 Oct. 1763, Box 124, Folder 5, RMM.

75 "Journal of the Indian Congregation at Gnaden-Hutten for January and February, 1747," quotes: 1 Apr., 4/5 Jan., Box 116, Folder 8, RMM.

sulated from outside influence and kept at arm's length from the Moravians themselves.[76]

Once they joined a mission, Indians alienated themselves from their non-Christian kin. Relatives urged them to stay away from the missions; Gottlieb's friends threatened to "knock his Brains out" if he went back. Their work was foreign to them. Men who had always been taught that raising crops was women's work were now expected to labor in the fields. The Brethren, in turn, regarded the converts as economic incompetents when they discovered they were unable to complete a task. In one case a missionary noted that "[s]everal Indians [that] we thought could help themselves Respecting plowing we find are not able," so that one of the Moravians had to plow their seven acres for them. Most Indians remained menial laborers; only rarely did they learn skilled trades. The men still hunted, but their trips were limited to brief excursions into the nearby countryside. When one convert tried to maintain his economic independence by practicing the traditional craft of canoe-making in his spare time, his wife asked the Brethren to make him stop. He was selling the canoes to colonists, and according to his wife he sometimes made "a bad use of the Mony being not always able to govorn himselfe."[77] As economic dependents and social inferiors, the mission Indians occupied an increasingly vulnerable place in the Pennsylvania landscape, depending as it did on the aid and goodwill of the Europeans among whom they resided.

*   *   *

Thus the Illinois country and Pennsylvania followed very different patterns of territorial development. Historians have sometimes attributed these differences to vaguely defined attributes of temperament or culture, but close attention to the dynamics of colonization suggests another explanation. French and British officials had comparable goals in the two regions, but the population histories of their colonies diverged decisively. In the Illinois country, intensive agricultural settlement failed and the French towns remained small, isolated outposts in a trading empire. As a result, colonists and Indians developed one kind of intercultural symbiosis, unstable in certain ways but essential to the survival of

---

[76] Gnaden-Hutten Journal, 6/17 Feb. 1747, Box 116, Folder 8, RMM; Powell to Spangenburg, 8 Aug. 1755, Box 118, Folder 6, RMM. The Indian village and that of the Brethren stood on opposite sides of the river to maintain this separation.

[77] Petition of Indians at Nain and Wechquetank to the Governor, 27 July 1763, Box 124, Folder 7, RMM; Powell to Spangenburg, 5 and 20 May 1755, Box 118, Folder 5, RMM; Gnaden-Hutten Journal, 11/22 Jan. 1747, Box 116, Folder 8, RMM.

the French outposts. In Pennsylvania, immigration overwhelmed the early patterns of intercultural contact and trade; rapid territorial development demanded a different kind of intercultural symbiosis, one premised on the need to transfer land quickly and efficiently from Indian to European owners and to dampen the potential for conflict inherent in that process.

Each system achieved a measure of success in the first half of the 18th century, but each also suffered from characteristic forms of instability. For the French, instability was rooted in the increasingly anemic condition of its overseas trading empire, which strained relations with Indian allies and made a British connection appealing for many of them. The British steadily gained influence in trade after 1740, but their unceasing need for territorial accommodation presented a different, and graver, threat to the Ohio Valley Indians by midcentury.

CHAPTER FOUR

The Alchemy of Property

A FTER the middle of the 18th century, Indian relations in the British empire were increasingly strained by unbearable pressures – pressures generated by the alchemy of property in British America. That alchemy worked according to a simple calculus: as population grew, so did demand for land; as demand for land grew, so did its value; as its value grew, efforts to capture and control it became more aggressive, more frenzied, more grandiose. Land hunger was not a new phenomenon in the British colonies – it was, in fact, one of the most persistent patterns of the colonial era – but in the early eighteenth century, not only in Pennsylvania but throughout the colonies, British and Indian leaders established increasingly effective diplomatic means for resolving conflicts over land. The attempt to extend Britain's territorial empire into the Ohio Valley, which originated about 1750, overreached existing structures of diplomacy and required new agreements with the Indians of the Ohio Valley – Indians who had already been dispossessed once, many thought unjustly, of their lands.

These pressures burst into the open in the Seven Years' War. As France and Britain sought to control the Ohio Valley, the Ohio Indians looked for a way to maintain their autonomy and power, an effort that shaped both their wartime alliances and their postwar initiatives. Britain's victory placed enormous new administrative demands on the empire; to succeed in managing affairs in the Ohio Valley, its agents needed far-sighted policies and cooperative, influential Indian leaders. But the complex demands of western development defeated administrators' efforts to devise a workable imperial strategy, and powerful, accommodating Indian leaders were hard to come by, both because such traditions of leadership had eroded in the region's trading communities and because many of the valley's residents had prior experience with British land hunger and were no longer in an accommodating mood.

Under these circumstances, the terrible energies of colonial adventurers and Indian warriors overwhelmed attempts to impose structure on imperial expansion, and in place of mediation the aggressive initiatives of ambitious individuals increasingly shaped intercultural relations in the Ohio Valley.

I

The Seven Years' War was the watershed event that defined relations between British subjects and Indians in the Ohio Valley. Before its outbreak, the Anglo-American trading empire had made steady inroads into the valley and eroded the loyalties of many formerly French-allied Indians. Pennsylvania's "chain of friendship" with the Ohio Indians extended from the Susquehanna Valley, to the Allegheny, and down the Ohio as far as the new trading town of Pickawillany, which in turn drew Indian traders from the Illinois and Miami towns along the Wabash and the Mississippi. In 1748 more than fifty Indian representatives from the Ohio, including a Miami delegation from Pickawillany, traveled hundreds of miles to confirm their alliance with Pennsylvania. (They met colonial officials at Lancaster, the predominantly German village that had sprung up at the center of the rich new farms on the Tulpehocken lands.) As late as 1750, Indian spokesmen at Logstown were requesting that either Pennsylvania or Virginia erect a fort on the Ohio "to secure the Trade, for they think it will be dangerous for the Traders to travel the Roads for fear of being surprised by some of the French and French Indians, as they expect nothing else but a War with the French the next Spring."[1]

At this point, many Ohio Indians preferred a British alliance to a French one. During the 1740s, especially in the years when French shipping was disrupted by war, French traders and commanders had often been unable to supply their allies with articles of trade and gifts. At the same time, the crisis of France's trading empire in the Ohio Valley had made its officers increasingly jealous of French territorial claims there; thus the voyage of Céloron in 1749, to bury lead markers asserting French territorial control where none, in fact, existed. In the Indians' calculus of interest, it was Britain's empire that appeared most beneficent in 1750. British trade was thriving in the west, while French commerce grew increasingly desiccated; at the same time, the occupied lands

---

[1] *Minutes of the Provincial Council of Pennsylvania*, 16 vols. (Harrisburg, 1838–1853) [hereafter *Pa. Col. Recs.*], vol. V, pp. 307–319; George Croghan to Gov. Hamilton, 16 Nov. 1750, in Reuben G. Thwaites, ed., *Early Western Travels, 1748–1846*, 32 vols. (Cleveland, 1904–1907), vol. I, pp. 53–57.

of British America were separated from the Indian territories of the west by a forbidding range of mountains and millions of acres of undeveloped land, while France was now claiming, suddenly and aggressively despite all evidence to the contrary, to control – to own – the lands upon which the Ohio Indians lived.

But refugees from the Delaware and Susquehanna Valleys among the Ohio Indians had also learned to be wary of British intentions. The British, one Shawnee commented, were "like Piggons[:] if [they] sufferid a paire . . . to reside [among them,] thayd Draw to them whole Troopes & take from [the Indians] all [their] Land[.]" The arrival of a stranger from the British colonies in the fall of 1750, who carried no trader's merchandise but kept a notebook and carefully measured his courses of travel, raised some eyebrows in Logstown. Christopher Gist covered for himself by keeping his measurements secret – "I understood it was dangerous to let a Compass be seen among these Indians" – and by announcing that he carried a message to the Indians from the king of England, by order of the governor of Virginia. In fact he was an agent of the recently formed Ohio Company of Virginia, instructed to explore the upper Ohio Valley, note its paths and rivers, and discover a "large Quantity of good, level Land" suitable for the company's needs. As he traveled, however, he diverted attention from his task by spreading word of a "large present of Goods" that had been delivered by the king himself to Virginia, and that now awaited a gathering of Ohio Indians and representatives of the colony to be distributed.[2]

In the spring of 1752 this gathering finally took place at Logstown. The Ohio Indians hoped to hear that Virginia planned to build a small fort on the Ohio to protect the traders, as they had requested, but it quickly became apparent that Gist had misrepresented the nature of the conference. It was sponsored not by the colony but by the Ohio Company itself, a land speculation venture organized by a circle of prominent Virginians who were angling for a half-million-acre grant from the crown that they hoped to locate on the upper Ohio. The company was formed following a 1744 treaty in which the Iroquois Confederacy relinquished its claim to any lands "that are or shall be by his Majesty's Appointment in the Colony of Virginia." Though this sounds like a limited concession, its bounds were potentially enormous. Virginia's western boundary was undefined, and its northern and southern limits

---

[2] Shamokin Diary, 6 Mar. 1748, Box 121, Folder 4, Records of the Moravian Mission Among the Indians of North America, Archives of the Moravian Church, Bethlehem, Pa. (microfilm); Christopher Gist's First Journal, entry for 20–23 Nov. 1750, and Gist's instructions, in Lois Mulkearn, ed., *George Mercer Papers Relating to the Ohio Company of Virginia* (Pittsburgh, 1954), pp. 9, 7.

opened in a wedge shape, so the colony's charter could be construed to include not only all of the Ohio Valley but also much of the present-day western United States, western Canada, and Alaska. The Iroquois delegation probably assumed it was ceding lands east of the Appalachians only, but the founders of the Ohio Company saw an opportunity and seized it. The Logstown conference was an attempt to confirm the validity of this earlier Iroquois cession and to purchase the compliance of the local Indian population. Thus in June 1752 Christopher Gist, who had by now completed a second reconnoitering expedition in the valley on the company's behalf, stood before representatives of the Mingo, Shawnee, Delaware, and Wyandot Indians at Logstown bearing a large shipment of English merchandise, and earnestly sought to convince them of his good intentions.[3]

The conference quickly reached an impasse. The Virginians explained the Iroquois cession of 1744 and told the assembled Indian leaders that they intended to "make a settlement of British subjects of the south East side of Ohio." In response, the Indians asked that the colony build a "strong house" to supply them with powder and lead, but they refused to approve any other construction or settlement. The Virginians assured the Indians that they would build such a fort, but argued that an adjoining settlement was needed to supply it with provisions. The Indian spokesman replied that the fort alone would be sufficient; with respect to its provisioning, "we will take care that there shall be no scarcity of that kind." Despite all the Virginians' efforts, the assembled Indians refused to approve a new settlement. As the conference neared its close, the Ohio Indians appeared to have faced down the Ohio Company.[4]

But an emerging division among the Ohio Indians gave the company one last opening. The Iroquois council had denied for years that the Ohio Indians could conduct diplomacy for themselves; Iroquois leaders continued to insist that the western Indians were only hunters, young men dependent on the Iroquois for political leadership. But affairs in the west had grown important in their own right, and in 1748 Pennsylvania

---

[3] The proceedings of the 1744 conference are in *Pa. Col. Recs.*, vol. IV, pp. 698–737; quote: p. 726. The Iroquois received £200 worth of merchandise, an equivalent value in gold, and a warriors' right-of-way through Virginia in exchange for their concession. The treaty's context is discussed briefly in Mulkearn, ed., *Mercer Papers*, pp. 530–539, 398–403, and more generally in Francis Jennings, *The Ambiguous Iroquois Empire: The Covenant Chain Confederation of Indian Tribes with English Colonies from its beginnings to the Lancaster Treaty of 1744* (New York, 1984), especially pp. 356–362. Gist's two sets of instructions from the Ohio Company (one of them secret), along with both Minutes and Extracts of the Logstown Conference, are in Mulkearn, ed., *Mercer Papers*, pp. 52–66, 127–138, 176–177.

[4] Logstown minutes, Mulkearn, ed., *Mercer Papers*, pp. 127–138.

finally chose to bypass the Iroquois Council entirely in its dealings with the Indians on the Allegheny and Ohio. Conrad Weiser represented Pennsylvania in that 1748 meeting, also held at Logstown, and he noted the change. "You are now become a people of note & grow very numerous of late years," he told the assembled Indian leaders, "& it becomes you to act the part of wise people & be more regular than you were some years ago, when only a few young hunters lived here." The Iroquois council was infuriated by this development, insisting that the western Indians "were but hunters, and no counsellors, or chief men; and they had no right to receive presents that was due to the Six Nations, although they might receive a share; but that share they must receive from the Six Nations chief under whom they belong." But despite the protests of Iroquois leaders, the Ohio chiefs had already established a measure of political independence from Onondaga; if the Iroquois council did not act quickly to reassert its authority among the Ohio Indians, Iroquois power in the west might soon be eclipsed altogether.[5]

Sometime around 1748 the Iroquois council attempted to do just that. It appointed Tanaghrisson, a Seneca chief, "Half King" for the western Indians. As his title suggests, Tanaghrisson's status was ambiguous: Iroquois leaders expected him to remain subordinate to the Iroquois council, but to be pre-eminent among the Ohio Indians. And indeed, Iroquois power on the Ohio was still substantial enough for Tanaghrisson's new status to be taken seriously by the Indians there; he acted as their chief spokesman at the 1752 conference with the Ohio Company. Publicly he could only express the consensus view of the assembled Indian leaders and resist the Ohio Company's settlement plans. But privately, if the minutes of the conference are to be believed, he expressed a more conciliatory position. Before the company's representatives departed, Tanaghrisson had signed an acknowledgment of the Lancaster deed on behalf of the Ohio Indians.[6]

Following the 1752 conference, mistrust and dissatisfaction toward the British only increased. Although the Virginians promised to build a fort, they soon demonstrated that they were more interested in schemes to engross the Ohio lands than they were in helping the Indians to protect them. While they neglected plans for a fort, agents of the Ohio Company busied themselves with plats, surveys, and maps of the Monongahela region and sought royal approval for a series of grants that would have given it control of the entire eastern half of the Ohio

---

[5] Entry for 17 Sept., Conrad Weiser's Journal, 1748, Weiser Collection, Historical Society of Pennsylvania, Philadelphia; Iroquois Great Council to Weiser, 17 Sept. 1750, quoted in Charles Hanna, *The Wilderness Trail*, 2 vol. (New York, 1911), vol. I, p. 348.

[6] Logstown minutes, Mulkearn, ed., *Mercer Papers*, pp. 127–138.

Valley. The failure to protect the western traders proved costly, as the Logstown chiefs had predicted it would. Between 1749 and 1753, French soldiers and allied Indians from the Great Lakes posts attacked many British trading parties, plundering them of skins, furs, and merchandise, sometimes taking the traders to Canada or even to France as prisoners, and seriously disrupting the Ohio Valley trade. In all, about £48,000 in merchandise, capital, and credit were lost in the French raids, but – to the incredulity of the Ohio Indians – neither Pennsylvania nor Virginia acted to defend the western traders.[7]

The balance of Indian interests on the upper Ohio thus swung decisively against the British colonies between 1752 and 1754, despite the fact that France, too, was asserting its territorial interests in the region more aggressively than ever in these same years. The Marquis Duquesne assumed the governorship of Canada in 1752; a career military man, he was chosen for the post because of his experience and skill as a strategist and a commander. Early in the spring of 1753 he dispatched an expedition of more than a thousand soldiers and *habitants* to build a string of forts from Lake Erie to the forks of the Ohio, in order to secure the French claim to the west. Four posts were built in 1753 and 1754: Forts Presque Isle, Le Boeuf, Machault, and, at the forks of the Ohio, Duquesne. The new outposts offered what the Ohio Indians wanted most: bases for trade and military support, without the threat of territorial expansion. New France had already proven its inability to support an expansive territorial empire; now that it was reasserting its power in the Ohio Valley, the new forts might serve both as protection against British encroachment and as a reliable alternative source of trade goods and diplomatic gifts. The string of French posts was an imposing presence, but it was nevertheless consistent with the Indians' desire to defend their Ohio lands.[8]

Support among the Ohio Indians for a British alliance had already seriously eroded by early 1754; the earliest engagements of the Seven Years' War only accelerated this process and alienated even strongly

---

[7] For the Ohio Company in these years, see Mulkearn, ed., *Mercer Papers*, pp. 66–73, 438–439; for Indians' exasperation at the lack of a fort, Croghan to Richard Peters, 3 Feb. 1754, in Samuel Hazard, ed., *Pennsylvania Archives* [1st Ser.], 12 vols. (Philadelphia, 1852–1856), vol. II, p. 118; for the "suffering traders," Kenneth P. Bailey, ed., *The Ohio Company Papers, 1753–1817: Being Primarily Papers of the "Suffering Traders" of Pennsylvania* (Arcata, CA, 1947); the value of the losses is calculated from pp. 36–162.

[8] For context and narrative, see Francis Parkman, *Montcalm and Wolfe* [orig. pub. 1884], in *France and England in North America* (New York, 1983), vol. II, pp. 903–905 and following; and Francis Jennings, *Empire of Fortune: Crowns, Colonies & Tribes in the Seven Years War in America* (New York, 1988), pp. 50–52 and following.

pro-British leaders like Tanaghrisson. George Washington twice visited the Ohio – first, in the fall of 1753 (when he was only 21 years old) as a representative of Virginia's governor sent to deliver a message to the French, then as the commander of a force of Virginia militia in 1754 – and discovered that the supposedly British-allied Indians there received him with cool suspicion. Tanaghrisson, Washington's only strong supporter among the Ohio Indians, dismissed him as "a good-natured man [who] had no experience." In the following year Major General Edward Braddock's march on Fort Duquesne, which ended in a disastrous defeat, confirmed to the Indians that the British were indifferent to, even contemptuous of, their interests. The imperious, stubborn Braddock assured Shingas, "king" of the Ohio Delawares, that "No Savage Should Inherit the Land" Britain was fighting for. He so alienated every Indian leader he met that, in the end, only eight warriors marched with his army. With near unanimity, the Indians on the upper Ohio concluded that a British alliance was useless to them. The only question that remained was whether to stay neutral or to take up arms against Pennsylvania and Virginia.[9]

A majority of the Pennsylvania Indians on the Susquehanna, who remained in close contact with colonial officials, chose neutrality. Pennsylvania had, on balance, been a good ally to them and they preferred peaceful accommodation with the colony in the emerging conflict between Britain and France. But for the Ohio Indians the imperial war played into old grievances with Pennsylvania, which had never respected Indian land rights; farms now stood everywhere on lands the Indians had been forced to sell. For many warriors on the Ohio, the war between France and Britain offered an opportunity to redress these losses; armed with French weapons, they marched against Pennsylvania to dramatize their sense of displacement and loss. Their enemy was not an army; it was a growing, swarming horde of settlers that seemed to spill everywhere onto lands they once knew as their own.

Beginning in the fall of 1755, war parties from the Ohio descended on the settlements of western Pennsylvania. The colony's frontier had a civilian, rather than a military, character: it was no strong wall of defense, but only a widely scattered, thinly populated stretch of agricultur-

[9] On Washington and the disaster at Fort Necessity in 1754—generally regarded as the first battle of the Seven Years' War, and an embarrassing defeat for the Virginians under his leadership – see Jennings, *Empire of Fortune*, pp. 65–68, quote: p. 66; for defections among the Mingos and Shawnees, Duquesne to Minister, 3 Nov. 1754 and 31 May 1755, in Sylvester Stevens and Donald Kent, eds., *Wilderness Chronicles of Northwestern Pennsylvania* (Harrisburg, 1941), pp. 83–85 and 89–90; on Braddock, see Scarouady's account of his defeat at Turtle Creek in 1755, in Hanna, *Wilderness Trail*, vol. I, p. 233; for the speech to Shingas, Jennings, *Empire of Fortune*, pp. 154–155.

al villages and solitary farms. Under attack there was nowhere to hide. Fearful, distressed inhabitants fled in terror – on Penn's Creek, "some allmost naked and without any thing to support them, reporting that every Indian was our Enemy" – as warriors surprised them in their homes. Everywhere on the frontier people experienced "the utmost confusion imaginable one flying here & the other there for Safety[.]" "News no like," according to Conrad Weiser, "was heard before in pensilvania." Residents petitioned the government for protection, but aid was delayed as the Assembly quarreled with the proprietor, John Penn, about whether his estates could be taxed. The deadlock was broken in November, when a bill to raise £55,000 without taxing proprietary estates was supplemented by a £5,000 gift from Penn. The Assembly immediately created a committee headed by Benjamin Franklin to manage the colony's defense. Its first act was to raise 300 frontier rangers to build and defend a series of blockhouses. Soon the frayed nerves of frontier residents were soothed somewhat by the construction of a string of forts guarding the passes through the Kittatinny Mountains, manned by hastily mustered militia forces.[10]

But the colony's new defenses were quite porous. Frontier raiding persisted and intensified for two years, and in that time the rhythms of the war, and the political developments they inspired, shook the colony to its foundations. In April, 1756, Governor Morris formally declared war on the hostile Delawares and their allies, and offered bounties for Indian scalps and prisoners. The decision outraged Pennsylvania's Quakers and strengthened a movement within the sect favoring withdrawal from politics. Most Quakers in the Assembly chose not to stand for re-election in October, ending the Quaker domination of provincial politics that dated back to the founding of the colony. In the meantime, the raiding only intensified; that summer, French and Indian raiders destroyed Fort Granville on the Juniata River and burned everything but the fort at Lebanon, within 75 miles of Philadelphia itself. Hundreds of captives and scalps flowed from the Pennsylvania backcountry to Fort Duquesne. While Quaker leaders channeled their energies into the new-

[10] On Pennsylvania's scattered settlement pattern generally, see James T. Lemon, *The Best Poor Man's Country: A Geographical Study of Early Southeastern Pennsylvania* (New York, 1972), especially ch. 4. Quotes: Conrad Weiser to Gov. Morris, 5 Jan. 1756, Weiser Collection, vol. I, p. 63, HSP; Timothy Horsfield to Gov., 27 Nov. 1755, Horsfield Papers, vol. I, pp. 67–68, American Philosophical Society, Philadelphia; Weiser to Morris, 5 Jan. 1756. Petitions: see, e.g., James Read, Conrad Weiser, et al. to Gov., 31 Oct. 1755, and Timothy Horsfield to Gov., 26 Nov. 1755, Horsfield Papers, vol. I, pp. 33–34, 55–58, APS. Assembly debates: *Pa. Col. Recs.*, vol. VI, pp. 738–743. Defenses: Franklin to William Parsons, 5 Dec. 1755, and Horsfield to Parsons, 25 Jan. 1756, Horsfield Papers, vol. I, pp. 78–88, 99–100, APS.

ly created Friendly Association for Regaining and Preserving Peace with the Indians by Pacific Measures, seeking to open diplomatic channels with the Ohio Indians through the Delawares who still remained in the Susquehanna Valley, the colony strengthened its commitment to the war.[11]

For two years the war intensified as ferocious raids repeatedly struck into the Pennsylvania countryside, menacing long-established communities and terrorizing backcountry residents. In August, 1756, Pennsylvania forces mounted their only significant counteroffensive of the war when Colonel John Armstrong led three hundred provincials against Kittanning, the principal Delaware town on the Allegheny River for more than 30 years and home to Shingas and Captain Jacobs, two of the most troubling Delaware war leaders. Armstrong's men suffered considerably – they absorbed perhaps 40 casualties – but they recovered 11 captive colonists and came away with 12 or so Indian scalps. They also killed Captain Jacobs himself, then burned the entire town. The attack set Kittanning's residents to flight and the townsite was abandoned, but the raids against Pennsylvania only grew worse.[12]

Quaker negotiators were pursuing, at the same time, a more promising route to peace. They had opened negotiations with the eastern Delaware spokesman Teedyuscung, who saw in their overtures an opportunity to strengthen his people's hand in their relations with Pennsylvania. Recognizing that his ability to mediate an agreement between the colony and the Ohio Indians gave him considerable leverage, Teedyuscung cooperated with the peace effort in order to strengthen the eastern Indians' position. His principal concern, and one in which he was supported by the anti-proprietary Quakers who were organizing negotiations between the eastern Delawares and the colony, was to force the Penns to admit that the Walking Purchase had been fraudulent, and to win a compensatory grant of more than two million acres in the Wyoming Valley on the upper Susquehanna. Though he received no guarantees, Governor William Denny promised to re-open the Indian trade at Fort Augusta, near the Susquehanna trading town of Shamokin, to review the circumstances of the Walking Purchase, and to ensure that

---

[11] Robert Davidson, *War Comes to Quaker Pennsylvania, 1682–1756* (New York, 1957), pp. 175–196; Theodore Thayer, *Israel Pemberton, King of the Quakers* (Philadelphia, 1943); Jack Marietta, *The Reformation of American Quakerism, 1748–1783* (Philadelphia, 1984), pp. 150–168. The colony offered £150 for male prisoners above 10 years; £130 for women and children captured alive or for scalps of males over 10; and £50 for scalps of women and children.

[12] For a good account of the war see Stephen Auth, *The Ten Years' War: Indian-White Relations in Pennsylvania, 1755–1756* (New York, 1989); Davidson, *War Comes to Quaker Pennsylvania*, pp. 185–186.

ample hunting grounds would be reserved for the eastern Delawares.[13]

These negotiations eventually opened the door to talks with the formerly Pennsylvania-allied Ohio Indians. As with the eastern Delawares, the war had badly strained the resources of the Ohio Indians. For three years their lives had been disrupted by war. After being driven from Kittanning in 1756, in the summer of 1758 a force of Ohio warriors and their French allies were defeated at Fort Ligonier, a loss that "caused the utmost consternation among the natives." Half a dozen or more villages on the Allegheny and upper Ohio, including Logstown, were abandoned following the battle. Their residents burned houses and fields behind them and moved to the Muskingum River a hundred and fifty miles to the west. Early in the fall of the same year, as General John Forbes began to prepare for a full-scale assault on Fort Duquesne, Pennsylvania sent a Moravian missionary named Christian Frederick Post to discuss the possibility of a peace settlement with the Ohio Indians.[14]

In General Forbes' mind an agreement with Pennsylvania's former allies was critical to the success of his campaign against Fort Duquesne, and he pressured Governor Denny to offer them terms. For the Ohio Indians, the offer was appealing. Their frontier raids had inflicted considerable damage on backcountry settlements, but their own strategic position had only deteriorated; now, with Forbes' army on the march, they faced the possibility that Britain might be able to impose conquerors' terms on them. The negotiators, on the other hand, offered an agreement that promised to recognize and secure the interests of the Ohio Indians in a way that Britain's colonies had never before been willing to do. For decades the Ohio Indians had struggled to free themselves from Iroquois domination and to gain independent recognition as sovereign authorities over their own affairs. The peace overture that came in the fall of 1758 offered the Ohio Indians the possibility that Iroquois hegemony might finally be broken, and that they would be recognized as autonomous actors, sovereign in their own political affairs.[15]

---

13 For these negotiations see especially Anthony F. C. Wallace, *King of the Delawares: Teedyuscung, 1700–1763* (Syracuse, 1990 [orig. pub. 1949]), and Auth, *Ten Years' War*, pp. 62–76.

14 "The Narrative of Marie LeRoy and Barbara Leininger, for Three Years Captives Among the Indians," *Pennsylvania Magazine of History and Biography*, 29 (1905), 410–412. For accounts of the Forbes campaign see Parkman, *Montcalm and Wolfe*, vol. II, pp. 1132–1134, 1285–1307; and Jennings, *Empire of Fortune*, pp. 200, 406–411. The journals kept by Post during his two trips to the Ohio between July 1758 and January 1759 are printed in Thwaites, ed., *Early Western Travels*, vol. I, pp. 175–191.

15 For an excellent discussion of the complex politics of this campaign and its implications for Pennsylvania's Indian relations, see Jennings, *Empire of Fortune*, pp. 369–404.

At the last moment Pennsylvania officials made a key concession that seemed to confirm this possibility. In 1754, in an effort to forestall the purchase of the Wyoming Valley by a company of Connecticut adventurers, Conrad Weiser had hastily arranged with a group of Iroquois leaders to buy nearly all of present-day Pennsylvania west of the Susquehanna on behalf of the colony, including the Allegheny and the forks of the Ohio. Such a purchase agreement with the Iroquois implicitly denied the western Indians' claim to own those lands, and reinforced the diplomatic fiction of the Covenant Chain. In the fall of 1758, with the prospect of a truce at hand, Governor Denny and his council publicly repudiated the purchase and returned the lands west of the Allegheny Mountains to the Ohio Indians. With that measure of assurance that they would be masters of their own affairs in dealing with the British colonies, the Indians on the upper Ohio, led by Tamaqua and his brothers, Shingas and Pisquetomen, abandoned the French and re-allied themselves with the British crown.[16]

The decision by the leaders of the Ohio Indians to accept Pennsylvania's offer "struck the French a stunning blow." The commander of Fort Duquesne, undermanned and ill-supplied, was forced by their defection to abandon the post without a fight. His men destroyed the fortification, burned the buildings, and fled during the night.[17] This victory was a crucial turning point for the British war effort in the American theater; the Ohio Indians hoped that it would mark a turning point in their relationship with Britain and its American colonies as well.

II

The peace of 1758 suggested the possibility that Britain and its colonies might establish a new equilibrium in their relations with the Ohio Indians. The Seven Years' War dramatized the need for a new settlement, one that placed a premium on better communication, adjudication, and conflict resolution between Indians and colonists; it also served as a catharsis for dispossessed Indians, who lashed out against past grievances but also held out hope for a better future. But for backcountry set-

---

[16] The initial purchase is described in *Pa. Col. Recs.*, VI, pp. 110–123. The agreement to return the Ohio lands came at the Easton treaty in October; the treaty minutes are in *Pa. Col. Recs.*, VIII, pp. 174–223; references to the land cession are on pp. 218–219 and following. The best account of these events is in Michael McConnell, *A Country Between: The Upper Ohio Valley and Its Peoples, 1724–1774* (Lincoln, NE, 1992), pp. 113–141; see also Paul A.W. Wallace, *Conrad Weiser: Friend of Colonist and Mohawk* (Philadelphia, 1945), pp. 350–363, 551.

[17] Henry Bouquet to William Allen, 25 Nov. 1758, quoted in Parkman, *Montcalm and Wolfe*, vol. II, p. 1306.

tlers, the war was no catharsis; it was an unparalleled catastrophe that clearly demonstrated the folly of cooperating with Indians. For settlers, the peace of 1758 created an opening, not to restore equilibrium, but to resume the pursuit of Indian lands. Despite the potential inherent in the peace of 1758, the war experience poisoned intercultural relations in the Pennsylvania backcountry; the events that followed only deepened the gulf between Indians and colonists, and clarified the distinction between those in each group that advocated accommodation, on the one hand, and those arguing for aggressive separatism on the other.

Initially, Ohio Indian leaders contemplated a postwar settlement that would have guaranteed their sovereign control over the Allegheny and Ohio lands, at the same time that it implied a substantial degree of Indian acculturation to a European form of political economy. Delaware leaders seem to have been particularly drawn to this formula, perhaps because their long history of peaceful assocation with Europeans in Pennsylvania allowed them to avoid the extreme hostility that circulated in some dispossessed Indian groups. Thus, even at the height of the border raids during the Seven Years' War, the Delaware chief and war leader Shingas was formulating an acceptable postwar settlement. What he wanted sounds deceptively simple: he wanted the British colonies to respect the independence of the western Indians and their right to control their own lands. In the Ohio Valley, after all, the Delawares and Shawnees had established a liberating distance from the colonial settlements that had displaced them. Hunters and warriors had returned to supposedly traditional pursuits, and enjoyed extraordinary success in them. After the war, Shingas hoped his people could follow these pursuits without interference.[18]

There was a paradox in this vision, which Shingas recognized and tried to account for. The revival of apparently "traditional" and autonomous Indian communities in the Ohio Valley was driven by opportunities to trade for European goods, and the efficiency of Indian hunters was tremendously enhanced by their use of European weapons. The hunter-trader culture of the Ohio Valley was erected on the foundation of European trade, and to maintain it required a steady supply of European goods. Shingas did not advocate withdrawal from European influence. On the contrary, he hoped that the colonies might be persuaded to send a handful of craftsmen among the Ohio Indians, who could manufacture gunpowder, smelt lead and iron, weave blankets, and make and mend guns. In the longer term, Shingas thought, some of these skills

---

[18] This and the following paragraphs are based on the conversation reported in "The Captivity of Charles Stuart, 1755–1757," Beverley W. Bond, Jr., ed., *Mississippi Valley Historical Review*, 13 (1926), 58–81; quotes: pp. 64–65.

might be taught to the Indians themselves by Englishmen who would "Come and Settle among them with their Families and Promote Spinning for Shirts and in Gen[era]l . . . Bring all Kinds of Trades among them that they might be Supplied with what they want near home." Throughout this experiment in intercultural cooperation, Shingas expected – in yet another faint echo of William Penn – that the Ohio Indians and the small group of Englishmen among them ought to be able to "Live Together in Love and Freindship and Become one people[.] But the Indians," added the Pennsylvanian who recorded his conversation with Shingas, "did not Insist nor Desire that the English sho[ul]d Be obliged to Intermarry with them[.]"[19] Ambivalent to the end, Shingas grappled with the problem of how to maintain autonomy and exchange at the same time.

His ambivalence was characteristic of the Indians who settled the peace with Pennsylvania in 1758. Even as they withdrew from the French alliance, they sought guarantees that their territorial rights would be respected. Immediately they found themselves at odds with British leadership. The Indians, "always jealous the *English* will take the land from us," wanted the British troops to withdraw from the Forks. Instead Forbes named the spot Pittsburgh to honor the mastermind of the British war effort, and set his men to the task of building a fort of their own. Several Indian leaders, including the Delaware Pisquetomen, indignantly objected. They were reassured by George Croghan, Andrew Montour, and Christian Frederick Post, who insisted that the British had no designs on their lands. Like Fort Duquesne, this would be a military and trading outpost without territorial implications. And "you know yourselves," Post reminded the Delaware leaders, "that you cannot do without being supplied with such goods as you stand in need of."[20]

And indeed, the prospect of hospitality at Fort Pitt helped to offset the Indians' concerns. It had always been understood that western posts existed at the sufferance of the local Indians, and one of the ways European post commanders enacted their awareness of this fact was through a familiar round of gift-giving occasions: gifts to confirm alliances or seal treaties, to supply allied Indian warriors, or simply for the sake of hospitality to traveling parties of hunters or warriors. By late 1758 the Indians in the upper Ohio Valley badly needed hospitality. The fighting had disrupted both agriculture and hunting; their deprivation was so severe that they were periodically "forced to live on acorns, roots, grass,

---

[19] "Captivity of Charles Stuart," p. 65.
[20] Post's second journal, 3 Nov. 1758 (quoting Pisquetomen) and 27 Nov. 1758, in Thwaites, ed., *Early Western Travels*, vol. I, pp. 240, 272.

and bark." For many Indians of the upper Ohio, diplomatic conferences at Fort Pitt became opportunities for sustenance. George Croghan arrived at the fort in the summer of 1759 as deputy to William Johnson, recently appointed the crown's first superintendent of Indian affairs for the northern colonies; Croghan was familiar both with the plight of the Ohio Indians and with their expectations, and he ordered large stocks of goods to be dispensed at every diplomatic occasion he sponsored. Following his first official conference with the Ohio Indians, large encampments of Shawnees, Delawares, and Mingos remained at the fort for a week. Colonel Hugh Mercer, the fort's commander, explained to his superior officer that the Indians were "starving when at home, thro' the loss of their Corn felds last fall, and come with Shoals of useless fry to prey upon us" when the opportunity arose. "It is not in my power," he wrote anxiously on another such occasion, "to prevent an Extravagant Consumption of Provisions."[21]

Croghan's extravagance could soon be quantified by the accounts he sent to his superiors. In the first five months of 1760, in *addition* to the large stocks of goods he dispensed on official occasions, Croghan spent more than £1,500 on randomly distributed gifts. In the summer of 1761, Croghan and Johnson sponsored a particularly expensive meeting with the Indians in the vicinity of Detroit; their accounts caught the eye of General Jeffery Amherst, Britain's supreme commander for North America, and spurred him to promote a more stringent regimen of economy in Indian relations.[22] A conqueror rather than a counsellor, Amherst possessed few of the skills and little of the wisdom expected of a peacetime leader in the west. Nor was he attuned to the messy ambiguities of intercultural alliances. Compulsive and detail-oriented, Amherst turned to the problem of economy with characteristic energy and pusillanimity. Issues of economy led him to consider questions of morality, questions of morality to systems of regulation. In the end, the problem of Indian expenses led Amherst to formulate a new regulatory system for Indian affairs, which radically changed the nature of diplomatic relations and the terms of intercultural trade in the Ohio Valley.

21 "Narrative of Marie LeRoy and Barbara Leininger," p. 410; Mercer to Bouquet, 15 Aug. and 8 Jan. 1759, in S.K. Stevens et al., eds., *The Papers of Henry Bouquet*, 5 vols. (Harrisburg, 1972–1984), vol. III, pp. 565–566, 23–24.

22 For expensive treaties see, e.g., Conference Minutes, 7 Aug. 1759, at Pittsburgh, *Bouquet Papers*, vol. III, pp. 507–511, and Horatio Gates to Croghan, 8 June 1760, Cadwallader Collection, Box 6, HSP. £1,500: "The Crown to George Croghan . . . for Goods Purchased . . . ," Cadwallader Collection, Box 5, HSP. Detroit treaty: Johnson to Amherst, 7 June 1761; Amherst to Johnson, 11 June 1761; conference minutes, 9–11 Sept. 1761; Johnson to Amherst, 7 Jan. 1762; in James Sullivan et al., eds., *The Papers of Sir William Johnson*, 14 vols. (Albany, 1921–1965), vol. X, pp. 277–279, 284–286; vol. III, pp. 474–493, 598–601.

Amherst was troubled by both the expense and the moral implications of imperial largesse. As he began to consider the problem, he concluded that small presents to Indian allies were acceptable on occasion,
but he preferred "Steady, Uniform, and friendly" dealings to extravagant displays. It was especially important to Amherst that the British
not be reduced "to purchasing the good behavior" of their erstwhile allies if their loyalties were otherwise questionable. "[W]hen men of what
race soever behave ill," he wrote to Johnson, "they must be punished
not bribed." Amherst did not want the British to appear overindulgent
or weak. Nor did he want to encourage the Indians to believe that they
could get what they needed from the British for free, so that they would
"grow remiss in their hunting." As his initial musings hardened into
policy, the idea of substituting rewarded labor for largesse assumed a
central role in his thinking. In August 1761 he officially outlawed all
gift-giving at the western posts. In part he seems to have believed that
this policy would provide Britain's Indian allies with a good moral lesson, but he was also making a strategic calculation. If the Indians had to
hunt and trade for European merchandise, he reasoned, they would be
"more Constantly Employed by means of which they will have less time
to concert, or Carry into Execution any Schemes prejudicial to his
Majestys Interests." At the same time, Amherst instructed Johnson to
oversee a new system for regulating the Indian trade. He left most of the
details to Johnson, but specified that it should include a provision to
keep the Indians "scarce of Ammunition." In the end, he persuaded
himself that a policy of economy, in addition to its obvious benefits to
the crown, would also make better, less scheming allies of the Ohio Indians.[23]

Whatever the need for economy in the British empire, in this last calculation Amherst could not have been more self-deceived: Indian relations were irremediably soured by his new policies. Most destructive
was the effort to keep the Ohio Indians short of ammunition. Gifts of
powder and lead were prohibited outright, and limits were placed on
their trade. Beginning in the fall of 1761 each customer at a British post
was allowed a maximum of five pounds of powder and five pounds of
lead per visit. The policy also included provisions to make the new regulations easier to enforce. At Pittsburgh, for example, trading was prohibited after sundown. Even more damaging to established practices
was a ban on trading with the Indians in their own villages; traders'
passes now stipulated that they could do business only at British gar-
risons. These regulations were surely violated in countless ways – sever-

[23] Amherst to Johnson, 22 Feb. 1761, 11 June 1761, and 9 Aug. 1761, *Johnson Papers*,
   vol. III, pp. 343–347; vol. X, pp. 284–286; vol. III, pp. 514–516.

al traders headquartered at Pittsburgh, in fact, did very well in these
years – but long-established patterns of trade were seriously disrupted,
and the Ohio Indians had to shoulder taxing new burdens. To trade,
they had to travel to the posts; to hunt, they had to husband their powder and lead with extraordinary efficiency. Many could no longer make
ends meet. Simon Levy, one of Pittsburgh's most prominent traders, was
forced to stop extending credit to his customers when they began to fail
regularly in their obligations, "producing dissatisfaction on both
sides."[24]

In the lower valley conditions were even worse. Thomas Hutchins
toured the western posts in his capacity as assistant Indian agent and
found their residents unhappy and suspicious of British policy. At
Kekionga near Fort Miamis, at Ouiatanon, and at the Shawnee town of
Chillicothe, he heard the universal complaint that "the Traders [were]
not allowed even to take so much Ammunition with them as to enable
those Indians to kill game sufficient for the Support of their families."
Their earlier experience with the French only sharpened the Indians' dissatisfaction; Hutchins wrote that they had been accustomed to receive
"great Presents three or four times a Year, and always a sufficient Quantity of Ammunition at the Posts." Amherst's abrupt decision to cut off
diplomatic gifts and restrict trade appeared "very Strange."[25]

At the same time, the Indians on the upper Ohio observed a steady
erosion of their territorial control as British encroachments proceeded
with remarkable speed. "Piggons" indeed: colonists followed one another in flocks. Beginning in 1759, despite the terrors of the recent war, settlers repopulated western Pennsylvania with astonishing speed. Braddock's and Forbes' Roads, which cut passable swaths through the
forested mountains beyond the Susquehanna, each served as a vital axis
along which settlement progressed all the way to the Forks of the Ohio.
Almost overnight a village grew up outside the walls at Fort Pitt; by the
summer of 1761, fields of corn, hay, and other crops surrounded the
town, a sawmill and an open-pit coal mine were operating, and soldiers
at the fort were quarrying stone and lime and baking bricks. In the
spring a census of households already listed a hundred and sixty houses.
Nor did the colonists confine themselves to the land around the fort.

---

[24] "The Journal of James Kenny, 1761–1763," John W. Jordan, ed., *Pennsylvania Magazine of History and Biography*, 37 (1913), 28; Johnson to Amherst, 24 Nov. 1762, and
Croghan to Amherst, 5 Oct. 1762, *Johnson Papers*, vol. III, pp. 884–886, vol. X, pp.
543–544; Kenny's Journal, 1761–63, 163. For one exception to the ban on sending
traders to Indian towns, see "George Croghan's Journal, 1759–63," Nicholas B. Wainwright, ed., *PMHB*, 71 (1947), 417.

[25] "Journal and Report of Thomas Hutchins," 4 Apr.-24 Sept. 1762, *Johnson Papers*, vol.
X, pp. 521–529; quotes: p. 529.

Virginians and Pennsylvanians began appearing singly, in pairs, in small groups, in isolated river valleys and meadows beyond the Alleghenies. Some suffered for their presumptions; two Virginians who set up a squatter's camp on a tributary of the Monongahela were soon discovered dead. "It grieves ye Indians," the trader James Kenny observed when he heard this news, "to see ye White People Settle on these Lands & follow Hunting or Planting."[26]

The Indians around Fort Pitt reacted to British presumptions by trying to undermine the security of their settlements, by seeking to confuse, threaten, frighten, and sometimes kill the trespassers among them. In the final stages of the Seven Years' War, the officers at Fort Pitt employed Delawares, Mingos, and Shawnees as spies. It was a baffling and unsuccessful experiment: the Indians withheld information, provided inconsistent reports of French activities, and created false alarms at the fort. "It is much easier to relate the Intelligence I receive," Mercer wrote with some exasperation, "than [to] reconcile the Inconsistencies of it." If a resident of the fort was mysteriously killed while he was out on his own, it was assumed that he was killed by a French-allied war party – but no one could be entirely sure. Horses disappeared from the fort with alarming frequency. Occupants of Fort Pitt anxiously studied the moods and comportment of visiting Indians, who seemed always to be *en masque*. Some were "sulky," "saucy," "churlish," "threatening"; others "seemed well pleased," "came . . . singing," "appear[ed] very hearty in our interest." Subtle shadings of temper were read like omens, as fort residents anticipated the possibility of attack without knowing for sure who the enemy might be. After several months of such experiences, Mercer wrote angrily to his superior that he could "promise you little, from the Indians this way. They speak fair to us, and at home are full of Caballs, and propagate a thousand lies, to sharpen each others resentment against us."[27]

The cabals, lies, and resentments reflected the Indians' deep misgivings about British encroachments in the valley. Not satisfied with a foothold at Fort Pitt, soldiers were soon pressing still farther into the valley in search of strategic fort sites. In 1762 a detachment from Fort

---

[26] Kenny's Journal, 1761–1763, pp. 6, 14, 27–29, 152; "List of Houses and Inhabitants at Fort Pitt," 14 Apr. 1761, *Bouquet Papers*, vol. V, pp. 407–421.

[27] Forbes to Bouquet, 14 Jan. 1759, and Mercer to Bouquet, 17 Feb. 1759, *Bouquet Papers*, vol. III, pp. 49–54, 129–131; Croghan to Bouquet, 10 Dec. 1762, *Johnson Papers*, vol. X, pp. 596–598; "James Kenny's 'Journal to Ye Westward,' 1758–1759," John W. Jordan, ed., *PMHB*, 37 (1913), pp. 422–424 and following; Mercer to Bouquet, 12 May 1759, *Bouquet Papers*, vol. III, p. 277.

Pitt went to build a blockhouse at Sandusky, about 150 miles northwest of Pittsburgh on the shores of Lake Erie. They were not received kindly. The lieutenant in charge reported that the local residents (likely a mixed population of Wyandots, Mingos, and perhaps Delawares) "fretted him much, wanting Gifts, Provissions &c which he had not to give them." He and his men managed to finish their job without coming to harm, but the lieutenant "says he would sooner be discharg'd then go on such Business again."[28]

Nor was the army the only aggressor; by 1762, Moravian missionaries were moving into the valley, where a few baptized Indians had already relocated and other potential converts seemed close at hand. They did not encounter hostility to their gospel, so much as deep-seated misgivings about their uses of the land. After John Heckewelder and Christian Frederick Post arrived in the town of Tuscarawas on the Muskingum River, they hired a man to help them clear a three-acre plot for planting corn. The Indians immediately became "alarmed": "instead of instructing us or our children," the local Delawares complained, "you are cutting trees down on our land! you have marked out a large spot of ground for a plantation, as the white people do everywhere; and bye and bye another, and another, may come and do the same." Eventually, they predicted, "a fort will be built for the protection of these intruders, and thus our country will be claimed by white people."[29]

But despite their misgivings, the Indians at Tuscawaras did not drive Heckewelder and Post off. Instead, the Delaware council granted them a 50-pace-square garden plot. What they could not grow there they would have to obtain from the Indians – a difficult proposition, at least for the moment, since a famine currently prevailed and there was no corn to spare. Post, who had some experience with the Ohio Indians, also warned Heckewelder that he must not let the Indians see him reading or writing. They believe, Post told Heckewelder – in a tradition that recalled the Walking Purchase, as well as Christopher Gist's travels in the valley – "that it concerns them or their territory. They say that they have been robbed of their lands by the writing of whites." Heckewelder lasted a year at Tuscarawas, but it was a miserable year, full of uneasiness and hardship, which he survived only through the ocasional hospitality of a group of traders who maintained a post nearby. Finally he fled in

---

[28] Kenny's Journal, 1761–63, 39–40.
[29] John Heckewelder, *A Narrative of the Mission of the United Brethren Among the Delaware and Mohegan Indians, from Its Commencement, in the Year 1741, to the Close of the Year 1808* (Philadelphia, 1820 [repr. New York, 1971]), pp. 59–64; quotes: pp. 61–62.

response to rumors of an impending uprising against the British intrusions into the valley.[30]

The rumors were not without foundation. The years since 1758 had been increasingly desperate and dispiriting ones for the Ohio Indians. Throughout the winter and spring of 1759, the villages of the upper Ohio suffered the effects of crop loss as a result of the previous year's fighting. In 1762 famine and disease worked together in the valley and struck especially hard in the west. Ouiatanon, Kekionga, and Chillicothe were paralyzed by sickness and hunger. The men of the villages, as Thomas Hutchins noted, being "mostly sick[,] ... could not hunt to support their families." Nor could women plant, which would mean hunger for the future as well as the present. At Ouiatanon nearly everyone was sick, and many had recently died; by fall the epidemic had killed 150 men at Chillicothe – more than a third of the adult male population – and a comparable number of women and children.[31]

Everywhere, privation and disease were blamed in part on the severe restrictions on trade and gifts at the British posts. To restore the health and strength of the Ohio Indians, shamans concluded that it was necessary to purge their lands of the British affliction. At Pittsburgh, and also at Fort Ligonier in western Pennsylvania, holy men cursed the soldiers and settlers; at Ligonier a subtle poison was introduced "with much difficulty" into the water supply – all "to no effect." One possible conclusion was that Indian witchcraft could not harm Europeans; these failures gave some Ohio Indians "a Strong opinnion of ye White People," according to one report.[32] But another possibility was that the afflictions and powerlessness of the Indians reflected their own failings: They were suffering the effects of cultural impurity, introduced by their willingness to embrace European ways and to forget their own culture. To resist British encroachments, the Ohio Indians had to reaffirm the sources of their own spiritual authority and cultural power.

Cultural purification required visions of renewal. To discover such visions, the Indians of the upper Ohio did not have far to look. Prophetic traditions had been circulating for more than a decade among some Delawares – particularly in places that had experienced extensive contact with British traders and Christian missionaries – which had particular relevance for the circumstances in which the Ohio Indians now

[30] Paul A.W. Wallace, *Thirty Thousand Miles With John Heckewelder* (Philadelphia, 1958), pp. 36–68; quote: p. 64.

[31] Hutchins' Journal, *Johnson Papers*, vol. X, pp. 521–529; Kenny's Journal, 1761–1763, 177–178.

[32] Post's Journal, 1758, Thwaites, ed., *Early Western Travels*, vol. I, p. 230; Kenny's Journal, 1761–1763, 19.

found themselves. As Gregory Dowd has demonstrated, visionary movements began to gain influence at least as early as 1745, when the encroachment of colonists on Delaware lands created new pressures for the Indians on the Susquehanna River. These visions offer an extraordinary example of cultural cross-fertilization; though they were espoused by people Dowd terms "nativists" – prophets interested in restoring "traditional" ways in the face of growing European influence – in content and form they were often deeply marked by the influence of Christian missionaries, who sought to transform the spiritual world of the Delawares through their preaching. It is one of the rich ironies of this era of intercultural contact that the most powerful calls for a return to a purer, "traditional" culture among the Ohio Indians were themselves shaped in fundamental ways by Christian visionary and preaching traditions.[33]

The earliest of these Indian prophets preached relatively apolitical messages. Most emphasized the evils of the alcohol trade, and insisted that Indians' spiritual power was sapped by its enervating effects. For the sake of alcohol, these preachers argued, Indians overhunted the land and drove away the game; under its influence their communities fell into violent discord. Influenced by visions of the Master of Life, Indian prophets began to preach abstinence and sought to ban alcohol from their communities. This simple message could be a very powerful one – the disorders alcohol caused in Indian towns could be severe – and a few of the prophets gained influence among their people. Gradually their prescriptions for change became more comprehensive and more radical. As early as 1751, one Delaware prophetess was arguing that the Master of Life, the Great Power, had created not a single race of man, but three distinct races – "the indians, the negro, and the white man" – and that each had its own proper forms of worship and ways of life.[34] Such a message directly challenged those who advocated accommodation with the colonies. Separate creations implied separate societies, separate territories, and separate cultures. If cultural differences were fundamental and not the result of historical developments, then political accommodation and cultural borrowing no longer appeared to be a benign way

---

[33] Gregory Dowd, *A Spirited Resistance: The North American Indian Struggle for Unity, 1745–1815* (Baltimore, 1992), pp. 27–33; Anthony Wallace was the first historian to comment upon the "syncretic" qualities of this prophetic tradition in his discussion of the Delaware Neolin; see *The Death and Rebirth of the Seneca* (New York, 1970), pp. 117–121. On this point see also Richard White, *The Middle Ground: Indians, Empires, and Republics in the Great Lakes Region, 1650–1815* (New York, 1991), pp. 279–281 and following.

[34] On the alcohol trade, its effects, and Indian temperance see Peter Mancall, *Deadly Medicine: Indians and Alcohol in Early America* (Cornell, 1995); Dowd, *Spirited Resistance*, pp. 27–30; quote: p. 30.

to avoid conflict. Instead they were evil, violations of a sacred boundary that separated distinct peoples from one another. The radical potential of this doctrine would be fully realized 12 years later in the Ohio Valley.

The man most closely identified with calls for cultural renewal among the Ohio Indians in the early 1760s was a Delaware prophet named Neolin. From his home on the Tuscarawas River, Neolin's reputation and influence spread quickly in the era of hardship following the French evacuation of Fort Duquesne. His moral authority stemmed from a vision in which the Master of Life appeared to him. The Master of Life confirmed Neolin's fears that his people were slipping into evils that would destroy their communities and sap their spiritual power. He described the universe as it had been at the creation, catalogued the errors into which Neolin's people had fallen, and offered a prescription for moral reform and spiritual renewal. To represent the vision to listeners, Neolin drew a map depicting the pathway of the soul to heaven. The Indians had once enjoyed a direct and simple route to heaven, according to Neolin, but Europeans had introduced them to "sins and vices" – represented by white slashes across the old way – that blocked their ascent and forced them to discover a new path. The drawing also illustrated this second path, which required the Indians to adopt new rituals and disciplines in order to avoid the temptations of European vices.[35]

What is initially most striking about Neolin's prescription for renewal is the extent to which it departed from earlier practices and conceptions – from "traditional" Delaware notions of spirituality – even as it promised to restore "traditional" sources of power and authority. Neolin was guided to his knowledge of the universe, not by a manitou – a personal spirit – but by a supreme being. (He condemned the standard invocation of a manitou in a warrior's preparation for battle – a manitou, according to the Master of Life, was "an evil spirit who prompts you to do nothing but wrong" – and advocated prayer to the Master of Life himself in its place.) The earthly world Neolin described was bounded by heaven and hell, and moral imperatives were central to the message he carried to his followers. One of those imperatives was the by-now familiar injunction against drinking, but Neolin also condemned taking more than one wife and Indians' quarreling among

---

[35] The most comprehensive description of the vision, upon which this account is based, is in [Robert Navarre], "The Journal of Pontiac's Conspiracy," in Milo M. Quaife, ed., *The Siege of Detroit in 1763* (Chicago, 1958), pp. 8–17; the map is described in Kenny's Journal, 1761–1763, 171–173. See also John Heckewelder, *History, Manners, and Customs of the Indian Nations Who Once Inhabited Pennsylvania and the Neighboring States*, rev. ed., Memoirs of the Historical Society of Pennsylvania, vol. XII (Philadelphia, 1876 [orig. pub. 1818]), pp. 291–293.

themselves. Like earlier prophets, he believed that Indians and Europeans were created as different peoples, with distinct territories and cultures. Europeans who sought to take possession of Indian lands violated
the balance of the universe and invited the wrath of the Master of Life;
but the Indians, too, were responsible for violating the natural order.
They now relied on guns and powder as a substitute for the bows and
arrows that the Master of Life had given their forefathers; as a result,
game was driven "to the depths of the forest," and would return only
when the Indians returned to the path the Master of Life had established
for them.[36]

To restore power to the Delaware people, Neolin devised a regimen
that was adopted "by their Whole Nation" in 1763. For seven years,
Delaware boys were to be trained in the use of a bow and arrow; during
this time, they would live entirely upon dried meat, and they would
drink a bitter black drink made with roots, plants, and water – an emetic intended to purge the young men of European impurities. At the end
of their seven-year training, the young Delawares, it was hoped, would
be freed from their dependence on Europeans; they were expected to
"quit all Commerce with ye White People & Clothe themselves with
Skins." Here Neolin's emphasis on moral reformation among Indians as
individuals – clearly an inheritance of Christian influence – merged with
a more traditional emphasis on ritual observances that could serve to restore spiritual power to the group as a whole.[37]

The appeal of Neolin's syncretic, nativist gospel was contagious
among the Ohio Indians. He traveled widely throughout the upper valley in the early 1760s, and his map of the universe was copied and
passed from hand to hand among his followers. As his message was dis-
seminated, its emphases also shifted. Neolin's initial concern was for reform among the Delawares; for example, he declared that the bitter
emetic he introduced among them would be a poison to members of
other tribes. But his teachings were double-headed, and could be interpreted another way: The Master of Life emphasized the differences between Indians and Europeans, not those among various Indian tribes; in
fact, he advocated intertribal peace and cooperation. Above all, in Neolin's rendering, the Master of Life wanted Indians to cooperate in resisting European cultural influences and in combatting – by force, if necessary – British encroachments onto Indian lands. This strain of Neolin's
message deeply influenced many Indians around Fort Pitt, and also at
Detroit, where Amherst's innovations in imperial policy created hard-

[36] [Navarre], "Pontiac's Conspiracy," pp. 14–16.
[37] Kenny's Journal, 1761–1763, 188.

ship and resentment among people long accustomed to close contact with the French.[38]

Then, in early 1763, came news that the Seven Years' War was finally over: France had given up the fight and was now negotiating a peace. (Later in the year, in the Treaty of Paris, France would cede all of its territorial claims in North America east of the Mississippi to Great Britain.) Word of France's defeat panicked many formerly French-allied Indians; it appeared essential that the Indians set aside their various conflicts and unite to oppose British power in the Ohio Valley with force. Secret belts had been passed from village to village throughout the west for several years advocating just such a union, but to no effect. The French loss provided a new, stronger motive for resistance: British power was now unopposed by any other European nation in the west. Neolin's gospel helped to sacralize and validate the cause of resistance. It certainly influenced a young Ottawa at Detroit named Pontiac, who led an uprising against the British post there in May of 1763. Word of that uprising, in turn, helped to spark further uprisings and sieges. By summer's end, every British post in the west had been beseiged, and most were captured at least temporarily by Indians; it would take the British army two years to reassert its control over all the western posts.[39]

The uprisings had an ambiguous political legacy for the Ohio Indians. On the one hand, they created a framework for intertribal cooperation that would be employed repeatedly in times of crisis in the years to come. But on the other hand, even as ties were forged across lines of tribal or communal identity, the uprisings also sharpened divisions within tribes and communities. Among the Delawares, for example, Tamaqua, Shingas, and Pisquetomen opposed the uprising against Fort Pitt on the grounds that the British were too powerful to resist with force; they were convinced that negotiation was the best way to secure Delaware interests. Netawatwees (or Newcomer) emerged in the years

---

[38] Kenny's Journal, 1761–1763, 188; [Navarre], "Pontiac's Conspiracy," pp. 15, 17 and following.

[39] The most recent book-length study of the uprisings remains Howard Peckham, *Pontiac and the Indian Uprising* (Princeton, 1947), but historians' understanding of them has changed substantially since Peckham wrote. See especially White, *Middle Ground*, pp. 269–314; McConnell, *A Country Between*, pp. 159–206; and Gregory Dowd, "The French King Wakes Up in Detroit: 'Pontiac's War' in Rumor and History," *Ethnohistory*, 34 (1990), 254–278. For the passing of belts see White, pp. 275–277; though he emphasizes that the belts traveled in three distinct circuits – one connecting Senecas, Delawares, Shawnees, and Mingos; a second circulating around Detroit; and a third sponsored by French traders – it is also clear that the lines among these various circuits were somewhat blurred, and that communications were circulating widely throughout the valley. See, e.g., Donald Campbell to George Croghan, 10 Mar. 1761, Cadwallader Coll., Box 5, HSP.

just prior to the uprising as a rival Delaware leader who had grown impatient with their commitment to accommodation. A prominent leader of the uprising, by the mid-1760s his aggressive anti-British stance made him a legitimate rival to the older leadership of the tribe.[40] Though the peace of 1758 initially promised to facilitate a new era of cooperation between the British colonies and the Ohio Indians, which might have strengthened the hand of conciliatory leaders among the Indians, events soon undermined that possibility and brought war leaders with a jaundiced view of British intentions once again to the fore.

III

Just as events after 1758 undermined accommodationist visions among Ohio Indians, they also produced a wrenching turn in Pennsylvania's Indian relations. Before the war accommodation was the touchstone of the colony's Indian policy, however the pressures of demographic growth might have strained the principle. But the war initiated a culture of Indian-hating, especially in Pennsylvania's outlying settlements, that took root with astonishing speed. The new hostility to Indians flared brilliantly in the reaction to the western uprisings of 1763, and – like the rise of militant leaders on the Ohio – served as a troubling harbinger of future developments in the colonial backcountry.

The intercultural dynamics of the Seven Years' War were complicated by the distinction between the western Delawares, Shawnees, and Mingos who allied with the French, and the eastern Indians, primarily clustered along the upper Susquehanna, who chose to remain neutral. Initially, Pennsylvania officials worked hard to protect the colony's neutral Indians. For their part, the eastern Indians recognized that they were doubly endangered. Pressured by western war parties to join in raids on the colony or, failing that, at least to allow the warriors to pass through their lands, the Susquehanna Indians also knew that, even if they refused to help, they might be blamed by colonists for the attacks. To protect their reputations as neutrals, the Susquehanna Indians regularly passed along information to the colony about the plans and movements of the French-allied war bands. In several cases, Indians who were themselves threatened by the possibility of attack were maintained at the colony's expense. When the Moravian mission at Gnadenhutten was razed in November, 1755, Governor Morris told the Christian Indians who fled to Bethlehem that, "[a]s you have made it your own choice to become Members of our Civil Society and Subjects of the same Government and determine to share the same Fate with us, I shall make it my

---

[40] McConnell, *A Country Between*, pp. 180–184.

Care to extend the same protection to you as to the other Subjects of his Majesty." At George Croghan's home in the western Pennsylvania hamlet of Aughwick, a group of neutral Indians gathered in a hastily-built, makeshift fort and waited, along with Croghan, for support from the colony. Likewise at Fort Allen, built near the site of Gnadenhutten to guard one of the principal passes through the Kittatinny Mountains, small parties of Indians regularly sought shelter and provisions.[41]

Gradually, though, the terrors of war altered colonists' perceptions of their Indian neighbors. It had never been the custom of Pennsylvanians to speak of Indians as savages, at least in public discourse, but the fear and uncertainty of war created a new language for the colony. As the raids began, Governor Morris expressed "great concern to see that a few merciless Savages can by reason of the defenceless state of the province, perpetrate such horrid cruelties and murders on poor innocent people living peaceably in their habitations." This image of the war worked its way into the collective imagination of the colony. By the time the worst of the fighting was past, the war seemed like no war at all. A soldier expressed his "great Grief" for the residents of the northeastern frontier, who had been subjected, he thought, not to battles but to "Murders, committed . . . by our Cruel and Savage Enemy the Indians." As the raids gradually slowed to a halt, the rangers at the frontier forts looked for signs of Indians almost as if they were stalking wild game. "[S]ome few Sculking Indians keeps round us every day," wrote one. "[W]e discover their fresh tracks but cannot, come up with them."[42]

As colonists learned to despise and dehumanize their attackers, the distinction between friendly neutrals and hostile warriors became increasingly difficult to maintain. Colonial hatred was categorical; under its pressure, the biological continuities that seemed to unite all Indians effaced the political and cultural variations that divided them. The

---

[41] Susquehanna Indians: examinations of Christian Seidle and David Zeisberger, 10 Nov. 1755, Phillip Wesa and Godfrey Wesler, 10 Nov. 1755, and John Schmick and Henry Fry, 15 Nov. 1755, Horsfield Papers, vol. I, pp. 39–42, 45–58, 51–54, APS; Timothy Horsfield to William Parsons, 3 July 1756, Horsfield Papers, vol. I, pp. 161–164; Weiser to Parsons, 28 Oct. 1755, Horsfield Papers, vol. I, pp. 69–72. Bethlehem: Gov. Morris to Gnaddenhutten Indians at Bethlehem, 4 Dec. 1755, Horsfield Papers, vol. I, pp. 81–84; Aughwick: Croghan to Richard Peters, 16 Oct. 1754, and to [?], 23 Nov. 1754, Cadwallader Collection, Box 5, Folder 19, HSP; Fort Allen: Timothy Horsfield to William Parsons, 7 July 1756, Horsfield Papers, vol. I, p. 177; Gov. Morris to Horsfield, 9 July 1756, Horsfield Papers, vol. I, p. 193; Capt. Reynolds to Parsons, 12 Aug. 1756, Horsfield Papers, vol. II, pp. 261–262; and the months of July and August 1756 throughout in this collection.

[42] Gov. Morris to William Parsons, 29 Nov. 1755, Horsfield Papers, vol. I, pp. 73–74, APS; James Hyndshaw to Conrad Weiser, 31 May 1757, Weiser Collection, vol. II, p. 65, HSP.

Moravian Indians experienced the change. When the frontier raids that had destroyed Gnadenhutten and, later, Bethlehem itself appeared to have subsided, the Moravian converts cautiously returned to the countryside in 1758 to settle two new villages, Nain and Wechquetank. In concert with the western uprisings of 1763, Pennsylvania's frontiers – now pushed far to the west, especially along Forbes' Road – were once again besieged. The Moravian Indians emphatically assured their neighbors that they had no ties to the hostile western Indians. To make it possible for them to hunt without being mistaken for hostile warriors, the Moravians issued to their neighbors a list of "Marks distinguishing peacable from wild Indians," which was intended to allow for easy visual identification. Peaceful Indians would be fully clothed, unpainted, with "natural" hair and guns displayed on their shoulders; "wild" Indians, by contrast, "go only in a shirt," wear paint and a feather, shave their heads, and conceal their guns. The Moravian Indians began to carry hunting passes issued by the colony. Nevertheless, any acts of violence in the neighborhood tended to be blamed on them. In October 1763 the residents of Nain and Wechquetank hastily fled to escape the vigilante justice of a group of "Irish Volunteers." A short time later they were taken into government protection and sequestered in Philadelphia, to the outrage of Indian-hating frontiersmen throughout the colony.[43]

In December, a party of about fifty armed men from the town of Paxton (formerly Paxtang) attacked the nearby village of Christian Indians on the Conestoga Manor, killing and scalping the six residents they found at home – two men, three women, and a child. Fourteen others who were away at the time of the attack were quickly taken into protective custody in Lancaster. Two weeks later another armed party rode into Lancaster, silenced the sheriff and coroner, and killed all 14. The residents of Lancaster county championed the attackers, who were soon known popularly as the Paxton Boys; in early February, 1764, in what must have been an extraordinary scene, hundreds of their supporters marched on Philadelphia to rid the colony of the Moravian Indians who were housed there. They soon discovered that royal troops and citizen volunteers, about seven hundred in all, had gathered to oppose their march, and they disbanded without reaching Philadelphia. The march

---

43 Grube's Journal, 22 Sept. 1763, Box 124, Folder 4, Records of the Moravian Mission Among the Indians of North America, Archives of the Moravian Church, Bethlehem, PA (microfilm); Petition, 27 July 1763, Box 124, Folder 7, RMM; Oberlin and Franke, "The Case . . . ," 15 Oct. 1763, Box 125, Folder 5, RMM; "Marks . . . ," Summer 1763, Box 124, Folder 7, RMM; Grube's Journal, 6 Sept., 20 Sept., 8–11 Oct., 1763; trial records, Box 124, Folder 6, RMM; B. Bachler to Gov. Hamilton, 10 Oct. 1763, Box 127, Folder 5, RMM. See also Heckewelder, *Narrative of the Mission*, pp. 56–75.

nevertheless confirmed that the Paxton Boys had widespread support, and upon their return home the aggrieved Lancastrians articulated their concerns in the form of a petition to the colony.[44]

The Paxton Boys' petition politicized Indian-hating in Pennsylvania. Most generally, it insisted that no Indians were neutral, and none could be allies in war. "Experience has taught us," the petitioners argued, "that they are all perfidious, & their Claim to Freedom & Independency, puts it in their power to act as Spies, to entertain & give intelligence to our Enemies, and to furnish them with Provisions and Warlike Stores." To limit the power of the neutrals to injure the colony, the petitioners thought that all interaction between colonists and Indians should be curtailed. Trade should be cut off until peace was restored. As for the Moravian converts under the government's protection, they should be removed from the province "and for the Future no Indians be allowed to live within the Inhabited parts of the Province whilst we are at War with Indians." Finally, the petition proposed renewing the system of bounties for Indian scalps; in this way, colonial officials who were secure in their Philadelphia homes might show their support for the "volunteer Parties" who "go out and reduce those Savages to Peace."[45]

The colony chose a middle way in responding to the petition. Though liberal-minded commentators like Benjamin Franklin fulminated against the ignorant hatreds of the westerners ("If an *Indian* injures me, does it follow that I may revenge that Injury on all *Indians*?"), the governor recognized that the petitioners' sentiment was too widespread to be ignored. He refused to remove the Moravian Indians from his protection, but in midsummer of 1764, in response to the prolonged rebellion in the west, he proclaimed the Delaware and Shawnee Indians to be "enemies, rebels, and traitors," and Pennsylvanians were required by the terms of his proclamation "to embrace all opportunities of pursuing, taking, killing, and destroying" any of them they might meet. The proclamation still contended that "sundry Delaware, Nanticoke, and other Indians," along with the Iroquois, were acting in the interests of the colony and were excepted. But since they had removed themselves from the "inhabited Parts of the Country," any Indian a colonist spotted was fair game – literally, since the governor also used this occasion to reinstate the policy

---

[44] *Pa. Col. Recs.*, vol. IX, pp. 89–134; *Pa. Arch.* [1st Ser.], IV, pp. 147–163. For the barrage of pamphlets that followed, see John R. Dunbar, ed., *The Paxton Papers* (The Hague, Netherlands, 1957); among the many discussions of these events, see especially Alden T. Vaughan, "Frontier Banditti and the Indians: The Paxton Boys' Legacy, 1763–1775," *Pennsylvania History*, 51 (1984), 1–29.

[45] Petition, Feb. 1764, Box 127, Folder 5, RMM.

of offering bounties for Indian prisoners and scalps. Ordinary citizens would now receive 150 Spanish dollars for an adult male prisoner, or $134 for his scalp, while a woman or child brought $130 or $50 for a scalp. Soldiers were entitled to half bounties.[46]

About a year later, the Moravian Indians were finally released from protective custody. As always, they were caught without an idiom in which to express themselves. To thank the governor for his hospitality, they explained, they "did not come with a String or Belt of Wampum agreable to the Custom among Indians," nor were they able to address him in his own tongue. Instead a memorial was written on their behalf in German and then translated into English, "hoping you will accept of it in your usual Benevolence from Your poor Indians." They well understood that they would no longer be welcome in their old settlements, nestled in the fertile and now well-populated valleys of the Delaware River and its tributaries. Instead, they announced that they would "go back into the Woods" to a new settlement on the upper Susquehanna. Soon they moved again, to the Ohio Valley.[47] This double remove dramatized the central lesson of the Seven Years' War in Pennsylvania: the incompatibility of Indians' settlements, however acculturated or eager to adapt their residents might be, with those of European colonists. For the frontier settlers, the war had been a baptism by fire; Indian-hating became a core tenet of their new civil religion.

But this is not the whole story of the war experience. However strained and violent the competition for frontier lands had become, moderating forces remained. The Moravian Indians left peacefully, after passing a year and a half as wards of the colony. Hated and resented by some, they were embraced by others as an enduring symbol of the colony's enlightened liberality. Above all, government emerged as a restraining force in the crisis, dampening the blows of injustice in a time of crisis. From the end of the Seven Years' War until the outbreak of the American Revolution, it was here that the efficacy of government would be repeatedly tested: in its capacity to mediate among antagonists in their various struggles for western land.

IV

Yet it was precisely in this context that government failed most dramatically in the late 1760s and early 1770s. First in their attempts to damp-

---

[46] Franklin, *Narrative of the Late Massacres, in Lancaster County* (Philadelphia, 1764), quoted in Vaughan, "Frontier Banditti," 5; Governor John Penn's Proclamation, *Pennsylvania Gazette*, 12 July 1764.

[47] Address of Christian Indians to Gov. Penn, 19 Mar. 1765, Box 127, Folder 5, RMM.

en conflicts between settlers and Indians around the Forks of the Ohio, and later in the effort to establish an orderly, limited framework for western growth, the officers of Britain's empire struggled to manage affairs in the Ohio Valley but were overwhelmed by the vast complexities they faced and the soaring ambitions they were always unable to keep in check.

Following the uprisings of 1763–1765, opportunistic squatters from Pennsylvania and Virginia once again pressed, remarkably quickly, onto Indian lands. This time they came as Indian-haters, hardened by the experience of war and organized for self-defense. Thomas Gage, Amherst's successor as supreme commander of British forces in North America, reported early in 1766 that "[s]everal Nations of Indians have lately been assembled at Fort-Pitt, to lay their Grievances before us." The Indians charged that settlers began to cross the Alleghenies and take up land on Redstone Creek – a tributary of the Monongahela, and the focal point of the Ohio Company's efforts before the war – "the Moment they had made Peace with us," and violence had followed almost immediately. Several Indians, according to their spokesmen at the fort, had recently "been murthered by the Inhabitants of Virginia, Pennsylvania, and the Jerseys, besides three upon the Ohio, and no Satisfaction given them." Gage concluded that, "if effectual Measures are not speedily taken to remove the Settlers from Red Stone Creek, and the several Governments [of the colonies]...do not pursue vigorous Measures, to prevent Inhabitants from Murthering the Indians, we shall be involved in another general War." "It grieves me," Benjamin Franklin wrote in another indictment of his colony's Indian-hating westerners, "to hear that our Frontier People are yet greater Barbarians than the Indians, and continue to murder them in time of Peace."[48]

Within two years, notwithstanding the complaints voiced at Fort Pitt and the evident concern of General Gage, the illicit settlements of western squatters had spread. From their first center on Redstone Creek they pushed onto choice lands on the Youghiogheny and Monongahela Rivers as well. The Ohio Indians pressed officials of Pennsylvania and the crown to force the squatters out and to devise a new, general land agreement for the territories between the Alleghenies and the Ohio.[49] Responsibility for such an agreement came to rest with William Johnson, whose supervisory role in Indian affairs throughout the northern colonies gave him unique authority to address the interlocking problems of Indian relations in the region. The power of individual colonies

---

[48] Gage to Conway, 24 June 1766, CISHL, vol. XI, p. 325; Franklin to William Johnson, 12 Sept. 1766, CISHL, vol. XI, p. 377.

[49] *Pa. Col. Recs.*, vol. IX, p. 539.

waned in these years as officers of the crown tried to forge a unified Indian policy for the British empire in America.

In many ways, Sir William Johnson was ideally suited to this role. He was widely experienced in Indian affairs, and by the end of the Seven Years' War he was well known to crown ministers, colonists, and Indians alike. Like his assistant Croghan, Johnson was a Scots-Irish emigrant to the American colonies. He arrived in 1738 and settled on a parcel of land belonging to his uncle, Peter Warren, in the Mohawk Valley, on what was then the far western frontier of New York. Over the next two decades he became the central figure in his colony's diplomacy with the Iroquois confederacy, in which capacity he won the trust of the pro-English faction of the Mohawks. In the dark days of the Seven Years' War, the personal loyalty Mohawk leaders felt toward Johnson was critical in preventing the Iroquois confederacy from abandoning the British alliance altogether. In 1763 he built an imposing new manor house, Johnson Hall, which quickly became an important center for Anglo-Iroquois conferences. After the western uprisings, Johnson was generally regarded in ruling circles of the British empire to be the most capable and informed expert on Indian affairs in the northern colonies.[50]

The next several years were crucial ones in Johnson's career and in the formation of a coherent British policy in the west. Suddenly discovering himself thrust to the center of imperial affairs, Johnson struggled unsuccessfully with his ambitions. In his public role as superintendent of Indian affairs, he was expected to act as an impartial mediator. But privately, opportunities arose to forge ties of patronage and interest with some of the most influential and powerful men in Britain and the colonies, and to parlay those connections into vast western landholdings. These private temptations were too great for Johnson to resist (as they also were for his assistant, George Croghan), and they shaped his response to affairs in the Ohio Valley. Moreover, Johnson's influence among the Indians was rooted in his Mohawk connections and closely tied to the increasingly archaic idea of the Covenant Chain. Thus although Johnson brought much more insight and experience to his role in Indian affairs than Amherst had, his rise to power had ominous implications for the Ohio Indians.

[50] The best biography of Johnson is Milton W. Hamilton, *Sir William Johnson: Colonial American, 1715–1763* (Port Washington, New York, 1976), but it is the first of two projected volumes and therefore breaks off in 1763. See also Arthur Pound, *Johnson of the Mohawks* (New York, 1930). James Flexner, *Mohawk Baronet: Sir William Johnson of New York* (New York, 1959), is a colorful (if not lurid) account of Johnson's life that Hamilton has criticized for its many inaccuracies.

As early as 1763 Johnson argued that the most pressing concern in Indian relations was to settle, in some comprehensive way, the land disputes that were quickly proliferating everywhere – not just near the headwaters of the Ohio, but all along the western boundaries of the British colonies. Such a settlement, he believed, would immeasurably improve Britain's Indian alliances, and at the same time strengthen its own frontier settlements. Johnson worried that the British colonies had, "from a mistaken notion" of the Indians' strength, "greatly dispised them, without considering," (here he may have had an image of Amherst before his eyes) "that it is in their power at pleasure to lay waste and destroy the Frontiers." If Britain did not reform its Indian relations and strengthen its alliances, he predicted that the western uprisings would be only a prelude to "a general Defection of all the Indians of North America."[51]

To prevent this catastrophe, colonial officials had to do two things. In the short run, they needed to examine the many disputes over land ownership and boundaries along the fringes of colonial settlement – often the result of fraudulent purchases or opportunistic grabs – to adjudicate the disagreements and pay reasonable settlements where they were due. In the longer term, Johnson argued that good Indian relations required a policy of slow, steady colonial growth regulated by land purchases that were publicly negotiated in advance. He was convinced that a gradual expansion of the colonies would be acceptable to the Indians, who were already accustomed to periodic land cessions, as long as sales were timely and reckless speculation could be avoided. The first step toward such a policy, in Johnson's view, was a boundary line between British and Indian lands that would run the entire length of the northern colonies. Future land sales beyond the line would then be negotiated between the crown and the Indian nations who owned the land, while private purchases and cessions to individual colonies would be disallowed. This policy would be doubly beneficial. First, it "would encourage the thick settlement of the Frontiers, oblige the proprietors of large grants to get them Inhabited," and force the colonies to make economical use of the lands they held, instead of permitting backcountry settlements to sprawl across broad and indefensible frontiers. Second, publicly negotiated land sales would reduce the problem of land fraud and "secure the Indians from being further deceived by many who make a practice of

---

[51] Johnson to the Lords of Trade, 13 Nov. 1763, in E. B. O'Callaghan and Berthold Fernow, eds., *Documents Relative to the Colonial History of the State of New York*, 15 vols. (Albany, 1856–1887) [hereafter *NYCD*], vol. VII, p. 574; [William Johnson], Advice to the Board of Trade, 1764, Cadwallader Collection, Box 5, HSP.

imposing on a few Indians with liquor and fair promises to sign Deeds, which are generally disavowed by the Nation."[52]

Johnson's proposal for a coherent, centralized western land policy accorded with the ministry's own efforts to address the problem. In a royal proclamation issued in 1763, the king's ministers had themselves sought a remedy for the colonists' unregulated occupation of western lands. The Proclamation of 1763 traced a western boundary along the entire length of Britain's seaboard colonies (following the Allegheny Ridge along much of its course) that was intended to separate colonial settlements from Indian lands. The Proclamation Line, as it was soon called, reflected the divided counsels of the king's advisers. Conceived by Charles Wyndham, the Earl of Egremont, and drafted by the Earl of Shelburne, the Proclamation was originally intended as a prelude to further western development. It included provisions for granting land warrants to officers and soldiers who had served in the Seven Years' War, to be located on the western side of the Proclamation Line; the line itself was to be simply the first step in ensuring limited and orderly western expansion and development.[53]

But Shelburne and Egremont had to contend with another powerful faction in the ruling circle, identified especially with the Earl of Hillsborough, which was much less enthusiastic about the prospect of western development. Eclipsing Shelburne just as the Proclamation took effect, Hillsborough chose to interpret the line as a more permanent western limit for the colonies. He was convinced that western growth would only damage the empire: inland settlements could never serve mercantilist interests in the same way that seaboard colonies did; they would create enormous, costly new administrative and defensive burdens for the crown; and if they succeeded they would only threaten to depopulate more useful parts of the realm – Irish estates (in which Hillsborough, not coincidentally, had a major interest) and profitable colonies, in particular.[54]

Johnson was caught between these two currents of policy, and at a remove of several thousand miles was not always in a position to judge their relative strength clearly. He was also becoming captivated by the

---

[52] Johnson to Lords of Trade, 13 Nov. 1763, *NYCD*, vol. VII, p. 578.

[53] The Proclamation is in *Johnson Papers*, vol. X, pp. 976–985; the discussion of British politics here and in the following paragraph is based on Jack Sosin, *Whitehall and the Wilderness: The Middle West in British Colonial Policy, 1760–1775* (Lincoln, NE, 1961), pp. 27–78 and following.

[54] In addition to Sosin (cited above), for Hillsborough see Bernard Bailyn, *Voyagers to the West: A Passage in the Peopling of America on the Eve of the Revolution* (New York, 1986), pp. 29–36.

alchemy of property. The possibility of western development had been attracting attention for a number of years already – at least since the formation of the Ohio Company of Virginia – but now, with one ruling faction apparently receptive to new trans-Appalachian development schemes, interest in large-scale land speculation ventures reached new heights. In Virginia, three pre-war land companies had been revived by 1763 – the Ohio, the Loyal, and the Greenbriar Companies – and all were petitioning for new grants or for recognition of old ones. In Pennsylvania the "suffering traders" (so called because they requested a land grant as restitution for the losses of Indian traders before the Seven Years' War) were organized in December of 1763 to press for a grant of their own. By 1766 Connecticut's leading military officer from the Seven Years' War, Phineas Lyman, was proposing that five or six colonies be created along the Mississippi – though he himself would be satisfied with the proprietorship of only one, to be located at the confluence of the Ohio and Mississippi Rivers, where he promised to settle thousands of Connecticut veterans within four years. And in the same year George Croghan masterminded the formation of the Illinois Company, a spinoff of the "suffering traders" group. A partnership that included both Croghan and Johnson, as well as William and Benjamin Franklin, Joseph Galloway, and the Philadelphia merchants John Baynton, Samuel Wharton, and George Morgan, the Illinois Company sought a grant of more than a million acres at the confluence of the Mississippi and Ohio Rivers, which they proposed would absorb the French settlements there and lay the foundation for a large new British colony in the far west.[55]

The personal motives of Johnson and Croghan in these years are highly suspect. Each dreamed of becoming a new kind of American aristocrat, whose fortunes would be made by the great "feudal revival" that appeared to be at hand. For the first time in decades, vast new tracts of American "wilderness" were about to fall into the hands of a lucky few – well-placed, well-informed men who recognized the opportunity and were astute enough to take advantage of it. Given their humble backgrounds, the possibility of a great proprietorship in league with men like Galloway and the Franklins represented a stunning apotheosis of both men's ambitions. Johnson's speculations are not easily reconciled with

---

[55] For a brief discussion of these companies see Sosin, *Whitehall and the Wilderness*, pp. 42–44, 136–146; for a fuller account, see Clarence Alvord, *The Mississippi Valley in British Politics*, 2 vols. (New York, 1959 [orig. pub. 1916]). On the Illinois Company, see the company's Articles of Agreement, 29 Mar. 1766, and [William Franklin], "Reasons for Establishing a Colony in the Illinois," 1766, CISHL, vol. XI, pp. 203–204, 248–257.

his earlier argument for slow, carefully regulated growth, much less with his responsibilities as Indian superintendent. Johnson and his partners fully recognized the conflict between his public role and private interests; when the Illinois Company made its proposal, the partners decided it would be prudent to keep Johnson's membership in the company a secret.[56]

Croghan's swirling involvements in speculative schemes went to his head as well. After a trip to London in 1764 that brought him in contact with a number of well-connected agents and administrators for colonial affairs, he returned to Pennsylvania with a sudden and insatiable appetite for finery. Despite his lifelong flirtation with insolvency, he purchased a large estate outside Philadelphia called Monckton Hall and immediately filled it with unconscionably expensive things: carpets from Scotland; Irish linens; furniture that included, as one of his biographers has enumerated with bewilderment, "a dozen mahogany chairs upholstered in green damask, . . . mahogany tables, desks, bookcases, commodes, backgammon tables, and, of all things, an expensive spinet." Thanks to his unique familiarity with western lands, Croghan also found himself corresponding with some of the brightest lights in the English-speaking world. Here, too, he was in over his head. In a letter to Benjamin Franklin purportedly from Croghan but clearly written by another hand, he was made to say that he was "much gratified, That the Elephant Bones [which Croghan had collected in Kentucky and sent to Franklin] were acceptable to you; and with your opinion on those animals once inhabiting this part of the Globe."[57] A reader can only suspect that the sentiment of this letter, no less than its orthography, lay outside the most pressing interests of Croghan's supremely practical mind.

In conjunction with the Illinois Company scheme, Croghan also convinced the Philadelphia merchant firm of Baynton, Wharton, and Morgan to risk a fortune in an effort to capture the Indian trade in the Illinois country. In an era of ill-advised schemes, this, as it turned out, was one of the worst. Croghan persuaded the partners in the wake of the western uprisings that traders would soon be allowed to re-enter the west, and the first merchant house to establish itself would be in the strongest position. His enthusiasm was infectious, and Baynton, Whar-

56 Sosin, *Whitehall and the Wilderness*, p. 141. On the idea of a "feudal revival" in the late colonial period more generally, see Rowland Berthoff and John Murrin, "Feudalism, Communalism, and the Yeoman Freeholder: The American Revolution Considered as a Social Accident," in Stephen Kurtz and James Hutson, eds., *Essays on the American Revolution* (Chapel Hill, 1973), pp. 256–288.

57 George Wainwright, *George Croghan: Wilderness Diplomat* (Chapel Hill, 1959), pp. 210–211; Croghan to Franklin, 12 Feb. 1768, Cadwallader Coll., Box 5, HSP.

ton, and Morgan spent an enormous sum – more than £75,000 in less than a year – on merchandise, shipping, and a thousand details of preparation. George Morgan himself accompanied their first cargo to the Illinois country, where he set himself up as the company's agent in Kaskaskia. He encountered nothing but trouble. He clashed with the French traders already doing business there, and also with the newly installed British commander. He failed to win either the local military contracts or those with the Indian department; local traders largely ignored him; and the Illinois Company floundered. Morgan, stranded in Kaskaskia, watched in helpless frustration as his company's investments dried up.[58]

All of this speculative activity created enormous pressures for western development. The longer the ministry delayed its decisions regarding western grants, the more numerous and grandiose the proposals became. The pressures came to a head at Fort Stanwix, New York, in 1768, where Johnson presided over a great gathering of Indians, including representatives from the upper Ohio, Detroit, and the Iroquois confederacy. His instructions were clear and limited. He was to negotiate an adjustment to the Proclamation Line that would establish a new boundary further west: the proposed line jutted west from the upper Susquehanna, met the Allegheny River and traveled downstream past Pittsburgh and along the course of the Ohio as far as the mouth of the Great Kanawha River, then proceeded due south across the Virginia and North Carolina backcountry.[59]

Hillsborough reluctantly agreed to the westward adjustment of the Proclamation Line on the grounds that the original line failed to describe the actual westernmost extent of colonial settlement. If the Proclamation Line was to be a permanent, stable boundary between colonies and Indians, it needed to be adjusted, drawn, and surveyed accordingly. The Delawares and Mingos who claimed the land at the headwaters of the Ohio, where squatters were settling illegally, arrived at Fort Stanwix prepared to sell the lands that had already been settled. But the proposed line went far beyond such a limited adjustment; it embraced millions of acres of choice, unsettled lands on the upper Ohio. Johnson compounded this feature of the sale when he agreed privately to negotiate for additional lands on behalf of various speculative interests. As it was finally negotiated, the boundary did not stop at the Great Kanawha; it followed the Ohio all the way to the Tennessee River. In addition, a tract within this larger grant was specifically set aside for the

---

[58] Max Savelle, *George Morgan: Colony Builder* (New York, 1932), pp. 20–75.
[59] This and the following paragraphs are based on Sosin, *Whitehall and the Wilderness*, pp. 165–180.

"suffering traders," which clearly violated the ministry's prohibition of land sales to private purchasers. By bringing such a vast territory into play, the Fort Stanwix treaty could only alienate the western Indians, who were increasingly concerned about Britain's apparently insatiable appetite for Ohio Valley lands.

Moreover, Johnson refused to negotiate directly with the western Indians. Instead he adhered to the conventions of the Covenant Chain. The private deliberations that set the stage for the conference were held with Iroquois leaders alone; during the conference itself, Iroquois leaders spoke on behalf of all the Indians present, while the western Indians were expected to remain silent; and payment for the ceded lands went directly to the Iroquois chiefs, who were permitted to distribute whatever presents they chose to the western Indians represented at the conference.[60]

The Fort Stanwix agreement was especially galling to the Shawnees in attendance. The land south of the Ohio was their hunting ground, and they denied that the Iroquois could claim it by right of ancient conquest. But they were shut out of all deliberations. Before the conference ended, Shawnee leaders took the extraordinary step of circulating among the western leaders to suggest that they "unite and attack the English as soon as the latter become formidable." Their proposal won support among at least some of the Delaware and Mingo leaders, and in the fall of the following year a delegation visited Detroit to put their case to leaders of the local Ottawas, Wyandots, Chippewas, and Potawatomis. The Shawnees also persuaded leaders of both the Miami and Illinois Indians to join them. In 1770, a large gathering of western Indians from throughout the valley converged on Chillicothe to discuss the Fort Stanwix treaty and to formulate an appropriate response. Colonial officials were astonished to learn through their informants that this great assembly, dubbed the Scioto Confederacy, agreed not only to cooperate with one another but also to seek peace with the Cherokees, the Creeks, and the other southern tribes in order to create a single, united front of Indian resistance to British power on the continent.[61]

In response, William Johnson nervously urged the Iroquois council to reassert its control over the western Indians. Thomas King, a respected Oneida elder, left in the summer of 1770 at the head of a delegation

60 The minutes of the conference, which ran from late September until early November, 1768, and the text of the treaty are in *NYCD*, vol. VIII, pp. 111–137.
61 *NYCD*, vol. VIII, p. 123; Croghan to Gage, 1 Jan. 1770, Gage Papers, American Series, V. p. 89, Clements Library, Ann Arbor, MI; Gage to John Stuart, 16 Oct. 1770, and to the Earl of Hillsborough, 12 Nov. 1770, in K.G. Davies, ed., *Documents of the American Revolution, 1770–1783*, 19 vols. (Shannon and Dublin, Ireland, 1972–1981), vol. II, pp. 203–204, 253–255.

bearing a hundred belts of wampum, on a journey that would take them west to the Scioto River and south as far as Charleston, South Carolina. The mission took a year and a half to complete. At Scioto the Iroquois delegation extracted a vague agreement to maintain peace with the colonists, but an observer concluded that the western Indians were harboring some plan "for which matters did not appear during the congress sufficiently ripe." To Johnson, the signs were ominous. "[I]f a very small part of these people have been capable of reducing us to such straits as we were in a few years since," he pointedly asked Hillsborough (to whom he had recently had to answer for overstepping his instructions at Fort Stanwix), "what may we not expect from such a formidable alliance as we are [now] threatened with?"[62] Indeed, the officers of the crown faced unprecedented obstacles in the Ohio Valley. Brought together by more than a decade of harsh experience with British power, many of the region's Indians appeared willing to abandon accommodation and unite in a military confederacy, founded on their common interests, that was dedicated to keeping British settlers off of their lands at all costs.

IV

For the Ohio Indians, the Fort Stanwix Treaty marked the culmination of a period of particularly ill-advised British policy in the west. The succeeding years saw the empire's power in the Ohio Valley collapse altogether. That collapse can be read in two acts. The first was the decision to abandon the western posts; in December, 1771, General Gage received instructions to withdraw from Fort Pitt and Fort Chartres as a concession to economy. Thus the British army was removed as a restraining power in the Ohio Valley. The second act, less precisely datable but no less decisive in its effects, was the ministry's failure to provide for limited land development beyond the Proclamation Line. By stalling indefinitely in its deliberations over various proprietary schemes, the ministry guaranteed that impatient, unscrupulous, or opportunistic adventurers would take the lead in western development and compound the confusions and conflicts that were already developing over western lands.

Though Fort Pitt was imposed on the Indians of the upper Ohio

---

[62] Dorothy Jones, *License for Empire: Colonialism by Treaty in Early America* (Chicago, 1982), pp. 104–105; Edmonstone to Gage, 24 Aug. 1772, and McKee's Journal, 28 Apr.-1 July 1772 (enclosed), Gage Papers, Am. Ser., vol. V. p. 105, Clements Library; Johnson to the Earl of Hillsborough, 18 Feb 1771, in Davies, ed., *Docs. Am. Rev.*, vol. III, pp. 39–42.

against their will, it served as an important center of diplomatic accommodation and, at least in theory, as an important restraint on the activities of western squatters. Squatting was becoming epidemic in these years, particularly along the Monongahela and its tributaries. In response to requests from Indian leaders, the fort commander, Charles Edmonstone, repeatedly warned settlers off of Indian lands; in the summer of 1767 a detachment of soldiers from the fort chased away hundreds of squatters and destroyed "as Many Hutts as they could find." Though well-intentioned, these initiatives were only temporary deterrents. By 1771, according to George Croghan's estimate, "Nott less than five thousand familys of his Majestys Subjects" had "seated themselves down in an ungovernable Manner" between the Alleghenies and the Ohio River.[63]

Throughout 1770 and 1771 Indian spokesmen conferred repeatedly with Johnson, Croghan, and Edmonstone to urge colonial authorities to control both the growth of squatter settlements and the "vast quantity of liquors" that the local traders plied, distilled from their own surplus corn and rye. But they received only weak assurances. These were difficult years for British authorities throughout the American colonies, and the ministry was growing steadily more detached from the hard problems of western administration. Pressed by crises in the colonies' port towns and the need for imperial economy, the king's advisers were more interested in saving money than solving problems in the west. To this end, troops dismantled, razed, and abandoned Fort Pitt.[64] For the Ohio Indians, as strange as it may seem given their earlier opposition to the fort, this was an ill-timed and ominous development. But now squatters and land developers were everywhere, and the withdrawal of British power made the Ohio Valley a kind of Hobbesian world, where only sheer force could effectively determine the outcome of events.

Having abandoned direct military supervision of the west, the ministry might still have imposed some order on western development by granting land to a privately capitalized proprietary venture. But that possibility, too, came to nothing in the end. By the early 1770s all the most powerful land interests in Virginia, Pennsylvania, and London had come together in a single, vast speculative enterprise known as the Wal-

---

[63] Johnson to Gage, 11 July 1767, and Gage to Shelburne, 24 Aug. 1767, CISHL, vol. XI, pp. 582, 595; Croghan to Samuel Wharton, 2 Nov. 1771, Cadwallader Collection, Box 5, HSP. See also more generally Alfred P. James, "The First English-Speaking Trans-Appalachian Frontier," *Mississippi Valley Historical Review*, 17 (1930–1931), pp. 55–64.

[64] For the abandonment of Fort Chartres, see Hamilton to Gage, 8 Aug. 1772, Gage Papers, Amer. Ser., v. 113, Clements Library; for Fort Pitt, Edmonstone to Gage, 11 Oct. 1772, Gage Papers, Amer. Ser., vol. V, p. 114. The decision is discussed more generally in Sosin, *Whitehall and the Wilderness*, pp. 221–222.

pole Company, which sought a charter for the proposed colony of Vandalia (named in honor of the queen, said to be descended from the Vandals). This was the biggest western colony yet conceived; it would extend across more than twenty million acres on the southern bank of the upper Ohio. In August, 1772, over the strenuous objections of Lord Hillsborough, the Board of Trade approved the Vandalia grant. But just when it appeared that surveying and settlement could proceed, a final obstacle emerged. The king's Law Officers objected to the vague boundaries of the grant, and to uncertainties surrounding the plan for collecting quitrents, and delayed their approval indefinitely. This delay doomed the Vandalia Company. When the Revolutionary War broke out nearly three years later, its members still awaited permission to proceed with their plans.[65]

Into the vacuum of authority on the upper Ohio were poured the competing energies of various charlatans and adventurers. A confusing jumble of ventures arose during the interminable period of ministerial indecision. Old and now invalid Indian grants to individual colonists were converted into real estate and sold off in lots; the governor of Virginia defied royal authority to pursue the interests of speculators (including himself); eager to establish their own claims to the land without having to buy it from self-appointed proprietors, squatters pushed ever farther into the valley. The Ohio Indians were infuriated by all the activity, but the collapse of British authority left them no diplomatic recourse.

The first person to advertise and sell land titles without authorization from either the crown or a colony was the irrepressible George Croghan. In 1749 he was granted 200,000 acres near the headwaters of the Ohio by the Iroquois council, which always seemed eager in those years to give away land it did not really own. It was a flawed transaction, to say the least: the bounds of the grant were cloudy; it was never approved by the Ohio Indians; and neither the crown nor the colony of Pennsylvania accepted the validity of grants to individuals without royal or proprietary approval. Nevertheless, late in 1770 Croghan set up a private land office in Pittsburgh and began offering to sell land titles, whose legitimacy he guaranteed, for tracts of any size to anyone who would pay for them. To squatters who had taken up lands without any authorization, and also to opportunistic speculators, Croghan's offer was the best available. He sold tracts ranging in size from a few hundred acres up to large speculative purchases of twenty thousand acres, while he circulated optimistic reports of the progress of his sales as a further encouragement to skeptics. He was aided by Michael Cresap, a Mary-

[65] Sosin, *Whitehall and the Wilderness*, pp. 181–210.

lander who was one of the earliest squatters on the Monongahela. Cresap told settlers that Pennsylvania's western boundary, which had not yet been surveyed, did not extend as far west as Pittsburgh. This allowed him to argue that Croghan's title to the land at the headwaters of the Ohio constituted the area's only legitimate source of jurisdiction.[66]

Croghan's initiative spurred a group of Virginians to act more aggressively. Virginia soldiers in the Seven Years' War were promised land by Governor Dinwiddie, and the ministry made a similar promise following the war to provincial officers throughout the colonies. George Washington was enlisted to pursue these claims on behalf of the First Virginia Regiment, and he also amassed a large speculative stake in soldiers' bounties. His friend William Crawford, who knew the land around Pittsburgh well, went to the headwaters of the Ohio on Washington's behalf and began locating choice tracts for him. Then Virginia's new governor, John Murray, the Earl of Dunmore, offered to patent 200,000 acres on behalf of the soldiers and enlisted Crawford to do the surveys. Crawford executed a series of surveys on the Monongahela and Great Kanawha Rivers in the summer of 1772, many conflicting with Croghan's claims and some including lands that had already been, or would soon be, taken up by squatters. In 1773 Dunmore sent another Virginia surveyor, Thomas Bullitt, farther downriver to survey lands opposite the Scioto River – lands included in the Fort Stanwix purchase, but lying just across the river from the center of Shawnee settlement in the Ohio Valley.[67]

Dunmore's iniatives hopelessly complicated an already confused situation. The surveys around Pittsburgh challenged not only Croghan's specious title, but the long-standing assumption that Pittsburgh fell within the boundaries of Pennsylvania. Dunmore also, by implication, dismissed the ministry's deliberations on behalf of the Walpole Company; he acted as if energetic initiative would eventually be rewarded, however it might conflict with official policy.

Brash opportunism at the top was mirrored in the behavior of thousands of aspiring small landholders below. In these same years ordinary farmers organized exploratory expeditions and survey parties in grow-

---

[66] Wainwright, Croghan, pp. 26–28, 275–277; Sosin, Whitehall and the Wilderness, pp. 195–196.

[67] See C.W. Butterfield, ed., The Washington-Crawford Letters (Cincinnati, 1877), especially Crawford to Washington, 20 Apr. 1771, 2 Aug. 1771, and 15 Mar. 1772, pp. 18–21 and 24–25; and Washington to Crawford, 6 Dec. 1771, pp. 23–24; Washington to Dunmore, 15 June 1772, in John C. Fitzpatrick, ed., The Writings of George Washington, 39 vols. (Washington, DC, 1931–1944), vol. III, pp. 85–87 and 87n; Croghan to Thomas Wharton, 11 May 1773, "Letters of Colonel George Croghan [to Thomas Wharton]," Pennsylvania Magazine of History and Biography, 15 (1891), 434.

ing numbers, or simply took up new land wherever they could, along the entire length of the Pennsylvania, Virginia, and Carolina frontiers. From the Monongahela and its tributaries squatters pressed west to the Ohio itself; by the early spring of 1774, settlements reached all the way to the mouth of Wheeling Creek. To the south Virginians were exploring other promising river bottoms beyond the Allegheny Ridge. Surveying teams had already begun to lay out claims along the Greenbriar and the Great Kanawha; in the fall of 1772 a "colony" had reportedly been established on the Ohio with its "seat of Government at the mouth of Newriver [where it meets the Kanawha] & the Quitrents 1/2 [d.?] sterling per Acre." Still farther south of these exposed and isolated valleys, in the late 1760s North Carolinians began to cross the Allegheny Ridge from the Yadkin River settlements to take up lands on the Watauga River; by 1771 North Carolinians and Virginians were both moving into the valleys of the Clinch and Holston Rivers, the upper tributaries of the Tennessee. Population grew rapidly on the Clinch and Holston and spread from there into Powell's Valley and onto the upper reaches of the New River.[68]

Late in 1773 Major-General Frederick Haldimand lamented the growing "spirit of emigration" sweeping the region. He wrote that a constant stream of families was going downriver from Pittsburgh to settle along the Ohio, some of them traveling as far as two hundred miles. The press onto western lands, he mused, "seems to threaten a great many inconveniences." The emigrants were certain to "irritate" the Indians; in the face of such wholesale incursions, violence was inevitable. Nor was that the only danger. "[S]uch settlements as these," Haldimand warned, "so far remote from all influence of the laws, will soon be the asylum of the lawless."[69]

Events would bear out both of Haldimand's predictions. The movement of settlers and surveyors down the Ohio raised the anxieties of many Ohio Indians to a new level. A Shawnee delegation traveled to Pittsburgh to protest the Virginia surveys opposite the mouth of the Scioto, while Mingos and Delawares began to abandon some town sites in the upper valley. They withdrew toward the Wabash River on the invitation of the Miami Indians, "with a view," according to William Johnson, "of becoming more formidable to us." On the south side of the river, the Cherokees, whom the Shawnees were trying to draw into

[68] Reuben G. Thwaites and Louise P. Kellogg, eds., *Documentary History of Dunmore's War, 1774* (Madison, WI, 1905), pp. xi–xiv; Angus McDonald to Hancock Taylor, 11 Mar. 1774, Taylor Family Papers, Filson Club, Louisville, KY; Robert Doack to William Preston, 20 Nov. 1771 and 28 Oct. 1772, Draper MSS 2QQ128, 2QQ137, Historical Society of Wisconsin, Madison.

[69] Haldimand to Dartmouth, 3 Nov. 1773, Davies, ed., *Docs. Am. Rev.*, vol. VI, pp. 237–238.

the Scioto Confederacy, were also beginning to react more aggressively to colonists; in the fall of 1773 a party of Cherokee warriors attacked seven surveyors in Powell's Valley. Accommodationist Cherokee leaders insisted that they wanted to preserve peace with the British, but John Stuart, superintendent of Indian affairs for the southern colonies, suspected that the Cherokees were seriously considering the invitation to join forces with the Scioto confederates.[70]

As events approached a crisis in the valley, they also embodied the enduring paradox of Britain's colonial enterprise. Officers of empire and Indian leaders had consistently sought, through long years of association, to create patterns of leadership and diplomacy that would mute conflict and encourage accommodation. But in this effort they were always less successful than the French and their Indian allies. In part this was a result of the enormous demographic pressures of British colonization, and the encouragement those pressures offered to Indian-hating and the racialist ideology of difference it inspired. In part, too, the failures of British policy stemmed from the fact that the British officers who were best situated to act as effective negotiators – particularly Johnson and Croghan – were themselves so bewitched by the alchemy of property that they became duplicitous and self-interested actors. As a result, the burdens of mediation fell on Indian leaders; they, too, were largely ineffective, both because they were relatively powerless and because their interests were always too partial to serve as an effective frame of reference for comprehensive mediation. In the French sphere, the fictional father figure Onontio stood for genuinely impartial mediation; in the British sphere, no effective counterpart to Onontio was ever devised.

The collapse of British authority in the Ohio Valley dealt the final blow to the already badly weakened principles of accommodation and mediation. The expansive dynamics of British colonization had always been inadequately controlled and channeled by imperial authorities. By the 1770s, chaos reigned in the Ohio Valley, and aggressive opportunism was the rule. Anyone viewing events from the perspective of the British empire would have regarded this pattern as a failure of public order, but the American Revolution altered this perception. By war's end, aggressive opportunism would be legitimized in an entirely new way; in the effort to invent an American empire of liberty, this dubious inheritance of the colonial experience would gain new force and credibility as an organizing principle for national policy.

---

[70] Address of Shawnee deputies to Keashuta and Alexander McKee, 28 June 1773, Davies, ed., *Docs. Am. Rev.*, vol. VI, pp. 166–167; Croghan to Thomas Wharton, 15 Oct. 1773, "Croghan-Wharton Letters," 434–436; interview with James Chambers, Draper MSS 3S75; Johnson to Dartmouth, 22 Sept. 1773, and Stuart to Dartmouth, 2 Aug. 1774, Davies, ed., *Docs. Am. Rev.*, vol. VI, pp. 224–225, vol. VII, pp. 156–157.

The Ohio Valley on the Eve of the Revolution

O N THE eve of the American Revolution, three constructions of colonialism overlapped in the Ohio Valley. Trade was the oldest imperial form in the region, and evidence of a trading culture remained wherever an observer looked. It still shaped the social and cultural dynamics of Ohio Valley towns, provided a livelihood for many valley residents, and brought diverse peoples together in complementary pursuits. Overlaid on this trading culture, the complex legacy of French and British efforts to create viable empires of land could be read in the landscape and in the attitudes of both Europeans and Indians; trading relations were beginning to sour in many communities as colonists interested in land as a commodity began to appear in the valley. Emerging alongside these two imperial forms was a third, more volatile and unpredictable than the first two. By 1774 a growing number of colonists saw themselves as participants in an empire of liberty. As effective governance lapsed, settlers entered the valley in ever greater numbers and carried with them distinctive new attitudes toward the land and the peoples of the Ohio Valley. The keystone of those attitudes was their faith in liberty as the organizing precept of western society.

At the end of the colonial era, trade remained the most important agent of intercultural cooperation in the Ohio Valley. In the Illinois country, where British soldiers finally occupied Fort Chartres in 1765 and immediately introduced new regulations to govern the Indian trade, the local residents voted with their feet against the British. In overwhelming numbers, both the French and the Indian population chose to abandon their communities, leaving homes, fields, and public buildings behind, to cross the Mississippi, where the new towns of St. Louis and Ste. Genevieve quickly became two of the most important fur trading centers in the world. British soldiers and administrators were astonished to see the residents abandon their homes and property so readily. (One observer speculated that the Frenchmen must be "Ignorant of our Constitution" to be so reluctant to live under British rule.) Kaskaskia, Prairie du Rocher, Chartres, and Cahokia all stood half-empty, "which," a visitor noted, "makes provisions very Scarce." At St. Philippe, only a single *habitant* remained. The Illinois Indians, too, abandoned their villages and fields and crossed to the Spanish side of the river. The commander at Fort Chartres reported soon after his arrival that the Kaskaskias, Michigameas, Peorias, and Cahokias with whom he had conferred, representing an estimated two thousand Indians – nearly the entire population of the confederacy – also intended to make the move.[1]

From their new base of operations across the river, the French merchants and traders of St. Louis and Ste. Genevieve enjoyed immediate success. With France's loss of Canada and the northern trade to Great Britain, its merchants and traders instead channeled their energies into the commercial network that brought furs to New Orleans from the Arkansas, Missouri, Mississippi, Illinois, and Wabash Rivers and the lower Great Lakes posts. Furs and skins quickly became New Orleans' principal export; in 1765 alone nearly a million pelts were shipped from its wharves to France. St. Louis and Ste. Genevieve developed an increasingly prominent class of merchant-traders, among whom the foremost was Pierre de Laclède Liguest, of Maxent, Laclède and Co. William Johnson wrote of him that "a Frenchman is now established [in St. Louis] who carries on a vast Extensive Trade, and is acquiring a great influence over all the Indian Nations." Laclède's trading network reached to every post from Detroit to Missouri, and Johnson feared that he would "Engross all the Trade in them parts." The shift to New Orleans permitted the *coureurs* of the Illinois country to maintain their old patterns with remarkably little disruption. They continued to travel up the Missouri River, where they enjoyed a "very considerable" trade with the Missouri tribes; they also crossed the Mississippi to ascend the Ohio, in violation of British regulations, to trade at the Wabash and lower Great Lakes posts.[2]

---

[1] Lieut. Fraser to Gen. Gage, 16 Dec. 1765; John Jennings' Journal, 4 Apr. 1766; Stirling to Gage, 15 Dec. 1765; in Clarence Alvord and Clarence Carter, eds., *The New Regime, 1765–1767*, Collections of the Illinois State Historical Library, vol XI (Springfield, 1916), pp. 130–131, 176–177, 126–127. On the migration generally, see also "Journal of Capt. Harry Gordon, 1766," in Newton D. Mereness, ed., *Travels in the American Colonies* (New York, 1916), pp. 472–475; and Philip Pittman, *The Present State of European Settlements on the Mississippi, with a geographical description of that river illustrated by plans and draughts* (Gainesville, FL, 1973 [orig. pub. London, 1770]), pp. 46–50.

[2] "Journal of Capt. Harry Gordon, 1766," pp. 483, 475; Aubry to the Minister, 27 Jan.

Further east, British traders remained active as well. The jumping-off point for the valley's trade was at Pittsburgh, a small, boisterous village dominated by an active and extraordinarily fluid trading community. Burghers, boatmen, packhorse drivers, traders, travelers, and feckless adventurers, many of them only passing through, rubbed elbows in its dirty, crowded streets. "Part of the inhabitants are agreeable and worthy of regard," a traveling clergyman decided after a short stay in the town, "while others are lamentably dissolute in their morals." Indians were everywhere, selling skins and furs and buying merchandise in the local stores. Boatloads of goods also departed regularly for the towns down-river. The crews of the distinctive Ohio River trading boats, overgrown canoes that might be sixty feet long, frequently included both Indians and colonists, and a traveler on the river who needed a guide or an interpreter was as likely to hire an Indian as a colonist for the job.[3]

Below Pittsburgh, the towns of the Ohio Valley were deeply influenced by intercultural commerce. By the early 1770s a cash economy prevailed in the valley; it was an exceptional village in which money was not expected in exchange for provisions or services. When David Jones, a Baptist preacher who tried unsuccessfully to start a mission among the Shawnees, traveled through the valley in 1772 and 1773, he learned that he needed cash – and plenty of it – everywhere he went: 25 dollars for a horse; corn at a "very expensive price"; "milk at nine-pence a quart, and butter at two shillings a pound"; 6 dollars to hire a pilot to see him from a Delaware town on the Muskingum River to the Ohio (this fee despite the fact that his guide, as it turned out, "knew not the course" and had to rely on a sketched map Jones was carrying). Most of the Ohio Valley towns had stocks of domesticated animals. Although the traditional combination of maize, squash, beans, and wild game remained central to local diets, beef, pork, butter, and milk were remarkably common. Imported luxuries that came to valley towns through the transatlantic market occasionally enlivened meals, as when Jones breakfasted on the exotic combination of "fat buffalo, beavers tails and chocolate." The material culture of the valley towns was stamped by European influence as well: clothes and jewelry, as we have seen, were

1766, CISHL, vol. XI, p. 144; William Foley and C. David Rice, *The First Chouteaus: River Barons of Early St. Louis* (Urbana, IL, 1983), pp. 1–12; Johnson to Lords of Trade, 16 Nov. 1765, CISHL, vol. XI, p. 120; Gage to Conway, July 15, 1766, in Mereness, ed., *Travels*, p. 477; Pittman, *Present State*, p. 2.

[3] David Jones, *A Journal of Two Visits Made to Some Nations of Indians on the West Side of the River Ohio, in the years 1772 and 1773* (New York, 1865 [orig. pub. 1774]), pp. 20, 39, 108–109. For another contemporary description of Pittsburgh see David McClure, *Diary of David McClure, Doctor of Divinity, 1748–1820*, ed. Franklin Dexter (New York, 1899), p. 45 and following.

most often made of European cloth, silver, and beads, and in many towns European-style cabins could be found alongside traditional long-houses.[4]

Colonists were present in every Ohio Valley town of any size, and their interactions with local Indians were varied and complex. When Jones arrived in Chillicothe in mid-January, he found about twenty traders, artisans, and shopkeepers from the colonies living there. John Irwin operated a store at Chillicothe out of a building that he rented from one of the local Indians, and he made his home in the nearby village of Blue Jacket's Town. Moses Henry was a gunsmith and trader from Lancaster, Pennsylvania, who had lived in Chillicothe for years. His Shawnee wife was herself a former colonist, captured as a young girl and raised in the community. At Pickaweeke, another small settlement near Chillicothe that Jones called "the most remarkable town for robbers and villains" he had ever known, he found an old acquaintance from Pittsburgh, Joseph Nicholas, who welcomed him into his home and offered him a meal. When Jones discovered that David Owens, the man whom he had hoped would serve as his interpreter with the Shawnees, had gone downriver with a hunting party and would not return for several months, a "foreigner" named Caesar was recommended in his place. Caesar was, in fact, almost certainly a former slave who had been captured and adopted by the Shawnees, and he reputedly "understood something about religion" as well as about languages.[5]

Some towns in the valley reflected even more clearly the unique characteristics of its trading culture. The principal settlements on the Muskingum River stood some seventy miles upriver from its mouth, but at the spot where it met the Ohio a small village named Connor's Town had appeared to serve the needs of traders and Indians passing up and down the valley. Connor's Town was a joint venture. It was named for a Maryland man who kept "a sort of tavern" for travelers; in early 1773 he was also making plans to plant an experimental wheat crop in the fall. His partner was an Indian who was regarded as a chief by the Delaware and Shawnee residents of the town; the two men were married to sisters, captured from the colonies in childhood and raised among the Ohio Indians. A short distance downstream, another village settled by Delawares and Shawnees was led by a Shawnee woman "who

[4] Jones, *Two Visits*, pp. 84, 87, 101, 104, 108–109, 53, 83–84; in only one case did Jones remark on the need to barter because "these Indians as yet have not the use of money"; see 85. See also Michael McConnell, *A Country Between: The Upper Ohio Valley and Its Peoples, 1724–1774* (Lincoln, NE, 1992), pp. 207–232.

[5] Jones, *Two Visits*, pp. 39–63.

is esteemed very rich," and who owned several black slaves to maintain her large herds of livestock.[6]

As cattle and pigs, poultry and wheat made their way into the Ohio Valley alongside articles of trade, the territorial dimension of colonialism gained a foothold even before significant numbers of European settlers did. Another transitional dimension of colonialism was embodied in the activities and communities of Moravian missionaries, who constituted a significant presence in the upper valley on the eve of revolution. It is possible to regard the Moravians either as the shock troops of empire, or as a buffering force that offered the Indians of the upper valley important adaptive skills and values. However their presence is interpreted, there is no question that these missionaries, and the communities they helped to create, found themselves at the center of the controversy raging among the Ohio Indians over how best to respond to the growing interest of European colonists in Indian lands.

The arrival of the Moravians initially threatened to divide Indian communities on the upper Ohio. Between 1770 and 1773 three Moravian towns were founded – Friedenstadt on the Beaver River, and Gnadenhutten and Schoenbrunn on the Muskingum – and each triggered disagreements and defections. The settlement of Friedenstadt created dissension in the nearby Kuskuskies towns, where the Mingo leader Kiashuta and the Munsee Delaware leader Custaloga both discovered that the Moravians undermined their authority and drew followers away from their towns. Custaloga's chief advisor, Glikkikan, suddenly chose to be baptized and took the name of Isaac. But for a variety of reasons, most Indian leaders on the upper Ohio looked sympathetically on the efforts of the Moravian communities and preferred to allow them to settle nearby. For one thing, many of the converts were kinsmen; for another, the Moravians brought valuable skills to the Indians they worked with. This combination eroded the initial hesitation of most Ohio chiefs. The most influential Delaware leaders, Netawatwees and Tamaqua, decided to allow the Moravians to settle among them; and even Netawatwees' younger advisers, White Eyes and Killbuck, who remained more militant than their aging counterpart and who were more suspicious of Moravian intentions, eventually conceded that the Moravians and their followers might be a positive influence among the Indians on the upper Ohio.[7]

In particular, the Moravians offered the Ohio Indians valuable tools for coping with their deepening economic crisis. The trading economy

---

[6] Jones, *Two Visits*, pp. 87–88.
[7] Paul A. W. Wallace, *Thirty Thousand Miles with John Heckewelder* (Pittsburgh, 1958), pp. 93–114; McConnell, *A Country Between*, pp. 226–229.

of the valley, especially its upper reaches, had been gradually souring for many years. Though game populations could still fluctuate significantly in this period, deer and other game were particularly scarce in the early 1770s. And although the trading regulations promulgated by Amherst had fallen into abeyance, the imperial crisis of the early 1770s was wreaking havoc on the colonies' transatlantic trade. As Parliamentary revenue initiatives prompted non-importatation agreements throughout the colonies, the imported dry goods that had been central to the valley's commerce became increasingly scarce. In place of well-connected traders plying abundant merchandise, Indians were left more and more often to do business with the growing population of small farmers squatting on backcountry lands. The only merchandise they had in abundance was alcohol. In these years home-distilled whiskey made from surplus farm produce became a significant article of intercultural trade for the first time; rum, distilled in the colonies, came to dominate the merchandise available even from more established traders. Alcohol was cheap, easy to make or obtain, convenient to transport, and highly profitable. "[E]very farmer is a sutler [or provisioner]," George Croghan wrote to Thomas Gage in an effort to explain the dramatic growth of the liquor trade, "and the Traders not being able to get Goods these two years past has employed their horses in bringing little else but Rum."[8]

For the Ohio Indians this was bad news coming and going: fewer skins and pelts, which were being disproportionately absorbed by the liquor trade. White Eyes, soon to succeed Netawatwees as the leading chief of the Ohio Delawares, thought he could see the handwriting on the wall. He told a visitor that "their way of living would not answer much longer – game grew scarce – they could not much longer pretend to live by hunting, but must farm, &c." In this context, the Moravians could be a valuable resource. Their villages were the first in the Ohio Valley to adopt intensive agricultural practices, like fencing fields and using iron plows; in Schoenbrunn's second spring the community managed to sow eighty acres. Soon non-Christian towns followed suit. After a disastrous famine in the summer of 1772, Jones noted in the following year that the Delawares at Geckelemuchpekink "have begun to farm [in the European style], to which they are much assisted by a Jersey Indian, who is not only their smith, but also makes their ploughs." In craft skills, too, Indian leaders believed that the Moravians might make a contribution to their commmunities; Custaloga initially welcomed the

---

[8] Croghan to Gage, 8 Aug. 1770, Gage Papers, American Series, vol. V. p. 94, Clements Library, Ann Arbor, MI.

settlement of Friedenstadt in part because he believed the missionaries might be able to teach his people to manufacture gunpowder.[9]

Delaware leaders were even receptive to the Moravians' interest in the moral life of Indian communities. Their emphasis on temperance was especially welcome in these years, when traders were trying to drown the Indian towns in liquor. In the summer of 1773 the Delaware council followed the lead of the Moravian communities and outlawed liquor in their towns. White Eyes was convinced that a European-style education was necessary if Indian leaders were ever to learn how to deal effectively with the colonies; in 1773 his friend Killbuck was raising money for a trip to England, where he intended to ask the king to appoint a schoolmaster and an Anglican minister to serve in Geckelemuchpekink. Killbuck was even persuaded that his people needed to learn the art of debt collection. "[H]e saw the necessity of a magistrate to recover debts," according to Jones, "and said, that by and by, he expected that they would have one; but as yet their people did not understand [such] matters."[10]

Temperance, education, frugality: the strategies adopted by Delaware leaders in the years just before the Revolution are reminiscent of earlier experiences with Pennsylvania; once again they raise the question of whether the Delawares could withstand the growth of a territorial empire by adapting to European ways. The tensions implicit in their acceptance of the Moravians run parallel to the tensions in the indigenous prophetic tradition that was gaining strength in the 1760s. In both cases, Indian leaders experimented with a partial adoption of European values in order to preserve the essential features of Indian identities. Further to the southwest, the Shawnee towns were much less receptive to this trade-off. When Jones proposed to establish a Christian mission there, he was so strongly mistrusted that he barely escaped from the Shawnee settlements with his life.

But these responses must also be placed in a larger context. They were part of a struggle by the Ohio Indians to retain political autonomy and to bolster the authority of their leaders. In its first incarnation, the imperial framework for the Ohio Valley was trade. Such an empire weakened the structures of chieftainship even as it contributed to a kind

---

[9] Jones, *Two Visits*, p. 89; David Zeisberger, *Schoenbrunn Story: Excerpts from the Diary of the Reverend David Zeisberger, 1772–1777 at Schoenbrunn in the Ohio Country*, August C. Mahr, trans., Daniel R. Porter, ed. (Columbus, Ohio, 1972), entries for 7 May 1772 and 17 June 1773, pp. 1, 5; Jones, *Two Visits*, p. 106; McConnell, *A Country Between*, p. 227.

[10] Jones, *Two Visits*, pp. 89, 97–99, 103–105, 107; see also Zeisberger, *Schoenbrunn Story*, p. 24; Edmund de Schweinitz, *The Life and Times of David Zeisberger* (Philadelphia, 1871), pp. 384–385; and Wallace, ed., *Thirty Thousand Miles*, pp. 101–102.

of renaissance among the Ohio Indians. The second incarnation of empire was territorial, and it should have worked in the other direction – indeed, for a time it did: territorial conflicts encouraged the Ohio Indians to strengthen and consolidate their leaders' power. But the emergence of mediators in the Ohio Valley turned out to be short-lived; the British empire overreached its grasp in the far west, and the collapse of British authority made the efforts of accommodationists irrelevant. In place of the accommodationists, who failed, a new generation of militant war leaders would rediscover the truth that the only way to preserve their autonomy was to fight for it.

PART THREE

Empire of Liberty

T O CONSTRUCT an American empire of liberty, it was first necessary to stand European imperial principles on their head. In both
the French and British empires, landed development required
central control; without that, the benefits of empire would not flow toward its center. If imperial elites were to gain anything by colonization,
the process had to be carefully governed. Thus imperial government
came to function as a restraining force on the activities of colonists; if
settlers pressed onto Indian lands, colonial officials were expected to act
as mediators. It was at least theoretically within the power of government to restrain opportunistic colonists, to legitimize Indian land claims
in English law, and to aid Indian leaders by taking their concerns and
complaints seriously. However imperfect these operations were in fact,
in principle the weight of imperial authority supported efforts to ensure
order, create legitimate boundaries, and protect the established interests
of both Native and European Americans along the boundaries of settlement.

It was precisely the immensity of this task that defeated the British
empire in the Ohio Valley. Centralized control of policy was difficult
enough to attain for the seaboard colonies; in the continental interior
the complexities were still more baffling. The result, as we have seen,
was withdrawal and collapse. An unprecedented burst of immigration
in these same years compounded the effects of that collapse. In an experience that paralleled that of Pennsylvania during the proprietary hiatus
of the 1720s, the hiatus of imperial authority in the early 1770s coincided with a rush of European immigrants, many of whom were seeking
lands of their own. Most of these immigrants came to the mid-Atlantic
and Chesapeake colonies; whether they came as free men and women or

had to fulfill a term of servitude, nearly all were aspiring landholders within a few years of their arrival.[1] The obvious outlet for their ambitions lay in the Ohio Valley. Rumors of development schemes swirled through the colonies, and travelers' accounts suggested that the valley held lands of mythic fertility and abundance.

The American Revolution ushered in a new era of imperial development in the Ohio Valley, one in which individuals exercised a new kind of authority and legitimacy. The creation of an empire of liberty was pushed forward by the activities of thousands of land-hungry western settlers; revolutionary governments at both the state and the confederation level, for reasons of strategy as well as theory, chose to follow their lead and support their efforts. This was a dramatic inversion of the earlier model of imperial development, which was directed from the center and governed by elites. Now government followed in the wake of individual initiative, picking up the pieces of imperial expansion and trying to shape them into something coherent and principled. While this inversion has been lauded for its capacity to unleash the creative energies of ordinary people, in the Ohio Valley violent and destructive impulses were unleashed as well. As in the frontier wars of the Seven Years' War, destruction generated hatred; for both Europeans and Indians, a racialized understanding of cultural difference gained influence as combatants struggled to make sense of their experiences.

These twin legacies of the Revolution – decentralized, atomized political authority and deeper, sharper lines of racial separation and hatred – reshaped the society and culture of the Ohio Valley. The Revolution, with all of its horrors, established the earliest and most salient context for the invention of a collective American identity. At the center of that shared identity was a commitment to rapid western expansion, racial separation and removal, and, when it seemed necessary, the extirpation of Native American peoples in the valley. Collective Indian rights and identities lost their force in American law, and the foundation was laid, first, for decades of racial conflict, and second, for the dispossession of Indians from their place in the American landscape.

[1] See Bernard Bailyn, *Voyagers to the West: A Passage in the Peopling of America on the Eve of the Revolution* (New York, 1986).

CHAPTER FIVE

Land and Liberty

THE American Revolution did not emerge in the Ohio Valley out of events taking place on the seaboard. War was already underway in the west, and the coming of the Revolution shifted its context and meaning without altering its fundamental character. The colonies' break with royal authority was, however, a powerful spur to the progressive dissolution of order and escalation of conflict in the valley. For colonists who were already beginning to settle there without authorization, the language, the ideas, and the urgency of the American Revolution all helped to validate their scramble for western lands. For the region's Indians, the Revolution accelerated the process by which peace chiefs and accommodationists lost ground to war leaders and their followers. As the war progressed, it undermined and invalidated the social patterns that had earlier emerged out of the British and French empires of trade. In their place, a hardening pattern of racial separation and conflict defined the fundamental character of the region's society and culture.

This hardening of racial hostility is such a familiar part of America's early national history that it is difficult not to take it for granted. But if the American Revolution in the valley had been freed from its moorings in the collapse of public authority and the scramble for land, its events might have proceeded very differently. In any competition between colonies and empire, alignments of interest in the region should have been complex, shifting, and difficult to foresee or rely upon – and that is true for both colonists and Indians. The Ohio Valley was not an obvious seedbed for revolutionary sentiment. Among the colonists, it was a common destination for thousands of loyalists to the crown who were fleeing the coercion, hostility, and humiliation of their neighbors in well-established communities. The Ohio Valley fell under the jurisdiction of Quebec, which had not joined the Revolution, and its communities were

so new that their political temper remained indeterminate.[1] Western settlers were often very recent migrants to the colonies; it has been argued
that they might have had stronger attachments to the idea – the habit –
of loyalty to a sovereign king than their American-born counterparts,
and in more settled parts of the backcountry this argument was borne
out by events.[2] Moreover, both the administration and the economy of
the Ohio Valley had especially strong ties to Great Britain and the
crown: many of its leading figures were royal officers, and others were
especially dependent on overseas trading connections for their economic
livelihoods.[3] In all these ways, the valley remained in a distinctly colonial state; it was farther from achieving political or economic self-suffi-
ciency than the longer-settled parts of the colonies, and its residents
were natural candidates for resisting the independence movement.

The interests of the Ohio Indians in the emerging imperial crisis were
also by no means immediately clear. Britain's Indian policy had alienated many native groups; Pontiac's Rebellion was only the most obvious
expression of the widespread sense among the region's Indian population that Britain was an unreliable and inconstant ally. By comparison,
an indigenous American source of political authority might be very appealing. A government in America could be expected to be more sensitive to the problems and complexities of Indian relations; it would not
suffer from the breakdowns in communication and the instability of
personnel and policy that seemed to plague the empire. Its Indian agents
would be experienced men who would enjoy more direct access to the
centers of political authority. In this light, the prospect of an alliance
with the United States initially appeared promising. The politics of Indian affairs in the Ohio Valley were also complicated by the enormous
complexity and diversity of its Indian population. It was home to more

---

[1] This is an underdeveloped theme in the literature on loyalism, but see Wilbur H. Siebert,
"The Dispersion of the American Tories," *Mississippi Valley Historical Review,* 1
(1914), 185–197; Siebert, *The Loyalists of Pennsylvania,* The Ohio State University Bulletin, vol. XXIV (Columbus, 1920); and Reuben G. Thwaites and Louise Kellogg, eds.,
Frontier Defense on the Upper Ohio, 1777–1778 (Madison, WI, 1912), throughout.

[2] In the near backcountry of the Carolinas, Virginia, and Pennsylvania, loyalist sentiment
and support was considerable wherever British military leadership appeared; in the famous battle of King's Mountain, for example, more than a thousand colonists fought
against the patriots. See Lyman C. Draper, *King's Mountain and Its Heroes* (Cincinnati,
1881), pp. 237–238. See also William Preston's correspondence related to loyalist activity in backcountry communities, esp. during the summer of 1780, Draper MSS
5QQ27–50, Historical Society of Wisconsin, Madison; and more generally Jeffrey Crow
and Larry Tise, eds., *The Southern Experience in the American Revolution* (Chapel Hill,
1978).

[3] See, e.g., Siebert, *Loyalists of Pennsylvania,* pp. 14–15.

than a dozen tribal groups, who had combined in bewildering patterns in a series of multiethnic villages. Throughout the valley, it was increasingly difficult to say with any confidence who, if anyone, wielded political power for a particular community or tribe, or what alliances might emerge out of the pressure of events. As time passed, the weight of political power could swing from one village to another in unpredictable ways. In an emerging contest of power between European rivals, the possibility that pro-American and pro-English factions would have emerged, or that the Ohio Indians would have sought to play the two sides off against one another while they remained neutral, seems very likely. The complexity of Indian politics should have been reflected in the progress of the war.

But this is not what happened. The events of the war served not to heighten the complexity of the Ohio Valley's social and political contours, but to flatten it. The progress of events increasingly polarized the residents of the valley into two distinct groups, defined by race and driven to violence in the defense of their interests.

I

The American Revolution in the Ohio Valley had its origins, not with events in and around Boston in the spring of 1775, but in an obscure military campaign led by Virginia's governor, Lord Dunmore, against the Shawnees of the Ohio Valley a year earlier. Lord Dunmore's War, in turn, originated in the collapse of imperial authority in the vicinity of Pittsburgh.

When Fort Pitt was hastily constructed during the Seven Years' War, and the town of Pittsburgh grew up alongside it, Pennsylvanians assumed that both fell within their colony's jurisdiction; when the fort was abandoned in 1773 the Pennsylvania Assembly created a new county in the west to establish a framework for government at Pittsburgh. But Pennsylvania's western boundary had never been officially surveyed, and some Virginians – including George Washington, William Crawford, and Governor Dunmore – thought it was part of Virginia. When Croghan and Crawford each began surveying adjoining lands as if they had pre-emption rights in the region, this basic jurisdictional question became acute.

In and around Pittsburgh, the dispute between Pennsylvania and Virginia was refracted through a growing awareness that the squatters' encroachments onto Indian lands might provoke hostility with the Indians on the upper Ohio. Although Pennsylvania claimed to control the region, it had so far refused to rebuild the fort, provide for a western garrison, or even organize a local militia company. Early in 1774, Dunmore enlisted the aid of John Connolly, a friend of Croghan's and another veteran of the Ohio country, to press Virginia's claim on the Ohio. Connolly traveled to Pittsburgh, where he organized a militia company and placed himself at its head. As captain of the local militia, he then announced that he would appeal to Virginia to erect a new county there. Many landholders worried that this shift might invalidate their claims to land, but Croghan, who continued to enjoy considerable influence in the area, backed Connolly. A chaotic struggle for political control ensued between the competing appointees of the Virginia and Pennsylvania factions; each proceeded to survey and grant lands on its own authority, while individual settlers contested with one another over the ownership of particular holdings. A series of arrests and counterarrests, evictions and confrontations soon threw the entire region into confusion and created a panic among its inhabitants.[4]

Virginia's claim to the upper Ohio gained strength in March and April of 1774, when several violent conflicts between colonists and Indians raised new concerns about military preparedness. Rumors of an impending Indian war were common along the Ohio River during the early spring. In some remote areas residents chose to flee eastward; other squatters, comforted by their numbers and the recent organization of the militia at Pittsburgh, chose to stay where they were.[5] In mid-April, a party of traders was waylaid by Cherokees as it carried a canoeload of merchandise down the Ohio to the Shawnee towns on the Scioto; the canoe was plundered and one of the three traders was killed. A short time later the same Pittsburgh merchant made a second attempt to ship goods to the Shawnees, this time entrusting them to two Indians "who were well known to be good men" and two colonists, who were to make the trip together. As they passed near the mouth of Wheeling Creek, the canoe they rode in was fired upon from the shore by a party of squatters led by Michael Cresap, and both Indians were killed. Cresap followed this attack with one against a group of Shawnee leaders returning home from a visit to Pittsburgh, in which he killed one man and wounded two others. Within a few days of these attacks came another unprovoked assault, this time on nearby Yellow Creek, against a group

[4] Arthur St. Clair to Gov. Penn, 2 Feb. 1774, and to Joseph Shippen, 25 Feb. 1774, Croghan to David Sample, 4 Apr. 1774, Aeneas Mackay to Gov. Penn, 4 Apr. 1774, Andrew McFarlane to Gov. Penn, 9 Apr. 1774, and Thomas Smith to Joseph Shippen, 13 Apr. 1774, Samuel Hazard, ed., *Pennsylvania Archives* [1st Ser.], 12 vols. (Philadelphia, 1852–1856), vol. IV, pp. 476–478, 481–489; Francis Wade to William Johnson, Mar. 6, 1774, James Sullivan, et al., eds., *The Papers of Sir William Johnson*, 14 vols. (Albany, 1921–1965), vol. VIII, pp. 1062–1066.
[5] Dan Smith to William Preston, 22 Mar. 1774, Draper MSS 3QQ15.

of friendly Mingos. Estimates of the number killed vary widely, from nine or twelve to thirty or forty.[6]

Word of the attacks spread quickly. At Pittsburgh, Connolly and his allies recognized that the growing fear of retaliation strengthened their cause; they circulated a report that the Ohio Indians had already decided to go to war, and responded by mobilizing the militia. In fact, despite the violent anger of a few Indians – most notably that of a Mingo named Chief Logan who lost his entire family in the attack on Yellow Creek – and demands by the Shawnees that their grievances be addressed, all the principal leaders of the Ohio Indians tried to preserve the peace and advised their warriors against seeking vengeance. Parties of traders in the Delaware and Shawnee towns who were in danger of being attacked by Logan were given protection and safe guidance back to Pittsburgh. Nevertheless, neither Indian leaders nor their imperial counterparts could restrain small parties from retaliating for the attacks of March and April, and rumors of an impending war persisted and intensified. In early June, a Pittsburgh resident reported that "an Indian war is commenced, and the out Inhabitants are all Forting [up or] Fleeing in."[7] Those who chose to "fort up" initiated a process that would remain characteristic of the valley's Euroamerican residents in the face of war for two decades. Having removed beyond the effective range of government protection, support, and control, they were forced to provide for their own defense. Frontier residents in the Revolutionary era thus compensated for the crown's failure to create a new colony in the west by staking a *de facto* claim to the land and organizing locally to defend it.

The dynamics of this process were clearly revealed for the first time in the spring and summer of 1774, when colonists along the Pennsylvania and Virginia frontiers busied themselves with two apparently con-

---

6 There are many accounts of the events on the upper Ohio in March and April, and their details vary widely. I have relied primarily on a contemporary account written by a Pittsburgh resident who was not directly involved in the violence and appears to have been relatively impartial in his judgments: Devereaux Smith to Dr. William Smith, 10 June 1774, in Jack M. Sosin, ed., *The Opening of the West* (Columbia, S.C., 1969), pp. 11–14. For other versions, see the later accounts from the Draper MSS printed in Reuben G. Thwaites and Louise P. Kellogg, eds., *Documentary History of Dunmore's War, 1774* (Madison, WI, 1905), pp. 9–19, and Dunmore to Dartmouth, 24 Dec. 1774, in K.G. Davies, ed., *Documents of the American Revolution, 1770–1783*, 19 vols. (Shannon and Dublin, Ireland, 1972–1981), vol. VIII, pp. 252–270.

7 Devereaux Smith to William Smith, 10 June 1774, Sosin, ed., *Opening of the West*, 13–14; Abraham Hite, Jr. to William Preston, 3 June 1774, Draper MSS 3QQ35. For rumors of war, see, e.g., Dan Smith to Preston, 22 Mar. 1774, Draper MSS 3QQ15; John Floyd to Preston, 26 Apr. 1774, Draper MSS 3QQ19; William Russell to Preston, 26 June 1774, Draper MSS 3QQ46.

tradictory activities. On the one hand, squatter communities banded together to construct makeshift forts, create local militia units, and thus
defend themselves against the possibility of attack. On the Clinch and
Holston Rivers, the inhabitants built a series of small log forts – by July,
there were seven on the Clinch River alone – and organized a militia pa-
trol "to protect the Frontiers & annoy the Enemy." Connolly and Dunmore recommended that a chain of posts be built along the Ohio itself,
to ensure the protection of the settlers and to provide a base from which
to organize an offensive against the Ohio Indians, if that became necessary. A new fort was constructed at Pittsburgh to replace Fort Pitt,
which Connolly named Fort Dunmore; downriver they built two more
outposts, one at the mouth of Wheeling Creek, the other on the Hock-
ing River. Elsewhere, small parties of westerners were left to make whatever provisions they saw fit. A Virginia officer who traveled through the
backcountry in the summer of 1774 commented that "most of the people in this country, seem to have a private plan of their own, for their
own particular defense." While Indian leaders tried throughout the
spring and summer to ensure peace, the colonists' preparations for war
took on a momentum of their own. One observer tersely captured the
mood among the western settlers. "Ye inhabitants of our Fruntier is in
ye Grate Confusion," he wrote; "they are all gathered in forts[.]"[8]
    On the other hand, even as frontier residents took an unprecedented
series of precautions to defend the lands they had staked out, surveyors
and explorers were more active in the Ohio Valley in 1774 than they
had ever been before – many of them with the direct approval and encouragement of Dunmore and his deputies. William Bullitt and John
Floyd, acting on behalf of the Virginia officers in the Seven Years' War,
each led surveying teams down the Ohio as far as the Kentucky and Salt
Rivers and laid off vast expanses of choice lands. William Thompson
led a similar expedition on behalf of the Pennsylvania officers. Independent parties split off from these larger groups to stake claims of their
own: James Harrod led a group of men to the future site of Harrodsburg on the Kentucky River, where they built a small cluster of
makeshift cabins to stake their claim, while the Hite and McAfee brothers laid private claims to some Salt River lands. Taken together, the various exploratory activities in the Ohio Valley in the summer of 1774

[8] William Russell to William Preston, 13 July 1774, Draper MSS 3QQ64; Col. Christian
to Preston, 12 July 1774, Draper MSS 3QQ63; map of Clinch forts based on William
Smith's sketch of 8 July 1774, Draper MSS 25C10; Bryce Russell to Preston, 2 July
1774, Draper MSS 3QQ52; Preston to Christian, 27 June 1774, Draper MSS 3QQ47;
Dunmore to Preston, 3 July 1774, Draper MSS 3QQ53; Arthur Campbell to Preston, 6
Oct. 1774, Draper MSS 3QQ116; Charles Lewis to Preston, 9 July 1774, Draper MSS
3QQ59.

added immensely to the available fund of knowledge about the lands and transportation routes on the south side of the Ohio between the Great Kanawha and Salt Rivers. The officers' representatives also completed surveys for hundreds of individual warrants and laid off, in all, about 100,000 acres of choice Kentucky lands, even though most of their activity took place in a region that the Shawnees continued to regard as their own, and to which the crown had granted no access for such purposes. The surveying season ended early that summer, after two of the Virginia parties were attacked by Shawnee warriors in July.[9]

The combination of locally devised defenses and aggressive exploration and surveying of western lands might be called the first phase of Lord Dunmore's War. Its second phase, which culminated in an energetic but indecisive campaign against the Shawnees, carried the military organization of the frontier settlements to a higher plane. The Shawnees were recognized to be the Indian group most strongly opposed to the occupation of Kentucky lands; they still regarded those lands as their rightful hunting territory, and considered the Treaty of Fort Stanwix, in which the Iroquois ceded all the northern Indians' claims to the region, to be invalid. By mid-summer, Governor Dunmore had concluded that an offensive against the Shawnees would give invaluable aid to the Virginians' cause. Dunmore justified the campaign by invoking the recent episodes of sporadic violence and repeated rumors of war, but its larger context was the collapse of royal authority in the west. Dunmore himself serves as the paramount symbol of that collapse, as a royal appointee who ignored his responsibilities to the crown and pressed an ever more ambitious and ill-conceived campaign to occupy the Kentucky basin by force.[10]

Though his plan was approved neither by the crown nor the Virginia Assembly, Dunmore began to recruit a volunteer force for the Shawnee campaign in the summer of 1774. Without the Assembly's sanction he was unable to guarantee pay, but the recruitment letter that circulated in the western settlements assured prospective soldiers that "the plunder of the Count[r]y will be valuable, & it is said the Shawnees have a great stock of horses." With this encouragement, Dunmore mounted a force

---

[9] Jack M. Sosin, *The Revolutionary Frontier, 1763–1783* (New York, 1967), p. 77; Deposition of James Douglas, 28 Oct. 1778, Draper MSS 1CC188–191; Neal O. Hammon, "Land Acquisition on the Kentucky Frontier," *The Register of the Kentucky Historical Society*, 78 (1980), 300–304.

[10] The best survey of Dunmore's War is Thwaites and Kellogg, eds., *Dunmore's War*; the editors' introduction briefly contextualizes the campaign, while its documents offer a good overview of the progress of the war. See also the brief treatment of the campaign in Michael McConnell, *A Country Between: The Upper Ohio Valley and Its Peoples, 1724–1774* (Lincoln, NE, 1992).

of about 2,400 militiamen. A number of Shawnee chiefs, led by Cornstalk, counseled peace, but most of the Shawnee warriors chose to resist
the Virginians by force. As a military affair the campaign was indecisive.
In the Battle of Point Pleasant, the only open engagement of Lord Dunmore's War, Shawnee warriors attacked the Virginians and inflicted
some casualties, but failed to drive them off. When the Virginians
marched directly on the Scioto towns and established a camp nearby,
Cornstalk and some of his followers accepted provisional terms to prevent a direct attack on their homes. The Shawnees and Virginians
agreed to negotiate a permanent settlement at a peace conference to be
held in the following spring, and in the meantime the Shawnee leaders
agreed to give up their claims to Kentucky. This agreement became a
point of considerable controversy: the outbreak of the Revolution pre-
empted the peace conference at which permanent terms were to be discussed; in the meantime the Virginians believed they had won Kentucky
with their blood and nerve, while most Shawnee warriors regarded the
settlement to be invalid. Following the campaign the exultant Virginia
army immediately dissolved into small parties, and despite the
Shawnees' reservations many of them scouted new lands on their return
trips home.[11]

As events carried the American colonies toward a rupture with Great
Britain, the ragged backcountry settlements of Pennsylvania, Virginia,
and North Carolina were peculiarly well prepared to receive the news.
For years they had experienced the effects of the ministry's neglect, inef-
ficiency, and delays; during the crisis of 1774, they were left to shape the
defense of their isolated communities as best they could. Dunmore's War
confirmed the growing sense that neither colony nor crown controlled
their affairs. In the days following the Shawnee campaign, a backcountry resident captured this sentiment in a provocative explanation of the
recently concluded war. "When without a king," he wrote, "[one] doeth
according to the freedom of his own will."[12] It is a startling image, appearing as it does months before the first commonly recognized battle of
the Revolution and a year and a half before the colonies formally declared their independence from royal authority. The decade of ministerial neglect following the Seven Years' War prepared the ground for western independence; Lord Dunmore's War was the liberating event that
defined the contours of the revolution in the west before the actual Revolution had even begun. It confirmed for western squatters the notion

---

[11] Circular letter to militia captains from William Preston, 20 July 1774, Draper MSS
3QQ139; Thwaites and Kellogg, eds., *Dunmore's War*, throughout; Dunmore to Dartmouth, Davies, ed., *Docs. Am. Rev.*, vol. VIII, pp. 252–270.
[12] William Doack to Preston, 22 Nov. 1774, Draper MSS 3QQ101.

that they could proceed according to the freedom of their own collective will, and thus guaranteed that the war in the Ohio Valley would turn on competing claims to the land.

II

The spring and summer of 1774 comprised an extraordinary season in the Ohio Valley: military preparations, surveys, and the precipitous campaign against the Shawnee towns proclaimed a new spirit of determination among western squatters. Beginning early in 1775 a full-scale land grab followed. Parties of surveyors, settlers, and would-be proprietors and speculators took up lands throughout central Kentucky, under a variety of auspices and with many forms of more or less specious authority. The colony of Transylvania, a shoestring proprietary venture, competed with individual adventurers and coteries of former officers to control the settlement of Kentucky's best lands. Their efforts created a complex patchwork of surveys, claims, homesteads, and clusters of log cabins; by late summer of 1775, more than half a dozen towns had been founded in central Kentucky – some of them were little more than a single structure at a crossroads, others included a dozen or more buildings – and more than a thousand aspiring landholders had established property claims in the Kentucky and Salt River basins.

Without even waiting for spring weather, parties of prospective settlers began to leave their homes in western Virginia, Pennsylvania, and North Carolina to establish claims in the Kentucky bluegrass. James, Robert, and George McAfee set out from their Botetourt County, Virginia farms on February 20 and made their way to a spring at the headwaters of the Salt River, where they had scouted land two summers earlier. James Harrod – who spent the years following the Seven Years' War as a trader on the Ohio River, had traveled as far west as Kaskaskia, and had enjoyed many opportunities to explore the rich lands south of the river – led a party of more than forty Virginians from the squatter settlements along the Monongahela River down the Ohio to the cluster of cabins he and his companions had built, also on the upper Salt River, in the previous year. John Floyd, a Virginia surveyor who laid off officers' lands during the summer of 1774, guided a group of about thirty men from the Holston River settlements to the headwaters of Dick's River, where they founded the town of St. Asaph's. A fourth party of adventurers came from North Carolina under the leadership of Thomas Slaughter; they arrived in early May and joined Harrod's settlement.[13] These

[13] William Stewart Lester, *The Transylvania Colony* (Spencer, IN, 1935), p. 57; Kathryn Harrod Mason, *James Harrod of Kentucky* (Baton Rouge, 1951), pp. 30–52, 68–79;

earliest groups of squatters on Kentucky lands coexisted uneasily with each other; they all established town sites in close proximity to one another and competed for good land, but they were also conscious of participating in a common enterprise with an uncertain future, in which cooperation might be vital to the success of their individual undertakings.

These squatter parties were soon joined by representatives of the Transylvania Company. The animating spirit of the venture was Richard Henderson, a backcountry lawyer and superior court judge from Granville, North Carolina who had dreamed for years of a western colony in Kentucky. He had hired Daniel Boone to make a series of exploratory surveys west of the Cumberland Mountains, beginning as early as 1764. After several false starts, Henderson finally assembled the Transylvania Company investors in January, 1775, and pressed ahead with his carefully planned settlement scheme. With the Iroquois cession at Fort Stanwix, and the defeat of the Shawnees in Dunmore's campaign, Henderson calculated that all the claims of the northern Indians to the Kentucky lands had been extinguished. The Cherokees were the only southern tribe with a reasonable claim to the region, since parts of Kentucky had been claimed as a Cherokee hunting ground. In the treaties of Hard Labor (1768) and Lochaber (1770) the Cherokees ceded a large swath of eastern Kentucky to Great Britain, extending west from the Allegheny Ridge as far as the Kentucky River. Henderson's plan was to make an additional purchase of land from the Cherokees on the southwest side of the Kentucky River line – a purchase that would embrace all of the earliest squatter communities in Kentucky – and in March of 1775 he arranged a meeting with several Cherokee leaders to propose the sale. Following a brief (and, some critics suggested, peremptory) four-day conference, the Cherokees, led by the Little Carpenter, Dragging Canoe, and the Raven, agreed to part with their claims to all the land lying between the Kentucky and Cumberland Rivers. In exchange for about £10,000 worth of cloth, metal goods, guns and ammunition, food, and liquor, the Transylvania Company acquired what its members regarded as a legitimate deed to between seventeen and twenty million acres of land in the heart of Kentucky.[14]

Before the Cherokee conference had drawn to a close, Daniel Boone

Charles Gano Talbert, *Benjamin Logan: Kentucky Frontiersman* (Lexington, KY, 1962), pp. 15–17.

[14] One reason for the Cherokees' willingness to part with their western hunting grounds was probably the tenuousness of their claim to them. William Johnson thought the Iroquois claim to the Kentucky lands pre-empted that of the Cherokees; the lands purchased by Henderson and the Transylvania Company were, moreover, far afield from the center of Cherokee settlement in the Carolina mountains. For Henderson, the Transylvania Company, and the Cherokee purchase at Sycamore Shoals, see Lester, *Transyl-*

was already leading an advance party through the Cumberland Gap and northwestward across eastern Kentucky as far as the Kentucky River, where they settled the town of Boonesborough on its southern bank. The Transylvania colonists, like the other parties of settlers, immediately faced the need to choose between individual and collective enterprises. Should their time be spent in staking land claims and erecting cabins and fences, or should the labor of the group be devoted to building a fort and clearing land while the proprietors laid out streets, created town lots, and established an orderly framework for granting lands? Unsurprisingly, the Transylvanians overwhelmingly favored private pursuits over community projects. Henderson wrote with some concern in early June that the Boonesborough settlement stretched along the river for nearly two miles, and its residents worked "in their different lots . . . without care or caution." When Boone's party first arrived at the Kentucky River they began to build a small fort, but the project was quickly abandoned in favor of the private pursuit of land. Now, Henderson wrote, it needed only two or three days' effort to be completed, but neither he nor Boone could persuade their settlement party to do the work. Henderson speculated that the fort might never be finished, "unless the Indians should do us the favor of annoying us, and regularly scalping a man every week until it is performed."[15]

By summer's end new settlements dotted the Kentucky landscape, and thousands of hastily marked land claims spread out from the center of activity just south of the Kentucky River to embrace all the most desirable land in the area. Well-watered, fertile grasslands with access to good springs were coveted as farmland, while key points on major waterways, where ferries or portages would delay travelers, made especially promising sites for future towns. Most of the adventurers who came to Kentucky in 1775 were not content to stake out a single claim or accept a modest plot in one of the new communities; instead, they spent their spare time riding through the woods, exploring the river bottoms, searching out valuable lands. Thus Slaughter and his men complained, when they arrived in Harrodsburg, that Harrod's group "had Secured every good spring in a Country of 20 odd miles in length and almost as broad." While many poorer aspirants to western land did their own legwork, men of means employed agents and surveyors to seek out choice

vania, pp. 1–47. For Boone, see John Mack Faragher's engaging biography, *Daniel Boone: The Life and Legend of an American Pioneer* (New York, 1992).

[15] Lester, *Transylvania*, pp. 58–82; Henderson to the [Transylvania] Proprietors in North Carolina, 12 June 1775, in George W. Ranck, *Boonesborough: Its Founding, Pioneer Struggles, Indian Experiences, Transylvania Days, and Revolutionary Annals*, Filson Club Publications no. 16 (Louisville, 1901), Appendix L, pp. 188–189.

lands on their behalf. It was among the more well-to-do speculators in western lands – former militia officers, substantial landholders, and successful merchants – that the interest was highest in anticipating the future town sites of Kentucky. It was universally agreed that the most promising of these lay at the falls of the Ohio, about midway between the mouths of the Kentucky and Salt Rivers (where, in fact, the town of Louisville would soon stand). Although the land alongside the falls was marshy and poor, it was surveyed repeatedly between 1773 and 1778, and as migrants moved into Kentucky it was subjected to countless overlapping and conflicting claims, until the entire area was covered by a bewildering web of artificial lines that were supposed to denote possession.[16]

If there is security in numbers, the flood of prospective settlers into Kentucky should have been secure in the possession of the land they acquired; but in fact they knew no sure method of guaranteeing the legitimacy of their claims. Former militia officers who held warrants for western lands hoped that the Bullitt, Floyd, and Thompson surveys would be upheld against any later encroachments. The view held most widely by the western squatters was that they could secure a claim to land by marking its boundaries clearly, building a cabin, and planting a crop of corn. Others had chosen to cast their lots with the Transylvania Company by purchasing a title to land from its proprietors, while some who were dubious of the Transylvania claim nevertheless hedged their bets by purchasing a deed from the company. It is impossible to estimate the number of prospective landholders who followed each of these courses, or to know how many acres of Kentucky land were surveyed or marked during the summer of 1775. But by the end of the year the Transylvania Company alone had granted more than nine hundred deeds within the bounds of its purchase; the towns of Boonesborough, Harrodsburg, Boiling Spring, and St. Asaph's had all been founded within a month or two of one another, and taken together they had an estimated population of three hundred residents by early summer; and smaller parties had established several one- or two-family outposts beyond this cluster of settlements.[17] Without official sanction or approval, the pri-

---

[16] The quote is from the Journal of Richard Henderson, entry for 7 May 1775, in Draper MSS 1CC49–51. Two groups made their way to the falls during the summer of 1775, one led by Thomas Bullitt, the other by John Connolly; both hoped to exploit the officers' surveys that had already been made in the region: see Henderson's Journal, Draper MSS 1CC101–102.

[17] Talbert, *Logan*, pp. 17–18; Henderson's Journal, Draper MSS 1CC41–45, 69–71, 89–91; John Williams' Report to the Proprietors, 3 Jan. 1776, Ranck, *Boonesborough*, App. S, p. 234.

vately sponsored occupation of Kentucky progressed with astonishing speed in 1775. It remained for its participants to secure and validate the infant communities that grew out of their efforts.

* * *

Coinciding as it did with the outbreak of the Revolution, the land rush in Kentucky gained legitimacy, support, and momentum from the political crisis that sundered the British empire in America. The progress of the Revolution, both as an ideological transformation and as a military enterprise, became inseparable from the steadily mounting pressure on western lands. As the writings of the settlers themselves make clear, the logic of rebellion resonated in important ways with the reasoning that led them to take up western lands in the first place; at the same time, strategic considerations made it imperative for Revolutionary leaders to offer support and defense to the scattered farms and settlements on the Ohio Valley frontier. At the outbreak of the war, westerners thus forged a relationship with the Revolutionary governments that gained its strength partly from shared ideological commitments and partly from calculations of mutual interest and convenience.

The spirit and language of the Revolution first received clear expression in the Kentucky settlements late in the spring of 1776, when a group of Harrodsburg residents began to object publicly to the actions of the Transylvania proprietors. A series of petitions to the Virginia Convention outlined their grievances; with these it is possible to trace the evolution of the settlers' reactions and ideas in a time of rapid change in politics and public discourse. The first petition, drafted in April or May and signed by 88 settlers, reflected little or no awareness of the imperial crisis; it could just as appropriately have been sent to a royal governor as to a revolutionary convention. Its purpose was to express local reservations about the Transylvania Company in light of recent developments. The most important of these was the decision by Henderson and his partners to increase land prices and fees sharply before the colony's second season of settlement. The price of a hundred acres jumped from twenty shillings to two pounds ten shillings; entry and warrant fees were set at two dollars, surveying fees at four dollars, and deed and annexation fees at two dollars; and a quitrent of two shillings per hundred acres was instituted, effective in 1780. These changes marked a surprising departure from the easy terms of the company's first season, and the petitioners hoped to distance themselves from the "gentlemen stiling themselves proprietors." The settlers were also concerned that Henderson's purchase from the Cherokees – and, by extension, the titles that many of them had purchased from him – might not even be valid. They therefore asked the Virginia Convention to recognize that their settlements were not tied to the Transylvania venture, and to offer them protection independent of it.[18]

Within a month the first Harrodsburg petition was supplemented by two others. Apparently inspired by the recently arrived George Rogers Clark, they reflect a much more acute awareness of the political and rhetorical opportunities that were presented by the Revolutionary movement. Clark was only twenty-four when he came to Harrodsburg, but he was immediately recognized as an important leader in the community. In the petitions he helped to draft, the Harrodsburg faction identified itself explicitly with the language and ideals of the Revolution. Henderson and his partners no longer "stiled" themselves simply as proprietors; they now "stile themselves the *true and absolute* Proprietors" of Transylvania. In the previous spring Henderson had sponsored a constitutional convention for the frontier communities, in which many of the petitioners had happily participated; now that process served as further evidence of the proprietors' malignant intentions. The petitioners complained that "in consequence of their Usurped authority officers both Civil and Military are appointed, Writs of Election issued[,] Assemblys convened, a Land Office opened, Conveyances made, [and] lands sold at an Exorbitant Price." In short, the proprietors had adopted a "System of Policy . . . which does not at all Harmonize with that lately adopted by the United Colonies." Indeed, the petitioners warned, if the Transylvania Company proceeded in its course, then "for ought yet appears this Fertile Country will afford a safe Asylum to those whose principles are Inimical to American Freedom."[19] To block the growth of an oppressive regime on Virginia's western border, the Harrodsburg group asked that the Virginia Convention invalidate the Transylvania purchase and extend its jurisdiction to include the western settlements.

The antiproprietary faction in Harrodsburg thus drew an unambiguous connection between its objections to the Transylvania Company and the objections raised by Revolutionary leaders against British rule. But that was not all: Interwoven with the idea that proprietary government was inimical to liberty was a second line of argument, which more accurately captured the spirit of Kentucky's settlement and offered an even more explosive rationale for the legitimacy of the Kentucky squatters' claims. For the Harrodsburg petitioners, freedom from oppression

---

[18] "Petition of Transylvanians to the Virginia Convention" [rec'd. May 1776], Ranck, *Boonesborough*, App. U, pp. 241–244; quote: p. 243.

[19] This and the following two paragraphs are based on two petitions, the first dated 7–15 June 1776, the second 20 June 1776; both can be found in James Rood Robertson, ed., *Petitions of the Early Inhabitants of Kentucky to the General Assembly of Virginia, 1769–1792*, Filson Club Publications no. 27 (Louisville, 1914), pp. 36–41. The emphasis in the first quotation has been added.

easily merged with the freedom to pursue their desire for western lands without restraint. Many of them, they noted, "became Adventurers in this part of the Colony in the year 1774, in order to provide a subsistance for themselves and their Posterity; but were soon obliged by our Savage Enemy to abandon their Enterprise." Virginia – and especially its backcountry adventurers – had, in the eyes of the petitioners, the best possible claim to Kentucky: "They Fought and bled for it." In the "memorable Battle at the Great Kanaway" (the inconclusive engagement at Point Pleasant that marked the high point of Lord Dunmore's campaign against the Shawnees), Virginia had won the right to claim Kentucky as its own. Now, with the approach of a war that might determine the fate of liberty in America, the Harrodsburg group pleaded for the opportunity to defend the cause of freedom. We "cannot but observe," they warned, "how impolitical it would be to suffer such a Respectable body of prime Rifle men" to be forced to remain neutral, or even to fight for tyrants, because Virginia failed to act when it had the chance.

In theoretical terms, the American Revolution challenged the old monarchical assumption that political authority flowed from the top of society downward, from God's chosen regent, the king, through his appointed noble authorities, finally settling in a residual form among established landowners of the realm. The new American states went to war in part to establish the principle that sovereign authority flowed in the other direction, and originated with the people themselves.[20] In the Kentucky settlements, this principle seemed by extension to grant legitimacy to the victors in an unregulated contest for western land.

If Virginia took the Kentucky settlements under its wing, the Harrodsburg petitioners predicted that a glorious flowering of the west – which had hitherto been obstructed by the "Base proceedings of a Detestible, Wicked and Corrupt Ministry to prevent any more counties to be laid off" – would follow. If Virginia would simply validate the occupation of Kentucky, they predicted, "Every obstacle would be Removed, Population [would] increase and of consequence a Barrier to the interior parts of Virginia from the Indians [would be formed]." The growth of settlement in Kentucky would insulate Virginia against attack in the impending war with Great Britain and its Indian allies; but that was only the beginning. By creating a new zone of settlement in the Ohio Valley, Virginia could enjoy the fruits of its fertile soil and benefit from the opening of the Ohio River to free navigation, a consequence which

---

[20] The most sophisticated exploration of this principle is still found in Gordon Wood, *The Creation of the American Republic, 1776–1787* (Chapel Hill, 1969); see also his *The Radicalism of the American Revolution* (New York, 1992).

would surely follow closely on the heels of settlement. "A new source of wealth would then be opened, as Trade and Navigation under the auspices of Virginia would Flourish, in the Western world." For all these reasons – for the promise of the future, no less than the sacrifices of the past – the Harrodsburg settlers proclaimed their determination "to acquit our conscience and not entail *Slavery* upon our posterity by submitting to the pretensions and impositions of the pretended proprietors."

The Harrodsburg petitions succeeded in their aim. In the fall of 1776, the newly created House of Delegates in Virginia passed a bill to divide Fincastle County into three new counties – Kentucky, Washington, and Montgomery – and effectively extended its jurisdiction across all of the modern state of Kentucky. Another bill also divided the county of West Augusta in three; by this act Virginia forfeited its claim to Pittsburgh, but organized nearly all of the lands lying south of Pittsburgh along the Monongahela and Youghiogheny Rivers into Ohio, Monongalia, and Yohogania Counties (the last of which fell almost entirely within the modern borders of Pennsylvania).[21] Across the entire broad sweep of its newly organized frontier, Virginia immediately had to face the problem of defense. These settlements were illegitimate in the eyes of both the British empire and the local Indian population. Just as the Ohio Indians objected to the settlements along the Ohio River, the Cherokees actively opposed the settlers in the Clinch, Holston, Powell, and Watauga Valleys. The cost of defending these communities would be high, but the alternative was worse. The crown's ties to the west were potentially much stronger than Virginia's. It was difficult to assess the influence that its alliances and diplomatic gifts, its knowledgeable and respected Indian agents, and the overriding importance of its transatlantic economy would have on western loyalties, but there was obvious reason to be concerned. The settlers represented an important potential counterweight to the British empire in the west, but it was left to the leaders of the rebellion to secure them to the Revolutionary movement. By validating the occupation of western lands and providing for the settlers' defense, the leaders of the Revolution took an important step toward improving their prospects in the war with Great Britain.

For Virginia's Revolutionary government, the decision to organize six new western counties was thus based largely on considerations of military strategy. Through the county governments, militia units were quickly organized to serve the Revolutionary cause. The settlers also

---

[21] For the laws themselves, see William Hening, ed., *The Statutes at Large; Being a Collection of all the Laws of Virginia, from the First Session of the Legislature in the Year 1619*, 13 vols. (New York, Philadelphia, and Richmond, 1819–1823), vol. IX, pp. 257–266; see also the drafts and editorial note in Julian P. Boyd et al., eds., *The Papers of Thomas Jefferson* (Princeton, NJ, 1950–), vol. I, pp. 564–576.

benefitted from the arrangement: by extending its jurisdiction westward, Virginia's House conferred legitimacy upon their western settlements and supported their local efforts at self-defense. Beginning in the
spring and summer of 1776, Virginia also began to supply the western
settlements with more elemental forms of defensive support – powder,
lead, and manpower. In May the Virginia Committee of Safety dispatched 600 pounds of gunpowder, "over & above that already allocated," to the frontier counties of Fincastle, Botetourt, and Pittsylvania. In
June George Rogers Clark and John Gabriel Jones traveled from the
Kentucky settlements to Williamsburg; arriving after the Convention
had adjourned, they nevertheless convinced the Council to give them
500 pounds of gunpowder. Virginia regularly offered military support to
the western settlements thereafter. Occasionally the eastern counties
even provided manpower to relieve to Kentucky settlers; in the fall of
1777, for example, when the three principal fortifications in Kentucky
were all under siege, Colonel John Bowman led a detachment of about
200 militiamen from the eastern settlements to relieve them.[22] In all of
these actions, Virginia's Revolutionary government committed itself to
the defense of the heretofore illegitimate western settlements.

The Continental Congress was also quick to recognize the strategic
importance of the Ohio Valley in its war effort, and soon acted to defend its communities. In July 1776 Congress notified the governor and
council of Virginia that it would man and maintain the three forts on
the upper Ohio: one at Pittsburgh and one each at the mouths of Wheeling Creek and the Great Kanawha River. In the fall it assigned a battal-
ion of continental troops to Fort Pitt, supplemented four months later
by an additional 200 men. To support these troops as well as the local
militia, Congress allocated two tons of powder, four tons of lead,
enough boats to transport 1,500 men down the Ohio, if necessary, and
food to support 2,000 men for six months. When conditions deteriorated in the following spring, Congress stepped up its aid. It sent 1,000 ri-
fles and another ton of lead to Fort Pitt, allocated $4,000 to improve the
fortifications there, and asked the Virginia House to commit an additional four tons of lead for the defense of the upper Ohio.[23]

---

[22] Order of the Virginia Committee of Safety, 27 May 1776, Draper MSS 4QQ48; Clark
to John Brown, [1791], quoted in John E. Selby, *The Revolution in Virginia,
1775–1783* (Williamsburg, VA, 1988), p. 141; for Bowman's expedition, see, e.g.,
Humphrey Marshall, *The History of Kentucky, Including an Account of the Discovery,
Settlement, Progressive Improvement, Political and Military Events, and Present State
of the Country* (Morehead, KY, 1971 [orig. pub. 1812]), pp. 29–30; and for additional
aid in 1777, Patrick Henry to General Edward Hand, 27 July 1777, Draper MSS
18J26.

[23] Worthington C. Ford et al., eds., *Journals of the Continental Congress, 1774–1789*, 34
vols. (Washington, 1904–1937) [hereafter *JCC*], proceedings for 11 July 1776, vol. V,

Just as the land rush of 1775 and 1776 triggered a supportive response in the Virginia House and the Continental Congress, the actions of the Revolutionary governments encouraged, in turn, a much larger second wave of emigration into the Ohio Valley. Beyond its willingness to provide for frontier defense, the Virginia House of Delegates passed two laws in 1779 that created a legal framework for the occupation of western lands. These bills – one that settled old land claims and another that established the procedure for claiming lands in the future – left a complicated legacy, and historians have long debated their merits and shortcomings. They made land widely and easily available, but their complex provisions were difficult for men without means to satisfy; in general, therefore, they favored ambitious middling speculators over either great land companies, on the one hand, or poor settlers on the other.[24]

The law that settled preexisting claims to western lands appeared to favor those who had actually settled in the west – the squatters who had "fought and bled" for the land – but it prescribed such an intricate and confusing set of procedures that its easy terms soon appeared chimerical to many prospective landholders.[25] First priority was given to claims that were based on actual settlement; those who had taken up lands prior to January 1, 1778 were entitled to claim four hundred acres as their own. Where military or company surveys overlapped with settlement rights, the settlers had a superior claim, but where such surveys embraced otherwise unclaimed lands they had priority over all other claims. Aspiring purchasers who arrived after 1778 could claim any lands that were not preempted by earlier settlers' or officers' claims.

But to hold a valid claim in theory was only the beginning of a bureaucratic odyssey for anyone seeking a title to land. Whether one was an early settler, a military officer, or a later purchaser, it was necessary to follow a bewildering series of procedures that might take one first to Kentucky, to locate a claim, then to the treasurer's office in Richmond, to pay the patent fee, then to the auditor's office, where one received a certificate for the treasurer's receipt, then to the land office, where the auditor's certificate for the treasurer's receipt entitled one to a land war-

---

p. 542; 12 Sept. 1776, vol. V, p. 752; 8 Jan. 1777, vol. VII, pp. 20–22; 9 and 15 Apr. 1777, vol. VII, pp. 247, 270.

[24] The laws are printed in Hening, ed., *Statutes at Large*, vol. X, pp. 35–65; on their formulation, see also Boyd et al., eds., *Jefferson Papers*, vol. II, pp. 133–167. For an assessment of the laws, see especially Fredrika J. Teute, "Land, Liberty, and Labor: Kentucky as the Promised Land," (Ph.D. diss., Johns Hopkins, 1988), which is the most sustained consideration of their effects.

[25] This and the following two paragraphs are based on Hening, ed., *Statutes at Large*, vol. X, pp. 35–65.

rant. Once the paperwork in Richmond was complete, of course, the prospective landholder had to return to Kentucky and make good on his still-theoretical right to the land. He would begin by registering his land office warrant with the county surveyor and requesting that the tract be officially surveyed. The surveyor would perform the survey at his convenience, register the survey and warrant, and issue a plat and certificate, along with the endorsed warrant, to the prospective landowner. The landowner was then expected to return both the plat and the certificate to the land office in Richmond, and in exchange would receive (at last) a valid title to his lands.

Confusion was only the first barrier to land ownership; the long process of securing a warrant, survey, and title could be an expensive gamble. In addition to the small fees that were due in the land office and to the surveyor for performing their duties, a prospective landowner had to pay "consideration money" to the state of Virginia for the land. The price was set at ten shillings sterling per hundred acres – not an exorbitant price, but not an amount that was likely to be readily available to many cash-poor western farmers either. Moreover, to fulfill the terms of the new law a westerner working alone would have to make two trips to Richmond, which were expensive both in traveling costs and in lost working time. Many claimants were forced to hire an agent who could help them acquire a warrant and register their survey. (For this reason, those who were best served by the new laws were both well-informed and well-connected: they understood the provisions of the laws clearly, and they had friends in the state capital who could help them with the legwork and paperwork required.) Even if he could overcome the costs involved, a prospective claimant still had to meet deadlines that might ruin his venture; both preemption rights and certificates of survey could expire if a land claimant failed to act on them within twelve months. Finally, of course, any claim could be disputed. Land commissioners were appointed to settle conflicting claims, but their work was only the beginning; even after Kentucky was admitted as a state, litigation over land clogged its courts for decades.[26]

The 1779 laws thus made land widely available, but they favored men with the cash, connections, and information necessary to exploit them – especially lawyers and surveyors, the two groups that dominated Virginia land speculation in the colonial period. For poor settlers, especially those who arrived after the beginning of 1778, the prospects for acquiring land on easy terms were quite limited. But aspiring landhold-

---

[26] On the importance of land litigation in the early development of Kentucky, see Mary K. Bonsteel Tachau, *Federal Courts in the Early Republic: Kentucky, 1789–1816* (Princeton, NJ, 1978), especially pp. 167–190.

ers responded to the fact that titles were legally available in the Ohio Valley for the first time, without carefully calculating their own chances. An unprecedented number of migrants made their way down the Ohio River and through the Cumberland Gap in 1779 and 1780. One contemporary observer estimated that nearly 3,000 people had moved to Kentucky in 1779, and he wrote in the following March that another 3,000 "Claimrs" had already gathered in Pittsburgh, where they were "detained by the Frost" before setting out to claim their own patch of Kentucky ground. In all, more than 20,000 people were believed to have moved into Kentucky in 1779 and 1780.[27]

Virginia's land laws, and the support offered to western settlers by both the Virginia House and the Continental Congress, encouraged squatters and prospective landholders to believe in the legitimacy of their desire for free and abundant land; even when the law worked against them they moved west in record numbers. As policymakers abandoned the principle of proprietary direction in western development, which emphasized control and order over individual liberty and opportunity, they unleashed a chain of events that permanently altered the relationship between settlers and the land in the new American republic. Less than a year after the passage of Virginia's 1779 land laws, William Trent (who was not an impartial observer, since he was deeply involved in several great speculation companies) wrote to a friend in Virginia to voice his misgivings about the new direction in policy:

Every Thing . . . I prophecied respecting your State opening an Office for the Sale of the back Lands has come to pass. It has depopulated a great Part of your interior Counties, lowered your Estates in Value, put it out of your Power to furnish your Quota of Troops, to defend your Selves against an attack on the Sea Coast, and encouraged a Number of Men to take Possession not only of the unlocated lands, but those that have been appropriated without paying a Farthing and most probably will set up a new state for themselves; Besides these evils you have brought on yourselves, so many Men are gone & going from the Other States as far Eastward as N York that it will be difficult if not impossible to reconect the Army. This is the blessed Effects of political Expediency.[28]

There was one more effect Trent failed to mention: the effect of the new policy on Indian relations in the Ohio Valley. The Revolutionary

---

[27] "Colonel William Fleming's Journal of Travels in Kentucky, 1779–1780," in Newton D. Mereness, ed., *Travels in the American Colonies* (New York, 1916), pp. 636–637; Robert B. McAfee, "History of the Rise & Progress of the New Providence Church" [extracts], Draper MSS 4CC25. On the law's tendency to favor the well-connected see Teute, "Land, Liberty, and Labor."

[28] Trent to Edmond Randolph, 9 Nov. 1779, in Kenneth P. Bailey, ed., *The Ohio Company Papers, 1753–1817: Being Primarily Papers of the "Suffering Traders" of Pennsylvania* (Arcata, CA, 1947), pp. 334–335.

governments tried to secure the confidence, or at least the neutrality, of the Ohio Indians at the same time that they offered military support for the western settlements. Though many Indian leaders were initially predisposed to follow their advice, it quickly became clear that the Revolution in the west presented a fundamental challenge to the sovereignty of the western Indians.

III

The outbreak of the Revolution did not initially prompt a clear or unified response among either Indians or Europeans in the Ohio Valley. While moderate factions of Ohio Indians led by the most prominent chiefs in the region sought to preserve peace through diplomacy, small parties of disaffected warriors opposed the new communities in Kentucky and continued to harass the settlers on the Monongahela, Youghiogheny, and upper Ohio Rivers. The warriors' actions had no direct and immediate connection to the Revolutionary War itself, but they played off of it and fed into it in important ways. By the same token, the new western settlements were not clearly loyal to either the Revolution or the empire. Despite the political connection that was forged between the Revolutionary governments and the west, many western settlers remained loyal or neutral. The pressures of the Revolutionary era, however, gradually led members of both groups to see the events of the war through the lens of racial difference. For Europeans and Indians alike, the common experiences of the Revolution gradually encouraged a coordinated and aggressive response. The broad range of interests and attitudes that characterized the early period were steadily compressed into increasingly intransigent and mutually opposed postures, defined by race and defended with hostility and violence.

The Revolution opened a new chapter in the ongoing tug-of-war between Ohio Indians who advocated accommodation with the advance of Euroamerican settlement and those who favored aggressive resistance. For the leading accommodationists, neutrality appeared to be the most sensible reaction to the imperial crisis. Among a minority of disaffected warriors, however, the large-scale occupation of western lands following Dunmore's War demanded an aggressive response, and after 1775 they were increasingly willing to break away altogether from leaders who advocated peace.

Initially these tensions and divisions ran mostly beneath the surface. Leading spokesmen for the Ohio Indians adopted a conciliatory tone in their dealings with both the crown and the rebellious colonies; they were concerned, above all, to maintain regular diplomatic relations and avoid an open war with either side in the emerging conflict. Negotiation, not war, appeared to them to be the surest means of holding onto Indian lands. White Eyes, who had risen from his role as advisor to Netawatwees to become the Delawares' most influential spokesman by 1775, hedged his bets by proclaiming his solidarity with both royal representatives and the Continental Congress. He sent a belt and a reassuring message to Governor Dunmore in the early summer of 1775, to which Dunmore – from his shipboard residence-in-exile in the Chesapeake Bay – responded in kind. "[Y]ou may rest satisfied," he told White Eyes, "that our foolish men shall never be permitted to have your Lands, but on the contrary, the Great *King* will protect you and preserve you in the possession of them." Immediately following his negotiations with Dunmore's agent, White Eyes conferred with representatives of Virginia's Revolutionary government and the Continental Congress. Spokesmen for the Shawnees, Mingos, Wyandots, and Ottawas were also in attendance at Fort Pitt, and the leaders of each of these groups declared their commitment to peace and neutrality.[29]

But the leaders who participated in these conferences, like their predecessors in Pennsylvania, were by definition accommodationists. The diplomatic system depended on the success of negotiation, compromise, and consensus, and its failure would reflect badly on the leaders who were responsible for maintaining it. In order to succeed, Indian leaders had to do more than present a united and acquiescent face to congressional negotiators; they also had to quiet – or mask – the discontent of their followers. During the negotiations at Fort Pitt in the fall of 1775, Cornstalk, the chief spokesman for the Shawnees, reported to the congressional delegation that "some of my foolish Young Men have Burned Several Houses at the Mouth of the big Kanhawa[.]" He promised to dispatch two messengers "to direct my People to sit still and do no mischief while we are doing Business[.]"[30] By attributing episodes of violence to their "foolish Young Men," tribal leaders downplayed their significance and reassured negotiators that they continued to control the affairs of their people. This was the traditional rhetorical stance of Indian diplomats, one that depended upon their ability to persuade warriors to desist by procuring gifts or concessions from the Europeans with whom they negotiated.

Even as early as 1775, however, rebellious factions concluded that such concessions were not forthcoming; they rejected the advice of their

---

[29] Dunmore to White Eyes, enclosed in John Connolly to John Gibson, Aug. 1775, *Pa. Arch.* [1st Ser.], vol. IV, pp. 683–684; minutes of the Fort Pitt conference, 7–19 Oct. 1775, in Reuben G. Thwaites and Louise P. Kellogg, eds., *Revolution on the Upper Ohio, 1775–1777* (Madison, WI 1908), pp. 81–127.

[30] Fort Pitt conference, 10 Oct. 1775, Thwaites and Kellogg, eds., *Revolution on Upper Ohio*, p. 3.

leaders and opposed the European occupation of the Ohio Valley. These factions drew their strength from every tribal group in the valley, and their activities reflected the extent to which tribal structures of authority had themselves deteriorated into near irrelevance there. Although Cornstalk had formally agreed at the end of Dunmore's War that the Shawnees would not cross to the southeast side of the Ohio River, many communities with substantial numbers of Shawnees still regarded Kentucky as their hunting ground. A Shawnee headman named Kishanosity, who was known as Hardman or the Rock, complained to a visitor "of the Encroachments of the Virginians[. H]e said they were now settling in Great Numbers in the Midst of their Hunting Grounds." He was soon leading raids against the Kentucky settlers.[31]

As the Kentucky settlements began to receive military aid, this pattern grew still more pronounced. Kishanosity had heard that "the People of Virginia were all determined upon War with the Indians except the Governor who was for peace but was obliged to fly on board of a ship to save his own life[.]" Throughout 1775 and 1776, small parties of warriors crossed the river to attack the Kentucky settlements. The leaders of these parties were often younger sons of tribal leaders or lesser local headmen, and the parties were often made up of young warriors from several tribes acting together. Although the most influential counsellors of his tribe had agreed to a policy of neutrality, for example, a local Delaware chief named Catfish conducted at least one attack against the Kentucky settlements. One of the most active of these early war leaders was Pluggy, the son of a Mingo headman, and Pluggy's Town quickly became infamous as a staging ground for attacks against the Kentucky towns.[32]

In February 1777 a party of Mingo, Shawnee, Delaware, and Wyandot warriors from Pluggy's Town conducted a series of attacks on several Kentucky settlements. In response the Continental Congress and Patrick Henry, the governor of Virginia, formulated plans for a military campaign against the town, which was located on the lower Scioto. The idea was abandoned, however, after George Morgan and John Neville, who were serving as Indian commissioners at Fort Pitt for the Continental Congress, wrote to discourage any military offensive in the Ohio Valley. "[W]e apprehend the inevitable consequences of this Expedition," they warned, "will be a general Indian War." Morgan and Neville were persuaded that "many Persons among ourselves wish to promote a War

---

[31] Journal of Capt. James Wood, 2 Aug. 1775, Thwaites and Kellogg, eds., *Revolution on Upper Ohio*, p. 6.

[32] Wood's journal, 31 July and 2 Aug. 1775, Thwaites and Kellogg, eds., *Revolution on Upper Ohio*, pp. 57, 60–61; Fort Pitt conference, 11 Oct. 1775, ibid., p. 102.

with the Savages," and they feared that during the expedition against Pluggy's Town "all Indians, without distinction, who may be found are to be massacred." As an alternative to the military offensive, they hinted that Virginia should consider a plan to "withdraw or confine" its western settlements to defuse the conflicts between settlers and Indians. The letter had its desired effect; the Continental Congress asked Henry to suspend the planned campaign indefinitely.[33] As long as Revolutionary leaders supported the accommodationists, their ends were at odds with those of the western settlers. For the latter, the goal of the Revolution was to open new western lands to settlement and to secure those that had already been settled. A "general Indian War" would serve that end much more successfully than diplomatic maneuvering ever could.

The makeshift raids of 1775 and 1776 gave way to more concerted military activity in late 1777 and 1778, as a larger and more committed anti-American faction took shape among the Ohio Indians. Many were driven into the anti-Revolutionary camp by several pivotal episodes of violence against peacefully inclined Indians, as when a detachment from Fort Pitt killed a number of Delawares – mostly women, all officially neutral – in undefended camps; or when the Shawnee chief Cornstalk (the Americans' most influential Shawnee ally) and his son were murdered while they visited Fort Randolph on a diplomatic mission; or when a delegation of Seneca diplomats was attacked by a mob as they approached Fort Pitt. At about the same time, the British began to recruit Indian allies for offensive strikes against the western settlements, and neutrality became, in effect, a pro-American policy. After the string of atrocities in late 1777 and early 1778, the Ohio Indians abandoned neutrality *en masse* and chose instead to fight.[34]

Even before the war faction won out in the Ohio Valley, representatives of the Ohio warriors tried to revive the far-flung Scioto Confederacy to oppose Anglo-American expansion. In the spring of 1776 a delegation of Ohio Indians traveled south to encourage the Cherokees and Creeks to take up arms against the "long knives" from Virginia who had invaded Kentucky.[35] The party of fourteen representatives – headed

[33] Proceedings for 27 Feb. and 25 Mar. 1777, *JCC*, vol. VII, pp. 166–167, 201; VA council minutes, 12 Mar. 1777; Henry to Morgan and Neville, 12 Mar. 1777; and Morgan and Neville to Henry, 1 Apr. 1777; in *Pa. Arch.* [1st Ser.], vol. V, pp. 258–261, 286–288. Nine months later, Congress instructed its Indian commissioners to see if the Six Nations could "oblige them [the warriors of Pluggy's Town] immediately to desist"; if not, they hoped the Iroquois might themselves threaten to attack the village. 3 Dec. 1777, *JCC*, vol. IX, pp. 998–999.

[34] Randolph Downes, *Council Fires on the Upper Ohio* (Pittsburgh, 1940), pp. 201–211.

[35] This paragraph and the one that follows are based on John Stuart's letter to Lord George Germain, 23 Aug. 1776, and the enclosed report from Henry Stuart to John

by a Mingo and a Shawnee, and including Ottawas, Nanticokes, and a single young Delaware – arrived in the Cherokee towns with blackened faces, spreading ominous reports of the state of the frontier. Along their route southward, "(which but very lately used to be the Shawnese and Delawares' hunting grounds, where they used to see nothing but deer, bear, and buffalo) they found the country thickly inhabited and the people all in arms." To reach the Cherokee towns, they had to "take a round of near 300 miles to avoid being discovered." In the eyes of the northern delegation, there was only one solution to the growth of the frontier settlements: all the Indians must "drop all their former quarrels and . . . join in one common cause."

The Shawnee deputy delivered an explicit call to arms to the Cherokees. Offering a war belt "of purple whampum, strewed over with vermilion" nine feet in length, he told his audience that "it was plain" the Kentuckians intended "to extirpate them." Arguing that "it [was] better to die like men than to dwindle away by inches," he implored the Cherokees to go to war with the Virginians who had crossed the mountains. He told his audience that the delegation intended to visit every southern nation of Indians to make the same request. "[T]hat nation which should refuse to be their friends on this occasion," he warned, "should forever hereafter be considered as their common enemy." The Shawnee speaker's message recalled the dream of the Scioto Confederacy, which had created a bond of mutual interest among the Ohio Indians and had even received a sympathetic hearing from the southern tribes, but had so far failed to generate any concerted plan of action. "[N]ow is the time to begin," he told his audience; "there is no time to be lost."

The effects of this mission were dramatic but short-lived. Although the Cherokees attacked several of the frontier settlements of Virginia and North Carolina shortly after the conference, they did so alone. The Creeks refused to join them, and the Ohio Indians were in no position to offer support. In the end the Cherokees were decisively defeated by the Virginia militia.[36] Though the idea of a united Indian front to Euroamerican expansion held growing appeal, as a practical matter the

---

Stuart dated 25 Aug., in Davies, ed., *Docs. Am. Rev.*, vol. XII, pp. 188–208; quotes: pp. 199, 202–203.

[36] This was the Cherokees' only concerted military effort of the Revolutionary War. Late in the summer of 1776, 2,000 warriors marched on the settlements of Watauga, Holston, Nolichucky, and Powell's Valleys. The settlers successfully defended themselves and mounted a counteroffensive. The Cherokees accepted peace terms with Virginia in 1777, and throughout the rest of the war the nation was officially neutral; only a small band of Overhill Cherokee warriors, led by Dragging Canoe, remained actively hostile. For this campaign and its outcome, see William Preston's correspondence, May 1776–June 1777, Draper MSS 4QQ38–157; Alexander Cameron to John Stuart, 23

Native American population west of the Appalachians was broken into regional cells, each of which had distinctly different territorial concerns and political interests. Only in the Ohio Valley did the pressures of colonization break down traditional structures of authority altogether and make tribal identity increasingly irrelevant to the political activity of its population.

*   *   *

The political loyalties of most western settlers at the outbreak of the Revolution, like those of the Ohio Valley's Indian population, were complicated and plastic. As we have seen, the Revolutionary governments in Virginia and Philadelphia took important steps to establish their support for the frontier communities in the earliest stages of the war. But the political and economic foundations of the Ohio Valley were shaped largely by crown policy and British markets, which meant that many of the region's most influential inhabitants were directly tied to the empire. On the other hand, leaders of the makeshift new squatter settlements of the Ohio Valley tended to identify more strongly with their colony than the crown; their most enduring attachments and most valuable connections were with the native elite that instigated and sustained the war for independence from Great Britain. But as the war progressed the issues of the Revolution were swallowed up in the more immediate conflict, which evolved into a race-based struggle for land. In their efforts to defend the new frontier communities against Indian attacks, loyalists and patriots alike were engaged in an increasingly fierce and indiscriminate war against the Indian population in the valley.

During the early years of the Revolution the region around Fort Pitt was a notorious hotbed of loyalist activity. Many of its most prominent residents retained their connections to the crown and worked quietly to undermine the activities of local patriot leaders. John Connolly conducted negotiations with the Ohio Indians at Fort Pitt in the spring of 1775 with the approval of the Virginia Convention at the same time that he secretly pursued an ambitious scheme to recapture the Ohio country for the crown. His plan failed when a group of patriots detained him and discovered an outline of his proposed military venture; he spent most of the next five years in jail. Another plot was uncovered in August 1777 among a group of loyalist sympathizers near the old Redstone settlement on the Monongahela. Colonel Zackwell Morgan learned that a substantial number of the local residents had "sworn allegiance to the King of Great Britain, & that some of the leading men at Fort Pitt are to

Sept. 1776, in Davies, ed., *Docs. Am. Rev.*, vol. XII, pp. 229–230; and Stuart to Germain, 24 Nov. 1776, ibid., vol. XII, pp. 253–254.

be their rulers & heads." When the militia sought them out in earnest, some of the loyalists fled into the Allegheny Mountains; others presumably made whatever excuses or reparations were necessary and remained in their communities. Henry Maggee, one of the leaders who retired to the mountains, later claimed that he and his associates had enlisted 431 men in the king's service before their plan was discovered.[37]

In the spring of 1778 several groups of Pittsburgh residents chose to migrate to Detroit, which remained under British control. A handful of the most prominent traders in the Ohio Valley were among them: Alexander McKee, Simon and James Girty, Matthew Elliott, Robert Surphlitt, and John Higgins all volunteered their services to the crown. McKee was appointed a deputy agent for Indian affairs, Elliott a captain in the Indian Department, and Simon Girty an interpreter and agent in the secret service. During March and April 40 soldiers also deserted from the garrison at Fort Pitt; one group of them reportedly left with a party of local settlers. All of them were apparently also taken under the protection of the British garrison at Detroit.[38]

All of this loyalist activity serves to remind us that the Revolutionary movement was by no means a consensual event in the American colonies. On the contrary: opposition was widespread, but the rebels' superior local organization forced much of the loyalist sentiment and activity underground. On the local level, the Revolution was a paradoxical event. While the independence movement was theoretically an expression of the unitary will of the people, colonists were deeply divided on the question of taking up arms against their king.[39] For many, the rebellion was an unconscionable crime against public order and the social contract.[40] The local divisions that grew out of this disagreement struck many participants in the Revolution as strangely aberrant; Zackwell Morgan, for one, was deeply unsettled by the loyalist activity he uncovered. He acted quickly "to put a stop to this unnatural unheard of

---

[37] Siebert, *Loyalists of Pennsylvania*, pp. 9–14; Morgan to Gen. Hand, 29 Aug. 1777, in Thwaites and Kellogg, eds., *Frontier Defense*, pp. 52–53.

[38] Siebert, *Loyalists of Pennsylvania*, pp. 14–15.

[39] Because rebellion was an extraordinary step that was only justified by an extreme abuse of power, unanimity was an important dimension of the Revolutionary movement. Jonathan Mayhew, for example, wrote, "For a nation thus abused to arise *unanimously* and to resist their prince . . . is not criminal, but a reasonable way of vindicating their liberties and just rights." From *A Discourse Concerning Unlimited Submission* (Boston, 1750); quoted in Bernard Bailyn, *The Ideological Origins of the American Revolution* (Cambridge, MA, 1967), p. 93 [emphasis added]. This conception of the popular interest as unitary was carried forth in Revolutionary political theory; see Wood, *Creation of the American Republic*, pp. 57–58 and following.

[40] For an explication of this view see Janice Potter, *The Liberty We Seek: Loyalist Ideology in Colonial New York and Massachusetts* (Cambridge, MA, 1983).

frantick scene of mischief that was in the very heart of our country."[41]
As long as the bonds of loyalty in a community were hidden from view,
the unity of the population – and the legitimacy of the Revolutionary
movement itself – remained in doubt.

But while these dynamics tore many communities apart, in the Ohio
Valley divisions between patriots and loyalists were quickly overwhelmed by the primary importance of local defense against Indian attacks. When the British began arming and advising Indian warriors in
1778, loyalism became a dead letter in the Ohio River settlements. Especially at the isolated outposts of Kentucky, questions of political allegiance were superseded as the war progressed by the more fundamental
problem of ensuring the survival of the communities themselves. The increasingly systematic and sustained Indian attacks of 1777 and 1778
forced would-be loyalists and patriots to cooperate in order to defend
their place in the Kentucky landscape.

The pressures of Indian attacks forced settlers to organize and regiment their communities to accomplish the most basic tasks of survival.
Teams of people traveled to fields to tend or harvest crops; hunting,
wood-gathering, and salt-making parties made carefully planned forays
into the Kentucky countryside; and, of course, both defensive and offensive military operations were coordinated and collective efforts. In 1779
a group of Boonesborough residents adopted a formal plan for tending
a crop of corn. "Whereas we the subscribers," their articles of association began, "being willing and desirous of making a crop of corn at the
station of Boonesborough, on the Kentucky, do think it essentially necessary for our own safety and the public good, to enter into rules that
may be obligatory on each subscriber." The articles of association
named three overseers for the operation, and required the subscribers to
appear every morning, at the beat of a drum, to receive their orders.
While some of them worked in the fields, others were employed as spies
and guards. Boonesborough's association only formalized a process that
was common to each of the Kentucky communities during the years of
fighting, when local leaders regularly made arrangements to ensure that
their townspeople were provided with food and other necessities.[42]

---

[41] Morgan to Hand, 29 Aug. 1777, in Thwaites and Kellogg, eds., *Frontier Defense*, p. 53.

[42] "Association for the Settlers of Boonesboro, in 1779, for Making a Crop of Corn," 15 Apr. 1779 [from the Kentucky Historical Society], Draper MSS 1CC207. Descriptions of communally organized activities are ubiquitous in the early histories of Kentucky; for the organizational role played by community leaders, see, e.g., Talbot, *Logan*, espe-cially pp. 31–67; Mason, *Harrod*, pp. 91–129; Faragher, *Boone*, pp. 141–225.

The core institution in this process of community regimentation was the militia. Although the earliest tendency of the Kentucky squatters was to fend for themselves, the experience of occasional Indian attacks soon taught them the value of preparedness and cooperation. That spirit was formalized in March, 1777, when Virginia's Kentucky County held its first formal militia muster. Three communities participated: Harrodsburg, Boonesborough, and Logan's Station. They had a total population of 280 settlers, with 121 men available to defend them.[43] As Indian attacks intensified in the summer of 1777, militia duty became the paramount activity of the Kentucky men.

Beginning in 1778, the Kentucky settlers also periodically organized offensive military campaigns against the Ohio Indians' towns. Frontier residents were often deeply ambivalent about such expeditions, since marching off to fight meant leaving their own homes unprotected. Commanding officers therefore discovered that, the more ambitious their own plans were, the less willing the settlers were to follow them. George Rogers Clark, who had a penchant for grand military adventure, was consistently unpopular with the frontier population even though his superiors regarded him as a capable strategist and brilliant leader. His scheme to capture Detroit appeared foolhardy to a population that was primarily interested in defending its own lands from Indian attacks, and they deserted in large numbers when they discovered his intentions.[44] The response to locally planned expeditions against Indian towns that harbored raiding warriors, on the other hand, was much more positive. Such counterraids served two purposes: the settlers could avenge earlier attacks; they might also gain valuable plunder in horses and furs. Thus when John Bowman organized an expedition to march against the Shawnee town of Chillicothe in the summer of 1779, the residents of the Kentucky towns willingly participated in the attack.[45] Whatever the political inclinations of the Kentucky settlers at the outbreak of the Revo-

---

[43] Faragher, *Boone*, pp. 145–146.

[44] Desertion was a problem even in Clark's first campaign in the west, in 1778–1779; see Selby, *Revolution in Virginia*, pp. 189–198. His reputation among the western population deteriorated as the war progressed, and he had even more difficulty raising men for campaigns in 1781 and 1786. See Thomas Scott to Joseph Reed, 19 Oct. 1781, and Clark to Reed, 4 Aug. 1781, Draper MSS 46J66–67; Marshall, *History of Kentucky*, pp. 289–291. Clark was vilified in Kentucky for his abuses of the public trust; see the anonymously penned charges sent to Col. William Fleming, in 1778 and again in 1780, in the Draper MSS 46J10, 58.

[45] Marshall, *History of Kentucky*, pp. 116–120; on plunder see, e.g., Chester R. Young, ed., *Westward into Kentucky: The Narrative of Daniel Trabue* (Lexington, KY, 1981), p. 57.

lution, the dynamics of the war largely effaced the distinction between loyalists and patriots and replaced it with a racially defined sense of identity and interests. In the long run, nothing the British crown did during the course of the war could have alienated the settlers in the Ohio Valley as completely as its decision to arm the Ohio Indians.

By war's end, loyalism was identified almost exclusively with Indian traders who lived beyond the frontiers of settlement and maintained mysterious relations with the Indian population of the Ohio Valley. Indeed, a number of leading Ohio Valley traders had taken up the British cause, and in the context of war even traders who professed neutrality could be regarded as enemies. Suspicion automatically attached itself to trading houses, where Kentucky residents thought hostile Indians were probably receiving arms and supplies even if they protested that their activities and intentions were peaceful. The frontier communities also developed a deep and abiding fear of spies. Although much of the information that came to Indian leaders and British officers at Detroit was probably gathered by parties of Indian scouts, Kentuckians also blamed loyalists for the knowledge accumulated by their enemies. To associate or be identified with Indians or the Indian trade was to invite the suspicion and hostility of the settlers. Newcomers to the frontier communities, on the other hand, although they might initially be regarded with caution, were quickly drawn into the regimen of local activities and assumed to be loyal to the Revolutionary cause.[46] Simply by identifying themselves with the effort to settle the west, strangers in the Kentucky towns proved themselves loyal and trustworthy citizens.

IV

Just as the need to organize community affairs during the early stages of the Revolution brought settlers together in common cause, the vivid and terrifying experiences they shared as the war dragged on left an indelible mark on their collective identity. The fear, hardship, and suffering that the western settlers endured together forged a common set of values that gave shape and meaning to their shared social world.

The squatters who took up land in Kentucky beginning in 1775 only gradually comprehended how precarious their position really was. Indian attacks were an object of sensation and concern during the first season and a half of settlement, but they were too sporadic and isolated to

---

[46] For suspicions attached to trading houses see, e.g., the interview with Daniel Higgins Sr., Draper MSS 3S131. For the fear of loyalist spies, William Preston to [Gov. James Monroe], 26 Apr. 1782, Draper MSS 5QQ108; interview with James Chambers, Draper MSS 3S102.

inspire a sustained reaction from the settlers. Although several encounters resulted in single deaths, their infrequency made them seem almost accidental. In mid-July of 1776, one of the most celebrated and frequently recounted events of the Revolutionary period drove home to the Kentuckians the extent of their isolation and vulnerability. Three young girls, Jemima Boone and Betsy and Frances Calloway, were kidnapped by a party of six Shawnees and Cherokees while they played along the river near Boonesborough. A rescue party recovered the girls two days later, but the event aroused alarm and encouraged the widely dispersed Kentucky settlers to reassess their priorities. The fort-building projects that had languished in every town in the Kentucky basin suddenly gained new life; by summer's end substantial fort stockades had been built in Boonesborough, Harrodsburg, and at Benjamin Logan's settlement on Elkhorn Creek. At the same time, the occupants of isolated plantations who had nurtured dreams of expansive estates began to reconsider their plans. Many isolated farms were temporarily abandoned in favor of one of the fortified towns, and some groups of settlers, like the founders of Hinkston's Station on the south fork of the Licking River, decided to quit the country altogether and return to the relative safety of the eastern settlements.[47]

Once the attacks against the Kentucky outposts had begun, the older communities in the Ohio Valley – those in the vicinity of Pittsburgh – faced renewed assaults from Indian warriors as well. Along the Monongahela, the Youghiogheny, and their tributaries, where settlements had gone unchallenged for several years, Indian warriors revived the effort to drive the settlers off the land. The residents there, like their Kentucky counterparts, responded by building blockhouses and forts, organizing local patrols and militia units, and preparing to defend themselves.[48]

For nearly twenty years the settlers of the Ohio Valley fought with the Ohio Indians for control of the land. Throughout the years of conflict they spent long periods of time living in small and squalid forts, where they struggled to meet the most basic needs of their survival. When they escaped the confinement of their log forts, they were constantly exposed to the unforseeable dangers that plagued the Kentucky

[47] For scattered episodes of violence during 1775 and 1776 and the responses to them, see, e.g, Lester, *Transylvania*, pp. 62–63, 112–115, 162–170; Talbert, *Logan*, pp. 25–28. The kidnapping story appears in countless histories of Revolutionary Kentucky; the earliest printed version may be the one in Marshall, *History of Kentucky*, pp. 20–21. For an excellent account of the early settlement period, also see Faragher, *Boone*, pp. 98–140.

[48] See, e.g., the Narrative of Captain Spencer Records, 1842, Draper MSS 23CC7–8; interview with Isaac Bane, Draper MSS 2S11; interview with James Chambers, Draper MSS 3S72, 76–77, 82.

landscape. Though they were drawn to the west by the promise of apparently boundless opportunity, settlers instead found themselves almost constantly surrounded by perils and challenges unlike any they had ever known.

The rhythms of the frontier war, which overlapped with the Revolution but outlasted it by more than a decade, determined how closely the frontier population was tied to its forts. When hostilities waned, settlers could return for a time to their land claims; but when the attacks intensified, they were forced to endure long periods of time locked up together inside cramped log walls. In 1777, during the first phase of sustained Indian raids, all of the Kentucky settlers who remained in the west passed the entire year crowded into the only three substantial forts in the region. In later years the number of forts grew, but the population increased even faster. Throughout the war, the Kentucky settlers periodically struggled with the overcrowding, chronic hunger and disease, and destitution that accompanied fort life. Simply to survive these long periods of close confinement was a challenge of the first magnitude. Most of the Kentucky forts were poorly provided with water, and sanitation was almost entirely overlooked. Disease periodically plagued all of the forts; at some, poor location or bad planning made it an endemic feature of the community. At the falls of the Ohio, a bad water supply caused many of the inhabitants to complain in 1779 "of the fever and Ague and many of the Children dying." The Boonesborough fort was described as "a dirty place in winter like every other Station." At Harrodsburg, a local epidemic in the spring of 1780 was exacerbated by the situation of the fort, as a visitor explained. "The Spring at this place," he wrote,

is below the Fort and fed by ponds above the Fort so that the whole dirt and filth of the Fort, putrified flesh, dead dogs, horse, cow, hog excrements and human odour all wash into the spring which with the Ashes and sweepings of filthy Cabbins, the dirtiness of the people, steeping skins to dress and washing every sort of dirty rags and cloths in the spring perfectly poisons the water and makes the most filthy nauseous potation . . . imaginable.[49]

The most basic needs of the Kentucky settlements were met only with great difficulty while their populations were sequestered in forts. During the growing season the inhabitants tried to raise enough grain to feed themselves, but when they forted up their crops were often concentrated in one or two fields nearby. They were a common, and easy, target of Indian attacks. Livestock, too, was at constant risk and was impossible to defend. A group of Kentucky petitioners lamented to the Virginia As-

---

[49] John Bowman to General Hand, 12 Dec. 1777, Draper 18J50; Fleming's Journal, 1779–1780, Mereness, ed., *Travels*, pp. 621, 626–627, 630.

sembly in 1779 that "many of us that brought good stocks of both Horses and cows, now at this juncture have not so much as one cow for the support of our familys." The price of food fluctuated wildly according to availability and demand. These depended, in turn, on several variables: The effects of raids and weather on a summer's corn crop and on livestock; the success or failure of the occasional hunting expeditions that went out from the forts; the availability of salt to dry and preserve meat; the severity of the winters; and variations in population. In the spring of 1780 provisions were especially scarce. By mid-March, the price of corn had risen to 100 dollars a bushel at Harrodsburg, salt was selling for 500 dollars a bushel, and meat was completely unavailable. Three weeks later, when a shipment of grain from the eastern settlements finally made its way down the Ohio to Louisville following the spring thaw, the price of corn in that community instantly fell from 150 to 40 dollars a bushel.[50]

At their worst, the periods of confinement could be nearly intolerable. As the first winter of fort life in Harrodsburg drew to a close, its inhabitants pleaded with the Virginia assembly for support during the approaching spring and summer. Looking back on the previous two seasons of settlement, the frontier dwellers lamented the misfortune and poor judgment that had marooned them in Kentucky. "During all this time," they wrote, "internal commotions & savage wars have rendered the property of its too sanguine adventurers very precarious, & themselves unhappy. We can look back at no period that is not stained with the blood of some fellow adventurer; no spot of our infant country which doth not exhibit us some monument of savage fury." The increasingly active war parties that now plagued their settlements, even "in the dead of winter," had forced the petitioners to abandon their homes at McClellan's Fort and take refuge at Harrodsburg "as a place of more strength." Given the opportunity to reflect on their fates, the Harrodsburg group concluded that "[o]ur situation is truly alarming: We are at least two hundred miles from the frontier inhabitants. We are surrounded with enemies on every side; every day increases their numbers." Pressed upon from the outside by Indians, they felt from within the burdens of their own suffering. "Our Fort is already filled with widows and orphans," the petitioners wrote (with some exaggeration); "their neces-

---

[50] Bowman to Hand, 12 Dec. 1777, Draper MSS 18J50; Petition, Summer 1779, in Robertson, ed., *Petitions of the Early Inhabitants of Kentucky*, pp. 45–57, quote: p. 46; Fleming's Journal, 1779–1780, Mereness, ed., *Travels*, pp. 636, 642. The depreciation of Virginia's paper currency also played a role in the cost of provisions; $4 in December 1777 had the same value as $75 in December 1780, and $1000 by December 1781. See the scale of depreciation in Draper MSS 46J68.

sities call upon us daily for supplies." Moreover, the Harrodsburg inhabitants worried that the worst was yet to come; "[t]he apprehension
of an invasion in the ensuing spring," they concluded, "fills our minds
with a thousand fears."[51]

As it happened, their concerns were prophetic. The spring, summer,
and fall of 1777 constituted a period of unprecedented misery, fear, and
deprivation in the lives of the Kentucky settlers. On the first of May,
198 people were living within the walls of Harrodsburg's fort. They included 85 white men and 24 women, along with 12 older children and
the extraordinary number of 58 children under ten years of age. There
were, in addition, 12 black slaves and seven of their children. Beginning
in March and continuing until mid-September, an inhabitant's journal
notes countless sightings of small parties of Indians or the discovery of
"signs" of their presence, and the news from the other forts was likewise
dominated by reports of sightings and attacks. Although the presence of
Indians was an obsessive preoccupation of the fort's occupants, relatively few people were actually killed during the long months of confinement; the diarist recorded the deaths of only nine of his fellow residents
and five Indians, although his journal spanned more than six months of
one of the war's most active periods of hostility. The constant threat of
attack nevertheless weighed heavily on the minds of the frontier population, and the Indians' presence had a real effect on the communities'
ability to provide for themselves.[52]

At the end of the difficult year of 1777, John Bowman wrote that the
Indians' attacks on the Harrodsburg fort had been "fruteless." He nevertheless remained gravely concerned about the community's future.
The Indians had left the settlers "almost without Horses," which hin-
dered them from tending their crops, hunting, making salt, or otherwise
gathering provisions for the town "out of the woods." The local food
supply was badly disrupted as a result. "Our corn," Bowman wrote,
"the Indians have burned all they could find the Past Summer, as it was
in Cribs at Deferent Plantations sum distance from the Garisons and no
horses to bring it in on." As he wrote, spring was still more than three
months away; yet "we have not more than two months bread." Like the
petitioners who hoped to elicit sympathy and aid 10 months earlier,
Bowman emphasized that the community had somehow to care for
nearly 200 women and children, many "widows with small children
destitute of necessairy Clothing."[53]

---

[51] Petition from the Committee of the County of Kentucky to the Governor and Council
   of VA, 27 Feb. 1777, Draper MSS 4CC29–30.
[52] John Cowan's Journal, Mar.-Sept., 1777, Draper MSS 4CC30.
[53] John Bowman to Gen. Hand, 12 Dec. 1777, Draper MSS 18J50.

The hardships of fort life in Kentucky did little to dissuade new settlers, however. The great influx of aspiring landholders that followed the passage of Virginia's land laws was reflected in an explosion of new settlements that fanned out from the earliest communities in the Kentucky basin. At Louisville, a traveler found during the winter of 1779 a "great number of Cabbins here and a considerable number of Inhabitants tho many of them were absent." Within a few miles of the central settlement, two smaller satellite communities had sprung up. Like every other satellite village constructed in the Revolutionary era, they were built in the form of "stations," or clusters of cabins connected by palisades; this arrangement provided the entire village with an outer wall that served as a small fort when the need arose. Beyond the two stations near Louisville, called Brashear's and Floyd's Stations, the traveler encountered a series of comparable settlements in the vicinity of Harrodsburg and Boonesborough. McAfee's Station on the Salt River; Bryan's Station on Elkhorn Creek; Todd's Station and, nearby, the newly founded town of Lexington; Bowman's Station near Dick's River; Ruddle's, Wilson's, Grant's, Whitley's, and English's Stations – all were new communities in 1779, and many of them arose, almost literally, overnight. At Bryan's Station, all but four of the 50 families living there in the winter of 1779 had arrived just that summer. Bowman's Station was populated by a core group of 20 families that came together to Kentucky from Roanoke, Virginia.[54] Kentucky's first historian, Humphrey Marshall, offered an insightful description of these settlements. "Their original population," he explained,

generally small, was various, and depended on the party which could be gotten together; often upon the popularity of the leader. They were recepticles for emigrants, and many of them, by the accession of numbers, and new cabins, swelled into villages in the course of a year or two; and were as suddenly depopulated, when no longer influenced by surrounding danger.[55]

Stations, in short, offered a defensive refuge to prospective landholders; their inhabitants would have preferred dispersed settlement on private plantations, but the Ohio Indians' unyielding opposition to their presence in Kentucky made forted villages an unfortunate necessity.

Despite all their precautions, the lives of the Kentucky settlers were punctuated by the grim reality of death at the hands of their enemies. After the great spurt of population growth in 1779 and 1780, it became increasingly difficult for the settlers to protect themselves. Though their

[54] Fleming's Journal, 1779–1780, Mereness, ed., *Travels*, pp. 621, 619–631, 635–636, 644, 647.
[55] Marshall, *History of Kentucky*, p. 115.

towns were fortified compounds, they still had to plant, tend, and harvest outlying fields, care for livestock, hunt for wild game, and travel from community to community to share news or to trade. When they went to their fields or took to the roads, the possibility of attack was an ever-present reality. One of the most striking documents to survive the frontier Revolution, and one that captures with vivid clarity the omnipresent sense of danger in the settlers' lives, is a journal kept by Colonel William Fleming during two visits to Kentucky, one in the winter and spring of 1779–1780 and another in 1783. Fleming was a prominent figure in western Virginia throughout the Revolutionary era; a veteran of the Seven Years' War, he raised a regiment in Botetourt County for Dunmore's 1774 campaign and served as a lieutenant colonel during the Revolutionary War, although he was disabled during the Shawnee campaign and could not serve actively thereafter. For two and a half years during the Revolution he represented the western counties in the Virginia Senate. A man of wealth, influence, and learning, Fleming was thus deeply engaged in the progress of the Revolution, and his own fate was inextricably tied to its outcome.

Nevertheless, in all of Fleming's daily entries during the time he spent in Kentucky, which span 10 months and run to more than 50 printed pages, there is not a single reference to the war against Great Britain. Nor are there expressed any musings on the wider implications of the Revolutionary movement, or speculations about the capacity of Kentuckians for self-government. Instead, at times on a daily basis, terse entries recount the immediate dangers that arose to threaten the Kentucky settlements. In Boonesborough on Christmas day in 1779 Fleming noted that two people were killed and two boys taken prisoner near the mouth of Floyd's Creek, and he wrote that "[p]eople hourly arrived with accounts of the distresses of Families on the road." With the spring thaw, reports of killings and scalpings multiplied. On March 14, he wrote, "We this day had confirmation of Col. Calaways and Pempertons being kild and scalped, and two negroes taken prisoners"; on the 20th "we had information that a man was kild betwixt Mr. Floyds and the Falls." April brought more bad news. On the 4th they "[w]ere informed that three men were kild and scalped at Levi Todds Station"; two days later he noted three more killings.[56]

In the pages of Fleming's journal, what is first reported with shock and horror gradually becomes accepted as an unpleasant but inescapable reality; through repetition, the descriptions of violent death gradually take on the character of a litany. The web of atrocity tales that runs through the pages of the journal also ran through the communities

---

[56] Fleming's Journal, 1779–1780, Mereness, ed., *Travels*, pp. 626, 635, 637, 641–642.

that Fleming visited, imparting a grim significance to the experience of daily life. "This evening two men came over from Lexington and informed us that one Nourse was kild there the third instant[.] [T]hey had shot him in the thigh and taken him off 8 miles towards Licking [River] before they kild him." "[W]e heard of a man and a negro being part of a larger Comp[an]y from the falls being kild and scalped Eight miles from Ja[me]s McAfees." "This morning [I was] informed that two men from King and Queen on their return were scalped on Rockcastle." "Col. Logan . . . brought . . . intelligence that two men that went hunting on Muddy Creek a branch of Kentucky above Boonsburg was kild last Monday. We likewise heard that the same day a man was knocked down by an Indian at Levi Todds Station but the people in the Fort firing on the Enemy the man escaped."[57] In these and countless other diary entries, Fleming described his progress through the Kentucky settlements as he recorded the process by which he gradually steeled himself to face the cruelty and the immediacy of the Kentuckians' embattled existence. The tales of horror that became an integral part of the settlers' lives served as bleak inspiration in their struggle to persevere; they also shaped a common set of social values as they imparted vivid texture to the fabric of community life.

At its worst, the experience of the frontier war in Kentucky was almost too much for the settlers to bear. "This Country seems a good deal like Br[e]aking," John Bowman wrote to a correspondent following the disastrous battle of Blue Licks in 1782. "Nay Many would remove themselves into the settlements but ar[e] not able[;] that is the Greates[t] reason of our sticking together." Throughout the spring and summer of the year, Indian attacks had taken their toll on the settlements. In April, William Preston lamented that "the savages have began their usual Depredations upon the unhappy Inhabitants of our Frontiers." He noted that "the People are in the utmost Consternation and talk of removing their Families." The fears of 1782 only echoed those of 1777, 1778, and 1780; in each of those years, Indian attacks and rumors of worse things to come frightened many Kentuckians into abandoning their stake in the far western frontier and moving east to safer ground. Each time, correspondents predicted that the Kentucky settlements would be substantially depopulated as a result. In 1780, John Taylor wrote that a band of Indian warriors "Fell in at James Roark's where they scalped seven of his children and his wife. They are all dead only one girl. . . . This part of ye County is in a scene of Confusion," he continued. "And I make no doubt but the Country will Break up without they Can Gett some assistance." After the defeat at Blue Licks, even Bowman himself

---

[57] Fleming's Journal, 1779–1780, Mereness, ed., *Travels*, pp. 643–644.

considered getting out. "I have sume thoughts of selling all my clame of lands on the Kentucky and moving into the State of North Carolina," he informed a friend. "Should you incline to purchase pray give the Earliest notice you can."[58]

Not surprisingly, the population of the Kentucky settlements fluctuated widely from year to year, season to season, and even at times from week to week throughout the war. Even as late as 1783, during William Fleming's second visit to Kentucky, he discovered that several communities had been abandoned, or almost so, following the setbacks of the previous summer. McAfee's Station "was deserted, the people having suffered greatly by the Indians last summer," while Kincheloe's Station "was entirely destroyed by the Enemy last summer, . . . excepting two dirty huts in which we could not lodge." Even at Louisville, Fleming reported that "we found the place almost deserted of Inhabitants." In the long run, however, these brief and localized declines in Kentucky's population were more than matched by waves of arriving newcomers, as contemporary population estimates make clear. In 1777, a visitor guessed that 5,000 people had established themselves in Kentucky; five years later, the figure had risen only to 8,000. Thereafter, though, western growth took off. In 1783 the population was estimated at 12,000, and in 1784 it had reached the astonishing level of 30,000. Three years later, Kentucky reportedly held 50,000 residents, and by the time of the first federal census in 1790 its population stood at 73,677.[59]

The burst in population growth coincided with word that a peace agreement between Great Britain and the United States was imminent. The news came at a low point in Kentucky's brief history, and it contributed enormously to the resurgent interest in western lands.[60] But although the agreement that ended the war with Britain also officially ended the Indian war on the Ohio Valley frontier, British diplomats could not speak for their Indian allies in the region. To the Ohio Indians the peace agreement was a betrayal; it came at just the time when their military ascendancy over the Kentucky settlers appeared to have been

---

[58] For quotes see Bowman to Isaac Hite, 30 Aug. 1782, Clark-Hite Papers, folder 116, Filson Club, Louisville, KY; Preston to Gov. James Monroe, 10 Apr. 1782, Draper MSS 5QQ107; John Taylor to William Preston, 23 Mar. 1780, Draper MSS 5QQ26. See also, e.g., William Breckenridge to William Preston, 1 June 1780, Draper MSS 5QQ31; John Hetcher[?] to David Hartas[?], [June 1780], Draper MSS 5QQ32; Preston to [Monroe], 26 Apr. 1782, Draper MSS 5QQ108; Alexander Breckenridge to Preston, 21 Oct. 1782, Draper MSS 5QQ112.

[59] Fleming's Journal, 4, 5, and 9 Jan. 1783, Mereness, ed., *Travels*, pp. 661–663; Evarts B. Greene and Virginia D. Harrington, eds., *American Population Before the Federal Census of 1790* (New York, 1932), p. 192.

[60] See, e.g., McAfee, "History, Rise, and Progress" [1782], Draper MSS 4CC64–65.

established beyond question.[61] For more than a decade after the Peace of Paris, Ohio warriors – now, ironically, more united than they had ever been before – rejected the treaty's provisions and continued their assault on the frontier settlements. As the seaboard states finally enjoyed a respite from war, the animosity between Europeans and Indians that was rooted in years of border warfare reached full flower in the Ohio Valley.

In this climate of a half-concluded war, the frontier residents of the new American nation set about the process of reinventing their embattled communities. In so doing they mapped a new construction of empire, at once more open-ended in its conception and more totalizing in its effects than anything previously attempted by Europeans on the American continent.

---

[61] See Randolph C. Downes, "Indian War on the Upper Ohio," *Western Pennsylvania Historical Magazine*, 17 (1934), pp. 93–115. Downes argues that the Peace of Paris led to "that great paradox of 1783, the acquisition by a nation whose armies had been continually beaten of lands whose Indian inhabitants had successfully defended them against that nation."

CHAPTER SIX

Empire Ascendant

A T WAR'S end national leaders hoped, above all, to rationalize and discipline the chaotic social forces of the Ohio Valley, to align its energies with the Revolutionary republican ideals that were being institutionalized in the seaboard states. But this was more easily envisioned than accomplished. The clarity and simplicity of nationalist blueprints for a new American empire came up against the complicated social patterns and tangled histories of settlers, Indians, traders, and British agents and officials who already occupied the region. As a result the goal of a rationalized and disciplined west was compromised. The political ascendancy of the United States, initially established in the region by the military support of revolutionary governments, was again extended in the 1780s and early 1790s by the force of arms, directed against the region's Indians in the interest of protecting western settlers. The United States Army succeeded in reshaping the Ohio Valley in ways policymakers could not.

The violent conflicts of the preceding decades indelibly stamped postwar culture. Even as they remained divided on a wide range of social and political questions, the Euroamerican residents of the Ohio Valley could unite in support of aggressive national expansion. Expansion was premised, in turn, on two theoretical innovations of the Revolutionary era: a territorial system that permitted Congress to extend national boundaries westward indefinitely, and a new definition of citizenship that was exceedingly generous toward Euroamericans but heightened the legal boundaries associated with race. In the end, national leaders and western settlers established a complicated pattern of mutual support, which served as the foundation for a new relationship between state and society in the west – one that sapped, with remarkable speed, Native American autonomy and power.

I

During the course of the war, western lands became central to Revolutionary visions of national development. The Revolution may have begun on the seaboard, but it would be really tested in the west, where the confederated republic might become a republican empire. To succeed, the United States needed not simply to gain independence from Great Britain, but also to create a viable national state to which all Euroamericans in the former colonies and their hinterlands would declare their loyalty. This would require, in turn, that Congress capture the west, both to prevent a rival power from gaining a foothold and to establish a frontier for future national development. The west presented a monumental opportunity, but also myriad theoretical and practical problems – problems upon which creative minds expended enormous energy.[1]

The first efforts to conceptualize an American empire of liberty began in the late 1770s, when nationalist spokesmen urged all states whose charters gave them a claim to western lands to forfeit them to the national government, so that Congress could formulate a coherent western policy. These lands would then, in the words of an early resolution, "be disposed of for the common benefit of the United States, and be settled and formed into distinct republican states, which shall become members of the federal union, and have the same rights of sovereignty, freedom and independence, as the other states." This radical conception of the new nation – liberal in its offer to share power with states whose existence was still conjectural, revolutionary its vision of a nation-state with elastic boundaries – promised to create a United States bounded only by the limits of its military power and the continued voluntary adherence of its citizens.[2]

This was a dramatic departure from earlier models of empire. Traditionally, European states were fixed geographical entities. By the late middle ages, theorists of royal authority had postulated a metaphysical correspondence between the king's own body and that of his realm. Each was bounded by limits that had been divinely preordained. However events might have modified the limits of a kingdom in fact over time, in theory its extent was constant, tied to an ideal conception of people, land, and crown bound together into a single, coherent organ-

---

[1] For the importance of the west generally see especially Drew McCoy, *The Elusive Republic: Political Economy in Jeffersonian America* (Chapel Hill, 1980).

[2] Resolution introduced 10 Oct. 1780, in Worthington C. Ford et al., eds., *Journals of the Continental Congress, 1774–1789*, 34 vols. (Washington, D.C., 1904–1937) [hereafter *JCC*], vol. XVII, p. 915; for a full discussion of the nationalist effort to gain control of western lands, see Peter Onuf, *The Origins of the Federal Republic: Jurisdictional Controversies in the United States, 1775–1787* (Philadelphia, 1983).

ism by ligaments of personal allegiance. Even when a king claimed new dominions, as in conquest or colonization, the limits of the realm remained intact. Instead of larger, coherent political entities, the empires of early modern Europe created "composite states," whose outlying or peripheral dominions were separate from the realm and governed independently, according to locally derived principles. In the colonies, local power was subordinate to that of the central state. This pattern of expansion, in which peripheral dominions existed apart from and inferior to core states, placed an important brake on colonization. Colonies were by definition second-class territories, constrained by their ambiguous constitutional status and ancillary economic functions.[3]

In its initial deliberations over western land, the Continental Congress envisioned a very different form of national expansion. It was left primarily to Thomas Jefferson, who had earlier shaped Virginia's western land policy and had perhaps considered the problem of the West more carefully than any other member of Congress, to formulate a proposal that could embody this vision. In April 1784 Jefferson's Plan of Government for the Western Territory was adopted by Congress; though its provisions were never acted upon, it served as the framework for the Northwest Ordinance of 1787. In its premises Jefferson's vision for the west was breathtaking in scope; nothing conveys its totality as clearly as the map that illustrates the plan. Where earlier cartographers had labored for years to portray the complicated reality of the Ohio Valley's human and geographic forms, Jefferson's proposal swept away the region's complexities; instead it depicted the eastern half of the continent as a palimpsest, a blank slate upon which could be inscribed the boundary lines of a new American empire (Figs. 5 and 6). The plan divided the trans-Appalachian west into 16 states, separated by straight-line boundaries that reflected no appreciation of the region's geographical contours. 10 of the 16 states bore names that either echoed revolutionary glories, like Washington and Saratoga, or offered a Latinate gloss for local characteristics, like Polypotamia ("land of many rivers").[4]

---

[3] For the metaphorical significance of the king's body and its connection to the body politic, see Ernst Kantorowicz, *The King's Two Bodies: A Study in Medieval Political Theology* (Princeton, 1957), especially pp. 193–272; for composite states see Edward Countryman, "Indians, the Colonial Order, and the Social Significance of the American Revolution," *The William and Mary Quarterly,* 3rd ser., 53 (1996), and H. G. Koenigsberger, "Composite states, representative institutions, and the American Revolution," *Historical Research,* 62 (1989), 135–153.

[4] "Plan for Government of the Western Territory," 3 Feb.-23 Apr. 1784, in Julian P. Boyd et al., eds., *The Papers of Thomas Jefferson* (Princeton, 1950–), vol. VI, pp. 581–617.

Figure 5. Thomas Hutchins' map of the Ohio Valley (1764) provides detailed information about the region's geography and population. Hutchins' "Map of the Country on the Ohio and Muskingum Rivers," from [William Smith], *An Historical Account of the Expedition Against the Ohio Indians* (London, 1766). Courtesy of the John Carter Brown Library, Providence, Rhode Island.

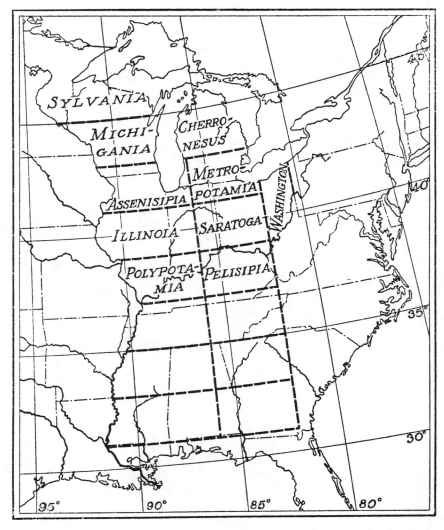

Figure 6. Map illustrating the boundaries proposed in Jefferson's "Plan for Government of the Western Territory" (1784), which simplified the west in order to claim dominion over it. From Julian P. Boyd et al., eds., *The Papers of Thomas Jefferson* (Princeton, N.J., 1950–   ), vol. VI, p. 591. Reproduced by permission of Princeton University Press.

Neither these precise boundaries nor Jefferson's names survived, but in a more general way his conception of the west shaped the Northwest Ordinance, which reinvented empire in a way that solved some of the most vexing problems British policymakers had earlier faced. In contrast to the traditional imperial system, in which colonial status was indefinitely prolonged, the Ordinance established criteria for carving states out of the Northwest Territory that would be placed "on an equal footing with the original States, in all respects whatever" once they reached a population of 60,000 free inhabitants. It also specified a form of government for the territory and procedures for selecting territorial officials. Perhaps most importantly, it established Congress's commitment to rapid, and theoretically unlimited, westward expansion. The Ordinance thus accomplished what the British ministry had failed to do for more than a decade following the creation of the Proclamation Line in 1763: it created a flexible, dynamic mechanism for settling Euroamericans on Ohio Valley lands.[5]

To establish such a mechanism was only the beginning, however. Congress also had to extend control over the lands it hoped to parcel out, in the first place by deciphering and extinguishing the complex pattern of Indian land claims in the region. The victory over Britain seemed to create an opportunity for just such an undertaking. In contrast to Britain's earlier reliance on the Iroquois as intermediaries and spokesmen, which had created innumerable confusions and disagreements over land, the Continental Congress instructed its Indian commissioners to meet with the Indian population of the northwest in its smallest constituent groups. "[A]s far as they shall find it convenient[,]" the commissioners were instructed "to treat with the several nations at different times and places." When they did meet with more than one nation at the same time, they were advised to "keep their treaties and conferences as distinct as may be." Even within the Iroquois confederacy, the commissioners were encouraged to "countenance every disposition in any one of the six nations to treat and act separately and independently." Unappreciative of the extent to which tribally defined lines of authority had themselves been blurred in the Ohio Valley, Congressional leaders expected that careful attention to each tribe's separate interests would allow the commissioners to negotiate unambiguous concessions and boundaries. At the same time, it would "discourage every coalition and

---

[5] The text of the ordinance is printed in *JCC*, vol. XXXI, pp. 669–672. For an annotated version, see Robert Taylor, ed., *The Northwest Ordinance 1787: A Bicentennial Handbook* (Indianapolis, 1987), pp. 31–77; and for a sustained history of its origins, Peter Onuf, *Statehood and Union: A History of the Northwest Ordinance* (Bloomington, IN, 1987).

consultation" that might lead the region's various Indian groups to band together in common cause.[6]

The commissioners were instructed to negotiate for cessions in an enormous tract north of the Ohio. It was defined by a "meridian line" running from the rapids of the Ohio "to the northern boundary of these United States," which took in nearly all of the modern states of Ohio, Indiana, and Michigan. This was only a rough guide; particular cessions would have to be arranged locally. But wartime migrations encouraged Euroamericans to view much of this land as conquered territory. By 1781 nearly all the village sites in the Muskingum and Scioto River watersheds had been abandoned as their residents moved west, to the Great Miami and Mad Rivers, or north, to the upper Sandusky. For the Revolutionaries, these removals confirmed that the Indians had been defeated and their land conquered; but the Ohio Indians did not regard themselves as a defeated or subject people, nor did they accept the principle that the lands abandoned during the war had been forfeited by the Indians or won by the United States.[7]

The effort to claim these lands was initially enacted in three treaties: One with the Iroquois, at Fort Stanwix in 1784; another with Delaware, Wyandot, Ottawa, and Chippewa spokesmen at Fort McIntosh in 1785; and a third, ostensibly with the Shawnees, at Fort Finney in 1786. The Fort Stanwix treaty set the tone for those that followed. The conference was poorly attended. The Iroquois had just met with representatives from New York, and a Mohawk spokesman complained that Congress had not given them sufficient notice to plan for another conference; in addition, many of his people were sick. As a result there was not a single Iroquois sachem in attendance. Proceedings stalled while the commissioners waited for more prominent leaders to arrive, but their patience finally ran out; a month after arriving at the fort, they announced that it was time to do business.[8]

The Mohawk spokesman, Aaron Hill, gamely tried to hold up his end of the bargain. I "beg your attention to the words of the Warriors," he began, "for there are no Sachems amongst us." Nevertheless, he claimed that the warriors' words were strong, and binding not only upon the six tribes of the Iroquois confederacy, but upon all of the western tribes they had once claimed to speak for under the auspices of the

---

[6] Resolution of 19 Mar. 1784, *JCC*, vol. XXVI, pp. 152–155.

[7] *JCC*, XXVI, p. 153; for wartime migrations see Helen Hornbeck Tanner, ed., *Atlas of Great Lakes Indian History* (Norman, OK, 1987), pp. 79–83.

[8] Neville B. Craig, ed., *The Olden Time*, 2 vols. (Pittsburgh, 1846–1848), vol. II, pp. 404–413; for another version of the proceedings see Brant's account, Draper MSS 23U1–11, Wisconsin Historical Society, Madison.

Covenant Chain. Now that the confederacy's tie to Great Britain was broken, Hill asserted that the Iroquois were "free, and independent, and at present under no influence," so they were willing to negotiate a peace with the United States. But Hill and Cornplanter, a Seneca warrior who was the other Iroquois speaker in attendance, hedged on its terms. The commissioners wanted the Iroquois to deliver up all their prisoners of war immediately; instead they suggested that Congress appoint representatives to travel through their towns and collect them. When the commissioners asked the Iroquois to suggest a new, comprehensive boundary line between Indian and United States lands, Cornplanter proposed the old boundary set at Fort Stanwix in 1768. "As to the territory Westward of" the Ohio, he averred, "you must talk respecting it with the Western Nations." Thus the Iroquois spokesmen tried to re-establish the authority of the Six Nations, but at the same time blunt the Americans' demands and avoid concessions they were not empowered to make.[9]

The commissioners would have none of it. The Iroquois were not independent, treating on equal terms with another power. "You are a subdued people," they informed the assembled delegates, defeated in war and subject to the will of the victors. Nor did the Iroquois spokesmen have the authority to speak for the western tribes. "[Y]ou have not shown us any authority either in writing or by belts, for your speaking in their names; without showing such authority, your words will pass away like the winds of yesterday that are heard no more." Even as they claimed more authority than they possessed, the assembled warriors responded unsatisfactorily to the commissioners' requests. "We shall now, therefore, declare to you the condition, on which alone you can be received into the peace and protection of the United States." The commissioners proceeded to dictate terms. They required the Iroquois immediately to deliver six hostages, who would remain in their custody until "all the prisoners white and black" had been released; and to cede all of their territory west of a line running from Lake Ontario to the Ohio River – which still left them, according the reproachful commissioners, with lands "as extensive . . . as they can in reason desire, and more than, from their conduct in the war, they could expect."[10]

The Iroquois delegates understood the outcome of the war differently. They had remained neutral as long as neutrality was tenable; but the war eventually divided the confederacy. Some fought with the British in recognition of their long-standing tie to the crown; others, with close ties to the colonies, supported the Revolution. Now that the war was

---

[9] Craig, ed., *Olden Time*, vol. II, pp. 416–423; quotes: pp. 418, 423.

[10] Craig, ed., *Olden Time*, vol. II, pp. 423–427; quotes: pp. 424, 423–24, 425, 426.

over, the Iroquois hoped they could resume an honorable and peaceful relationship with the United States on something like the same terms they had earlier known with Britain. Instead, a straggling group of warriors was being asked to concede to a fundamental revision of power relations, in which, among other things, they would sign away all the confederacy's interest in any land claims west of Niagara for all time. The commissioners came away with a tersely worded treaty document, signed by one or two delegates from each of the Six Nations, but the entire affair generated a wave of resentment and discontent in Iroquoia; two years later the confederacy council publicly repudiated the treaty.[11]

Two other meetings followed to establish a boundary with the Ohio Indians. The first, held three months later at Fort McIntosh with Wyandot, Delaware, Ottawa, and Chippewa delegates, again resulted in a brief treaty that stipulated the delivery of hostages, established the sovereign power of the United States, and created a boundary line between United States and Indian land. This line bounded a reserve, bordering on the south shore of Lake Erie, for the Delawares and Wyandots; by the terms of the treaty they forfeited their claims to all other lands in the Ohio Valley. In their negotiations the commissioners unwittingly exploited the fractured politics of the upper Ohio; the Indian signatories, led by the Delaware Captain Pipe and the Wyandot Half King, acted to protect the interests of their own communities but lacked the authority to make broader concessions on behalf of their tribes.[12]

The treaty infuriated neighboring communities, whose leaders felt betrayed by the Delaware and Wyandot delegates and feared that they, too, would soon be pressured to sign away their lands. A group of Shawnee and Mingo leaders at Shawnee Town lamented that the Fort McIntosh treaty ceded "the whole Shawanese Country" to the United States. "Father," they wrote to the British agent Alexander McKee, "You Now see Trouble is coming upon us fast." McKee soon reported that the Fort McIntosh treaty had divided the western Indians; a group of Shawnees and Delawares was headed west to revive plans for a re-

---

[11] The treaty is printed in Wilcomb Washburn, ed., *The American Indian and the United States: A Documentary History*, 4 vols. (New York, 1973), vol. IV, pp. 2267–2269. It was formally repudiated at Fort Schlosser on 27 Mar. 1786; see Draper MSS 23U32–33. See also Walter H. Mohr, *Federal Indian Relations, 1774–1788* (Philadelphia, 1933), pp. 122–124.

[12] The treaty text is in Washburn, ed., *American Indian and the United States*, vol. IV, pp. 2269–2271; for a summary of the commissioners' message to the Indians see Draper MSS 23U19–21; for the interests of the signatories of the Forts McIntosh and Finney treaties, and the reactions of other Ohio Indians, see (in addition to what follows) Richard White, *The Middle Ground: Indians, Empires, and Republics in the Great Lakes Region, 1650–1815* (New York, 1991), pp. 435–440.

gional confederacy. By August, 1785, McKee had heard that Congress was already preparing to begin surveys of its newly acquired lands, and that it planned to make treaties with the remaining Ohio Valley tribes as quickly as possible. Reflecting on the Stanwix and McIntosh treaties, McKee wrote, "It is indeed evident that the transactions at those two Meetings can not be permanent, as it will be found that refractory Tribes will never tamely submit to be deprived of A Country, on which they think their existance depends."[13]

The commissioners finally succeeded in cornering a Shawnee delegation at the mouth of the Big Miami River in January 1786. The mood was tense; an army detachment built a makeshift fort, Fort Finney, to protect the negotiators from hostile observers. Revealingly, the first Indian signers of the treaty that resulted from the meetings were the Wyandots Half King and the Crane, and the Delawares Captain Pipe, Buckongahelas, and Big Cat, all of whom had participated in the Fort McIntosh treaty. Their principal ally among the Shawnees was Molunthy, leader of the Mequashake Shawnees; the other Shawnee signers are obscure, and one spoke very critically of the treaty agreement during the negotiations. The document was nevertheless approved on the last day of January, 1786.[14]

These objectionable treaties created a temporarily unified Indian response. Late in 1786, a large gathering of delegates that claimed to represent the Iroquois confederacy and all the principal tribal groups on the upper Ohio and at Detroit convened on the Detroit River to formulate a message to Congress. Calling themselves the "United Indian Nations," they rejected all three treaties and called for a new, comprehensive agreement between the United States and all the Indians of the Northwest. Thus far, they contended, the American commissioners had caused nothing but "mischief and confusion." For the future, they asked that all treaties involve the entire "United Indian Nations," that they be conducted openly and without restraint, and that all land cessions be publicly and unanimously approved. All "partial Treaties" would be held by the Indians to be "Void and of no effect."[15]

Despite this show of unanimity, events soon demonstrated that it was impossible for the region's various sachems and would-be spokesmen either to reach agreement with one another, or to dictate the behavior of their supposed followers. The cycle of fragmentation and rebellion in

[13] Major Snake, Captain Johnny, Thomas Snake, and Chiaxy to Alexander McKee, 20 Mar. 1785, Draper MSS 23U16–21; McKee to John Johnson, 24 Apr. 1785, Draper MSS 23U22; McKee to Johnson, 6 Aug. 1785, Draper MSS 23U24.

[14] Draper MSS 23U34–37; White, *Middle Ground*, pp. 438–439.

[15] Draper MSS 23U51–56.

the Indian polities of the Ohio Valley, begun in the events leading up the Revolution, now only accelerated. In the fall of 1785, as a group of Detroit-area sachems worked to negotiate an acceptable agreement with the United States, they lamented that "some foolish young men" on the south side of Lake Erie "continue to carry on Depredations tending to Destroy the quiet of the Country, as well as the good works the General Council of our Confederacy are laboring to accomplish." They pleaded for wise men to assert themselves against the foolishness of the warriors, but their efforts had little effect.[16]

By 1789, when a conference was held at Fort Harmar to draft a new, comprehensive treaty agreement that could supersede the three "partial" and objectionable ones, the Indians' united front had crumbled. Attendance at the conference was dismal, and the proceedings accomplished nothing. One more treaty resulted, but instead of reflecting the Indians' desire for more limited land concessions, it confirmed the boundaries that had already been specified in the previous three treaties. Once again its signatories lacked the authority to cede land, and a serious lapse of protocol called the entire event into question.[17]

The failure at Fort Harmar conclusively demonstrated that the Northwest Ordinance had, in effect, made postwar Indian relations inherently unworkable. However willing national leaders might have been, in principle, to respect Indian claims and gain land by diplomatic means, in practice the creation of an expansive, open-ended nation made land acquisition by treaty at best a face-saving gesture, at worst a poorly disguised farce. The Northwest Ordinance undermined the presumption of Indian sovereignty, and at the same time granted implicit legitimacy to the expansionist impulses of the settler population. It thus perpetuated the condition of Kentucky's Revolutionary frontier, promising that, in time, even the most aggressive claims to Indian lands might be honored. As a result, conflict again overwhelmed the efforts of accommodationist leaders to negotiate a plausible peace, and the congressional bid to rationalize affairs in the Ohio Valley produced only bitterness, misunderstanding, and war.

II

To extend its authority into the Ohio Valley, Congress also had to capture the loyalties of western settlers – a task that proved to be nearly as difficult as formulating a workable Indian policy. While the Revolution established in the minds of eastern leaders a rationale for creating a dis-

---

[16] Draper MSS 23U29; see also Draper MSS 23U57–59.
[17] Draper MSS 23U75–157; White, *Middle Ground*, pp. 443–448.

ciplined national republic, it nurtured in the Ohio Valley intensely local loyalties and ambitions. The Revolutionary movement provided western settlers with a potent anti-authoritarian ideology, and the Indian wars forged experiences and fears alien to nationalist leaders in the east. Despite their enormous debt to the leaders of the Revolution, many Ohio Valley squatters regarded national power mistrustfully; despite their enthusiasm for the abstract principle of western development, national leaders often reacted with horror to the society that was already taking shape there.

For the settlers, the official end of the war did not bring the relief they hoped for. In Kentucky the treaty with Britain "was an event of great joy" to settlers, "as they had anticipated a suspension of their Indian wars, but in this they were mistaken." Despite the agreement with Britain, the Ohio Indians continued to raid settlements throughout the valley, killing, capturing, and terrifying Euroamericans wherever they went. Letters, journals, narratives, and remembrances from the 1780s are filled with references to the perpetual danger of Indian attacks. When Alexander Breckenridge struck out for Kentucky with a party of nineteen men in the fall of 1782, after word of the preliminary peace agreement had reached the former colonies, he encountered two "Advertisements" at the Laurel River warning travelers that Indians "were on the road, and have killed nine men at the big Flat Lick." William Christian was disappointed to discover several years later that the best land in Kentucky was too expensive, "unless on the outside where it is dangerous." Nor was livestock yet secure, as he reported with some anxiety to his correspondent. "I am afraid of losing my Horses every day by the Wabash Indians who keep about." Recalling their experiences decades later, settlers' memories were filled with stories of encountering or eluding Indians. Wherever they went, Kentuckians lived with the possibility that a party of Indians might set them suddenly and frantically to flight.[18]

The Indian warriors who troubled these prospective settlers were hard to identify and terrifying to face. During the war they perfected their raiding methods, and by the mid-1780s their routes into Kentucky were well-established. Nathaniel Hart later recalled that when he lived in Harrodsburg "the Indians who then annoyed that part of the country generally crossed the Ohio between the mouth of the Kentucky River &

---

[18] Robert B. McAfee, "History of the Rise & Progress of the New Providence Church" [extracts], Draper MSS 4CC64–65; Alexander Breckenridge to William Preston, 21 Oct. 1782, Draper MSS 5QQ112; William Christian to Col. Gilbert Christian, 13 Aug. 1785, Draper MSS 5QQ124; and see, e.g., the Narrative of Capt. Spencer Records, 1842, Draper MSS 23CC.

Louisville, passing up on the South side of the river, which was then a wilderness, to McAfee's Station." In older and more densely settled areas like the Salt River basin, raids became less frequent; but the residents remained wary. In the early 1780s they "continued to reside in the station & cultivate corn out on their farms as privately as possible, & always with guns in their hands."[19]

But despite all the threats and dangers, western settlers gradually gained confidence in their enterprise. Some worried that the land already under the jurisdiction of existing states – the land they had "fought and bled for" during the war – was now being engrossed by speculators. The Virginia land law, along with various proprietary ventures whose claims were still alive, were conspiring to take these lands away from ordinary settlers. Thus, even before the war with Britain was over, ad hoc associations of adventurers were forming to push farther onto Indian lands. Sometime in 1780, a group of several hundred Kentuckians asked Congress to let them move across the Ohio to escape the speculators. In the vicinity of Fort Pitt people began to discuss the possibility of moving into Indian country, where they could "establish a government for themselves." "There is now a paper handing about," William Croghan (nephew to George) wrote from Fort Pitt in the spring of 1782, "Encouraging people to go Settle on the Indians land[.] [U]pwards of 500 have sign'd it and say they will go over this summer[.]" Before most of the embattled Kentucky settlers could even emerge from their fortified stations, hundreds, perhaps thousands, of others were beginning to push across the Ohio in defiance of the region's Indians. Besides these Kentuckians, thousands of migrants a year began to arrive in the valley from the east as the end of the war approached. Within several years, the landscape north of the Ohio was dotted with squatter communities like Haglin's Town, Norris's Town, Amberson's Bottom, and Menzon's Town, and groups of settlers were moving in "by forties and fifties."[20]

By the time Congress began to deal with the Ohio Indians in earnest,

---

[19] Duncan to Harmar, 16 May 1786, Harmar Collection 3:48–49, William L. Clements Library, Ann Arbor, MI; Hart to Lyman C. Draper, 20 Dec. 1838, Draper MSS 2CC26; McAfee, "History of the Rise & Progress," Draper MSS 4CC61–62.

[20] Petition of Kentucky Settlers, cited in Andrew R. L. Cayton, *The Frontier Republic: Ideology and Politics in the Ohio Country, 1780–1825* (Kent, Ohio, 1986), p. 4, and dated in Patricia Watlington, *The Partisan Spirit: Kentucky Politics, 1779–1792* (Chapel Hill, 1972), p. 240; Gen. William Irvine to William Moore, 3 Dec. 1781, quoted in Cayton, *Frontier Republic*, p. 3; Croghan to Col. Dorsey Penticost, 28 Apr. 1782, Draper MSS 30J41; John Armstrong to Josiah Harmar, in William H. Smith, ed., *The St. Clair Papers: The Life and Public Services of Arthur St. Clair*, 2 vols. (New York, 1970 [orig. pub. 1881]), vol. II, pp. 3–4.

the growth of squatter communities across the river had become a pressing concern for two reasons. One was the provocation they offered to
the Indians. The other, more immediate, concern was that these communities threatened to undermine national interests in the valley. For one
thing, squatters appeared to be dangerously lacking in public spirit. The
ideals of the Revolution seemed to many leaders to require a reformation of manners. "The new Governments we are assuming, in every
Part," John Adams wrote, "will require a Purification from our Vices,
and an Augmentation of our Virtues or they will be no Blessings." But
western squatters remained impure, self-interested actors with only
weak attachments to the national experiment. They were "shiftless fellows" who wanted to throw off all forms of public authority and be responsible only to themselves. The ragged bands of self-reliant squatters
were often compared to Indians: they lived beyond settled communities
and seemed indifferent to civic values. Eastern critics argued that they
sought isolation instead of society, and preferred subsistence to market-
oriented agriculture; in manners, material comforts, and the outward
trappings of culture they appeared to degenerate as they moved west
and north.[21]

The Ohio adventurers also posed a more practical threat to national
interests. They were engrossing land before it could be surveyed and
sold by federal agents, thus leaching away the one significant resource
of an otherwise insolvent nation. George Washington thought the Ohio
squatters were perversely consumed with the pursuit of land. For men
without connections, influence, or money, the only way to get it was to
mark out claims beyond the bounds of public authority. Thus Washington found a "rage for speculating" in lands on the north side of the
Ohio in 1784, and complained, "Men in these times, talk with as much
facility of fifty, a hundred, and even 500,000 Acres as a Gentleman formerly would do of 1000 acres." A federal surveyor concluded that this
"lawless set of fellows . . . are more our enemies than the most brutal
savages of the country."[22]

These concerns led Congress to take a hard line against the squatters
north of the Ohio. Late in 1784, in the first military initiative undertak-

---

[21] Adams to Abigail Adams, 3 July 1776, quoted in Gordon Wood, *The Creation of the
American Republic, 1776–1787* (Chapel Hill, 1969), p. 123; Peter Onuf, "Settlers, Settlements, and New States," in Jack Greene, ed., *The American Revolution: Its Character and Limits* (New York, 1987), pp. 171–196.

[22] Washington to Jacob Read, 3 Nov. 1784, in W. W. Abbot and Dorothy Twohig, eds.,
The Papers of George Washington: Confederation Series (Charlottesville, 1992–   ),
vol. II, pp. 118–123; Extract of a letter from a gentleman at Ft. Harmar . . . to his
friend in this town [Boston], July 26, 1786, *New Haven Gazette and Connecticut Magazine*, 5 Oct. 1786, quoted in Onuf, "Settlers, Settlements, and New States," p. 183.

en by Congress since the peace with Britain, three companies of American soldiers under the command of Lieutenant Colonel Josiah Harmar took up residence at Fort McIntosh at the mouth of the Beaver River. One of their responsibilities was to protect the various agents of the United States government that periodically entered the valley – Indian commissioners in 1785; a group of surveyors working under the direction of Thomas Hutchins, the geographer of the United States, in 1786, when they began laying off ranges of federal land ceded by the Delawares and Wyandots at Fort McIntosh. The army's other priority was to drive squatters out of the region, and this proved, at least initially, to be the more formidable task. Thousands of people had moved across the river until, as John Armstrong informed Harmar after an expedition down the Ohio to the Miami River, there was "scarcely one bottom on the river but has one or more families living thereon." He estimated that more than fifteen hundred families had already settled on both the Miami and the Scioto Rivers. Detachments from the fort periodically warned off settlers and burned their cabins, but most settlers returned as soon as the soldiers had gone. In the fall of 1785 the soldiers built Fort Harmar further downriver, at the mouth of the Muskingum, to put them closer to the illegal settlements, but by the end of the following year Harmar concluded that their efforts had been largely ineffectual.[23] The squatters had so far defeated every effort by the federal government to direct their actions or control the land they occupied.

In these same years, conflicts between Ohio Indians and western settlers escalated. The Fort Finney agreement generated a new wave of militant dissatisfaction in many Ohio Indian towns, and in the summer of 1786 warriors committed a series of raids on the Kentucky towns and murders along the river. In response, the Kentucky militia took matters into its own hands. George Rogers Clark organized a two-pronged attack on the villages that were staging the raids. Benjamin Logan was to lead one detachment against the cluster of towns on the Mad River, a tributary of the Great Miami, while Clark himself would march against the principal settlements on the Wabash. After observing Clark's preparations, four hundred Indian warriors rushed to the Wabash towns, leaving the Mad River villages largely unprotected. Clark's attack collapsed, but Logan led 888 men against Piqua, Mequashake, and several other Mad River towns. With few warriors to protect them, most of the residents fled. Only ten Indians were killed, but they included several

---

[23] Editor's introduction; Harmar to the President of Congress, 1 May 1785; Harmar to the Secretary of War, 1 June 1785; Harmar to Secretary of War, 12 July 1786; Armstrong to Harmar, April 1785; Harmar to Secretary of War, 22 Oct. 1785; Harmar to Secretary, 12 July 1786; in Smith, ed., *St. Clair Papers*, vol. II, pp. 1–7, 14–15, 3–4, 11–13, 14–15.

Shawnee, Delaware, and Wyandot chiefs who had cooperated with the United States. Molunthy, the principal Shawnee signatory of the Fort Finney treaty, raised the American flag over Mequashake and held out his copy of the document; he was initially taken prisoner, but an angry Kentuckian soon cleaved his skull with a tomahawk. His body was then burned and blown up with gunpowder. Before returning to Kentucky the militia force burned seven towns and laid waste to their fields of corn and produce. Three days later, Logan sent the Shawnees on the Mad River a letter inviting them to return all their prisoners and make peace. Otherwise, "you may soon expect another Army in your Country in order to Destroy every Town on this Side of the Lakes. Which I think it would be much to our Advantage to do."[24]

Under these pressures, the valley's Indian population steadily splintered and diminished. After the raid on the Mad River towns, many residents left the valley to resettle on the Tennessee River or in Spanish Louisiana. Those who remained once again moved north and west. After 1786 the Ohio Indians were primarily confined a corridor to the south and west of Lake Erie, where villages clustered on the Sandusky, Maumee, and Wabash Rivers.[25] Though their numbers were shrinking, those who remained were committed to recovering and defending their lands along the Ohio.

As in the Revolution, violence further weakened the influence of accommodationist Indian leaders and spurred the United States to provide military aid to the western settlers. Harmar dispatched two companies of federal troops to Louisville, where he instructed them to cooperate with the Kentucky militia to prevent a counterattack. At the same time, responding to reports of violence, Congress raised additional troops to send to the Ohio Valley. Soon they were posted at forts along most of the length of the river: at Venango on the Allegheny, Fort Pitt, Fort McIntosh at the mouth of the Beaver River, at Wheeling, Fort Harmar on the Muskingum, Fort Steuben opposite Louisville, and in Vincennes, where the Americans were just establishing themselves. The federal troops were supported by a force of 1,000 Kentucky militia who were instructed to help if they were needed.[26]

---

[24] See John Mack Faragher, *Daniel Boone: The Life and Legend of an American Pioneer* (New York, 1992), pp. 251–255, for a full and balanced account of this attack. There are conflicting versions of Molunthy's death; I have largely followed Faragher, adding the disposition of his body as it is described in Draper MSS 23U38; see also Harmar to Secretary of War, 15 Nov. 1786, in Smith, ed., *St. Clair Papers*, vol. II, pp. 18–19, and White, *Middle Ground*, p. 440. Logan to the Shawnees, 9 Oct. 1786, Draper MSS 23U38–39.

[25] Tanner, ed., *Atlas*, pp. 84–91.

[26] Harmar to the Secretary, 15 Nov. 1786 and 7 June 1787, in Smith, ed., *St. Clair Papers*, vol. II, pp. 18–19, 22–23; Mohr, *Federal Indian Relations*, p. 127.

Thus a growing federal military presence in the Ohio Valley emerged gradually in response to events. This development roughly coincided with a series of land sales in the valley. In 1787 Congress sold a million acres of land north of the Ohio to the Ohio Company of Associates, a consortium of former Revolutionary officers from New England; another million acres known as the Miami Purchase to John Cleves Symmes; and a third large tract to the Scioto Company. In the fall it auctioned another 72,934 acres in the first four ranges of public lands, which had been surveyed by Hutchins and his associates. The Northwest Ordinance, passed in the same year, created a framework of public authority for the new communities that would be settled north of the river.[27] Congress made all of these arrangements despite the persistent objections of a large segment of the Ohio Indians, and virtually guaranteed by its actions that violence would escalate further. As a result, although federal troops were originally posted in the Ohio Valley in part to drive off squatters, after 1787 the army's role changed: Now it offered protection to settlers as they moved onto land the local Indians still regarded as their own.

The years that followed were full of uncertainty and terror, worse even than the peak years of the Revolution. In part this was because the Euroamerican population was much larger and more difficult to protect. The Ohio River had become a major thoroughfare for settlers; in the twenty months from October 1786 to June 1788, officers at Fort Harmar counted more than 600 boats and over 12,000 people passing down the river.[28] These flotillas made easy marks for Indian warriors, slow and heavily laden as they often were. The Ohio Indians were also by this time experienced in frontier raiding, thoroughly familiar with the routes settlers followed, and well-equipped as a result of renewed British support. In certain limited roles the army could protect settlers effectively. Wherever forts stood, raids were less likely; those strategic points along the river thus became small protected zones, and nearby communities, like Louisville and Clarksville near Fort Steuben, enjoyed their benefits. When the Ohio Company partners founded Marietta, the first town within their purchase, they chose a site on the Muskingum directly across from Fort Harmar. And when Symmes and his associates founded the town of Cincinnati a short time later, General Harmar helped to ensure its survival by establishing Fort Washington nearby.

But there was also much that the army was powerless to do. Raids

---

[27] Malcolm J. Rohrbough, *The Land Office Business: The Settlement and Administration of American Public Lands, 1789–1837* (New York, 1986), pp. 10–11.

[28] Harmar to Secretary of War, 14 May 1787, 9 Dec. 1788, 15 June 1788, in Smith, ed., *St. Clair Papers*, vol. II, pp. 19–22, 37–38, 44–45.

into Kentucky and along the river continued, and were nearly impossible to prevent. When the Kentucky militia retaliated against the Wabash towns in the summer of 1788, Harmar and his subordinates were likewise unable to stop them. With a comprehensive Indian treaty scheduled for early 1789, Harmar simply hoped to keep the peace long enough to let diplomacy take its course. When the treaty failed, he had no choice but to follow the Kentuckians' lead and march an armed force against the Wabash towns. The result was disappointing; though he managed to burn several Indian towns, in two engagements he lost about two hundred men without winning a decisive victory. Rufus Putnam, reflecting on this turn of events, lamented, "Our prospects are much changed. in staed of peace and friendship with our Indian neighbours a hored Savage war Stairs us in the face." In 1791 Arthur St. Clair, the first governor of the Northwest Territory, again staged an attack on the Wabash. He suffered the most disastrous defeat any Indian force had ever inflicted on the United States Army: marching north from Fort Washington, his force of over 1,400 men was surprised and routed. More than six hundred men and about fifty female camp followers were killed, including thirty-seven officers; another three hundred were wounded.[29]

By 1792 the Ohio Indians were the dominant military power in the valley. Settlers in Kentucky and Ohio watched anxiously for raiding parties; no one was sufficiently protected to feel safe. "We daily expect to be attacked by them at one or other of our stations," Colonel George Clendenin wrote from Fort Randolph on the Kanawha River. "The frontier counties have never experienced so desperate a summer as this appears to be." Conditions were worst near the Ohio and on the fringes of settlement, but in these years everyone was affected by the military success of the Ohio Indians. In 1794 – two years after Kentucky was admitted as a state – Robert Todd, a surveyor and member of a prominent early Kentucky family, was killed by Indians "in view of Frankfort," the state capital, "immediately before the Legislature convened at that place."[30]

The Indians' ascendancy was short-lived. In response to the crisis in

---

[29] Arthur St. Clair to Secretary of War, 5 July 1788, in Smith, ed., *St. Clair Papers*, vol. II, pp. 48–49; Major Hamtramck to Harmar, 31 Aug. 1788, in Gayle Thornbrough, ed., *Outpost on the Wabash: Letters of Brigadier General Josiah Harmar and Major John Francis Hamtramck* (Indianapolis, 1957), p. 116; Putnam's *Memoirs*, quoted in Francis Paul Prucha, *The Great Father: The United States Government and the American Indians* (Lincoln, NE, 1995 [orig. pub. 1984]), 63; Richard Kohn, *Eagle and Sword: The Federalists and the Creation of the Military Establishment in America, 1783–1802* (New York, 1975), pp. 104–116; Cayton, *Frontier Republic*, pp. 38–39.

[30] Col. George Clendenin to the governor, 26 May 1792, Draper MSS 15C3 [copy]; Hart to Draper, 20 Dec. 1838, Draper MSS 2CC26.

the valley, the United States Army redoubled its efforts; in 1794, under the leadership of Anthony Wayne, its forces won an important and decisive victory at the Battle of Fallen Timbers. This outcome often obscures the prolonged terrors of the post-Revolutionary era in Kentucky and Ohio, but the escalating violence of the 1780s and early 1790s should not be dismissed too easily. In this period the settlers of the Ohio Valley learned that their local resources were not enough to challenge the power of the Ohio Indians, and that the national government could be an invaluable resource in protecting their interests. Because national leaders were willing to define United States territory very expansively in the Ohio Valley, and to commit considerable military resources to defend their claims, they strengthened national loyalties in a region that was otherwise intensely localist in its politics and outlook.

The Ohio Indians thus played a crucial role in aligning the interests of western settlers and national leaders. Without them, to organize western settlement under national auspices would have been a difficult and contested process. But the Ohio Indians, in effect, triangulated the conflict, offering the United States government and western squatters a common enemy and a common focus of concern. In the Indian wars of the 1780s and 1790s, the national government established a foothold in the region and shaped its early development in fundamental ways. Army forts protected contested sites and guaranteed the survival of new towns. The army pioneered a viable market economy for the region by buying up its produce and introducing large quantities of cash in return. It encouraged the development of communication and transportation networks. In a variety of ways, the army helped to secure Ohio Valley settlements and began to integrate them into a national infrastructure.[31] The federal soldiers who originally came to the Ohio Valley to dampen conflict between Indians and settlers became instead defenders and agents of an expansive new American empire. The army secured American claims to land, shaped and pushed forward settlement patterns, and laid the groundwork for the first viable market economy west of the Appalachian mountains that was not tied to the Indian trade.

[31] Andrew R. L. Cayton, "'Separate Interests' and the Nation-State: The Washington Administration and the Origins of Regionalism in the Trans-Appalachian West," *The Journal of American History*, 79 (1992), 53–54. Cayton cites Secretary of War Henry Knox's estimate that an army of 5,168 men would cost $1,026,477 annually to maintain, more than half of which would be spent in pay and subsistence and thus delivered directly to the Ohio Valley. By early June 1792 the residents of Marietta had cleared between 6 and 700 acres, and that year had already sold "10,000 bushels at 2 sh. 6 p. pr. bushel" to the commanding officer there, along with 40,000 lb. of pork. See John Heckewelder, *The First Description of Cincinnati and Other Ohio Settlements: The Travel Report of Johann Heckewelder (1792)*, ed. Don Heinrich Tolzmann (Lanham, MD, 1988), p. 30.

III

Migrants continued to stream into the Ohio Valley until, by 1800, it was home to a large and singularly diverse population. The earliest residents came primarily from backcountry communities in Pennsylvania, Virginia, and North Carolina. As the Revolution drew to a close, the stream of migration widened to include a much larger number of prospective settlers who were encouraged by the rapid pace at which valley lands were being opened to settlement. Some came on their own initiative; others were drawn along by the recruitment efforts of would-be proprietors, speculators, and territorial officials. The later arrivals included substantial numbers from New England, New York, and New Jersey. People came to the Ohio Valley from every seaboard colony, and they carried a wide range of experiences and expectations. For the national experiment to succeed in the region – for an empire of liberty to take effective shape – this widely disparate, often locally oriented population had to be united by a coherent social order that could establish meaningful connections among the valley's great diversity of settlers and communities.

Arthur St. Clair, the first governor of the Northwest Territory, perceptively described the challenge of integrating a bewilderingly complex region:

There are upon the Mississippi and Wabash Rivers a considerable number of People . . . accustomed to be governed by the laws & customs introduced by that Nation [France], or by the Arbitrary Edicts of British military officers – There are also some People in that Quarter who have migrated from Virginia – A settlement is begun between the great and little Miami composed of Emigrants from that state and from New Jersey. The reservation for the Virginia officers upon the Scioto has turned the attention of many to that part of the country and as soon as it shall be open for settlement, a settlement will be made there where People from that state or from the District of Kentucky where they have been used to the laws & customs of Virginia will predominate. Higher up the Ohio comes the country purchased by the Ohio Company, which being composed of chiefly adventurers from Massachusetts & Rhode Island – the first inhabitants are and will be from those states. Above them again are the range of townships that have been sold, and as they have become the property of People from NYork & Pennsylvania & NJersey the Settlements will be made to people from those states. To the northward again of the last is the Connecticut reservation and that State is now disposing of the sail.[32]

In the Ohio Valley, the full range of American diversity came together

32 "To the President of the United States[:] A Memorial respecting the Territory of the United States NW of the Ohio," 12 May 1789, Arthur St. Clair Papers, Box 3, folder 1, Ohio Historical Society, Columbus.

in a single place for the first time. It remained to be seen what patterns of economic and political power, what combination of social and cultural institutions, would serve most effectively to tie these highly differentiated subcommunities together and integrate them into a larger national context.

The earliest squatters in the valley were, in general, unpromising constituents for a nation-building project. Many had a long-standing attraction to the "westering tradition," a constant urge to move into areas newly opened to settlement. For such migrants, moving west was often part of an ongoing search for unencumbered land. Moving west was also a strategy common to "long hunters" like Daniel Boone who, like the Indian men they knew, relied upon extended hunting trips to provide them with furs and skins for the market; their families survived during their prolonged absences as subsistence farmers. The "westering" crowd was attracted by the elemental appeal of open, free land and by the challenge and opportunity associated with settling it. The families of many early Kentuckians moved repeatedly, over the course of two generations or more, in the search for free land.[33]

Backcountry residents consistently lacked political power or representation in colonial governments, and as they moved to the periphery they also sought political autonomy. They often challenged the authority of distant governments and absentee landlords, and sometimes invented makeshift systems of local authority. In the Revolutionary era, a series of self-governing communities and self-proclaimed independent states sprang up like mushrooms throughout the backcountry, encouraged in part by the anti-authoritarian rhetoric of the 1760s and 1770s. Settlers in Maine and Vermont organized to assert their local rights to self-determination; some western Pennsylvanians briefly supported the creation of the independent state of Westsylvania, while others formed the aptly named community of Fair Play; in the North Carolina backcountry the Watauga settlers declared their independence from the state and their loyalty to the Continental Congress; localist backwoodsmen of southwestern Virginia organized the state of Franklin and likewise applied for independent statehood. Among Kentuckians, the contest between the Transylvania proprietors and their Harrodsburg opponents dramatized the issue with particular clarity. Submitting to great landowners and distant sources of political authority constituted a

---

[33] The quoted phrase comes from Charles Gano Talbert, *Benjamin Logan: Kentucky Frontiersman* (Lexington, KY, 1962), pp. 1–11; Logan offers one example of the continuous search for land. For Boone and the tradition of "long hunting," see Faragher, *Daniel Boone*, pp. 9–67; see also Faragher's discussion of "American Tartars" in *Sugar Creek: Life on the Illinois Prairie* (New Haven, 1986), pp. 51–52.

species of slavery, inimical to the Revolution and destructive to the local pursuit of liberty and equality.[34]

Yet not all aspiring westerners were localists. The Ohio Valley also attracted the attention of well-connected men who hoped to capitalize on the expansive territorial claims of the United States in grand land speculation ventures, closely tied to the national territorial system and the authority of the federal government. After the Revolution, Congress was initially reluctant to sell land to large-scale proprietors because of the aristocratic overtones of such a method; the Land Ordinance of 1785 instead provided for sales directly to prospective settlers. But within two years Congress had changed course. The Northwest Ordinance laid the foundation for the proprietary schemes of the Ohio Company of Associates, John Cleves Symmes, and the Scioto Company. Congress set aside another huge piece of land along the river as a reserve for Virginia's military warrants, and a speculative market quickly developed in those certificates as well. The change in policy was inspired partly by practical concerns: the need for quick cash and the difficulty of coordinating large-scale, government-funded surveying operations. But it was also defensible in more principled terms. It embodied a Federalist vision for western development, one that placed a premium not only on economic development but also on the moral and social authority of gentlemen in an undisciplined and chaotic region. Speculative ventures like the Ohio Company promised to make large quantities of land available to individual settlers relatively quickly, at the same time that they empowered men of reputation and honor to shape western society. The economic influence of leading speculators was reinforced with the dignity of public office, as many of them were appointed to territorial offices and federal judgeships.[35]

Despite the advantages conferred upon them by Congress, however, these men soon discovered how difficult it could be to secure and exer-

---

[34] For Maine see Alan Taylor, *Liberty Men and Great Proprietors: The Revolutionary Settlement on the Maine Frontier, 1760–1820* (Chapel Hill, 1990); for Vermont, Michael Bellesiles, *Revolutionary Outlaws: Ethan Allen and the Struggle for Independence on the Early American Frontier* (Charlottesville, VA, 1993); for Westsylvania, Thomas Slaughter, *The Whiskey Rebellion: Frontier Epilogue to the American Revolution* (New York, 1986), pp. 31–37; for Fair Play, George D. Wolf, *The Fair Play Settlers of the West Branch Valley, 1769–1784: A Study of Frontier Ethnography* (Harrisburg, PA, 1969); for Watauga and Franklin, Malcolm J. Rohrbough, *The Trans-Appalachian Frontier: People, Societies, and Institutions 1775–1850* (New York, 1978), pp. 21–63; and see more generally Onuf, *Origins of the Federal Republic*, pp. 21–46.

[35] Rohrbough, *Land Office Business*, pp. 3–25. For Federalist gentlemen, moral authority, and territorial officeholding see Cayton, *Frontier Republic*. For post-Revolutionary land speculation in other contexts see Taylor, *Liberty Men*; Alan Taylor, *William*

cise economic power in the postwar west. None of their speculative ventures prospered. The Ohio Company, John Cleves Symmes, and the Scioto Group all entered the Ohio land market with the highest expectations, but their hopes were largely disappointed. With each group receiving a million acres or more, and with several ranges of public land going to auction at about the same time, so much Ohio Valley land came onto the market so quickly that it was impossible to control its surveying and settlement effectively, or to sell it for a good price. The Ohio Company and Symmes each managed to organize a core settlement and sell land in its immediate vicinity, but beyond those central communities sales proceeded very slowly. Nor were the settlers already living in Ohio and Kentucky eager to make purchases. This was still a squatter's paradise, and the adventurers who had already established themselves in the valley could afford to wait until the price was right.[36]

To stave off financial disaster, the speculators lowered their prices until they were selling almost at cost, offered generous credit, and gave substantial discounts to large purchasers. John Cleves Symmes established a standard selling price of a dollar an acre, even though this was the price he agreed to pay Congress for the best land in his purchase, and his average cost was nearly sixty-seven cents an acre. Rumors abounded that Congress would soon be selling land much more cheaply in the valley, and in 1791 the House passed a bill that would have offered it at 25 cents an acre. Though the bill never passed the Senate, it encouraged prospective settlers to hold out for better terms. Symmes reported in exasperation in 1795 that "all Kentucky and the back parts of Virginia and Pennsylvania are running mad with expectations of the land office opening in this country – hundreds are running into the wilderness west of the Great Miami, locating and making elections. They almost laugh me full in the face when I ask them one dollar per acre for first-rate land, and tell me they will soon have as good for thirty cents." Ironically, Congress eventually set a minimum price of two dollars per acre – double Symmes' asking price. When sales were disappointingly slow, the federal land law was modified in 1800 to extend more generous credit and to sell lots in smaller tracts, but the dream of twenty-five cents an acre was gone forever.[37]

Cooper's Town: Power and Persuasion on the Frontier of the Early American Republic (New York, 1995); and William Wyckoff, The Developer's Frontier: The Making of the Western New York Landscape (New Haven, 1988).

[36] Timothy J. Shannon, "'This Unpleasant Business': The Transformation of Land Speculation in the Ohio Country, 1787–1820," in Jeffrey P. Brown and Andrew R. L. Cayton, eds., The Pursuit of Public Power: Political Culture in Ohio, 1787–1861 (Kent, OH, 1994), pp. 15–30.

[37] John Cleves Symmes to Jonathan Dayton, 6 Aug. 1795, in Beverley Bond, ed., The

In the end, most of the aspiring proprietors of the great Ohio tracts were disappointed. Some were spectacularly ruined, others were simply unable to translate their holdings into great wealth. Though some members of the Ohio Company of Associates became prominent leaders of Ohio, none grew rich on their land speculations; John Cleves Symmes gained an appointment as a federal judge, but as a land speculator he was a sensational failure; and the Scioto Company, which hoped to recruit settlers in France, collapsed in a scandal of mismanagement and misinformation. These men had hoped to trade on their connections in Congress to benefit from the widespread impulse to emigrate to the West in the years following the Revolution. By selling enormous chunks of Ohio land to small coteries of well-connected men, and by appointing many of the same people to political office in the Northwest Territory, Congress showed itself remarkably willing to comply with their ambitions. Unintentionally, however, because it sold land to competing groups and made so much of it available at once, it created an economic environment so competitive that the speculative ventures could not survive.[38]

This competitive environment provided ordinary settlers with choices and opportunities that appeared to give them a substantial measure of control over their economic fates. In fact their control was limited, and to some extent illusory. The burgeoning population of the Ohio Valley did not find free land, available for the taking to anyone willing to fight and bleed, or at least chop and plow. It found, instead, a free *market* in land, which made it widely accessible but required a substantial economic commitment. To purchase a standard, 640-acre plot from a federal land office required a minimum of $1,280 in cash. After 1800 it was possible to buy 320 acres, and to extend payment over four years, but in either case a purchaser had to produce a considerable amount of cash in a relatively short time. The only way to do this, for poor farmers who came west without capital, was to clear and improve the land immediately and to begin raising crops for the market. Anyone who succeeded in turning a profit quickly could pay for their land and remain on it; anyone who failed lost it. The results of the land scramble in Ohio were sobering, just as they had been earlier in Kentucky. By 1810, only about 45% of Ohio's adult males owned land, while almost a quarter of its real estate was held by 1% of taxpayers. This was an improvement over European norms, and consistent with patterns elsewhere in the ear-

---

Correspondence of John Cleves Symmes (New York, 1926), pp. 171–175 and 152 n. 208; Rohrbough, *Land Office Business*, pp. 22–25.
[38] Shannon, "'This Unpleasant Business.'"

ly republic, but a far cry from the squatter ideal of rough equality. Instead, the land market was quickly dominated by a small coterie of men distinguished more by their sharp speculative instincts than by their social standing or political influence – again like the earlier experience of Kentucky. No one typifies this success more clearly than Nathaniel Massie, an ambitious and well-connected young Virginian who emerged as the leading speculator in the Virginia Military Tract.[39]

Ohio Valley lands exposed everyone, wealthy, middling, or poor, well-connected or obscure, to the risks and opportunities of the market. The market, in turn, began to sort out the social landscape by differentiating among the successful, the competent, and the impecunious. From its origins as a backwoods refuge from arbitrary authority, the Ohio Valley quickly developed a market infrastructure, until "by the middle of the nineteenth century," as two historians of the region have recently noted, "the Old Northwest was one of the most important centers of commercial agriculture in the world." The complex dynamics of Ohio Valley settlement turned the aspirations of proprietors and subsistence squatters alike into quaint, backward-looking fantasies. Britain's empire of land, which was shaped by a comparatively straightforward contest between common settlers and elite proprietors, gave way to a new economic and social system that was more open in the opportunities it created for small and middling landowners, more competitive in its dynamics, and more chaotic in its results.[40]

[39] Rohrbough, *Land Office Business*, pp. 22–23; Lee Soltow, "Inequality amidst Abundance: Land Ownership in Early Nineteenth-Century Ohio," *Ohio History*, 88 (1979), 133–151. Soltow finds this level of landownership and inequality to be essentially constant until at least 1850; see p. 147 n. 25, and compare Soltow, "Progress and Mobility among Ohio Propertyholders, 1810–1825," *Social Science History*, 7 (1983), 405–426. For the relationship between frontier settlement and the growth of capitalism see Allan Kulikoff, *The Agrarian Origins of American Capitalism* (Charlottesville, 1992), especially pp. 208–217. Kulikoff correctly emphasizes that frontier migration disproportionately attracted settlers who already had some capital; the move west was much more difficult, and more unlikely, for people without any means to begin with. For the relationship between land, freedom, and the struggle to control western resources see Alan Taylor, "Land and Liberty on the Post-Revolutionary Frontier," in David Konig, ed., *Devising Liberty: Preserving and Creating Freedom in the New American Republic* (Stanford, 1995), pp. 81–108. For Massie see Cayton, *Frontier Republic*, pp. 53–56.

[40] Andrew Cayton and Peter Onuf, *The Midwest and the Nation: Rethinking the History of an American Region* (Bloomington, IN, 1990), p. 35. For the importance of merchants, credit networks, and the market from the earliest period of settlement see Kim Gruenwald, "Merchants, Farmers, and Empire: The Establishment of a Market Economy in the Ohio Valley," paper presented at the Second Annual Conference of the Institute of Early American History and Culture, Boulder, CO, 31 May–2 June, 1996; Rohrbough, *Trans-Appalachian Frontier*, pp. 41–44; Mary K. Bonsteel Tachau, *Feder-*

The emergence of the marketplace as the central arbiter of social difference accorded well with one strain of Revolutionary thought, the tradition that Isaac Kramnick has identified as "bourgeois radicalism." For many radical theorists, the essence of the Revolutionary achievement was to free individuals from the circumstances of their birth and loosen the social order in a way that opened new opportunities to the able and ambitious. This tradition emphasized liberation from state dogmas and toleration of difference, doctrines that accorded well with the social complexity of the Northwest Territory. Kramnick identifies the "race of life" as a defining metaphor of this radical tradition, a metaphor that placed a premium on work, achievement, and self-advancement. These ideas provided a bridge between traditional republican conceptions of society, with their emphasis on collective enterprise, civic virtue, and the moral authority of prominent gentlemen, on the one hand, and the liberal doctrines of equal opportunity and individual enterprise that came to dominate the political life of the early republic on the other. In a region like the Ohio Valley, with an unformed social order and an extraordinary diversity of inhabitants, the liberal emphases of bourgeois radicalism were especially well-suited to local conditions. The valley's diverse and recent social origins virtually guaranteed the emergence of an intensely competitive economic environment.[41]

The metaphor of the "race of life" was much less significant in the region, however, than metaphors of openness and opportunity. Residents and commentators were impressed less by the competitiveness of their circumstances than they were by the apparently unlimited economic horizons that lay before them. A similar view prevailed throughout the new nation. "If we make a right use of our natural advantages," John Gardiner noted in a Fourth of July oration in Boston, "we soon must be a truly great and happy people. When we consider the vastness of our country, the variety of her soil and climate, the immense extent of her sea-coast, and of the inland navigation by the lakes and rivers, we find a *world within ourselves*, sufficient to produce whatever can contribute to the necessities and even the superfluities of life." In the Ohio Valley, the abundance of land suggested cornucopian possibilities. The region was,

al Courts in the Early Republic: Kentucky, 1789–1816 (Princeton, 1978), pp. 162–165, and on land litigation, pp. 167–190. For consumption patterns in early Kentucky, see Elizabeth A. Perkins, "The Consumer Frontier: Household Consumption in Early Kentucky," *The Journal of American History*, 78 (1991), 486–510.

41 Isaac Kramnick, *Republicanism and Bourgeois Radicalism: Political Ideology in Late Eighteenth-Century England and America* (Ithaca, 1990); see also Joyce Appleby, *Liberalism and Republicanism in the Historical Imagination* (Cambridge, MA, 1992), and Gordon Wood, *The Radicalism of the American Revolution* (New York, 1992).

in the judgment of Samuel Holden Parsons, a "terrestrial paradise," astonishing in its extent and fertility.[42]

Those who settled in the valley immediately recognized its vast commercial potential. Early arrivals often moved several times, searching for a "land of promise." The fortunate could eventually report to relatives that they had found "land aplenty not Entered and the richest I ever beheld and as for stock it is one of the finest places that is to be found." Once settled, farmers only needed access to markets to make their new lands pay. Thus commercial towns emerged alongside pockets of agricultural development. From the beginning farmers raised cash crops like hemp and tobacco as well as foodstuffs, and in the rapidly growing towns of the valley they also found an immediate market for their surplus corn, wheat, and livestock. To make ends meet, settlers needed merchants and markets; they also needed open transportation routes to the outside world.[43]

Other, more neglected parts of the American backcountry were plagued with threats of foreign conspiracies in these years. Where the United States failed to protect settlers against Indians, confer legitimacy on land titles, or support economic development, prominent men were surprisingly willing to ally themselves with foreign powers. Ira Allen, concerned that northern Vermont would languish under the United States, conspired with French officials to create the "republic of Reunited Columbia" in the northeast. Many leading southwesterners, including Daniel Boone, John Sevier, James Wilkinson, and Andrew Jackson, negotiated with Spain for land grants or support for secession after years of frustrating neglect from the national government. Others flirted with France during Edmond Charles Genet's American tour, while William Blount secretly pursued a British alliance to invade Louisiana and the Floridas. But in the Ohio Valley, the national government defended early settlements, established a viable political system that could confer legitimacy on officeholders, created a legal framework that validated land titles and supported economic development, and, in 1795, secured navigation rights to the Mississippi River. These actions laid the foundation for a steadily expanding economy and largely dispelled the

---

[42] John Gardiner, *An Oration, Delivered July 4, 1785* . . . (Boston, 1785), 35, quoted in Peter Onuf and Cathy Matson, "Toward a Republican Empire: Interest and Ideology in Revolutionary America," *American Quarterly*, 37 (1985), 517; Parsons to [William Samuel Johnson?], 26 Nov. 1785, quoted in Merrill Jensen, *The New Nation: A History of the United States During the Confederation 1781–1789* (New York, 1950), p. 114.

[43] A. C. Ramsey, "A Sketch of the Life and Times of Rev. A. C. Ramsey . . . ," and Hosea Smith to his father, quoted in Rohrbough, *Trans-Appalachian Frontier*, pp. 96, 94. For the early importance of commerce see note 40 above.

challenges to national ascendancy that were common to other back-country regions of the early republic.[44]

Thus rapid economic development in the west was effectively realized even as the economic ascendancy of Federalist gentlemen was challenged and largely eclipsed. Those same gentlemen also, and perhaps more importantly, hoped to set the tone and shape the character of public life in the Ohio Valley. In newly founded settlements of bewildering diversity and questionable moral character, territorial leaders hoped to create unifying public institutions that could undergird the social order and prepare settlers to be competent and responsible citizens. Many Federalists with pretensions to social and cultural preeminence favored a thoroughgoing program of social, cultural, and moral reform, in keeping with the classical republican ideals of the Revolutionary movement. Community-builders expected settlers to embrace the call to civic virtue and to cultivate the discipline, sobriety, and thrift characteristic of an emerging pattern of bourgeois values.[45]

In their calls for reform, Federalists ran up against a large segment of the region's population that was largely indifferent to the summons. This group identified more with the Revolution's promise of local control and individual liberty than with its emphasis on civic virtue. Its strength lay in more subsistence-oriented rural regions and among humble laborers like boatmen and mechanics; it drew upon older agrarian, laboring, and frontier traditions, and its members adhered to the male-dominated, rough-and-tumble values of a more rugged existence. At its most extreme, this culture verged into the violent, whiskey-addled "gouge and bite, pull hair and scratch" crowd upon whom foreign travelers in the west never failed to comment. But the Ohio Valley's localists were defined principally by their attachment to autonomous households

---

[44] For the broad outlines of this argument see especially Andrew R. L. Cayton, "'When Shall We Cease to Have Judases?': The Blount Conspiracy and the Limits of the 'Extended' Republic," in Ronald Hoffman and Peter J. Albert, eds., *Launching "the Extended Republic": The Federalist Era* (Charlottesville, 1996), and Cayton, "'Separate Interests' and the Nation-State." On foreign plots see also Jeanne Ojala, "Ira Allen and the French Directory, 1796: Plans for the Creation of the Republic of United Columbia," *WMQ*, 36 (1979), 436–448; Faragher, *Daniel Boone*, pp. 274–295; Robert Remini, *Andrew Jackson and the Course of American Empire, 1767–1821* (New York, 1977), pp. 102–106 and following; Reginald Horsman, *The Frontier in the Formative Years, 1783–1815* (New York, 1970), pp. 14–20.

[45] Cayton, *Frontier Republic*, pp. 12–32; Cayton and Onuf, *Midwest and the Nation*, pp. 50–51; and, more generally, Mary P. Ryan, *Cradle of the Middle Class: The Family in Oneida County, New York, 1790–1865* (New York, 1981); Nancy Cott, *The Bonds of Womanhood: "Woman's Sphere" in New England, 1780–1835* (New Haven, 1977); Paul Johnson, *A Shopkeeper's Millennium: Society and Revivals in Rochester, New York, 1815–1837* (New York, 1978).

and communities and individual freedom, not by a particular affinity for violent popular entertainments. Like the Daniel Boone of legend, inclined to move farther west when he could see the smoke from a neighbor's chimney, this segment of the region's population was suspicious of outside wealth and distant political authority, often preferred a religion of the heart to a religion of the head, emphasized patriarchal household authority, and expected its women to work hard outside the house as well as in. Many such ordinary settlers responded mistrustfully to the would-be architects of a new social order in the west.[46]

On fundamental questions of public order the reformers managed to win the day, at least in the region's market towns. By 1792 Cincinnati had already grown to more than 900 residents, with a large commercial interest. "The town," wrote one visitor, "is overrun with merchants and traders and overstocked with merchandise; there are already over 30 stores and warehouses here, and the one ruins others." It was poised to become a thriving center of regional trade. But Cincinnati's "respectable" inhabitants feared the influence of the "[i]dlers," who were "a multitude like the Sodomites" in the town. "It is however hoped," the visitor concluded, "that the place, as well as the other settlements on the north side of the Ohio, will in the course of time, and probably soon, be cleared of this bad element, for experience teaches, that as soon as they are brought under the hands of the law, they seek the shores of Kentucky (which lies directly across the Ohio), and if they are caught there, then they escape to the extreme borders of the Clinch or Cumberland River, or even to Orleans." Thus the reformers and improvers of the new Ohio towns hoped to banish vice to the hinterlands.[47]

To accomplish their aim, they brought law to bear on disorder. Beginning on Christmas eve 1792, and persisting into the new year, high-spirited Cincinnatians celebrated the holiday season in a most disturbing manner. "The Town is every night alarmed by an almost constant Discharge of Fire Arms," according to Territorial Secretary Winthrop Sargent, "accompanied with the most savage *yell*, and many houses bear the marks that *those arms* have been very highly charged with very deadly Weapons." Sargent called out a militia guard in response, "which has been opposed by Force and menaces," and discovered to his chagrin that the offenders included individuals from whom, according

---

[46] Elliott J. Gorn, "'Gouge and Bite, Pull Hair and Scratch': The Social Significance of Fighting in the Southern Backcountry," *The American Historical Review*, 90 (1985), 18–43; Michael Allen, *Western Rivermen, 1763–1861: Ohio and Mississippi Boatmen and the Myth of the Alligator Horse* (Baton Rouge, 1990); Frank Owsley, *Plain Folk of the Old South* (Baton Rouge, 1949).

[47] Heckewelder, *First Description of Cincinnati*, p. 45.

to "their standing in society and Dependence upon Civil Obligations[,] we should expect better Conduct." But Sargent was confident that force and justice would prevail; to justify his use of the militia, he recalled a similar situation at Marietta in its earliest days, when an overly exuberant holiday celebration produced a formal complaint that was aired in a special court session. Several offenders were convicted of disturbing the peace and, Sargent concluded, "from that time to this I have heard of no Complaint on similar offences in Washington County." Thus the battle between reformers and localists found expression in the earliest years in contests over law and order; in the increasingly respectable market towns along the river, the forces of order gradually prevailed.[48]

But this split also shaped the contentious politics of the postwar era, and here the localists continued to exert a strong influence. In both Kentucky and Ohio, people who regarded themselves as natural leaders found their initiative challenged on a series of fundamental questions; to maintain their leadership, they had to compromise their views and search out a new political language, less elitist and more popular in tone. Ordinary farmers and mechanics, on the other hand, experienced for the first time the power that accrued to humble people through broadly based voting rights, exercised in a context that was neither deferential nor coercive. They challenged Federalist assumptions of governance in the Ohio Valley and became core supporters of the Jeffersonian Republican program, with its emphasis on liberation from government and elites, in the late 1790s. Accompanying as it did the evolution of market relations, this development severed the connection that republican theorists emphasized between economic autonomy and political power. In the new nation, political power was granted to ordinary men even as the market drew them into new patterns of economic dependency upon neighbors, merchants, mortgageholders, and moneylenders. The empowerment of ordinary, unlettered men delayed even the most basic reforming measures. Public education, for example, which the

---

[48] Sargent to John Cleves Symmes, 6 and 13 Jan. 1793, Winthrop Sargent Papers, box 1, folder 7, OHS (emphasis in original). Such occurrences remained commonplace in outlying communities; they were also apparently more common in Kentucky than Ohio, but both states saw their share of violent popular entertainments. In 1796 Edward Christian wrote to Thomas Worthington from Martinsburg, Ohio, to describe "perhaps the greatest riott . . . that ever was known of in a civilized country. the Irish ag[ains]t the Buckskins. the attacks was brot. on by the Irish with double our force and armed with Swords and Clubs. We defeated them with great blood shed, one of the paddys is hourly expected to die this Gentleman I had the pleasure of thumping. tomo[rrow] they will be tried by a Jury of 12 men under the riot act, attend if possible and let not your Native Country be trampled upon by those irish Convicts." 18 Jan. 1796, Thomas Worthington Papers, box 1, folder 1, OHS.

drafters of the Northwest Ordinance considered the institutional corner-
stone of a responsible, enlightened, and integrated citizenry, was disre-
garded in the early years. It was not until the 1850s that public schools
received taxpayer support in the Ohio Valley.[49]

Thus in place of nationalist patriotism buttressed by republican institutions and values, the Ohio Valley developed regional cells of communities and farms bound together, loosely at first, by the market, but otherwise independent and localist in their orientation. Disputes between
Federalists and their Jeffersonian Republican opponents in the 1790s
anticipated later political battles between Whigs and Jacksonian Dem-
ocrats.[50]

Yet it would be a mistake to overemphasize the divisiveness of this
broad distinction. Lines were never so clear and simple in fact: ordinary
farmers and laborers could embrace reformist impulses, while even the
most commercially oriented merchants could favor the Jeffersonian program of small government and economic liberty. A common reliance on
the market drew hunters, boatmen, farmers, and merchants together in
a common web of mutual dependence. In the political sphere, a large
centrist core emerged that agreed on fundamental principles. The efforts
of established, well-connected men to control their social inferiors
through public institutions were largely defeated; to preserve their as-
cendance, prominent men had to maintain their standing in the marketplace. The middle-class desire for social reform found expression in private rather than public institutions, in a host of reform societies and religious organizations that quickly proliferated in the first half of the
nineteenth century. Government activism was largely restricted to the
economic realm, where rapid development could confer benefits on

---

[49] For political contests see Watlington, *Partisan Spirit*, where Watlington uses the labels
"articulate center" and "partisan" to distinguish between the two groups in Kentucky;
and Cayton, *Frontier Republic*, which contrasts Ohio's Federalist leaders, generally
from New England, with the populist liberalism of most early settlers, especially those
from Kentucky, Virginia, and North Carolina. See also Donald J. Ratcliffe, "The Experience of Revolution and the Beginnings of Party Politics in Ohio, 1776–1816," *Ohio
History*, 85 (1976), 186–230; Andrew R. L. Cayton, "'Language Gives Way to Feel-
ings': Rhetoric, Republicanism, and Religion in Jeffersonian Ohio," in Brown and Cayton, eds., *Pursuit of Public Power*, pp. 31–48; and more generally Kenneth Cmiel, *Democratic Eloquence: The Fight over Popular Speech in Nineteenth-Century America*
(New York, 1990). On the link between economic independence and political power
see J. G. A. Pocock, *The Machiavellian Moment: Florentine Political Thought and the
Atlantic Republican Tradition* (Princeton, 1975), and McCoy, *Elusive Republic*; on
public education see Carl Kaestle, *Pillars of the Republic: Common Schools and American Society, 1780–1860* (New York, 1983), pp. 182–192.

[50] For the later period see especially Charles Sellers, *The Market Revolution: Jacksonian
America, 1815–1846* (New York, 1991).

nearly everyone in the social order. Many ordinary farmers and settlers, once suspicious of distant political and economic power, were drawn into full participation in the national political order by the democratic emphases of Jeffersonianism.[51]

The postwar culture of the Ohio Valley was shaped less by the conscious efforts of self-identified elites than it was by the popular attitudes and beliefs of ordinary settlers. Preeminent among these beliefs was the faith that their triumph in gaining control of the West was not an accidental occurrence, but a manifestation of divine authority. This conviction took root in the harrowing experiences of the Indian wars, and only grew stronger as the Euroamerican population of the valley continued to grow. It was here, in the hardships of fort life and the terrors of Indian warfare, that the first elements of a shared regional culture took shape. These experiences intersected with and intensified the growth of evangelical religion in the early republic, helping to create in the Ohio Valley an unusually vibrant undercurrent of popular piety.[52]

Many early settlers were convinced that God had delivered them from their perils, and that the survival of their communities had been divinely ordained. Divine judgment can run both ways, of course. In the spring of 1774, with the storms of the Revolutionary era about to break, one westerner asked, "Do you not think that God is about to punish us for our sins with temporal Judgments? the expectation of a plentiful Crop is cut off, The indian Tribes commenc'd a War. the ministry at home intending to force Taxes upon us. I think it is time to cry, Help Lord, for vain is the help of man without he concurs." Faced with an impending crisis, God's judgments seemed dire indeed. But in the darkest days of the war even the smallest victories could appear divinely ordained. "Providence is daily working out strange deliverances for us," Arthur Campbell wrote in the summer of 1778. When a party of attacking Indians was "unexpectedly discomfited," he concluded that "the most hardened mind must see and admire the divine goodness in such an interposition." A short time later several hundred Indians attacked a settlement on the Greenbriar River, but a messenger "providentially got

---

[51] For the creation of a political middle ground see Cayton, *Frontier Republic*, pp. 51–80 and following, and Ratliffe, "Experience of Revolution"; for a comparable settlement in another context see Taylor, *Liberty Men and Great Proprietors*; for privatized reform see Ryan, *Cradle of the Middle Class*; for the reform of American law to facilitate economic development see Morton J. Horwitz, *The Transformation of American Law, 1780–1860* (Cambridge, MA, 1977).

[52] John Boles, *The Great Revival, 1787–1805: The Origin of the Southern Evangelical Mind* (Lexington, KY, 1972); Nathan Hatch, *The Democratization of American Christianity* (New Haven, 1989).

in two days before the Indians, and the whole settlement got into forts."
If a small number of armed men was able to hold a large body of attacking Indians at bay, it could be "regarded by the reflecting part of the Station as a Providential deliverance."[53]

In the early years, God's judgment of the Kentucky communities appeared to be mixed. "[T]he state of religious society was but very little
attended to" in the wartime stations, Robert McAfee later reflected;
"dancing & hunting constituted the general amusement of both young
& old, & being confined in the Fort was favorable to the gratification of
each." Yet hardship hardened faith. McAfee recalled that the death of
one young man "very much weighed upon" the minds of his family,
"but being destitute as yet of minsters of the gospel, impressions made
by the events of misfortune were not improved, and of course were soon
forgotten." When an army of Kentuckians was decisively beaten by Indians at the Battle of Blue Licks in 1782, however, the members of
McAfee's community clearly understood God's message. "The influence
of this defeat in a moral & religious point of view was considerable, &
brought the inhabitants to a serious sense of their duty & great obligation to their Creator." Then, "as a strong evidence of the continued care
of Providence to them," a minister named David Rice moved to Harrod's Run, near Danville, and began preaching in people's homes; a year
later Adam Rankin was called to Lexington. In the spring of 1785,
McAfee and his neighbors built a log cabin on the Salt River "for the
double purpose of meeting & school house," where Rice preached for
several years. They named their congregation New Providence, as a reminder of the many providential occurrences that had favored the inhabitants.[54]

McAfee's reactions to the war were not universally shared, but they
suggest that hardship could strengthen a sense of purpose among the
settlers. They also provide one model for understanding how the lessons
of experience could take institutional form. The Revolution conveyed
meanings that first became articles of faith, and later received concrete
expression in community-building enterprises. In the earliest Ohio Valley settlements, the Indian war was a defining experience that challenged western settlers to interpret their persistence in the landscape in
transcendent terms, and to define an enduring social order that gave institutional expression to those transcendent meanings.[55]

---

[53] John Brown to William Preston, 28 May 1774, Draper MSS 3QQ29; Campbell to Rev.
Charles Cummings, 10 June 1778, Draper MSS 18J77; McAfee, "History of the Rise
and Progress," Draper MSS 4CC61.

[54] McAfee, "History of the Rise and Progress," Draper MSS 4CC61–67; quotes: pp. 61,
64, 65, 66.

[55] For the institution-building impulse in frontier religious communities see T. Scott

As the valley's population quickly diversified in the late 1780s and the 1790s, religious institutions proliferated until the Ohio Valley became, in the judgment of one scholar, the first "testing ground" for religious pluralism in America. Moravians and Methodists, Lutherans of every description, General and Particular Baptists, Quakers and the Disciples of Christ, Anglicans, Presbyterians of several persuasions, and others were represented in the region at an early date. Yet even as these groups sought to retain their distinctive institutional identities, they also shared the "evangelical united front" that became as characteristic of the Ohio Valley as its pluralism. This united front was broadly Methodist in its orientation, and gained its strength from Wesleyan theology and evangelizing methods. In the early years it depended especially on the efforts of circuit-riding ministers and intense evangelical revivals. These revivals echoed the emotional structure and content of the Indian war experience: they emphasized the deplorable sinfulness of the human condition, with the dire threat it posed to the soul; the strength of grace; and the power of Christ to offer deliverance to suffering sinners. This sequence – danger, grace, deliverance – followed the morphology of the settlers' experience, which began with the mortal dangers of relocation and Indian war, proceeded through the uncertain phase of ad hoc cooperation and community-building, and culminated at last in the mastery of a new landscape, with its promise of an unbounded future. When the frontier population of the Ohio Valley writhed on the ground in an agonizing recognition of the mortal dangers to which they had exposed their souls, or fell tearfully to their knees to acknowledge their deliverance and salvation, the occasion gained much of its intensity from the specific earthly experiences of the pioneer generation.[56]

Beneath the tremendous diversity of Ohio Valley settlers lay the defining experience of conquest, which shaped regional lore and values and imparted a kind of cultural unity to the region. Memories and tales drawn from the years of Indian fighting, of danger, uncertainty, and triumph, undergirded a broadly shared regional identity. Richard Slotkin has described the residual cultural influence of frontier violence as a kind of regeneration; through their violent triumph in difficult times, valley settlers found reassurance and renewal. The nature of this regeneration could take different forms, depending on the audience. Some used past violence as a point of departure for a more orderly existence.

Miyakawa, *Protestants and Pioneers: Individualism and Conformity on the American Frontier* (Chicago, 1964).

[56] Timothy L. Smith, "The Ohio Valley: Testing Ground for America's Experiment in Religious Pluralism," *Church History*, 60 (1991), 461–479, quote: p. 466; Boles, *The Great Revival*; Hatch, *Democratization of American Christianity*; Sydney Ahlstrom, *A Religious History of the American People* (New Haven, 1972), pp. 431–439.

Robert McAfee's narrative of providential deliverances used the founding of New Providence Church to mark the beginning of a new and fundamentally different existence – a reformed and refined life, freed from the terrors and barbarities of earlier years.[57]

For others, the war hardened without refining; they, too, contributed distinctive qualities to regional identity and experience. Many years after the war, an elderly Kentucky resident recalled for an interviewer a particularly vivid memory from the years of conflict. Jonathan Leet told the story of a man who returned one day to his home on Whitley Creek to discover that his wife and two children had been murdered and scalped. In anguish, he chased and caught two Indians whom he believed to be responsible. A tanner by trade, the man then paused to skin one of his victims completely. Taking his trophy home, he tanned it and had it cut and stitched into a pair of pants and a vest, "which he would wear to Washington [Kentucky] on public days." In public occasions when this man displayed his grisly suit, no less than in the services of McAfee's New Providence church, a social group ritually commemorated its triumph over a savage and alien enemy.[58]

The war thus provided a storehouse of experience and lore sufficiently deep and varied to sustain multiple strains of culture and social experience. In the narratives of people like Robert McAfee and Jonathan Leet, memories of the Indian war penetrated the consciousness of Ohio Valley residents and preserved a sense of shared trials and common purpose.

IV

The Ohio Valley emerged from the Revolutionary era a distinctive region, united within itself by the powerful experiences of the war years and connected with the United States at large by ties of military and economic dependency. It was also increasingly connected with a larger national context by the emerging significance of race as the most fundamental marker of social difference in postwar society and law. Though eastern states first invoked race in citizenship law to guarantee that free blacks would remain non-citizens, in the west racial proscriptions were quickly broadened to apply to Indians as well, with significant implications for the extension of America's empire of liberty.

In a monarchy, the relationship between sovereign and subject was organic and "natural," part of the condition into which a person was

---

[57] Richard Slotkin, *Regeneration Through Violence: The Mythology of the American Frontier, 1600–1860* (Middletown, CT, 1973).

[58] Draper MSS 2S7.

born. But the Revolution transformed subjects into citizens. This decisive change, which members of the Revolutionary generation regarded
as supremely important, carried implications that contemporaries did
not yet fully grasp. Most fundamentally, citizenship status was volition-
al in a way that subjectship was not: a subject was born into a relationship with a sovereign, but a citizen, in theory, *chose* to be a member of
the republic. Citizenship was thus more malleable than subjectship; it
required identifying markers beyond the locus of one's birth. The Revolution dramatized the need for such markers when Congress grappled
with the problem of "naturalizing" foreign immigrants – a term held
over from the older, monarchical context and the view that political
membership was natal, not voluntary.[59]

The first American naturalization law, passed in 1790, introduced a
crucial innovation in legal language that creatively addressed the need
for "natural" markers of citizenship, and at the same time invented a
powerful new mechanism of race exclusion. Racial markers had been
used for many years in colonial law, in statutes that subjected blacks to
unique legal disabilities. But the naturalization law of 1790 established
a normative racial category, as opposed to a disadvantaged one, for the
first time. It held that any "free white person" who had resided in the
country for two years, could demonstrate "good character," and swore
to "support the constitution of the United States" could be admitted as
a citizen. The whiteness clause was uncontroversial – it was never mentioned in the Congressional debates on the bill – and was presumably included for the limited purpose of preventing free African-Americans
from claiming citizen status, but its implications went much deeper.
Making whiteness a necessary qualification for citizenship was a powerful innovation, strikingly inclusive in one way and exclusive in another.
Inclusive, because it postulated an essential, "natural" core of common
identity where none had previously existed: Whiteness could unite not
only Pennsylvanians with Virginians, but also native-born Euroamericans with immigrant Germans and Scots-Irish. Exclusive, because it
made racial boundaries theoretically absolute.[60]

As new states were carved out of the Northwest and Southwest, their

---

[59] James Kettner, *The Development of American Citizenship, 1608–1870* (Chapel Hill,
1978), pp. 173–247.

[60] The final version of the bill can be found in *United States Statutes at Large*, vol. I, pp.
103–104. For a history of race discrimination in the statute law of British America see
especially Winthrop Jordan, *White Over Black: American Attitudes Toward the Negro, 1550–1812* (Chapel Hill, 1968); for a thoughtful analysis of whiteness in American history see David Roediger, "Whiteness and Ethnicity in the History of 'White Eth-
nics' in the United States," in *Towards the Abolition of Whiteness: Essays on Race,
Politics, and Working Class History* (London, 1994).

constitutions and legal codes adopted and extended the principle that whiteness was necessary for citizenship. Property and tax-paying qualifications for voting were abandoned in Kentucky, Tennessee, and most of the territories that became states between 1796 and 1821. These states thus rejected the classical republican notion that political power should be tied to property ownership. But at the same time, five of the eight states admitted between 1796 and 1821 limited the vote to white men. A Michigan legislator explained that Indians and blacks were not members of what he termed the "great North American family."[61]

In practice, this exclusion was applied to Indians in an expedient and haphazard way. It was not always either easy or desirable to maintain a sharp distinction between white and nonwhite in a region with such a complicated past, as an Ohio Supreme Court case of 1842 made clear. Ohio was one of the states that restricted voting rights to "free white citizens." Under this law, the trustees of Zenia township tried to exclude a man named Parker Jeffries from voting. Jeffries was the son of a Euroamerican man and a *métis* woman, which, the trustees asserted, made him "a person of color." Technically, the trustees were right. But the chief justice chose not to apply a strict reading of the law because its effects would be deeply disruptive. "There have been, even in this state, since its organization," he noted, "many persons of the precise breed of this plaintiff, I mean the offspring of whites and half-breed Indians, who have exercised political privileges and filled offices, and worthily discharged the duties of officers." He did not have far to look for examples. "One such is now a clerk of this court, and two are now members of this bar, and disfranchisement, for this cause, will be equally unexpected and startling." Despite the strength of the trustees' claim, the court granted Jeffries the right to vote.[62]

The United States often defined whiteness even more loosely when it dealt with western Indians. In a long series of treaties spanning the nineteenth century, Indians of many different tribes were repeatedly offered the chance to become "white" before the law if they would give up their lands and their corporate identity. These agreements routinely stipulated that individual members of Indian tribes who would relinquish their tribal membership could be granted private land and citizenship rights.[63]

This standard treaty provision helps put racial proscriptions as they

---

[61] Chilton Williamson, *American Suffrage: From Property to Democracy, 1760–1860* (Princeton, NJ, 1960), pp. 208–222; quote: p. 219.
[62] *Jeffries v. Ankeny et al.* (1842), 11 Ohio 372.
[63] Kettner, *Development of American Citizenship*, pp. 292–293.

were applied to Indians in their proper context. Though years of frontier violence often made Indians popular objects of hatred and revulsion in the Ohio Valley, state and federal policies were not aimed primarily at singling them out for disadvantaged treatment within American society, as they were in the case of African Americans. For Indians, race was used instead primarily as a lever to pry them loose from their collective property claims. Once they abandoned their tribal identifications and the property rights they implied, Indians could often be readily accepted as "white." It was not their physiology that disqualified them as members of the "great North American family," but the obstruction they presented to the expansion of the United States' empire of liberty.

Thus when Ohio Valley communities were willing to be integrated into the American territorial system, the racial origins of their inhabitants were often of little consequence. In the Illinois country, for example, where settlers' lands had been held for generations at the sufferance of the local Indians and governed by French law and custom, and where communities were dominated by *métis* populations, Congress made special allowances to establish a continuous legal framework for property ownership. In 1791 it confirmed title to improved lands to those who occupied them, and granted 400 acres to any head of family who had been living in Vincennes or the Illinois country as of 1783 (thus legitimizing claims staked by Virginians during the Revolution, as well as older French ones). Through a process of self-selection, some residents of the French communities chose to remain, take up property under American law, and establish themselves as white citizens, while others chose to leave.[64]

Many – "by far the greater part," in the estimation of a Vincennes judge – decided to leave. He guessed that they had "neither patience nor, as they say, much confidence left in the promise of government," but his explanation did not fully account for their decision to emigrate. Of the estimated 10–15,000 *métis* living in the Ohio Valley in the early 19th century, many were unwilling to adapt to the American system of propertyholding. Often they had not claimed land at all under the French system; having grown up at the commercial nexus between two cultures, most *métis* preferred trade to farming and identified with the region rather than with a single, bounded plot of land. They thus possessed a weak sense of property rights by American standards, and, pressed by incoming officials and settlers to stake their claims to land, many pre-

[64] "An Act for granting lands to the Inhabitants and settlers at Vincennes and the Illinois country . . .", 3 Mar. 1791, *United States Statutes at Large*, vol. I, pp. 221–222; Paul W. Gates, *History of Public Land Law Development* (New York, 1979), pp. 87–88.

ferred simply to move on to someplace where land was not yet being parceled and commodified.[65]

Among those who successfully claimed land in the French settlements, many were relative newcomers. One of the largest claimants in Kaskaskia was the prominent merchant Pierre Menard, who was born near Montreal in 1766 and arrived in Kaskaskia only around 1790. He nevertheless managed to claim several thousand acres in the American Bottom. In all, 2,851 claims were confirmed in Ohio, Indiana, Illinois, and Michigan, conferring a total of 706,000 acres. For those who remained to be integrated into newly Americanized communities, the transition from *métis* to white society could be uncomfortable, even humiliating, but it was not especially difficult. In Green Bay, a very old trading community on Lake Michigan, circuit court judge James Doty called a grand jury to investigate local domestic arrangements. As a result, 36 of the community's most prominent men were charged with fornication, and two others with adultery, because they had been married according to local custom. Most quietly pleaded guilty and had their marriages legitimized by a justice of the peace, though two fought the charges in court. In later years, when *métissage* was thoroughly stigmatized and whiteness was an essential characteristic of respectability, the mixed racial origins of prominent families in trading communities could cause considerable embarrassment and energetic denial, but they were not grounds for legal dispossession of property or citizenship rights.[66]

But many residents of the Ohio Valley who identified primarily with Indian communities viewed the opportunity to become white before the law as a devil's bargain. Most Indians regarded themselves as members of separate, sovereign nations, and they resented the pressures of American expansion. In 1778, when the impact of the Revolution on the west was still poorly understood, a treaty between the United States and the Ohio Delawares stipulated that distinct, sovereign Indian states might coexist with a new American nation, and perhaps even become equal members of a federal union, once the American states had achieved independence from Britain.[67] It is tempting to regard such a proposal as

---

[65] Judge George Turner to St. Clair, 14 June 1794, box 4, folder 7, St. Clair Papers, OHS; Jacqueline Peterson, "The People in Between: Indian-White Marriage and the Genesis of a Métis Society and Culture in the Great Lakes Region 1680–1830," (Ph.D. diss., University of Illinois Chicago Circle, 1981), pp. 142–143.

[66] Gates, *Public Land Law*, pp. 92 and 92–93n; Irwin F. Mather, *The Making of Illinois: Historical Sketches* (Chicago, 1900); Peterson, "People in Between," pp. 1–12; on the complicated social legacy of *métissage*, see Jacqueline Peterson and Jennifer Brown, eds., *The New Peoples: Being and Becoming Métis in North America* (Lincoln, NE, 1985).

[67] For Indian attitudes toward the United States see especially James Merrell, "Declara-

fantastically far-fetched, but in 1778 an independent Delaware state in the west would have been one way for America's new revolutionary republic to extend legitimate public authority into the Ohio Valley. By the 1790s, however, such a possibility had been foreclosed. The precise relationship between Indian and American polities was contested for several more decades, but the foundation for Indian dispossession in the west was laid during the Revolution and its immediate aftermath. In that era, the rapid growth of squatter settlements was validated by revolutionary governments; the blueprint for a dynamic, expansive territorial system was devised; and the doctrine of racial exclusion first took shape in American law. These developments ensured that Native Americans would not be treated as fully sovereign entities by the new nation; what remained was to work out the precise logic by which they would be deprived of their authority.

It was left to the Supreme Court, in particular, to articulate this logic. *Johnson v. McIntosh* (1823) contested the sale of Ohio Valley lands to private purchasers by a group of Piankashaw Indians. This sale threatened federal control of western lands, and it would not be surprising for the court to hold that private purchasers could not buy Indian lands. The court did disallow the purchase, but it made the opposite argument: the sale was illegitimate, not because the purchasers lacked the authority to buy the land, but because the Indians did not have the right to sell it. The majority opinion argued that Indians were not sovereign owners of land, but "perpetual inhabitants, with diminutive rights." They were "an inferior race of people, without the privileges of citizens, and under the perpetual protection and pupilage of the government."[68]

This idea was developed most fully in the famous Marshall opinion in the *Cherokee Nation v. Georgia* (1831), which articulated the classic doctrine of Indian subordination to American national power. When Georgia tried and convicted a citizen of the Cherokee Nation for murdering another Cherokee within the bounds of the Cherokee Nation, the Cherokee Council objected that Georgia laws had no force in Cherokee territory. Their lawyer argued that they could sue Georgia as a foreign power, since the Cherokees were legally defined as aliens of the United States. But Marshall's opinion denied them the right to be treated as a foreign power. "An aggregate of aliens composing a state must, they say, be a foreign state," he wrote in summary of the plaintiffs' argument. "In

tions of Independence: Indian-White Relations in the New Nation," in Greene, ed., *American Revolution*, pp. 197–223; for the possibility of a distinct Indian state see the treaty between the United States and the Delawares, 17 Sept. 1778, Article 6, *United States Statutes at Large*, vol. VII, pp. 13–15.

[68] *Johnson v. McIntosh*, 8 Wheaton 543 (U.S. 1823); quote: 569.

general," he agreed, "nations not owing a common allegiance, are foreign to each other." But "[t]he condition of the Indians in relation to the United States is, perhaps, unlike that of any other two people in existence. . . . The Indian territory is admitted to compose a part of the United States. . . . They acknowledge themselves, in their treaties, to be under the protection of the United States," and accept the right of the United States to regulate trade with them. Rather than foreign nations, Marshall argued, Indian tribes "may, more correctly, perhaps, be denominated domestic dependent nations." As such, they had no standing before the court. "[T]he majority is of opinion," Marshall concluded, "that an Indian tribe or nation within the United States is not a foreign state, in the sense of the constitution, and cannot maintain an action in the courts of the United States."[69]

In the *Cherokee* decision, the principle of elastic national boundaries, which made even Indian lands belong to the United States, converged with the racialized definition of citizenship, which made Indians unfit for sovereign independence, to complete the dispossession of Indians, as tribal or national entities, in American law. Denied standing in the courts as corporate bodies, Indian groups could resist the loss of their lands only by violence. As individuals, too, Indians were disadvantaged before the law. Born as aliens, they did not enjoy a citizen's standing in the courts; denied recognition as foreigners, they were also barred from the kind of standing ordinarily accorded to non-citizens. As aliens they could not hold property, making their individual claims to land as tenuous as their corporate ones. In the Ohio Valley, and indeed throughout the west, the process by which nonwhites became nonpersons before the law was a welcome change for prospective white settlers. It ensured rapid access to western property, and made every white person in the west an effective agent of empire.

One such agent was William Conner, a *métis* Indian trader whose father had worked among the Delawares in Ohio decades earlier, and whose mother was a Delaware. Following in his father's footsteps, in 1802 Conner joined the White River Delawares in present-day Indiana. He married a Delaware woman named Mekinges, daughter of a local sachem, and established his own trading town. When Indiana was admitted as a state 14 years later, much of it was still claimed by Indians. State officials and Indian leaders needed intermediaries to negotiate land

---

[69] *The Cherokee Nation v. Georgia*, 5 Peters 1 (U.S. 1831); quotes: pp. 16, 17, 20. In the following year the Marshall court offered a more sympathetic interpretation of Indian sovereignty, but that came in relation to the state of Georgia rather than the United States; see *Worcester v. Georgia*, 6 Peters p. 515 (U.S. 1832). For a full consideration of these cases see Jill Norgren, *The Cherokee Cases: The Confrontation of Law and Politics* (New York, 1996).

sales, and Conner became a key negotiator for the Indiana Delawares. By October 1818 the deal was struck; the White River Delawares would move to Missouri. Though Mekinges and their children soon left, Conner stayed behind and petitioned Congress for a grant of land within the cession. Three months later, Conner married "possibly the only eligible [white] woman" on the White River. "Without breaking stride," his chroniclers have noted, "the old frontiersman became a builder in a new community." With his prior knowledge of the region and early arrival, Conner established a central economic role among the growing settler population and amassed a respectable fortune. When he died, Conner's Delaware family returned to Indiana to sue for a portion of his estate, but the court, following the now-familiar racial logic of 19th century law, ruled that they were ineligible to inherit any of his property.[70]

Thus the perameters of America's empire of liberty were established. Voluntarily constituted, racially defined, indefinitely expansive, and democratically governed, it was an empire with an extraordinary capacity to reap the benefits of its citizens' energies. Instead of seeking to hold expansion in check, as the British empire had done, the United States invented a system of governance that harnessed its fortunes to the aggressive, expansionist impulses of its western population. Within the republic's embrace, citizens enjoyed extraordinary liberties; beyond it, the systematic exploitation of nonwhite peoples was extended and deepened. In the Ohio Valley, that exploitation meant, in addition to the extension of slavery, the wholesale appropriation of Indian land. The legal disabilities of Native Americans guaranteed that violence would govern their relations with the United States until a continental empire was secured at the end of the nineteenth century; that is a pattern whose origins can be traced back to the process by which the Ohio Valley was first occupied in the years during and immediately after the American Revolution.

---

[70] John Lauritz Larson and David G. Vandersteel, "Agent of Empire: William Conner on the Indiana Frontier, 1800–1855," *Indiana Magazine of History*, 80 (Dec. 1984), 301–328; quotes: p. 313.

EPILOGUE

State Power and Popular Authority
in the New American Nation

A NEW kind of empire, linked to a new kind of state, originated in the
American Revolution, and the Ohio Valley was its first testing
ground. Earlier British and French attempts to master the region were
defeated by its size, the complexity of its human population, and the
troublesome independence of colonists and Indians alike. To extend empire into the continental interior seemed to require a more potent, centralized, authoritarian state, one that could effectively manage the complexities of the region and oversee intercultural relations, monitor economic affairs, and regulate social development. But an administrative
structure sufficiently strong and flexible to meet these challenges never
did emerge, in either the French sphere or the British. Though the region
was deeply affected by European imperialism – its social and economic
systems, its patterns of alliance and warfare, its communities and its culture all bore the deep impress of intercultural relations – and though individual colonists profited in their activities in the Ohio Valley, administrators and architects of empire wanted more. They wanted not simply
to oversee those processes, but to control them. That goal always eluded
European empire-builders in the Ohio Valley.

The United States succeeded where France and Britain failed. Ironically, its success was due in part to the weakness of the national state. In
a critical moment, when the direction of the Revolutionary War hung in
the balance, the Continental Congress offered sweeping power and authority to western settlers who had previously been regarded as outlaws
in the British imperial scheme. This was not a foregone outcome or a
necessary corollary of the Revolutionary movement; the common wis-

dom, in fact, held that expansion would destroy a republic.[1] But for strategic as well as ideological reasons, the states and the Continental Congress empowered westerners and thereby validated their pursuit of free land. Then, in extending national power westward in the 1780s and 1790s, a Federalist vision of controlled and orderly expansion was compromised by the ongoing pressures of settlement and by the disorder and violence that had become an endemic characteristic of intercultural relations. To retain westerners in its interest, the United States government had to define its territorial ambitions broadly and pursue them aggressively.

The result was to create, in Thomas Jefferson's felicitous phrase, an "empire of liberty."[2] The term embodies a paradox: "empire" implies the coercive dominion of state power; especially in the period immediately following the Revolution, the idea of empire carried powerfully negative connotations for most Americans. "Liberty" implies, in effect, the absence of precisely such power: though the word possesses complex shades of meaning, its essence is, presumably, freedom from the kind of restraint associated with the authority of empire. How could imperial power be reconciled with governance in a democratic republic? In the Ohio Valley, the United States liberated its citizens to pursue their own interests while it turned the power of empire against the region's Native American population; their experiences in the years after the Revolution contrasted sharply with the widespread growth of liberty and economic opportunity enjoyed by the many thousands of people who flocked to the Ohio Valley to take up lands in the new American empire.

Historians have often argued that, because the American Revolution institutionalized a national commitment to the enlightened principles of universal human liberty and equality, it is ungenerous and anachronistic to criticize the founding generation for their failure to abolish slavery or to protect Native American claims to sovereignty and property rights. By articulating universal principles that could stand as permanent national ideals, this argument contends, the founders set age-old patterns of inhumanity, injustice, and inequality on the road to extinction.[3]

---

[1] This idea was identified especially with Montesquieu and revived by the antifederalists; see, e.g., Cecelia Kenyon, "Men of Little Faith: The Anti-Federalists on the Nature of Representative Government," *The William and Mary Quarterly*, 3rd ser., vol. XII (1955), especially pp. 6–13, and Lance Banning, *The Jeffersonian Persuasion: Evolution of a Party Ideology* (Ithaca, 1978), pp. 106–107.

[2] Jefferson's earliest use of the phrase appears in a letter to George Rogers Clark, 25 Dec. 1780; see Julian P. Boyd et al., eds., *The Papers of Thomas Jefferson* (Princeton, 1950–), vol. IV, pp. 233–238; quote: p. 237.

[3] This argument has been made more prominently in relation to slavery than Indian policy; see especially William Freehling, "The Founding Fathers and Slavery," *The Ameri-*

While it is true that enlightened principles ultimately challenged the systematic exploitation of nonwhite peoples, the legacy of the American Revolution is more complicated than this generalization suggests. To begin with, the Revolution can lay no exclusive claim to humanitarian values. Slavery, after all, was abolished in Britain and its colonies thirty years before the Emancipation Proclamation was issued in the United States, at which time only Brazil, of all the former colonies of the western hemisphere, had not yet freed its slaves. It would be considerably longer until the United States moderated its hostility toward Native Americans and slowed its appropriation of Indian lands.

And despite the soaring prose of the Declaration of Independence, it is no accident that the exploitation of nonwhite peoples in the United States deepened and intensified before it began to be ameliorated. The Revolution liberated white men to pursue their economic and political independence. It would have been something quite different, much more difficult and at odds with that pursuit, to mediate interests in a state where *all* men (or all men and women), of whatever race, were theoretically equal. By defining the rights of white citizens broadly, Congress eased the potential for sharp divisions among Euroamericans even as it placed more pressure on the lines of racial difference. The dispossession of native peoples and the enslavement of African Americans were not invented in the Revolutionary era; both were characteristic of European colonization throughout the Americas. But the new American nation valorized economic opportunity and political power for white men, while it had neither the strength nor the will to challenge its citizens' desire to exploit nonwhites in their pursuit of opportunity and power. As a result, an empire of liberty in the broadest and truest sense remained elusive in the Ohio Valley and beyond, and the problem of race would continue to bedevil the inheritors of the American Revolution for many generations to come.

can Historical Review, 77 (1972), 81–93. For a critical response see Paul Finkelman, *Slavery and the Founders: Race and Liberty in the Age of Jefferson* (Armonk, NY, 1996), especially pp. 138–167.

Bibliography of Cited Materials

PRIMARY SOURCES

Archival Collections

American Philosophical Society, Philadelphia
    Burd-Shippen Papers.
    Horsfield Papers.
    Logan Papers.
    Miscellaneous MSS on Indian Affairs, 1737–1775.
Clements Library, Ann Arbor, Michigan
    Gage Papers.
    Harmar Papers.
Filson Club, Louisville, Kentucky
    Clark-Hite Papers.
    Edmund T. Halsey Collection.
    Preston Family Papers.
    Taylor Family Papers.
Historical Society of Pennsylvania, Philadelphia
    Cadwallader Collection.
    Croghan Papers.
    Gratz-Croghan Papers.
    Indian Records Collection.
    Logan Papers.
    Penn Papers.
    Taylor Papers.
    Weiser Collection.
Historical Society of Wisconsin, Madison
    Draper Manuscripts.
Huntington Library, San Marino, California
    Huntington Manuscripts.

Loudoun Papers.
National Archives of Canada, Ottawa
  MG1: Archives des Colonies (Paris)
      Series C.
      Series E.
      Series F2.
      Series F3.
      Series G1.
  MG2: Archive de la Marine (Paris)
      Series A.
      Series B2.
      Series B3.
      Series 3JJ.
  MG8: Documents relatifs la Nouvelle France et au Quebec.
  MG18.
The Ohio Historical Society, Columbus
  Arthur St. Clair Papers.
  Winthrop Sargent Papers.
  Thomas Worthington Papers.

Published Sources

Alvord, Clarence, and Clarence Carter, eds., *The New Regime, 1765–1767.* Collections of the Illinois State Historical Library, XI. Springfield, 1916.
Bailey, Kenneth P., ed., *The Ohio Company Papers, 1753–1817: Being Primarily Papers of the "Suffering Traders" of Pennsylvania.* Arcata, CA, 1947.
Blair, Emma H., ed., *The Indian Tribes of the Upper Mississippi Valley and Region of the Great Lakes.* 2 vols. Cleveland, 1911.
Bouquet, Henry. *The Papers of Henry Bouquet.* Edited by Sylvester K. Stevens et al., 5 vols. Harrisburg, 1972–1984.
Browne, William Hand et al., eds., *Archives of Maryland.* 72 vols. Baltimore, 1883–   .
Butterfield, C. W., ed., *The Washington-Crawford Letters.* Cincinnati, 1877.
Canadian Archives, 1904. Ottawa, 1905.
Canadian Archives, Supplement, 1899. Ottawa, 1901.
"The Captivity of Charles Stuart, 1755–1757." Edited by Beverley W. Bond, Jr. *Mississippi Valley Historical Review,* 13 (1926), 58–81.
Craig, Neville B., ed., *The Olden Time.* 2 vols. Pittsburgh, 1846–48.
Croghan, George. "George Croghan's Journal, 1759–1763." Edited by Nicholas B. Wainwright. *Pennsylvania Magazine of History and Biography,* 71 (1947), 305–444.
Croghan, George. "Letters of Colonel George Croghan [to Thomas Wharton]." *Pennsylvania Magazine of History and Biography,* 15 (1891), 429–439.
Darlington, Mary C., ed., *Fort Pitt and Letters from the Frontier.* New York, 1971.
Davies, K. G., ed., *Documents of the American Revolution, 1770–1783.* 19 vols. Shannon and Dublin, Ireland, 1972–1981.

Diffenderffer, F. R. "Early Local History as Revealed by an Old Document." *Papers of the Lancaster County Historical Society*, 2 (1897), 5–10.

Draper, Lyman C. et al., eds., *Collections of the State Historical Society of Wisconsin*. 31 vols. Madison, 1854–1931.

Dunbar, John R., ed., *The Paxton Papers*. The Hague, Netherlands, 1957.

Dunn, Jacob P., ed., "The Mission to the Ouabache." *Indiana Historical Society Publications*, vol. III (Indianapolis, 1902), pp. 255–330.

Dunn, Richard, and Mary Maples Dunn, eds., *The Papers of William Penn*. 5 vols. Philadelphia, 1981–1986.

Egle, William, ed., *Pennsylvania Archives*, 2nd Ser. 19 vols. Harrisburg, 1874–1893.

Eschmann, C. J., comp. and trans. "Kaskaskia Church Records." *Illinois Historical Society Transactions*, 1904 (Springfield, 1904), pp. 394–413.

Eshelman, H. Frank. "Assessment Lists and Other Manuscript Documents of Lancaster County Prior to 1729." *Papers of the Lancaster County Historical Society*, 20 (1916), 162–194.

Faribault-Beauregard, Marthe. *La population des forts français d'Amérique (XVIIIe siécle)*. 2 vols. Montreal, 1982–1984.

Ford, Worthington C. et al., eds., *Journals of the Continental Congress, 1774–1789*. 34 vols. Washington, 1904–1937.

Galbreath, C. B., ed., *Expedition of Celoron to the Ohio Country in 1749*. Columbus, OH, 1921.

Hazard, Samuel, ed., *Pennsylvania Archives* [1st Ser.]. 12 vols. Philadelphia, 1852–1856.

Hazard, Samuel, ed., *The Register of Pennsylvania*. 16 vols. Philadelphia, 1828–1835.

Heckewelder, John. *The First Description of Cincinnati and Other Ohio Settlements: The Travel Report of Johann Heckewelder (1792)*. Edited by Don Heinrich Tolzmann. Lanham, MD, 1988.

Heckewelder, John. *History, Manners, and Customs of the Indian Nations Who Once Inhabited Pennsylvania and the Neighboring States*. Rev. ed. Memoirs of the Historical Society of Pennsylvania, vol. XII. Philadelphia, 1876. Orig. pub. 1818.

Heckewelder, John. *A Narrative of the Mission of the United Brethren Among the Delaware and Mohegan Indians, from Its Commencement, in the Year 1740, to the Close of the Year 1808*. New York, 1971. Orig. pub. 1820.

Hening, William, ed., *The Statutes at Large; Being a Collection of all the Laws of Virginia, from the First Session of the Legislature in the Year 1619*. 13 vols. New York, Philadelphia, and Richmond, 1819–1823.

Hennepin, Louis. *Description of Louisiana Newly Discovered to the Southwest of New France by Order of the King*. Translated by Marian E. Cross. Minneapolis, 1938. Orig. pub. Paris, 1683.

Hays, John. "John Hays' Diary and Journal of 1760." Edited by William A. Hunter. *Pennsylvania Archaeologist*, 24 (1954), 63–84.

Innis, H. A., ed., *Select Documents in Canadian Economic History, 1497–1783*. Toronto, 1929.

Jefferson, Thomas. *The Papers of Thomas Jefferson*. Edited by Julian P. Boyd et al., Princeton, NJ, 1950– .

Johnson, William. *The Papers of Sir William Johnson*. Edited by James Sullivan et al., 14 vols. Albany, 1921–1965.

Jones, David. *A Journal of Two Visits Made to Some Nations of Indians on the West Side of the River Ohio, in the Years 1772–1773*. New York, 1865. Orig. pub. 1774.

Kellogg, Louise, ed., *Early Narratives of the Northwest, 1634–1699*. New York, 1917.

Kenny, James. "James Kenny's 'Journal to Ye Westward,' 1758–59." Edited by John W. Jordan. *Pennsylvania Magazine of History and Biography*, 37 (1913), 395–449.

Kenny, James. "The Journal of James Kenny, 1761–1763." Edited by John W. Jordan. *Pennsylvania Magazine of History and Biography*, 37 (1913), 1–47, 152–201.

Krauskopf, Frances, trans. and ed., "Ouiatanon Documents." *Indiana Historical Society Proceedings*, vol. XVIII (Indianapolis, 1955), pp. 135–234.

Margry, Pierre, ed., *Découvertes et Établissements des Français dans l'Ouest et dans le Sud de L'Amérique Septentrionale (1614–1754): Mémoires et Documents Originaux*. 6 vols. Paris, 1876–1886.

Marshall, Humphrey. *The History of Kentucky, Including an Account of the Discovery, Settlement, Progressive Improvement, Political and Military Events, and Present State of the Country*. Morehead, KY, 1971. Orig. pub. 1812.

McClure, David. *Diary of David McClure, Doctor of Divinity, 1748–1820*. Edited by Franklin Dexter. New York, 1899.

McDermott, John, ed., *Old Cahokia: A Narrative and Documents Illustrating the First Century of its History*. St. Louis, 1949.

Mercure de France. Reprinted Geneva, 1968.

Mereness, Newton D., ed., *Travels in the American Colonies*. New York, 1916.

Michigan Pioneer and Historical Society Collections. 40 vols. Lansing, 1874–1929.

Minutes of the Provincial Council of Pennsyvlania. 16 vols. Harrisburg, 1838–1853.

Mulkearn, Lois, ed., *George Mercer Papers Relating to the Ohio Company of Virginia*. Pittsburgh, 1954.

"The Narrative of Marie LeRoy and Barbara Leininger, for Three Years Captives Among the Indians." *Pennsylvania Magazine of History and Biography*, 29 (1905), 407–420.

O'Callaghan, E. B., and Berthold Fernow, eds., *Documents Relative to the Colonial History of the State of New York*. 15 vols. Albany, 1856–1887.

Pease, Theodore, and Ernestine Jenison, eds., *Illinois on the Eve of the Seven Years' War, 1747–1755*. Collections of the Illinois State Historical Library, vol. XXIX. Springfield, 1940.

Pease, Theodore, and Raymond Werner, eds., *The French Foundations, 1680–1693*. Collections of the Illinois State Historical Library, vol. XXIII. Springfield, 1934.

Pénicaut, André. *Fleur De Lys and Calumet: Being the Pénicaut Narrative of*

French Adventure in Louisiana. Translated and edited by Richebourg McWilliams. Baton Rouge, 1953.

Pittman, Philip. *The Present State of European Settlements on the Mississippi, with a geographical description of that river illustrated by plans and draughts.* Gainesville, FL, 1973. Orig. pub. London, 1770.

Quaife, Milo M., ed., *The Siege of Detroit in 1763.* Chicago, 1958.

Records of the Moravian Mission Among the Indians of North America. Archives of the Moravian Church, Bethlehem, PA. Microfilm.

Reichel, William C., ed., *Memorials of the Moravian Church.* 2 vols. Philadelphia, 1870.

Robertson, James Rood, ed., *Petitions of the Early Inhabitants of Kentucky to the General Assembly of Virginia, 1769–1792.* Filson Club Publications no. 27. Louisville, 1914.

Rowland, Dunbar, and Albert Sanders, eds., *Mississippi Provincial Archives, 1704–1743: French Dominion.* 3 vols. Jackson, MS, 1927–1932.

St. Clair, Arthur. *The St. Clair Papers: The Life and Public Services of Arthur St. Clair.* Edited by William H. Smith. 2 vols. New York, 1970. Orig. pub. 1881.

Smith, John. *Generall Historie of Virginia, New England, and the Summer Isles, 1624.* In Edward Arber, ed., *Travels and Works,* 2 vols. New York, 1966. Orig. pub. 1910.

Sosin, Jack M., ed., *The Opening of the West.* Columbia, SC, 1969.

Stevens, Sylvester K., and Donald Kent, eds., *Wilderness Chronicles of Northwestern Pennsylvania.* Harrisburg, 1941.

Symmes, John Cleves. *The Correspondence of John Cleves Symmes.* Edited by Beverley Bond. New York, 1926.

Thornbrough, Gayle, ed., *Outpost on the Wabash: Letters of Brigadier General Josiah Harmar and Major John Francis Hamtramck.* Indianapolis, 1957.

Thwaites, Reuben G., ed., *Early Western Travels, 1748–1846.* 32 vols. Cleveland, 1904–1907.

Thwaites, Reuben G., ed., *The Jesuit Relations and Allied Documents.* 73 vols. Cleveland, 1896–1901.

Thwaites, Reuben G., and Louise P. Kellogg, eds., *Documentary History of Dunmore's War, 1774.* Madison, WI, 1905.

Thwaites, Reuben G., and Louise Kellogg, eds., *Frontier Defense on the Upper Ohio, 1777–1778.* Madison, WI, 1912.

Thwaites, Reuben G., and Louise P. Kellogg, eds., *Revolution on the Upper Ohio, 1775–1777.* Madison, WI, 1908.

Trabue, Daniel. *Westward into Kentucky: The Narrative of Daniel Trabue.* Edited by Chester R. Young. Lexington, KY, 1981.

United States Statutes at Large. Washington, DC, 1789– .

Washburn, Wilcomb, ed., *The American Indian and the United States: A Documentary History.* 4 vols. New York, 1973.

Washington, George. *The Papers of George Washington: Confederation Series.* Edited by W. W. Abbot and Dorothy Twohig. Charlottesville, 1992– .

Washington, George. *The Writings of George Washington.* Edited by John C. Fitzpatrick. 39 vols. Washington, DC, 1931–1944.

Zeisberger, David. *Schoenbrunn Story: Excerpts from the Diary of the Reverend*

David Zeisberger, 1772–1777 at Schoenbrunn in the Ohio Country. Translated by August C. Mahr. Edited by Daniel R. Porter. Columbus, OH, 1972.

SECONDARY SOURCES

Books and Dissertations

Agnew, Jean-Christophe. *Worlds Apart: The Market and the Theater in Anglo-American Thought, 1550–1750.* New York, 1986.

Ahlstrom, Sydney. *A Religious History of the American People.* New Haven, 1972.

Allen, Michael. *Western Rivermen, 1763–1861: Ohio and Mississippi Boatmen and the Myth of the Alligator Horse.* Baton Rouge, 1990.

Altman, Ida, and James Horn, eds., *"To Make America": European Emigration in the Early Modern Period.* Berkeley, 1991.

Alvord, Clarence. *The Illinois Country, 1673–1818.* Springfield, IL, 1920.

Alvord, Clarence. *The Mississippi Valley in British Politics.* 2 vols. New York, 1959. Orig. pub. 1916.

Alvord, Clarence, and Lee Bidgood. *The First Explorations of the Trans-Allegheny Region by the Virginians, 1650–1674.* Cleveland, 1912.

Anderson, Fred. *A People's Army: Massachusetts Soldiers and Society in the Seven Years' War.* Chapel Hill, 1984.

Anson, Bert. *The Miami Indians.* Norman, OK, 1970.

Appleby, Joyce. *Economic Thought and Ideology in Seventeenth-Century England.* Princeton, 1978.

Appleby, Joyce. *Liberalism and Republicanism in the Historical Imagination.* Cambridge, MA, 1992.

Aquila, Richard. *The Iroquois Restoration: Iroquois Diplomacy on the Colonial Frontier, 1701–1754.* Detroit, 1983.

Armistead, Wilson. *Memoirs of James Logan.* London, 1851.

Auth, Stephen. *The Ten Years' War: Indian–White Relations in Pennsylvania, 1755–1756.* New York, 1989.

Axtell, James. *After Columbus: Essays in the Ethnohistory of Colonial North America.* New York, 1988.

Axtell, James. *Beyond 1492: Encounters in Colonial North America.* New York, 1992.

Axtell, James. *The Invasion Within: The Contest of Cultures in Colonial North America.* New York, 1985.

Bailyn, Bernard. *The Ideological Origins of the American Revolution.* Cambridge, MA, 1967.

Bailyn, Bernard. *Voyagers to the West: A Passage in the Peopling of America on the Eve of the Revolution.* New York, 1986.

Bellesisles, Michael. *Revolutionary Outlaws: Ethan Allen and the Struggle for Independence on the Early American Frontier.* Charlottesville, VA, 1993.

Belting, Natalia Maree. *Kaskaskia Under the French Regime.* Illinois Studies in the Social Sciences, vol. XXIX. Urbana, 1948.

Boles, John. *The Great Revival, 1787–1805: The Origin of the Southern Evangelical Mind.* Lexington, KY, 1972.

Bonsteel Tachau, Mary K. *Federal Courts in the Early Republic: Kentucky, 1789–1816*. Princeton, 1978.

Briggs, Winstanley. "The Forgotten Colony: *Le Pays des Illinois*." Ph.D. diss., Univ. of Chicago, 1985.

Brown, George W., gen. ed., *Dictionary of Canadian Biography*. Toronto, 1966– .

Brown, Jeffrey P., and Andrew R. L. Cayton, eds., *The Pursuit of Public Power: Political Culture in Ohio, 1787–1861*. Kent, OH, 1994.

Brown, Jennifer S. H. *Strangers in Blood: Fur Trade Company Families in Indian Country*. Vancouver, 1980.

Callender, Charles. *Social Organization of the Central Algonkian Indians*. Milwaukee Public Museum Publications in Anthropology no. 7. Milwaukee, 1962.

Cayton, Andrew R. L. *The Frontier Republic: Ideology and Politics in the Ohio Country, 1780–1825*. Kent, OH, 1986.

Cayton, R. L., and Peter Onuf. *The Midwest and the Nation: Rethinking the History of an American Region*. Bloomington, IN, 1990.

Choquette, Leslie. "French Emigration in the Seventeenth and Eighteenth Centuries." Ph.D. diss., Harvard Univ., 1988.

Cmiel, Kenneth. *Democratic Eloquence: The Fight over Popular Speech in Nineteenth–Century America*. New York, 1990.

Cooper, Irma Jane. *The Life and Public Services of James Logan*. New York, 1921.

Cott, Nancy. *The Bonds of Womanhood: "Woman's Sphere" in New England, 1780–1835*. New Haven, 1977.

Crane, Verner. *The Southern Frontier, 1670–1732*. New York, 1981. Orig. pub. 1928.

Cronon, William. *Changes in the Land: Indians, Colonists, and the Ecology of New England*. New York, 1983.

Crosby, Alfred. *Ecological Imperialism: The Biological Expansion of Europe, 900–1900*. New York, 1986.

Crow, Jeffrey, and Larry Tise, eds., *The Southern Experience in the American Revolution*. Chapel Hill, 1978.

Davidson, Robert. *War Comes to Quaker Pennsylvania, 1682–1756*. New York, 1957.

De Schweinitz, Edmund. *The Life and Times of David Zeisberger*. Philadelphia, 1871.

Denevan, William, ed., *The Native Population of the Americas in 1492*. 2nd ed. Madison, WI, 1992.

Doerflinger, Thomas. *A Vigorous Spirit of Enterprise: Merchants and Economic Development in Revolutionary Philadelphia*. Chapel Hill, 1986.

Dowd, Gregory. *A Spirited Resistance: The North American Indian Struggle for Unity, 1745–1815*. Baltimore, 1992.

Downes, Randolph. *Council Fires on the Upper Ohio*. Pittsburgh, 1940.

Draper, Lyman C. *King's Mountain and Its Heroes*. Cincinnati, 1881.

Dunn, Richard S., and Mary Maples Dunn, eds., *The World of William Penn*. Philadelphia, 1986.

Eccles, William. *The Canadian Frontier, 1534–1760*. New York, 1969.

Ekberg, Carl J. *Colonial Ste. Genevieve: An Adventure on the Mississippi Frontier*. Gerald, MO, 1985.

Emerson, Thomas, and R. Barry Lewis, eds., *Cahokia and the Hinterlands: Middle Mississippian Cultures of the Midwest*. Urbana, IL, 1991.

Faragher, John Mack. *Daniel Boone: The Life and Legend of an American Pioneer*. New York, 1992.

Faragher, John Mack. *Sugar Creek: Life on the Illinois Prairie*. New Haven, 1986.

Flexner, James. *Mohawk Baronet: Sir William Johnson of New York*. New York, 1959.

Foley, William, and C. David Rice. *The First Chouteaus: River Barons of Early St. Louis*. Urbana, IL, 1983.

Gates, Paul W. *History of Public Land Law Development*. New York, 1979.

Giraud, Marcel. *Histoire de la Louisiane française*. 5 vols. Paris, 1953–1987.

Giraud, Marcel. *A History of French Louisiana, Volume One: The Reign of Louis XIV, 1698–1715*. Translated by Joseph C. Lambert. Baton Rouge, 1974.

Giraud, Marcel. *A History of French Louisiana, Volume Two: Years of Transition, 1715–1717*. Translated by Brian Pearce. Baton Rouge, 1993.

Giraud, Marcel. *A History of French Louisiana, Volume Five: The Company of the Indies, 1723–1731*. Translated by Brian Pearce. Baton Rouge, 1991.

Gollin, Gillian Lindt. *Moravians in Two Worlds: A Study of Changing Communities*. New York, 1967.

Greene, Evarts B., and Virginia D. Harrington, eds., *American Population Before the Federal Census of 1790*. New York, 1932.

Greene, Jack, ed., *The American Revolution: Its Character and Limits*. New York, 1987.

Gutiérrez, Ramón A. *When Jesus Came, the Corn Mothers Went Away: Marriage, Sexuality, and Power in New Mexico, 1500–1846*. Stanford, 1991.

Hamilton, Milton W. *Sir William Johnson: Colonial American, 1715–1763*. Port Washington, New York, 1976.

Hanna, Charles. *The Wilderness Trail*. 2 vols. New York, 1911.

Harris, Richard Colebrook. *The Seigneurial System in Early Canada: A Geographical Study*. Madison, WI, 1968.

Hatch, Nathan. *The Democratization of American Christianity*. New Haven, 1989.

Heckscher, Eli. *Mercantilism*. Translated by Mendel Shapiro. 2 vols. London, 1935.

Hinderaker, Eric. "The Creation of the American Frontier: Europeans and Indians in the Ohio River Valley, 1673–1800." Ph.D. diss., Harvard Univ., 1991.

Hoffman, Daniel. *Brotherly Love*. New York, 1981.

Horsman, Reginald. *The Frontier in Formative Years, 1783–1815*. New York, 1970.

Horwitz, Morton J. *The Transformation of American Law, 1780–1860*. Cambridge, MA, 1977.

Howard, James. *Shawnee! The Ceremonialism of a Native Indian Tribe and Its Cultural Background*. Athens, OH, 1981.

Hufton, Olwen. *The Poor of Eighteenth-Century France, 1750–1789*. Oxford, 1974.

Innis, Harold A. *The Fur Trade in Canada: An Introduction to Canadian Economic History*. Rev. ed. Toronto, 1956.

Jennings, Francis. *The Ambiguous Iroquois Empire: The Covenant Chain Confederation of Indian Tribes from its Beginnings to the Lancaster Treaty of 1744*. New York, 1984.

Jennings, Francis. *Empire of Fortune: Crowns, Colonies & Tribes in the Seven Years War in America*. New York, 1988.

Jennings, Francis. *The Founders of America: How Indians Discovered the Land, Pioneered in It, and Created Great Classical Civilizations; How They Were Plunged into a Dark Age by Invasion and Conquest; and How They Are Reviving*. New York, 1993.

Jennings, Francis. *The Invasion of America: Indians, Colonialism, and the Cant of Conquest*. New York, 1976.

Jensen, Merrill. *The New Nation: A History of the United States During the Confederation 1781–1789*. New York, 1950.

Johnson, Joseph. "A Statesman of Colonial Pennsylvania: A Study of the Private Life and Public Career of James Logan to the Year 1726." Ph.D. diss., Harvard Univ., 1943.

Johnson, Paul E. *A Shopkeeper's Millennium: Society and Revivals in Rochester, New York, 1815–1837*. New York, 1978.

Jones, Alice Hanson. *Wealth of a Nation to Be: The American Colonies on the Eve of the Revolution*. New York, 1980.

Jones, Dorothy. *License for Empire: Colonialism by Treaty in Early America*. Chicago, 1982.

Jordan, Winthrop. *White Over Black: American Attitudes Toward the Negro, 1550–1812*. Chapel Hill, 1968.

Kaestle, Carl. *Pillars of the Republic: Common Schools and American Society, 1780–1860*. New York, 1983.

Kantorowicz, Ernst. *The King's Two Bodies: A Study in Medieval Political Theology*. Princeton, 1957.

Kellogg, Louise P. *The French Régime in Wisconsin and the Northwest*. Madison, WI, 1925.

Kent, Barry C. *Susquehanna's Indians*. The Pennsylvania Historical and Museum Commission, Anthropological Series, no. 6. Harrisburg, 1984.

Kettner, James. *The Development of American Citizenship, 1608–1870*. Chapel Hill, 1978.

Kimball-Brown, Margaret. *Cultural Transformations Among the Illinois: An Application of a Systems Model*. Publications of the Museum, Michigan State University, vol. 1 no. 3. East Lansing, 1979.

Kinietz, W. Vernon. *The Indians of the Western Great Lakes, 1614–1760*. Occasional Contributions from the Museum of Anthropology of the University of Michigan, no. 10. Ann Arbor, 1940.

Klein, H. M. J., ed., *Lancaster County Pennsylvania: A History*. 4 vols. New York, 1924.

Knittle, W. A. *Early Eighteenth Century Palatine Immigration*. Philadelphia, 1937.

Kohn, Richard. *Eagle and Sword: The Federalists and the Creation of the Military Establishment in America, 1783–1802*. New York, 1975.

Kramnick, Isaac. *Republicanism and Bourgeois Radicalism: Political Ideology in Late Eighteenth-Century England and America*. Ithaca, 1990.

Krech, Shepard III, ed., *Indians, Animals, and the Fur Trade: A Critique of Keepers of the Game*. Athens, GA, 1981.

Kulikoff, Allan. *The Agrarian Origins of American Capitalism*. Charlottesville, 1992.

Kulikoff, Allan. *Tobacco and Slaves: The Development of Southern Cultures in the Chesapeake, 1680–1800*. Chapel Hill, 1986.

Lemon, James T. *The Best Poor Man's Country: A Geographical Study of Early Southeastern Pennsylvania*. New York, 1976.

Lester, William Stewart. *The Transylvania Colony*. Spencer, IN, 1935.

Lewis, Arthur James. *Zinzendorf, the Ecumenical Pioneer: A Study in the Moravian Contribution to Christian Mission and Unity*. Philadelphia, 1962.

Leyburn, James G. *The Scotch-Irish: A Social History*. Chapel Hill, 1962.

Mancall, Peter. *Deadly Medicine: Indians and Alcohol in Early America*. Ithaca, 1995.

Mancall, Peter. *Valley of Opportunity: Economic Culture along the Upper Susquehanna, 1700–1800*. Ithaca, 1991.

Marietta, Jack. *The Reformation of American Quakerism, 1748–1783*. Philadelphia, 1984.

Martin, Calvin. *Keepers of the Game: Indian-Animal Relationships and the Fur Trade*. Berkeley, 1978.

Mason, Kathryn Harrod. *James Harrod of Kentucky*. Baton Rouge, 1951.

Mather, Irwin F. *The Making of Illinois: Historical Sketches*. Chicago, 1900.

McConnell, Michael. *A Country Between: The Upper Ohio Valley and Its Peoples, 1724–1774*. Lincoln, NE, 1992.

McCoy, Drew. *The Elusive Republic: Political Economy in Jeffersonian America*. Chapel Hill, 1980.

Merrell, James. *The Indians' New World: Catawbas and their Neighbors from European Contact Through The Era of Removal*. Chapel Hill, 1989.

Miller Surrey, Nancy M. *The Commerce of Louisiana During the French Régime, 1699–1763*. Columbia Studies in History, Economics and Public Law, vol. LXXI. New York, 1916.

Miyakawa, T. Scott. *Protestants and Pioneers: Individualism and Conformity on the American Frontier*. Chicago, 1964.

Mohr, Walter H. *Federal Indian Relations, 1774–1788*. Philadelphia, 1933.

Muller, Jon. *Archaeology of the Lower Ohio River Valley*. Orlando, FL, 1986.

Norall, Frank. *Bourgmont: Explorer of the Missouri, 1698–1725*. Lincoln, NE, 1988.

Norgren, Jill. *The Cherokee Cases: The Confrontation of Law and Politics*. New York, 1996.

Onuf, Peter. *The Origins of the Federal Republic: Jurisdictional Controversies in the United States, 1775–1787*. Philadelphia, 1983.

Onuf, Peter. *Statehood and Union: A History of the Northwest Ordinance*. Bloomington, IN, 1987.

Owsley, Frank. *Plain Folk of the Old South*. Baton Rouge, 1949.

Palm, Mary Borgias. *The Jesuit Missions of the Illinois Country, 1673–1763*. Cleveland, 1931.

Parkman, Francis. *France and England in North America*. 2 vols. New York, 1983.

Peckham, Howard. *Pontiac and the Indian Uprising*. Princeton, 1947.

Peterson, Jacqueline. "The People in Between: Indian–White Marriage and the Genesis of a Métis Society and Culture in the Great Lakes Region 1680–1830." Ph.D. diss., Univ. of Illinois Chicago Circle, 1981.

Peterson, Jacqueline, and Jennifer S. H. Brown, eds., *The New Peoples: Being and Becoming Métis in North America*. Lincoln, NE, 1985.

Pocock, J. G. A. *The Machiavellian Moment: Florentine Political Thought and the Atlantic Republican Tradition*. Princeton, 1975.

Potter, Janice. *The Liberty We Seek: Loyalist Ideology in Colonial New York and Massachusetts*. Cambridge, MA, 1983.

Pound, Arthur. *Johnson of the Mohawks*. New York, 1930.

Prucha, Francis Paul. *The Great Father: The United States Government and the American Indians*. Lincoln, NE, 1995. Orig. pub. 1984.

Quimby, George I. *Indian Culture and European Trade Goods: The Archaeology of the Historic Period in the Western Great Lakes*. Madison, WI, 1966.

Ranck, George W. *Boonesborough: Its Founding, Pioneer Struggles, Indian Experiences, Transylvania Days, and Revolutionary Annals*. Filson Club Publications no. 16. Louisville, 1901.

Remini, Robert. *Andrew Jackson and the Course of American Empire, 1767–1821*. New York, 1977.

Richter, Daniel. *The Ordeal of the Longhouse: The Peoples of the Iroquois League in the Era of European Colonization*. Chapel Hill, 1992.

Roediger, David. *Towards the Abolition of Whiteness: Essays on Race, Politics, and Working Class History*. London, 1994.

Rohrbough, Malcolm J. *The Land Office Business: The Settlement and Administration of American Public Lands, 1789–1837*. New York, 1986.

Rohrbough, Malcolm J. *The Trans-Appalachian Frontier: People, Societies, and Institutions 1775–1850*. New York, 1978.

Ryan, Mary P. *Cradle of the Middle Class: The Family in Oneida County, New York, 1790–1865*. New York, 1981.

Sahlins, Marshall. *Stone Age Economics*. New York, 1972.

Savelle, Max. *George Morgan: Colony Builder*. New York, 1932.

Schwartz, Robert. *Policing the Poor in Eighteenth-Century France*. Chapel Hill, 1988.

Schwartz, Sally. *A Mixed Multitude: The Struggle for Toleration in Colonial Pennsylvania*. New York, 1987.

Selby, John E. *The Revolution in Virginia, 1775–1783*. Williamsburg, 1988.

Sellers, Charles. *The Market Revolution: Jacksonian America, 1815–1846*. New York, 1991.

Sheldon, E. M. *The Early History of Michigan from the First Settlement to 1815*. New York, 1956.

Shepherd, William R. *History of Proprietary Government in Pennsylvania*. New York, 1896.

Siebert, Wilbur H. *The Loyalists of Pennsylvania*. The Ohio State University Bulletin, vol. XXIV. Columbus, 1920.

Slaughter, Thomas. *The Whiskey Rebellion: Frontier Epilogue to the American Revolution*. New York, 1986.

Slotkin, Richard. *Regeneration Through Violence: The Mythology of the American Frontier, 1600–1860*. Middletown, CT, 1973.

Smith, Bruce D., ed., *The Mississippian Emergence*. Washington, DC, 1990.

Smith, Bruce D., ed., *Mississippian Settlement Patterns*. New York, 1978.

Sosin, Jack M. *The Revolutionary Frontier, 1763–1783*. New York, 1967.

Sosin, Jack M. *Whitehall and the Wilderness: The Middle West in British Colonial Policy, 1760–1775*. Lincoln, NE, 1961.

Spangenberg, August Gottlieb. *The Life of Nicholas Lewis Count Zinzendorf*. Translated by Samuel Jackson. London, 1838.

Sturtevant, William C., gen. ed., *Handbook of North American Indians*, vol. XV: *Northeast*. Edited by Bruce G. Trigger. Washington, DC, 1978.

Talbert, Charles Gano. *Benjamin Logan: Kentucky Frontiersman*. Lexington, KY, 1962.

Tanner, Helen Hornbeck, ed., *Atlas of Great Lakes Indian History*. Norman, OK, 1987.

Taylor, Alan. *Liberty Men and Great Proprietors: The Revolutionary Settlement on the Maine Frontier, 1760–1820*. Chapel Hill, 1990.

Taylor, Alan. *William Cooper's Town: Power and Persuasion on the Frontier of the Early American Republic*. New York, 1995.

Taylor, Robert, ed., *The Northwest Ordinance 1787: A Bicentennial Handbook*. Indianapolis, 1987.

Teute, Fredrika J. "Land, Liberty, and Labor: Kentucky as the Promised Land." Ph.D. diss., Johns Hopkins, 1988.

Thayer, Theodore. *Israel Pemberton, King of the Quakers*. Philadelphia, 1943.

Thornton, Russell. *American Indian Holocaust and Survival: A Population History Since 1492*. Norman, OK, 1987.

Tolles, Frederick. *James Logan and the Culture of Provincial America*. Boston, 1957.

Trudel, Marcel. *L'Esclavage au Canada français: Histoire et Conditions de l'Esclavage*. Quebec, 1960.

Underhill, Ruth. *Red Man's Religion: Beliefs and Practices of the Indians North of Mexico*. Chicago, 1965.

Usner, Daniel H., Jr. *Indians, Settlers, and Slaves in a Frontier Exchange Economy: The Lower Mississippi Valley before 1783*. Chapel Hill, 1992.

Van Kirk, Sylvia. *"Many Tender Ties": Women in Fur Trade Society, 1670–1870*. Winnepeg, 1980.

Volwiler, Albert T. *George Croghan and the Westward Movement, 1741–1782*. Cleveland, 1926.

Wainwright, George B. *George Croghan: Wilderness Diplomat*. Chapel Hill, 1959.

Wallace, Anthony F. C. *The Death and Rebirth of the Seneca: The History and Culture of the Great Iroquois Nation, Their Destruction and Demoralization, and Their Cultural Revival at the Hands of the Indian Visionary, Handsome Lake*. New York, 1970.

Wallace, Anthony F. C. *King of the Delawares: Teedyuscung, 1700–1763*. Philadelphia, 1949.

Wallace, Joseph. *The History of Illinois and Louisiana Under the French Rule*. Cincinnati, 1893.

Wallace, Paul A. W. *Conrad Weiser: Friend of Colonist and Mohawk*. Philadelphia, 1945.

Wallace, Paul A. W. *Indians in Pennsylvania*. Rev. ed., Pennsylvania Historical and Museum Commission Anthropological Series, no. 5. Harrisburg, 1989.

Wallace, Paul A. W. *Thirty Thousand Miles With John Heckewelder*. Pittsburgh, 1958.

Watlington, Patricia. *The Partisan Spirit: Kentucky Politics, 1779–1792*. Chapel Hill, 1972.

Weslager, C. A. *The Delaware Indians: A History*. New Brunswick, NJ, 1972.

White, Richard. *The Middle Ground: Indians, Empires, and Republics in the Great Lakes Region, 1650–1815*. New York, 1991.

White, Richard. *The Roots of Dependency: Subsistence, Environment, and Change among the Choctaws, Pawnees, and Navajos*. Lincoln, NE, 1983.

Williamson, Chilton. *American Suffrage: From Property to Democracy, 1760–1860*. Princeton, NJ, 1960.

Wolf, George D. *The Fair Play Settlers of the West Branch Valley, 1769–1784: A Study of Frontier Ethnography*. Harrisburg, PA, 1969.

Wood, Gordon. *The Creation of the American Republic, 1776–1787*. Chapel Hill, 1969.

Wood, Gordon. *The Radicalism of the American Revolution*. New York, 1992.

Wood, Peter, Gregory Waselkov, and M. Thomas Hatley, eds., *Powhatan's Mantle: Indians in the Colonial Southeast*. Lincoln, NE, 1989.

Wyckoff, William. *The Developer's Frontier: The Making of the Western New York Landscape*. New Haven, 1988.

Zoltvany, Yves F. *Philippe de Rigaud de Vaudreuil: Governor of New France 1703–1725*. Toronto, 1974.

Articles and Conference Papers

Anderson, Virginia DeJohn. "King Philip's Herds: Indians, Colonists, and the Problem of Livestock in Early New England." *The William and Mary Quarterly*, 3rd Ser., 51 (1994), 601–624.

Benson, Evelyn A. "The Earliest Use of the Term 'Conestoga Wagon.'" *Papers of the Lancaster County Historical Society*, 57 (1953), 109–119.

Benson, Evelyn A. "The Huguenot Le Torts: First Christian Family on the Conestoga." *Journal of the Lancaster County Historical Society*, 65 (1961), 92–105.

Benson, Evelyn A. "James Logan as the First Political Boss of Lancaster County

When it Was the Wild Frontier." *Papers of the Lancaster County Historical Society*, 59 (1955), 57–77.

Berthoff, Rowland, and John Murrin. "Feudalism, Communalism, and the Yeoman Freeholder: The American Revolution Considered as a Social Accident." In Stephen Kurtz and James Hutson, eds., *Essays on the American Revolution*, pp. 256–288. Chapel Hill, 1973.

Blasingham, Emily J. "The Depopulation of the Illinois Indians." *Ethnohistory*, 3 (1956), 193–224, 361–412.

Briggs, Winstanley. "The Enhanced Economic Position of Women in French Colonial Illinois." In Clarence A. Glasrud, ed., *L'Héritage Tranquille: The Quiet Heritage*, pp. 62–69. Moorhead, MN, 1987.

Briggs, Winstanley. "Le Pays des Illinois." *The William and Mary Quarterly*, 3rd Ser., 47 (1990), 30–56.

Briggs, Winstanley. "Slavery in French Colonial Illinois." *Chicago History*, 18 (Winter 1989–1990), 66–81.

Cayton, Andrew R. L. "'Separate Interests' and the Nation-State: The Washington Administration and the Origins of Regionalism in the Trans-Appalachian West." *The Journal of American History*, 79 (1992),39–67.

Cayton, Andrew R. L. "'When Shall We Cease to Have Judases?': The Blount Conspiracy and the Limits of the 'Extended' Republic." In Ronald Hoffman and Peter J. Albert, eds., *Launching "the Extended Republic": The Federalist Era*. Charlottesville, 1996.

Coffman, Ralph J. "Pre-Columbian Trade Networks in the Missouri, Ohio and Mississippi River Valleys and Their Importance for Post-Columbian Contact." Paper presented at the Missouri Valley History Conference, Omaha, NE, March 1992.

Countryman, Edward. "Indians, the Colonial Order, and the Social Significance of the American Revolution." *The William and Mary Quarterly*, 53 (1996), 342–366.

Crane, Verner W. "The Tennessee River as the Road to Carolina: The Beginnings of Exploration and Trade." *Mississippi Valley Historical Review*, 3 (1916), 5–14.

Cutcliffe, Stephen H. "Colonial Indian Policy As a Measure of Rising Imperialism: New York and Pennsylvania, 1700–1755." *The Western Pennsylvania Historical Magazine*, 64 (1981), 237–268.

Davis, Natalie Zemon. "Iroquois Women, European Women." In Margo Hendricks and Patricia Parker, eds., *Women, "Race," and Writing in the Early Modern Period*, pp. 243–358. London, 1994.

Desbarats, Catherine. "The Cost of Early Canada's Native Alliances: Reality and Scarcity's Rhetoric." *The William and Mary Quarterly*, 3rd Ser., 52 (1995), 609–630.

Dowd, Gregory. "The French King Wakes Up in Detroit: 'Pontiac's War' in Rumor and History," *Ethnohistory,* 34 (1990), 254–278.

Downes, Randolph C. "Indian War on the Upper Ohio." *Western Pennsylvania Historical Magazine*, 17 (1934), 93–115.

Frost, J. William. "William Penn's Experiment in the Wilderness: Promise and Legend." *Pennsylvania Magazine of History and Biography*, 107 (1983), 577–605.

Gorn, Elliott J. "'Gouge and Bite, Pull Hair and Scratch': The Social Significance of Fighting in the Southern Backcountry." *The American Historical Review*, 90 (1985), 18–43.

Gruenwald, Kim. "Merchants, Farmers, and Empire: The Establishment of a Market Economy in the Ohio Valley." Paper presented at the Second Annual Conference of the Institute of Early American History and Culture, Boulder, Colo., May 1996.

Hammon, Neal O. "Land Acquisition on the Kentucky Frontier." *The Register of the Kentucky Historical Society*, 78 (1980), 297–321.

Hauser, Raymond E. "Warfare and the Illinois Indian Tribe During the Seventeenth Century: An Exercise in Ethnohistory." *The Old Northwest*, 10 (Winter 1984–1985), 367–387.

James, Alfred P. "The First English-Speaking Trans-Appalachian Frontier." *Mississippi Valley Historical Review*, 17 (1930–31), 55–64.

Jennings, Francis. "The Delaware Interregnum." *Pennsylvania Magazine of History and Biography*, 89 (1965), 174–198.

Jennings, Francis. "The Indian Trade of the Susquehanna Valley." *Proceedings of the American Philosophical Society*, 110 (1966), 406–424.

Jennings, Francis. "Iroquois Alliances in American History." In Jennings et al., eds., *The History and Culture of Iroquois Diplomacy*. Syracuse, 1985.

Jones, Maldwyn A. "The Scotch-Irish in British America." In Bernard Bailyn and Philip Morgan, eds., *Strangers Within the Realm: Cultural Margins of the First British Empire*, pp. 284–313. Chapel Hill, 1991.

Kent, Barry C., Janet Rice, and Kakuko Ota. "A Map of 18th Century Indian Towns in Pennsylvania." *Pennsylvania Archaeologist*, 51 (1981), 1–18 and endpaper.

Koenigsberger, H. G. "Composite states, representative institutions, and the American Revolution." *Historical Research*, 62 (1989), 135–153.

Larson, John Lauritz, and David G. Vandersteel. "Agent of Empire: William Conner on the Indiana Frontier, 1800–1855." *Indiana Magazine of History*, 80 (Dec. 1984), 301–328.

Matson, Cathy, and Peter Onuf. "Toward a Republican Empire: Interest and Ideology in Revolutionary America." *American Quarterly*, 37 (1985), 496–531.

Moogk, Peter. "Reluctant Exiles: Emigrants from France in Canada before 1760." *The William and Mary Quarterly*, 3rd Ser., 46 (1989), 463–505.

Nash, Gary. "The Quest for the Susquehanna Valley: New York, Pennsylvania, and the Seventeenth-Century Fur Trade." *New York History*, 48 (1967), 3–27.

Ojala, Jeanne. "Ira Allen and the French Directory, 1796: Plans for the Creation of the Republic of United Columbia." *The William and Mary Quarterly*, 36 (1979), 436–448.

Perkins, Elizabeth A. "The Consumer Frontier: Household Consumption in Early Kentucky." *The Journal of American History*, 78 (1991), 486–510.

Peterson, Jacqueline. "Women Dreaming: The Religiopsychology of Indian White Marriages and the Rise of a Metis Culture." In Lillian Schlissel, Vicki L. Ruiz, and Janice Monk, eds., *Western Women: Their Land, Their Lives*, pp. 49–68. Albuquerque, 1988.

Quaife, Milo M. "Detroit Biographies: The Sieur de Bourgmont." *Burton Historical Collection Leaflet*, 6 (1928), 49–63.

Ratcliffe, Donald J. "The Experience of Revolution and the Beginnings of Party Politics in Ohio, 1776–1816." *Ohio History*, 85 (1976), 186–230.

Siebert, Wilbur H. "The Dispersion of the American Tories." *Mississippi Valley Historical Review*, 1 (1914), 185–197.

Smith, Timothy L. "The Ohio Valley: Testing Ground for America's Experiment in Religious Pluralism." *Church History*, 60 (1991), 461–479.

Soltow, Lee. "Inequality amidst Abundance: Land Ownership in Early Nineteenth-Century Ohio." *Ohio History*, 88 (1979), 133–151.

Soltow, Lee. "Progress and Mobility among Ohio Propertyholders, 1810–1825." *Social Science History*, 7 (1983), 405–426.

Sugrue, Thomas. "The Peopling and Depeopling of Early Pennsylvania: Indians and Colonists, 1680–1720." *Pennsylvania Magazine of History and Biography*, 116 (1992), 3–31.

Taylor, Alan. "Land and Liberty on the Post-Revolutionary Frontier." In David Konig, ed., *Devising Liberty: Preserving and Creating Freedom in the New American Republic*, pp. 81–108. Stanford, 1995.

Tolles, Frederick. "Nonviolent Contact: Quakers and the Indians." *Proceedings of the American Philosophical Society*, 107 (1963), 93–101.

Turnbaugh, William A. "Wide-Area Connections in Native North America." *American Indian Culture and Research Journal*, 1 (1976), 22–28.

Usner, Daniel. "From African Captivity to American Slavery: The Introduction of Black Laborers to Colonial Louisiana." *Louisiana History*, 20 (1979), 25–48.

Usner, Daniel. "The Frontier Exchange Economy of the Lower Mississippi Valley in the Eighteenth Century." *The William and Mary Quarterly*, 3rd Ser., 44 (April 1987), 165–192.

Vaughan, Alden T. "Frontier Banditti and the Indians: The Paxton Boys' Legacy, 1763–1775." *Pennsylvania History*, 51 (1984), 1–29.

Wallace, Anthony F. C. "Woman, Land, and Society: Three Aspects of Aboriginal Delaware Life." *Pennsylvania Archaeologist*, 17 (1947), 1–35.

Zimmerman, Albright. "Daniel Coxe and the New Mediterranean Sea Company." *Pennsylvania Magazine of History and Biography*, 76 (1952), 86–96.

Zimmerman, Albright. "European Trade Relations in the 17th and 18th Centuries." In Herbert Kraft, ed., *A Delaware Indian Symposium*. The Pennsylvania Historical and Museum Commission Anthropological Series, no. 4. Harrisburg, 1974.

Index